T0383833

CONTEMPORARY ISSUES IN BUSINESS ECONOMICS AND FINANCE

CONTEMPORARY STUDIES IN ECONOMICS AND FINANCIAL ANALYSIS

Series Editor: Simon Grima

CONTEMPORARY STUDIES IN ECONOMICS AND
FINANCIAL ANALYSIS   VOLUME 104

CONTEMPORARY ISSUES IN BUSINESS ECONOMICS AND FINANCE

EDITED BY

SIMON GRIMA

University of Malta, Malta

ERCAN ÖZEN

University of Usak, Turkey

HAKAN BOZ

University of Usak, Turkey

emerald
PUBLISHING

United Kingdom – North America – Japan
India – Malaysia – China

Emerald Publishing Limited
Howard House, Wagon Lane, Bingley BD16 1WA, UK

First edition 2020

Copyright © 2020 Emerald Publishing Limited

Reprints and permissions service
Contact: permissions@emeraldinsight.com

British Library Cataloguing in Publication Data
A catalogue record for this book is available from the British Library

ISBN: 978-1-83909-605-1 (Print)
ISBN: 978-1-83909-604-4 (Online)
ISBN: 978-1-83909-606-8 (Epub)

ISSN: 1569-3759 (Series)

INVESTOR IN PEOPLE

CONTENTS

LIST OF FIGURES

LIST OF TABLES

ABOUT THE EDITORS

Simon Grima, PhD (Melit.), MSc (Lond), MSc (BCU), BCom (Hons) (Melit.), FFA, FAIA (Acad), is the Head of the Department of Insurance, in charge of the Bachelor of Commerce in Insurance, the Bachelor of Commerce (Honours) and Master's degrees in Insurance and Risk Management and a Senior lecturer at the University of Malta. He set up the Insurance Department in 2015 and started and coordinated the MA and MSc Insurance and Risk Management degrees. He served as the President of the Malta Association of Risk Management (MARM) between 2013 and 2015, and President of the Malta Association of Compliance Officers (MACO) between 2016 and 2018. Moreover, he is among the first Certified Risk Management Professional (FERMA), is the chairman of the Scientific Education Committee of the Public Risk Management Organisation (PRIMO) and a member of the curriculum development team of Professional Risk Managers' International Association (PRMIA) in 2014. His research focus and consultancy is on Governance, Regulations and Internal Controls (i.e. Risk Management, Internal Audit and Compliance) and has over 30 years of experience varied between Financial Services and with public entities in academia, Internal Controls, Investments and IT. He acts as an Independent Director for Financial Services Firms, sits on Risk, Compliance, Procurement, Investment and Audit Committees and carries out duties as a Compliance Officer, Internal Auditor and Risk Manager.

He has acted as Co-chair and is a Member of the Scientific Program Committee on some international conferences and is a chief editor, editor and review editor of some journals and book series. He has been awarded outstanding reviewer for *Journal of Financial Regulation and Compliance* in the 2017 Emerald Literati Awards.

Web Pages:
https://www.um.edu.mt/profile/simongrima
Web of Science Researcher ID: O-5299-2015
Loop profile: 348395
Scopus Author ID: 57151215400
ORCID: https://orcid.org/0000-0003-1523-5120
Emerald Insight Volume Editor: Contemporary Studies in Economic and Financial Analysis https://www.emeraldinsight.com/series/csef
Google Scholar https://scholar.google.com/citations?user=6L-kN98AAAAJ&hl=en
Research gate https://www.researchgate.net/profile/Simon_Grima

Previous Publications

Bonello, A. (2019). *Understanding the investor: A Maltese study of risk and behaviour in financial invest-ment decisions.* In S. Grima & J. Spiteri (Eds.). London: Emerald Group Publishing Limited.

Borda, M., Grima, S., & Kwiecien, I. (Eds.) (2020, Forthcoming). *Life insurance in Europe: Risk analy-sis and market challenges.* Springer.

Grima, S., Bezzina, F., Romanova, I., & Rupeika-Apoga, R. (2017). *Contemporary issues in finance: Current challenges from across Europe.* Contemporary Studies in Economic and Financial Analysis, Volume 98. London: Emerald Group Publishing Limited.

Grima, S., & Marano, P. (2018, July). *Governance and regulations' contemporary issues.* Contemporary Studies in Economic and Financial Analysis, Volume 99. London: Emerald Group Publishing Limited. ISBN: 978-1-78743-816-3.

Grima, S., & Thalassinos, E. (2018). *Contemporary issues in business and financial management in east-ern Europe.* Contemporary Studies in Economic and Financial Analysis, Volume 100. London: Emerald Group Publishing Limited.

Grima, S., Ozen, E., Boz, H., Spiteri, J., & Thalassinos, E. (2019). *Contemporary behavioural issues.* Contemporary Studies in Economic and Financial Analysis, Volume 101. London:Emerald Group Publishing Limited.

Grima, S., & Thalassinos, E. (2019, February 3, Forthcoming). *Financial derivatives: A blessing or a curse?* Emerald Group Publishing Limited. R. Dalli Gonzi & I. Thalassinos (Eds.).

Grima, S., Thalassinos, E., & Spiteri, J. (2019). Frontiers in applied mathematics and statistics math-ematical finance. *Research Topic Risk Management Models and Theories.*

Grima, S., & Boztepe, E. (2020, Forthcoming). *Contemporary issues in audit management and forensic accounting.* Contemporary Studies in Economic and Financial Analysis, Volume 102. Emerald Group Publishing Limited..

Grima, S., Ozen, E., & Boz, H. (2020, Forthcoming). *Contemporary issues in business, economics and finance.* Contemporary Studies in Economic and Financial Analysis, Volume 104. Emerald Group Publishing Limited

Grima, S., Sirkeci, O., & Elbeyoglu, K. (2020, Forthcoming). *Street economy: Micro enterprises & street vendors.* Contemporary Studies in Economic and Financial Analysis, Volume 103. Emerald Group Publishing Limited.

Grima, S., & Boztepe, E. (2021, Forthcoming). *Contemporary issues in public sector accounting and auditing.* Contemporary Studies in Economic and Financial Analysis, Volume 105 Emerald Group Publishing Limited.

Zammit, M. L., Spiteri, J. V., & Grima, S. (October 3, 2018). *The development of the Maltese insurance industry: A comprehensive study.* London: Emerald Group Publishing Limited.

Ercan Özen received his BSc in Public Finance (1994), MSc in Business-Accounting (1997) and PhD in Business Finance (2008) from University of Afyon Kocatepe. Now he is an Associate Professor of Finance in Department of Banking and Finance, School of Applied Sciences, University of Uşak, Turkey. His current research interests include different aspects of Finance. He has (co-) authored five book chapters and more than 35 papers, more than 25 conferences participation, member in International Program Committee of three conferences and workshops. He is Chair of International Applied Social Sciences Congress. He is also a Certificated Accountant, a Member of Agean Finance Association and a member of TEMA (Turkey Combating Soil Erosion, for Reforestation and the Protection of Natural Resources Foundation.)

Web Pages:
https://orcid.org/0000-0002-7774-5153
http://www.researcherid.com/rid/A-2697-2019

Previous Publications:
Grima, S., Ozen, E., Boz, H., Spiteri, J., & Thalassinos, E. (2019). *Contemporary behavioural issues*. Contemporary Studies in Economic and Financial Analysis, Volume 101. London: Emerald Group Publishing Limited. ISBN: 978-1-78769-882-6 eISBN: 978-1-78769-881-9.
Grima, S., Ozen, E., & Boz, H. (2020, Forthcoming). *Contemporary issues in business, economics and finance*. Contemporary Studies in Economic and Financial Analysis, Volume 104. Emerald Group Publishing Limited.

Hakan Boz is an Assistant Professor at Usak University, School of Applied Sciences. Prior to joining the academia, he has held various positions in the tourism and hospitality sector. He has over 10 years of managerial experience in the tourism and hospitality sectors. He has also acted as a consultant for a wide variety of businesses. He has published several journal articles and book chapters in high impact tourism and hospitality journals tourism with a special emphasis on human interactions both as consumers and as employees.

He is the Founder of the HB Lab, a lab carrying out scholarly and business research using psychophysiological tools such as fMRI, EEG, Eye Tracker, GSR, HR, Speech Recognition and Facial Expression Recognition. He is the Co-developer of a Facial Recognition software algorithm used in understanding consumer and employee behaviour. The software algorithm he has co-developed is currently used by various businesses and non-profit organisations.

Previous Publications:
Boz, H., Yilmaz, O., Arslan, A., & Koc, E. (2016). A comparison of depression and turnover intentions of hotel employees in all-inclusive and non all-inclusive hotels. In *Global issues and trends in tourism* (pp. 372–382). Sofia: ST. Klıment Ohrıdskı Unıversıty Press
Boz, H., & Koc, E. (2019). *Measuring emotional intelligence in tourism and hospitality*. Emotional Intelligence in Tourism and Hospitality (pp. 36–45). London: Cabi Publication.
Grima, S., Ozen, E., Boz, H., Spiteri, J., & Thalassinos, E. (2019). *Contemporary behavioural issues*. Contemporary Studies in Economic and Financial Analysis. Volume 101. London: Emerald Group Publishing Limited.
Grima, S., Özen, E., Boz, H., Spiteri, J., & Thalassinos, E. (Eds.). (2019). *Contemporary issues in behavioral finance*. London: Emerald Publishing Limited.
Grima, S., Ozen, E., & Boz, H. (2020, Forthcoming). *Contemporary issues in business, economics and finance*. Contemporary Studies in Economic and Financial Analysis, Volume 104. Emerald Group Publishing Limited.
Koc, E., & Boz, H. (2015). All-inclusive food and beverage operations In P. Szende (Ed.), *F&B/restaurant management*. London: Pearson Publication. ISBN-13:9780133258769.
Koc, E., Aydın, G., Ar, A.A., & Boz, H. (2017). Emotions and emotional abilities in service failures and recovery. In *Service failures and recovery in tourism and hospitality: A practical manual* (p. 42). London: Cabi Publication.
Koc, E., & Boz, H. (2018). How can consumer science be used for gaining information about consumers and the market? The role of psychophysiological and neuromarketing research. In *Case studies in the traditional food sector* (pp. 129–152). New York, NY: Elsevier Publication.
Koc, E., & Boz, H. (2019). *Emotions and developing emotional intelligence in tourism and hospitality businesses*. Emotional Intelligence in Tourism and Hospitality (pp. 16–35). London: Cabi Publication.
Koc, E., Taşkın, Ç., & Boz, H. (2019). *Risk and control in consumer behavior: A discussion*. Contemporary Issues in Behavioral Finance (pp. 1–13). London: Emerald Publication.

ABOUT THE CONTRIBUTORS

Semih Acikgozoglu is a Research Assistant at Afyon Kocatepe University, Faculty of Economics and Administrative Sciences, Division of Business Administration, Turkey. His primary research areas are marketing and consumer behaviour.

Hilmi Tunahan Akkuş is a Lecturer at Savaştepe Vocational School, Balıkesir University, Balıkesir, Republic of Turkey, as well as an Assistant Director in Savaştepe Vocational School. His main research areas include Islamic finance, financial markets and institutions, investments and portfolio management, behavioural finance, financial forecasting and modelling.

Nurgül Emine Barin received her BSc in Public Finance from University of Afyon Kocatepe (1993), MSc in Labour and Social Security Law (1997) and PhD in Labour and Social Security Law (2002) from University of Anadolu. She is an Assistant Professor at Afyon Kocatepe University, Faculty of Economics and Administrative Sciences, Department of Business Administration, Turkey. Her main research interests are individual labour law, collective labour law, labour law acts, workers' rights, occupational health and safety, and female workers.

Adem Boyukaslan is a Research Assistant with a Finance PhD at Afyon Kocatepe University, Faculty of Economics and Administrative Sciences, International Trade and Finance Department in Turkey. His primary research areas include risk management, corporate finance, behavioural finance and financial markets.

Olimpia Livia Preda Buzgurescu received her BSc in Faculty of Mathematics and Informatics, Department of Informatics (2013), MSc in e-Business Administration Department (2014) from University of Craiova, Romania. She is a PhD Student in Accounting at the University of Craiova. Her current research interests include aspects of finance and accounting. She has participated in many international conferences.

Vildan Saba Cenikli received her Bachelor's degree and Master's degrees in Economics from University of Dokuz Eylül in 2008 and 2010. She is a Research Assistant in Department of Economics in Faculty of Economics and Administrative Sciences 'University of Afyon Kocatepe, Turkey'. She is currently a PhD student in the Department of Economics at the Dokuz Eylül University in Turkey. Her field of research are money theories, high-technology in the economies, application of econometric models and the input–output analyses. She has participated in numerous international conferences both as a speaker and as an attendee. She has published papers in national and international journals.

Sevil Bektaş Durmuş was born on the 7 August 1985 in Bakırköy. Bektaş Durmuş received the Master's degree in Strategic Marketing and Brand Management in 2009 at Bahçeşehir University after graduating from university in 2007. After completing the Master's degree in 2011, she worked with the title of 'Lecturer' at Beykoz University, Public Relations and Advertising Department between 2011 and 2013. While working as a lecturer, she also started her PhD Program at Istanbul University, Department of Journalism in 2012. She continued her academic career as a Research Assistant at the Department of New Media and Journalism at Istanbul Yeni Yüzyıl University in 2014. She completed her PhD with her thesis that had the title 'Digital Activism in the Context of Determining Agenda Theory in Social Movements in New Media' on 31 July 2018, and in the same year, she was appointed as a Doctor Lecturer in the Advertisement Department at the Faculty of Communication at Istanbul Yeni Yüzyıl University. Bektaş Durmuş, who is currently working as a Doctor Lecturer at Istanbul Yeni Yüzyıl University, Faculty of Communication, is also the Educational Coordinator of the Faculty.

Negru Elena is a PhD Student in Accounting at the University of Craiova, Romania. She received her BSc in Finance (1999) from University of Craiova and MSc in Management of European Public Affairs (2004) from Bucharest University of Economic Studies. Now she is working in the finance domain in the local government.

Aslı Elgün was born in 1975 in Izmir and completed BA in Ege University's Faculty of Communication Department of Journalism and then received her Master's degree from Ege University Women's Studies Department and doctorate from Ege University's Department of Journalism. She worked part time at Ege University Women's Issues and Research Center during her graduate studies. After that, Elgun worked as a Research Assistant at the Department of Journalism in Ege University. Since 2014, she has been working as a Doctor Lecturer at the same university. She has been giving lectures on gender, alternative media, and community media at undergraduate and graduate level and has various studies and works on gender and alternative media. In addition, she takes part in the ongoing European Union Erasmus Plus Youth Project and carries out several projects at national level which are still being conducted.

Umut Eroğlu is an Assistant Professor at Canakkale Onsekiz Mart University, Biga Economics and Administrative Sciences/Department of Business Administration. He is studying specifically human resources management and published many articles in various scientific journals. He has conducted several PhD and Master's thesis, management- and organisation-related courses in undergraduate, graduate and postgraduate levels. He also gives consultant service to private sector organisations around managerial issues like developing human resource effectiveness, designing training and learning processes, structuring corporate universities and developing business strategies.

Simon Grima, PhD (Melit.), MSc (Lond), MSc (BCU), BCom (Hons) (Melit.), FFA, FAIA (Acad), is the Head of the Department of Insurance, in charge of the Bachelor of Commerce in Insurance, the Bachelor of Commerce (Honours) and Master's degrees in Insurance and Risk Management and a Senior lecturer at the University of Malta. He set up the Insurance Department in 2015 and started and coordinated the MA and MSc Insurance and Risk Management degrees. He served as the President of the Malta Association of Risk Management (MARM) between 2013 and 2015, and President of the Malta Association of Compliance Officers (MACO) between 2016 and 2018. Moreover, he is among the first Certified Risk Management Professional (FERMA), is the chairman of the Scientific Education Committee of the Public Risk Management Organisation (PRIMO) and a member of the curriculum development team of Professional Risk Managers' International Association (PRMIA) in 2014. His research focus and consultancy is on Governance, Regulations and Internal Controls (i.e. Risk Management, Internal Audit and Compliance) and has over 30 years of experience varied between Financial Services and with public entities in academia, Internal Controls, Investments and IT. He acts as an Independent Director for Financial Services Firms, sits on Risk, Compliance, Procurement, Investment and Audit Committees and carries out duties as a Compliance Officer, Internal Auditor and Risk Manager.

He has acted as Co-chair and is a Member of the Scientific Program Committee on some international conferences and is a chief editor, editor and review editor of some journals and book series. He has been awarded outstanding reviewer for *Journal of Financial Regulation and Compliance* in the 2017 Emerald Literati Awards.

Umut Halac is currently working in Yasar University, Department of Economics. He got his PhD and Master's degrees from Dokuz Eylul University, Institute of Social Sciences, Department of Economics. He has major on macroeconomics and minor on econometrics. His interests are macroeconomy and applied econometrics. He is an active member in national and international projects and cooperations.

Bahadır Ildokuz studied Economics and graduated from Boğaziçi University in 2006. At the same university, he finished his Master studies on Economics and Finance in 2008. He started his PhD studies on Finance in İstanbul University in 2012 and graduated in 2015. He has worked in several departments of different banks at different positions such as treasury marketing supervisor, product development supervisor, treasury operations manager and he is still the manager of economic research and private banking in EmlakBank. He was also an Assistant Professor in Toros University in 2018. He was a Lecturer of Finance and Economics for undergraduate, graduate and PhD classes. He gave lectures ranging from Economics to Finance Theory.

Sezer Bozkuş Kahyaoğlu is an Associate Professor at the Izmir Bakircay University, Faculty of Business Administration and Social Science, Accounting and Finance

Department. Sezer graduated from Bosporus University in 1993 with honour degree BSc in Management. Sezer had MA degree in Money Banking and Finance at Sheffield University and Certification in Retail Banking from Manchester Business School, both with a joint scholarship of British Council and Turkish Bankers Association. After finishing her doctoral studies, she earned her PhD degree in Econometrics from Dokuz Eylul University in 2015. In the period of 1993–2004, Sezer worked in banking sector in various positions of head office. Sezer worked at Turkish Derivatives Exchange (TurkDEX-VOB) for two years as the founding member and Head of Audit and Investigations Department. Also, Sezer worked in KPMG Risk Consulting Services as Senior Manager between 2007 and 2012. Afterwards Sezer joined in Grant Thornton as a founding partner of advisory services and worked there for two years. Since August 2014, she has been working in SMM Technology and Risk Consulting as a partner responsible for risk consulting. Sezer has certifications of CIA, CFSA, CRMA, CFE and CPA as well. Her research interests mainly include applied econometrics, time series analysis, financial markets and instruments, energy markets, corporate governance, risk management, fraud accounting and auditing.

Seda Mumlu Karanfil, Human Resources Specialist, completed her undergraduate degree in 2007 at Anadolu University, Department of Business Administration and her Master's degree in 2013 at Istanbul University's Human Resources Management Program. She is currently a PhD candidate in Human Resources Management at Istanbul University. During her doctoral studies, she conducted research on human resources management, transformative leadership, business values, personality traits, perception of job insecurity and organisational citizenship behaviour. Starting her career in a multinational bank, She worked in the field of Human Resources Recruitment, Training and Development. Most recently, and also worked as a Human Resources Specialist at Istanbul University Career Development Application and Research Center. Currently, She continues to pursue her academic studies.

İbrahim Kiray, MSc, was graduated from Çanakkale Onsekiz Mart University Biga Faculty of Economics and Administrative Sciences, Department of Business Administration in 2016 as the highest ranking student of the department. In the same year, he started his Master's degree in both Economics and Business Administration at Çanakkale Onsekiz Mart University, The Graduate School of Social Sciences. In 2018, he graduated from the Economics Program by presenting the Project titled 'The Relationship Between Democracy, Economic Developing Development and Poverty: A Comparison of Developed and Developing Countries'. In 2019, the thesis entitled 'A Study on Investigation of the Effect of Motivation Factors on the Motivation and Performance of Salesperson' was accepted and successfully completed the Master of Business Administration Program. In 2017–2018, he lectured for one year at Çanakkale Onsekiz Mart University Gelibolu Piri Reis Vocational School. He has participated in International Scientific events and presented papers.

Ayşegül Kirkpinar did her Bachelor's degree at Celal Bayar University, Department of Business Administration in 2009. She got her Master's degree in Accounting and Finance at the same university in 2011. Her Master's thesis was about artificial neural networks in finance. During her Master studies, she has also been as an international student in a language school in London for a couple of months. After Master's degree, she completed her Doctor of Philosophy degree in Finance at Dokuz Eylül University in 2018. Her dissertation thesis was regarding volatility spillover between commodity and bond markets of some emerging markets. Her research interests include financial modelling and forecasting, portfolio management and behavioural finance. She continued research in these areas. She is married and has a son. She is currently working at İzmir Katip Çelebi University, Faculty of Economics and Administrative Sciences, Department of Business Administration as an Assistant Professor.

Nihan Akincilar Köseoğlu graduated from the Department of Political Science and International Relations at Marmara University in June 2007. After that, she started an International Relations MA program – mainly focussing on Turkish–Greek relations at Istanbul Bilgi University in February 2008. She finished the MA program in June 2010 after writing her thesis called 'The European Communities' Reactions to Military Interventions in Turkey and Greece'. She began her PhD in the Department of European Union Politics and International Relations at the European Union Institute of Marmara University in September 2010. She finished her PhD program in July 2015 after writing her thesis called 'Europeanization of Minority Rights in Turkey and Greece: A Comparative Analysis'. Additionally, she has been working at several universities in Istanbul since 2009. Now she is working at Fenerbahçe University as an Assistant Professor at the Department of Political Science and International Relations since April 2018. Her academic working areas are the European Union, minority rights, human rights abuses, fight against discrimination, Europeanisation and Turkish-Greek Relations. She has several international and national publications while she knows also English, German and Greek languages.

Sabriye Kundak received her Bachelor's degree in Economics from University of Anadolu in 2005. She received her Master's degrees and Doctorate's degrees in Economics from University of Afyon Kocatepe in 2008 and 2015. She is a Research Assistant in Department of Economics in Faculty of Economics and Administrative Sciences 'University of Afyon Kocatepe, Turkey'. Her fields of research are international economics, growth, manufacturing industry, panel data analyses, application of econometric models and the input–output analyses. She has participated in numerous international both as speaker and as attendee. She has published papers in national and international journals.

Gamze Yıldız Şeren Kurular was born in 1987, from Elazığ, Turkey. She is an Assistant Professor at Namık Kemal University, Faculty of Economics and Administrative Sciences, Public Finance Department Tekirdag-Turkey. She received an undergraduate degree from Marmara University, Faculty of Economics and Administrative Sciences, Department of Public Finance (2008).

She holds Master's degree (MA) in Public Economics from Marmara University (2011) and PhD in Public Finance from Marmara University. Her doctorate thesis is on gender responsive budgeting and local government. Her main research fields focus on public finance, environmental economics, budgeting and gender.

Serdar Ogel is an Assistant Professor at Afyon Kocatepe University, Faculty of Economics and Administrative Sciences, Division of Business Administration, Turkey. His primary research areas include risk management, financial markets and investment tools.

İlkin Yaran Ögel is a Research Assistant at Afyon Kocatepe University, Faculty of Economics and Administrative Sciences, Department of Business Administration in English, Turkey. Her main research interests are brand management, global brands and brand culture. Secondary areas include international business management.

Ercan Özen received his BSc in Public Finance (1994), MSc in Business-Accounting (1997) and PhD in Business Finance (2008) from University of Afyon Kocatepe. Now he is an Associate Professor of Finance in Department of Banking and Finance, School of Applied Sciences, University of Uşak, Turkey. His current research interests include different aspects of Finance. He has (co-) authored five book chapters and more than 35 papers, more than 25 conferences participation, member in International Program Committee of three conferences and workshops. He is Chair of International Applied Social Sciences Congress. He is also a Certificated Accountant, a Member of Agean Finance Association and a member of TEMA (Turkey Combating Soil Erosion, for Reforestation and the Protection of Natural Resources Foundation.)

Alparslan Özmen is an Assistant Professor at Afyon Kocatepe University, Faculty of Economics and Administrative Sciences, Department of Business Administration, Turkey. His study fields range from brand management to city marketing, service marketing and international marketing.

Inna Romānova is a Professor and the Vice-Dean of the Faculty of Business, Management and Economics at the University of Latvia and the Director of a professional master degree program in Finance. Her academic interests are in corporate finance and financial sector development. She is an expert in Economics and Management Sciences of the Latvian Academy of Sciences. Inna is the author of a number of papers on Financial Sector Development, Financial Management and Asset Management published in international scientific journals. She is on the editorial board of several scientific journals. She has also a professional experience in banking and finance, both in Latvia and in Germany. She is also a Visiting Professor in several universities in Europe.

Ramona Rupeika-Apoga is a Professor in Finance at the University of Latvia and the Head of the Department of Finance and Accounting. She has leaded and participated in several studies and research projects internationally and locally.

She has more than 15 years of pedagogic experience in Latvian and European higher education institutions with specialisation in EU Economic and Monetary Integration, International Finance, Banking Economics and SMEs. She is an Expert in Economics and Management Sciences of Latvian Academy of Sciences and the author of a great number of articles in Access to Finance for SMEs, Financial Risk Assessment and Management, Financial Globalisation and more, published in several international journals. She participated, as a leader, in many European research projects, among them a Nordic–Baltic network in Corporate and International Finance, the research project 'Innovations in Latvian Companies and Industries for Competitiveness Enhancement within the Framework of Globalization', the think tank 'CERTUS' on the research project 'Riga as Financial Centre' and 'Access to Finance' and INTERFRAME project 'Latvian State and Society Challenges and Solutions in an International Context'.

She is an Editor at the *European Research Studies Journal, International Journal of Economics & Business Administration, Journal of Applied Economics and Business, Journal of Finance and Financial Law* and *International Journal of Business and Economic Sciences Applied Research.*

Metin Tetik, born on 8 April 1986, received his BSc in Economics (2009), MSc in Economics (2011), PhD in Economics (2017) from Pamukkale University. Now he is an Assistant Professor of Economics in the School of Applied Sciences, University of Uşak, Turkey. While his current research interests include macrofinance, macroeconomics, game theory and applied economics, his teaching interests include game theory and econometrics.

Rustem Baris Yesilay is currently at Ege University, Aviation Higher Vocational School. He is the Vice Director/Manager of the school and the Founding Head of Civil Aviation Management Program. He earned his PhD from Dokuz Eylul University, Institute of Social Sciences, Department of Economics, and he has Master's degree from Istanbul University, Institute of Social Sciences, Department of Fiscal Economics. He has 17 years teaching and research experience. He has publications on sustainable development, innovation, entrepreneurship and cluster management. He has taken active role as a coordinator/researcher at least in 10 national and international projects.

Hasan Hüseyin Yildirim was born in 1987 in Konya. He completed his previous education in a university in Konya and graduated from Istanbul University, Faculty of Business Administration in 2009. He received his Master's degree (2011) in Finance from Marmara University and obtained a PhD degree (2016) from Istanbul University. He is an Assistant Professor in the Burhaniye School of Applied Sciences at Balikesir University. His Master's and PhD theses are on the evaluation of investment projects. He is a Lecturer in Financial Analysis, Financial Management and International Finance courses in Banking and Finance Department and International Trade Department in undergraduate, graduate and Master classes. His research interests include the economy, finance and banking sector and renewable energy investments.

LIST OF CONTRIBUTORS

Semih Acikgozoglu	Afyon Kocatepe University, Turkey
Hilmi Tunahan Akkuş	Balıkesir University, Turkey
Nurgül Emine Barin	Afyon Kocatepe University, Turkey
Adem Boyukaslan	Afyon Kocatepe University, Turkey
Olimpia Livia Preda Buzgurescu	University of Craiova, Romania
Vildan Saba Cenikli	Afyon Kocatepe University, Turkey
Sevil Bektaş Durmuş	Istanbul Yeni Yuzyil University, Turkey
Negru Elena	University of Craiova, Romania
Aslı Elgün	Ege University, Turkey
Umut Eroğlu	Çanakkale Onsekiz Mart University, Turkey
Simon Grima	University of Malta, Malta
Umut Halac	Yasar University, Turkey
Bahadır Ildokuz	Emlakbank, Turkey
Sezer Bozkuş Kahyaoğlu	İzmir Bakırçay University, Turkey
Seda Mumlu Karanfil	İstanbul University, Turkey
İbrahim Kiray	Çanakkale Onsekiz Mart University, Turkey
Ayşegül Kirkpinar	İzmir Katip Çelebi University, Turkey
Nihan Akincilar Köseoğlu	Fenerbahçe University, Turkey
Sabriye Kundak	Afyon Kocatepe University, Turkey
Gamze Yıldız Şeren Kurular	Tekirdag Namık Kemal University, Turkey
Serdar Ogel	Afyon Kocatepe University, Turkey
İlkin Yaran Ögel	Afyon Kocatepe University, Turkey
Ercan Özen	Uşak University, Turkey
Alpaslan Özmen	Afyon Kocatepe University, Turkey
Inna Romānova	University of Latvia, Latvia
Ramona Rupeika-Apoga	University of Latvia, Latvia
Metin Tetik	Uşak University, Turkey
Rustem Barıs Yesilay	Ege University, Turkey
Hasan Hüseyin Yildirim	Balikesir University, Turkey

SERIES EDITOR'S INTRODUCTION

The Emerald book series: **Contemporary Studies in Economic and Financial Analysis**, edition CSEF104 includes studies on Contemporary Issues in Business Economics and Finance contributed mainly by authors invited from participants in the 3rd International Applied Social Science Congress (C-IASOS2019) held in Çeşme, İzmir, Turkey, between 4 and 6 April 2019.

An analysis of the existence of volatility spillover between the conventional stock index and participation-30 index based on the indexes in the Turkish Capital Markets BIST-30 and the Participation-30 indexes is carried out in Chapter 1. They find a strong correlation between the BIST-30 and Participation-30, which are affected by the same shocks, causality and volatility in both directions.

The authors of Chapter 2 identify models for carrying out bankruptcy risk analysis that have as variables relevant performance indicators to examine the bankruptcy risk of the Romanian industrial companies, to determine its predictability and significance, in order to avoid their potential bankruptcy.

In Chapter 3, the authors aim to support the employment of the female labour force and to show its share in the development and growth in the member countries of the Organisation of Islamic Cooperation (OIC). They find that female employment has a positive impact on economic growth for the selected OIC countries.

The author of Chapter 4 investigates the volatility spillover from oil to precious metals under high volatility and low volatility regimes. Accordingly, results showed that there were volatility spillovers from oil to palladium and platinum in low volatility regimes and from oil to platinum in high volatility regimes.

In Chapter 5, the authors reveal knowledge, report on perception level and look at the evaluation of exchange rate risk management techniques of enterprises registered to Afyonkarahisar Chamber of Commerce and Industry. The most important finding of this study is that the majority of the companies, which are operating in a competitive environment, are intensely exposed to foreign exchange risk but try to overcome the foreign exchange risk using traditional internal firm-level hedging methods instead of well-reputed external hedging methods or derivative instruments.

The authors of Chapter 6 demonstrate the effect of the CAMLS (C represents capital adequacy; A, asset quality; M, management adequacy; E, earnings; L, liquidity; and S, sensitivity to market risks) variables on the variable E. The study revealed the importance of the capital, management and liquidity variables, which are internal factors, in increasing the profitability of banks.

In the Chapter 7, the authors examine the interaction between experience, satisfaction and positive word of mouth within the context of city marketing. The findings of the study exposed an interaction between experience, satisfaction and positive word of mouth regarding a city. Additionally, it showed the mediator role of satisfaction on the relationship between experience and positive word of mouth.

The author of Chapter 8 aimed to determine the pros and cons of the Crowdsourcing concept through new media applications in the form of critical evaluations by examining sample case studies that use the Crowdsourcing concept. The study demonstrated that Crowdsourcing is becoming a worldwide business model and allows anyone with free time and internet connection to contribute to the economic productivity.

In Chapter 9, the authors analyse the effect of motivation factors on the performance of the salesperson and found that the dimensions of image and relations among five dimensions namely satisfaction, image, relations, knowledge of product and service and advertisement related to motivation factors have a significant effect on the task performance of salesperson.

The author of Chapter 10 focused on combining positive psychological capital and its assurances with seven different sources of motivation, as categorised in Allen and Fabian, in 2019. Based on input from managers of human resources department employees, job search behaviour was found to be high. The inability to optimise the skills of individuals and limited career opportunities in the institutions they work for are examples of factors that affect job search behaviour.

In Chapter 11, the author discussed tax as a tool for solving the issue of climate change. The author noted that a multidimensional policy instead of a one-_dimensional policy, an environmentally conscious society and state, and cooperation of policy actors on a global scale are the basic elements, which can play an important role in the solution of the climate change problem.

In Chapter 12, the author discussed the concepts of community media, sustainability and female-oriented non-governmental organisations (NGOs), and then explained the media usage habits and the factors that affect the sustainability of the preferred channels of the female-oriented NGOs. Conclusions show that the financial, content production related, technical, and legal factors affect the sustainability of community media.

The author of Chapter 13 investigates the EU's anti-discrimination policy for sports (i.e. the Treaty of Lisbon (2009)). In this study, the author raises awareness of this crucial and unending discrimination problem in sports.

In Chapter 14, the authors measure efficiency of national innovation systems (NIS) using the data envelopment analysis (DEA) method. This method is used on country samples of 18 Eastern European and Central Asian countries (EECA) and Turkey. Based on the key findings one can note that Kazakhstan, Turkey, Latvia and Uzbekistan are more efficient in innovation performance when compared to other EECA countries.

In Chapter 15, the authors investigate whether the BIST30 index acted in accordance with the overreaction hypothesis against the return changes in the Dow Jones Industrial Average (DJIA) index during the 2008 global financial crisis. Findings obtained using the CAR analysis show that the BIST30 index did not generally act in accordance with the overreaction hypothesis against the DJIA.

The last chapter (16) relates to the determinants of the Bank's Stability in Latvia post-transition. The authors confirm the results of other studies on bank stability of small economies, with some exceptions due to the unique situation in term bank business models applied by Latvian banks.

CHAPTER 1

VOLATILITY SPILLOVER BETWEEN CONVENTIONAL STOCK INDEX AND PARTICIPATION INDEX: THE TURKISH CASE

Sezer Bozkuş Kahyaoğlu and Hilmi Tunahan Akkuş

ABSTRACT

Introduction – *The rapid flow of information between the markets eliminates the possibility of diversifying the portfolio by bringing the markets closer, and may cause the volatility in a market to spread to another market. In this context, revealing the relationships between conventional and participation markets or financial assets is important in terms of portfolio diversification and risk management.*

Purpose – *The major aim of this work is to analyse the existence of volatility spillover between conventional stock index and participation index based on the indexes in Turkish Capital Markets. BIST-30 and Katılım-30 indexes are used as the representatives of conventional stock index and participation index, respectively.*

Methodology – *Firstly, the univariate HYGARCH (1,d,1) parameters are calculated, and secondly, the dynamic equicorrelation (DECO) methodology is applied. DECO model is proposed to simplify structural assumptions by introducing a structure in which all twosomes of returns take the same correlation for a given time period. In this way, DECO model enables to have an optimal portfolio selection in comparison to an unrestricted time varying-dynamic*

Contemporary Issues in Business, Economics and Finance
Contemporary Studies in Economic and Financial Analysis, Volume 104, 1–17
Copyright © 2020 by Emerald Publishing Limited
ISSN: 1569-3759/doi:10.1108/S1569-375920200000104002

correlation approaches and gives more advanced forecasting ability for the duration of the financial crisis periods compared to the various portfolios.

Findings – *There is a strong correlation between BIST-30 and Katılım-30. They are affected by the same shocks. We expect to see different investor behaviours for Katılım-30 and BIST-30. However, they seem to have almost the same investor profile. In addition, there is a causality in both ways and volatility spillover between them.*

Keywords: Participation index; volatility spillover; Dynamic Equicorrelation (DECO) model; HYGARCH model; Non-linear causality; Islamic stock index; Sharia-compliant equity; Islamic finance; conventional stock index

JEL classification: C58; G11; G32

1. INTRODUCTION

The financial deregulation and foreign openness process, which accelerated in the late twentieth century, increased trade relations between countries. Especially, the market collapse (Black Monday) in October 1987 and the 'Asian Financial Crisis' in 1997 made the integration of international stock exchanges more important (Kılıç & Buğan, 2016, p. 167). Along with technological developments, financial liberalisation accelerates the flow of information between markets and offers different investment opportunities in different geographical regions. However, the rapid flow of information between the markets eliminates the possibility of diversifying the portfolio by bringing the markets closer, and may cause the volatility in a market to spread to another market. In this context, revealing the relationships between markets or financial assets is important regarding the portfolio diversification and risk management.

Some of the new improvements in the global financial system are the establishment of Islamic banks, Islamic equities and bond markets, which are different from their counterparts (Ajmi, Hammoudeh, Nguyen, & Sarafrazi, 2014, p. 214). The Islamic financial system shows significant differences from the traditional financial system in terms of both principles and financial products (Hammoudeh, Mensi, Reboredo, & Nguyen, 2014, p. 190). The Islamic financial system requires all financial transactions to be made based on real assets, as well as sharing the profit and loss of the parties in the contracts (Rejeb, 2016, p. 2). Islamic law constitutes the basis of Islamic finance. In this context, the Islamic finance prohibits interest (riba) to be received and paid; performing overly ambiguous transactions (garar); gambling (maysir) including derivative transactions, which are not based on short sales, real transactions and speculation. In addition to these, Islamic finance is an asset-based financial system that differs from the interest-based conventional system and it establishes a principle to share profit and loss in the transactions (Hammoudeh et al., 2014, pp. 189–190; Shahzad, Ferrer, Ballester, & Umar, 2017, pp. 9–10). Islamic finance is identified with the concept of interest-free finance. Aydin (2012) stated that the compound interest rate in conventional finance is considered to be the eighth wonder of the world (p. 61).

Islamic stocks, one of the broadest range of investment products provided by the Islamic finance industry, have attracted the attention of international investors over the past few years. Portfolio managers and investors are increasingly interested in Islamic stocks that have different characteristics based on Islamic ethical values (Mensi, Hammoudeh, Sensoy, & Yoon, 2016, p. 2457). Stock markets definitely contain the risk-sharing component (Masih, Kamil, & Bacha, 2018, p. 1). Islamic stock indices comprise the shares of enterprises that meet the qualitative and quantitative criteria. However, these qualitative and quantitative criteria may differ between countries (Buğan, 2016, pp. 251–254). There is a difference between the criteria of the Kuala Lumpur Syariah Index (KLSI) Islamic indices in Malaysia and the criteria for the DJIMI and FTSEGII Islamic indices. While the income approach is preferred as the monitoring criteria rather than the activity approach in the DJIMI and FTSEGII Islamic indices, the situation for the KLSI indices is the opposite. According to the activity approach, the activities of the enterprises to be included in the Islamic index should be in accordance with the Islamic rules (Albaity & Ahmad, 2011, p. 163). However, as in the conventional finance system, the index selection for investments in Islamic finance is becoming more important as the global economic structure develops (Dania & Malhotra, 2013, p. 66).

The Islamic financial sector has improved significantly in recent years and it is foreseen that this development will not stop. According to the ICD-Thomson Reuters-published Islamic Finance Development Report-2018, it is estimated that, at the end of 2017, the total amount of global Islamic financial assets reached $ 2,438 billion and it will have reached $ 3,809 trillion by 2023 (ICD-Thomson Reuters, 2018). According to the report, the total Islamic financial assets in the world is dispersed as 71% Islamic banking, 17% sukuk, 6% other financial institutions, 4% Islamic funds and 2% takaful.

It is claimed that Islamic stocks represent a unique class of investment which is called as 'decoupling hypothesis', related to Islamic stocks and different from conventional stocks (Masih et al., 2018, p. 5). It is important to know how the investors in the market have differentiated from the conventional investors in terms of their investment preferences for portfolio diversification and risk management. Majdoub and Sassi (2017) stated that individual or institutional Islamic investor behaviour has an impact on market behaviour (Majdoub & Sassi, 2017, p. 16). It is thought that this effect may create different results on the volatility spillover in Islamic markets. Although there are various reasons behind the volatility spillover and the transmission of shocks between the markets, the Islamic financial sector brings different explanations to this situation. Indeed, this connection is expected to disappear as companies in 'Islamic stock exchange indexes' are assumed to contain low interest rates and low leverage ratios. In addition, the asset-supported financing rule, one of the basic principles of Islamic finance, provides that the real sector and financial sectors are interconnected, and this situation does not lead Islamic emerging markets to have volatility spillover in the US market (Majdoub & Mansour, 2014, p. 453). Due to the unique and conservative nature of Islamic investments, there is a common perception that 'Islamic financial assets' may provide a specific safeguard against the increased risk and instability in international financial markets. In addition, Islamic investment tools should be less sensitive to external shocks in comparison to their conventional counterparts due to low 'leverage ratios', investable sectors and restrictions on speculative activities (Shahzad et al., 2017, pp. 9–10). Within the scope of these explanations, theoretically, we do not expect any volatility spillover between both of these two Islamic and conventional indexes.

The volatility spillover, which can be expressed as the effect of volatility in a financial market or asset on a volatility of a different market or asset, is the fact that new information on a market or asset can be effective on another market or asset. Therefore, the volatility spillover is the assimilation of news in a market by another market (Gebka & Serwa, 2007, p. 204). Volatility spillover can be divided into two as contemporaneous and dynamic volatility spillover. The contemporaneous volatility spillover is the spread of volatility that very same day, which usually occurs between the markets in the same region. The dynamic volatility spillover occurs usually between capital markets in different regions. In this case, the information in a capital market will affect other markets the next trading day, that is, the volatility spread may occur the next day (Mulyadi, 2009, p. 5).

In this study, whether there is volatility spillover between the indices in the same market is investigated. For this purpose, Katılım-30 participation index and BİST-30 conventional index in Turkey were included. Thus, it will be revealed whether these indices can be put in the same basket for portfolio diversification or not. In addition, conventional and Islamic stock investors in Turkey will have information regarding the risk sources of stock indices that they are investing. In earlier studies on volatility spillover, no study was found on conventional and Islamic indices in Turkey. This issue demonstrates the authenticity of the study. In addition, dynamic equicorrelation (DECO) method developed by Engle and Kelly (2012) will be used in this study. The method is one of the newest methods developed in recent years.

In the second part of the study, the literature review will be included. In the third part, the method of the study will be explained. The data and preliminary statistics about the data will be explained in the fourth section. Empirical findings will be included in the fifth part of the study. The general conclusions of the study will be explained in the sixth and last sections.

2. LITERATURE REVIEW

Various studies have been carried out on the risk and return structure of Islamic and conventional investment tools and indicators (Dewandaru, Bacha, Masih, & Masih, 2015). However, the issue of volatility spillover is studied in many ways due to its importance in terms of risk management. However, evidence for volatility spillover from developed markets to emerging markets has usually been investigated in those studies. Similarly, there are various empirical works on the volatility spillover between 'Islamic and conventional markets'. Those studies were generally based on US markets, and the studies were carried out by linking US conventional markets with US Islamic markets (DJIM and MSCI Islamic indices). In our study, the effects of volatility spillover between 'Islamic and conventional stock indices' in the same market are investigated. For this purpose, the literature on the volatility spillover between Islamic markets and conventional markets is summarised in the following.

Mulyadi (2009) investigated the volatility spillover between capital markets in Indonesia, the USA and Japan. As a result of the study, one-way volatility spillover from the US market to Indonesian market and two-way volatility spillover between Indonesian and Japanese markets were determined.

Albaity and Ahmad (2011) investigated the return and volatility behaviours of three Islamic stock market indices (DJIMI, FTSEGII and KLSI) in three different countries (USA, UK and Malaysia). According to EGARCH and TARCH model results, one-way volatility spillover from the DJIMI and FTSEGII Islamic indices to the KLSI Islamic index was determined. In addition, while the leverage effect was determined in the DJIMI and FTSEGII Islamic indices, no effect was found in the KLSI Islamic index.

Dania and Malhotra (2013) investigated the dependence between the four global Islamic indices (North America, EU, Far East, Pacific Region) and the conventional indices in the same region. As a result of the study, 'positive and significant volatility spillover from conventional indices to Islamic indices' was determined. There was also an evidence of the asymmetric volatility transition between the relevant markets.

Hammoudeh et al. (2014) examined the dependence between DJIM index, 'three indexes of the global conventional stock exchanges' (Asia, Europe, USA) and global factors (oil prices, VIX, US 10-year treasury interest rates, 10-year European monetary union government bonds). The empirical findings showed that there is dependence between the Islamic market (DJIM) and the conventional markets and risk factors. Accordingly, the 'dissociation hypothesis', which shows differences between Islamic markets and conventional markets, is rejected.

In their study investigating the volatility spillover between US stock markets and five MSCI Islamic indices (Indonesia, Malaysia, Pakistan, Qatar, Turkey), Majdoub and Mansour (2014) have implemented three models including 'the multivariate GARCH-BEKK, DCC and CCC'. As a result of the study, conditional correlation estimations were found to be statistically significant in almost all cases, but it was determined that they were very low, that is, the shock transfers between these markets were not significant.

Nazlioglu, Hammoudeh, and Gupta (2015) examined whether there was volatility/risk transmission between 'the Dow Jones Islamic stock markets and the three conventional markets (the US, Europe and Asia)' before, during and after the 2008 global financial crisis. The study also explored the volatility spillover dynamics between the aforementioned markets and the US economic policy uncertainty index, oil prices, VIX and federal funding rate. As a result of the study, the presence of significant volatility spillover between 'Islamic and conventional indices' was determined.

In their study including 'three sub-periods as pre-crisis, crisis and post-crisis', Saadaoui and Boujelbene (2015) investigated the volatility spillover between 'the Dow Jones stock indices and six Dow Jones emerging Islamic stock indices (Hungary, Malaysia, Mexico, Peru, Poland, Turkey)'. As a result of the study, it was concluded that there was a spillover especially during the crisis period and the crisis affected all financial assets, whether Islamic or not.

Kılıç and Buğan (2016) investigated the spillover effects between the USA S & P-500 index and six Dow Jones regional indices (E1DOW, DJIEU, DJGCC, DJIGCC, DWAP, DJIAP). As a result of the study, apart from the relationship between Europe and Asia-Pacific regions, it was seen that there was a financial spillover effect in all relations between 'Islamic and conventional markets'. The findings also show that there is a high correlation between their returns. In the crisis period, this relationship is not persistently decreasing and reactions to shocks occur at different times. The overall result of the empirical work was that Islamic markets did not respond differently to financial shocks emerging from conventional markets and there were no safe zones for investors during the financial crisis.

Mensi et al. (2016) carried out their study on 10 'Dow Jones Islamic and conventional sector index' pairs ('basic products, consumer goods, consumer services, finance, health services, industrialists, energy, technology, telecommunications and public services'). As a result of the study, the Islamic-conventional financial sector index pairs were found to be related to the period from 2001 to 2015 despite the prohibitions of Islamic principles.

Rejeb (2016) investigated the existence of volatility spillover for crisis period and calm period between 10 conventional market indices ('developing markets', 'Arabian markets', 'Arabian markets except S. Arabia', 'GCC', 'Canada', 'UK', 'USA', 'Europe', 'Asia-Pacific', 'World market') and eight Islamic market indices ('developing Islamic market', 'general Islamic market', 'Canada Islamic', 'England Islamic', 'USA Islamic', 'Europe Islamic', 'Asia-Pacific Islamic', 'World Islamic'). As a result of the study, it was determined that Islamic markets were sensitive to financial crises, there was a strong dependence on Islamic markets from conventional markets and this dependence spreads among Islamic markets. These results show that the Islamic finance industry has failed to provide a strong safeguard against economic and financial shocks affecting conventional markets.

Majdoub and Sassi (2017) examined the volatility spillover and hedging effectiveness between China and Asian Islamic stock indices. As a result of the study, there was a significant positive and negative return on the Asian Islamic stock markets selected from China and a two-way volatility spillover between China, Korea and Thailand Islamic markets existed. This shows evidence of short-term predictability on Chinese Islamic stock market movements. However, there is no short-term volatility permanence in India, Indonesia and Malaysia.

In their study, Shahzad et al. (2017) contributed to the current debates on the empirical evidence of the hypothesis of the separation of Islamic stock markets from their basic peers. For this purpose, they investigated return and volatility spillover between three 'conventional stock markets (USA, UK and Japan)', the 'global Islamic stock index (DJIM)' and a number of important macroeconomic and financial variables ('VIX index', the 'US stock market uncertainty index', 'US 10-year Treasury bond yields' and 'crude oil prices'). As a result of the study, strong interactions between 'global Islamic stock market', 'conventional stock exchanges' and significant risk factors have been determined. This shows that the 'Islamic and conventional stock markets' are not decomposed.

Celik, Ozdemir, and Gulbahar (2018) examined the existence of return and volatility spillover through VAR-EGARCH model between the 'US and MSCI emerging markets' and 'Islamic stock index (Indonesia, Malaysia and Turkey)'. As a result of the study, it was found out that there was an asymmetric and multifaceted return and volatility spillover between developed countries and developing countries in terms of Islamic indices.

When the summary of the literature is examined, the studies on the volatility spillover between Islamic markets and conventional markets show that there is no differentiation between the markets. Only Majdoub and Mansour (2014) found a very low level of volatility relationship between Islamic markets and conventional markets, but evidence for strong volatility was found in other studies. Moreover, another point that is noteworthy in the literature is to explore the relationship between Islamic indices and developed markets such as the USA, Japan and European countries.

3. RESEARCH METHODOLOGY

It is a fact that the volatility of an asset is not directly observable so it is necessary to construct a model. The volatility is used as a measure of uncertainty or risk which plays an important role in financial market analysis. Hence, by means of a constructed model, the volatility can be easily measured and predicted. In the financial analysis literature, there are various volatility models which have been suggested to evaluate the characteristics of return for an asset. When the major characteristics of the high-frequency time series data are considered:

1. The volatility changes over-time in a continuous style.
2. The volatility clustering is the most common attribute with the periods of big changes in prices alternate with the periods during which small price changes or almost no changes occur. This leads to an asymmetric feature in the volatility.
3. In addition, excess kurtosis or fat-tailed feature is frequently observed.

The major aim of this work is to analyse the existence of volatility spillover between conventional stock index and participation index based on the indexes in Turkish Capital Markets, namely BIST-30, against Katılım-30 Participation Indexes. In this chapter, DECO approach is applied to capture the volatility of indexes. Based on the theoretical and conceptual framework, data and the empirical findings are discussed in the following and policy recommendations are made to contribute relevant literature.

3.1. Data

BIST-30 and Katılım-30 indexes are used as the representatives of conventional stock index and participation index, respectively. The daily return series of BIST-30 and Katılım-30 stock indexes are used for the period July 2014–October 2018.

The previous empirical literature examines the comparative behaviour of the Islamic financial markets and conventional markets (e.g., Al-Khazali, Lean, & Samet, 2014; Beck, Demirguc-Kunt, & Merrouche, 2013; Hayat & Kraussl, 2011; Jawadi, Jawadi, & Louhichi, 2014; Milly & Sultan, 2012) In this context, there are two major types of investor profiles, that is, faith-based stock investors and conventional-based stock investors (Umar, 2017). Faith-based investors only buy shares in Sharia-compliant equity and keep out traditional equities from their asset portfolio. On the contrary, the conventional investors' portfolio contains both Islamic and traditional equities. This information is critical for the interpretations of the empirical findings in the following sections.

3.2. Methodology

The major steps of modelling BIST-30 and Katılım-30 are given in Fig. 1 such that the first and second steps start with calculation of the descriptive statistics and the routine stationarity tests are applied. Third step is the estimation for univariate model by using HYGARCH (1,d,1). As the fourth step, DECO model is estimated for pairwise return series. Afterwards, robustness test is implemented to ensure the reliability of DECO model in the fifth step. Finally, the existence of relationship between BIST-30 and Katılım-30 are tested and also the direction of this relationship is investigated by using the nonlinear Granger Causality tests.

3.3. Descriptive Statistics

Both of the return series are not normally distributed and they are skewed to the right. The graphs of BIST-30 and Katılım-30 are shown in Fig. 2a and 2b, respectively.

3.4. Stationarity Tests

The time series analysis starts with testing the normality and stationarity of the data to proceed to the next steps. The 'Augmented Dickey Fuller (ADF) test' and 'Kwiatkowski–Phillips–Schmidt–Shin (KPSS) test' results of BIST30 and Katılım-30 are shown in Tables 1–4, respectively. It should be noted that the null

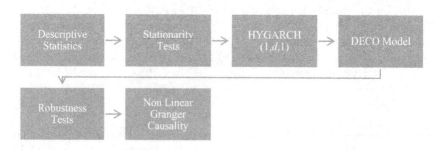

Fig. 1.   The Major Steps in Modelling BIST-30 and Katılım-30.

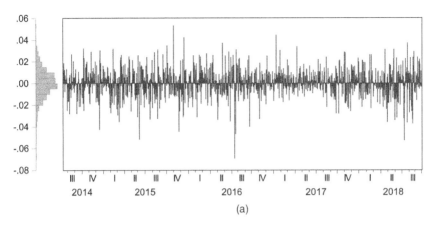

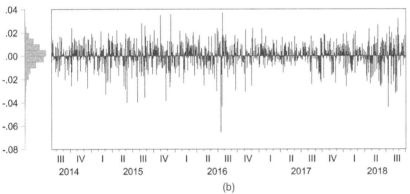

Fig. 2. (a) BIST-30 Return Series (2014–2018). (b) Katılım-30 Return Series (2014–2018).

Table 1. ADF Test Results of BIST-30.

	t-Statistic	Prob.
With constant	−32.9854	0.0000***
With constant and trend	−32.9705	0.0000***
Without constant and trend	−32.9904	0.0000***

Table 2. ADF Test Results of Katılım-30.

	t-Statistic	Prob.
With constant	−31.3642	0.0000***
With constant and trend	−31.3496	0.0000***
Without constant and trend	−31.3467	0.0000***

Note: ***Significant at %1 confidence interval.

Table 3. KPSS Test Results of BIST-30.

	t-Statistic	Prob.
With constant	0.0710	-
With constant and trend	0.0618	-

Table 4. KPSS Test Results of Katılım-30.

	t-Statistic	Prob.
With constant	0.0495	–
With constant and trend	0.0466	–

hypotheses for ADF test and KPSS test are the inverse and the KPSS test results are important to secure the stationarity requirements for robust model estimation process (Dickey & Fuller, 1979; Kwiatkowski, Phillips, Schmidt, & Shin, 1992).

According to ADF Test and KPSS Test results, BIST-30 and Katılım-30 series are stationary. Based on these test results, it is possible to proceed to the next stage to estimate individual HYGARCH $(1,d,1)$ processes for the variables.

4. HYGARCH $(1,d,1)$

The Nobel Prize winning Engle (1982) proposes that the heteroskedasticity of conditional variance can be expressed as a 'linear function of past squared errors' which is called 'autoregressive conditional heteroskedasticity (ARCH)' model. ARCH models are specifically developed to determine the volatility properties of high-frequency time series in financial markets. Engle's approach (ARCH) could be useful for clarifying market developments where turbulent periods, with big variation, are followed by stable periods, with modest variations. In addition to this, Davidson (2004) contributes to the literature by a new econometric model, that is, the 'hyperbolic GARCH,' or HYGARCH model as a generalisation of fractionally integrated GARCH model (FIGARCH) with hyperbolic convergence rates in order to give a more general framework to model the long memory characteristics in the series and overcome the limitations of infinite unconditional variance.

Davidson (2004) argues that HYGARCH does not put in force infinite variances, rather it permits the data to control the power of the heteroskedastic equation. In other words, HYGARCH has the expected property of the finite variance as the GARCH process while at the same time, its auto correlation function (ACF) decays hyperbolically. In this chapter, considering the characteristics of the return data, HYGARCH model is used for calculating individual alpha and beta parameters respectively (Conrad, 2010; Li Muyi et al., 2014).

The memory parameter generated from HYGARCH model has usually a value equal to/or between zero and one. When $d=1$, then the model reduces to a GARCH model and hence, non-negativity conditions are all the same for HYGARCH.

The first-order HYGARCH model equation is defined in the Eq. (1):

$$y_t = \varepsilon_t \sqrt{h_t}$$

$$h_t = \frac{\gamma}{1-\beta} + \left\{1 - \frac{1-\delta B}{1-\beta B}[1 - w + w(1-B)^d]\right\}y_t^2, \tag{1}$$

$$h_t = (1-w)h_{1,t} + w h_{2,t}$$

with

$$h_{1,t} = \gamma + \beta h_{1,t-1} + (\delta - \beta)y_{t-1}^2$$

and

$$h_{2,t} = \gamma + \beta h_{2,t-1} + [1 - \beta B - (1 - \delta B)(1-B)^d]y_t^2.$$

In our case, the d parameter is not statistically significant for any of the variables. The univariate HYGARCH $(1,d,1)$ calculations are shown in Tables 5 and 6. The sample 'mean of squared residuals' is taken to establish the repeated application. The positivity restriction for the GARCH $(1,1)$ is fulfilled for BIST-30 and Katılım-30, respectively. This restriction is expressed as 'alpha[L]/[1–beta(L)] >= 0'. The unconditional variance is '0.000215306' for BIST-30 and the unconditional variance is '0.000142614' for Katılım-30. The conditions are as expected: 'alpha[0] > 0', 'alpha[L] + beta[L] < 1' and 'alpha[i] + beta[i] >= 0'. Therefore, it is possible to proceed to the next stage to establish DECO model.

4.1. DECO Model

In this chapter, DECO model is proposed to simplify structural assumptions by introducing a form in which all twosomes of returns take the same correlation for a given period of time. On the other hand, by definition this correlation changes over time. Engle (2002) was the very first in the literature to introduce Dynamic Conditional Correlation (DCC) in order to simplify multivariate measurement. Engle and Sheppard (2005) claim that DCC can be successfully implemented for

Table 5. HYGARCH Parameter Estimations for BIST-30.

	Coefficient	SE	t-value	t-prob
Cst(M)	0.000420	0.00039113	1.074	0.2831
Cst(V) x 10^4	0.010442	0.0094158	1.109	0.2677
ARCH(Alpha1)	**0.022461**	**0.0077364**	**2.903**	**0.0038**
GARCH(Beta1)	**0.972689**	**0.0095317**	**102.0**	**0.0000**
No. Observations: 1,038				
No. Parameters: 4				
Mean (Y): 0.00013				
Variance (Y): 0.00018				
Skewness (Y): −0.28595				
Kurtosis (Y): 4.55355				
Log Likelihood: 3022.857				
Alpha[1]+Beta[1]: 0.99515				

Table 6. HYGARCH Parameter Estimations for Katılım-30.

	Robust Standard Errors (Sandwich Formula)			
	Coefficient	SE	t-value	t-prob
Cst(M)	0.000466	0.00030709	1.518	0.1294
Cst(V) x 10^4	0.011536	0.012072	0.9556	0.3395
ARCH(Alpha1)	**0.037838**	**0.014729**	**2.569**	**0.0103**
GARCH(Beta1)	**0.954073**	**0.021680**	**44.01**	**0.0000**

No. Observations: 1,038
No. Parameters: 4
Mean (Y): 0.00023
Variance (Y): 0.00011
Skewness (Y): −0.71081
Kurtosis (Y): 5.55839
Log Likelihood: 3267.790
Alpha[1]+Beta[1]: 0.99191

the high-dimensional assets up to 100 items. Engle and Kelly (2012) state that the DECO model is related to DCC model and in fact, it is a special type of the DCC model. The specialty could be defined as the fact that the correlations across all two-somes of assets are equal in DECO model. However, the common equicorrelation is time varying. DECO model provides consistent parameter estimates by using a quasi-maximum likelihood. Firstly, the model is constructed by calibrating individual volatilities. Afterwards the correlations are calculated. In this way, DECO model is designed to enhance the portfolio selection process compared to an 'unrestricted dynamic correlation' structure. In addition, Clements, Scott, and Silvennoien (2014) argue that DECO model gives more advanced forecasting ability for the duration of the financial crisis periods compared to the various portfolios.

The major advantage of DECO model is to minimise the computational and presentational difficulties for high-dimensional systems. This can be achieved by 'equicorrelated matrices' which have simple analytic 'inverses and determinants'. The probability computations are significantly simplified by DECO model and the optimisation is possible for large amount of assets. The DECO model is defined as Eq. (2), where ρt is the equicorrelation, I_n denotes the 'n-dimensional identity matrix', and J_n is the '$n \times n$ matrix of ones':

$$R_t = (1-\rho_t)I_n + \rho_t J_n, \qquad R_t^{-1} = \frac{1}{1-\rho_t}I_n + -\frac{\rho_t}{(1-\rho_t)(1+[n-1]\rho_t}J_n,$$

$$\det(R_t) = (1-\rho_t)^{n-1}(1+[n-1]\rho_t).$$

$$R_t = \begin{pmatrix} (1-\rho_{1,1,t})I_{n_1} & 0 & \cdots \\ 0 & \ddots & 0 \\ \vdots & 0 & (1-\rho_{K,K,t})I_{n_k} \end{pmatrix} + \begin{pmatrix} \rho_{1,1,t}J_{n1} & \rho_{1,2,t}J_{n_1 \times n_2} & \cdots \\ \rho_{2,1,t}J_{n_2 \times n_1} & \ddots & \\ \vdots & & \rho_{K,K,t}J_{n_K}, \end{pmatrix}, \quad (2)$$

where $\rho_{l,m,t} = \rho_{m,l,t} \;\; \forall l,m.$

Based on the DECO definition in Eq. (2), the multivariate model is estimated in Table 7.

According to the empirical findings in Table 7, all the DECO parameters are in the array of ordinary estimates from GARCH models, that is, alpha = 0.028 and beta = 0.96. In addition, the Rho is equal to 0.84 which indicates a strong correlation between BIST30 and Katılım-30 for the observed period. Afterwards, the Li and McLeod's Multivariate Portmanteau robustness tests are applied for the DECO model in order to determine the goodness-of-fit in model diagnostics.

The test results are given in Table 8 for BIST-30 and Katılım-30, respectively.

In this work, the final stage is defined as the 'nonlinear Granger causality test' for the two variables in the following section.

4.2. Nonlinear Granger Causality Tests

The causality concept, which represents an essential view for analysing dynamic interactions and the strength of relationships between time series, is introduced by the pioneering works of Wiener (1956) and Granger (1969). There are various types of Granger causality tests such as bivariate causality, multivariate causality, asymmetric causality, linear panel causality, nonlinear causality and non-parametric causality applied in the literature depending on the structure of sample data.

In order to determine the structure of data, the BDS test is performed on the residuals of the data. Based on the BDS test results, the fact that the linearity null hypothesis is rejected in all cases indicates the presence for the nonlinearity of the data. In this respect, the 'nonlinear Granger Causality test' is implemented for the data to investigate the nonlinear predictive power of the model depending on the sample period (2014–2018). The 'nonlinear Granger causality test' results from Katılım-30 to BIST-30 and vice versa are given in Table 9, respectively.

Table 7. DECO Model.

	Robust Standard Errors (Sandwich formula)			
	Coefficient	SE	t-value	t-prob
Rho	0.843690	0.035760	23.59	0.0000
Alpha	0.028275	0.011296	2.503	0.0125
Beta	0.960647	0.021595	44.48	0.0000
df	8.412142	1.3888	6.057	0.0000

Table 8. Li and McLeod's Multivariate Portmanteau Test Results.

BIST-30	Katılım-30
Li-McLeod(5) = 26.8409 [0.139]	Li-McLeod(5) = 22.0107 [0.231]
Li-McLeod(10) = 51.6499 [0.102]	Li-McLeod(10) = 43.9399 [0.234]
Li-McLeod(20) = 86.6999 [0.285]	Li-McLeod(20) = 80.7627 [0.392]
Li-McLeod(50) = 213.892 [0.238]	Li-McLeod(50) = 186.239 [0.715]

Table 9.   The Nonlinear Granger Causality Test Results.

From Katılım-30 to BIST-30	From BIST-30 to Katılım-30
The lag parameter: $p = 2$ The Granger causality Index: GCI = 0.111542 The value of the F-test: 30.7687 The $p\_$value: 3.06193e-024 The critical value at 5% of risk: 2.463	The lag parameter: $p = 2$ The Granger causality Index: GCI = 0.102792 The value of the F-test: 28.2291 The $p\_$value: 2.72063e-022 The critical value at 5% of risk: 2.463

These empirical findings in Table 9 show that there is a statistically significant mutual causality link between BIST-30 and Katılım-30 for the sample period.

4.3. Discussion on the Empirical Findings

There is a volatility spillover between BIST-30 and Katılım-30. It is a fact that conventional investors are free to prefer any asset for their portfolio, but it is not the case for faith-based investors. In other words, the faith-based investors could only invest in Shariah complying assets and they are required to eliminate conventional assets from their portfolio, whereas, the conventional investors' portfolio contains both Islamic and conventional equities. In our case, the investors of both indexes have similar attitude and risk appetite. Considering this theoretical framework and Shariah rules, investors may be even the same conventional investors who try to diversify their portfolio risks in BIST.

Considering the empirical findings in the relevant literature, there is mostly a significant causality between conventional investors and participatory investors. The summary of empirical findings is shown at Table 10. It is seen that conventional investors and participant investors are related and they have the power to

Table 10.   The Summary of Empirical Findings in the Literature.

Literature	Empirical Finding
Mulyadi (2009)	C ↔ C
Albaity and Rahman (2011)	P ↔ P
Dania and Malhotra (2013)	C → P
Nazlioğlu et al. (2013)	C ↔ P
Hammoudeh et al.(2014)	C ↔ P
Majdoub and Mansour (2014)	Insignificant relationship
Saadaoui and Boujelbene (2015)	C ↔ P
Kiliç and Buğan (2016)	C ↔ P
Mensi et al. (2016)	C ↔ P
Rejeb (2016)	C → P
Majdoub and Sassi (2017)	P → P
Shahzad et al. (2017)	C ↔ P
Çelik etal (2018)	C ↔ P

Source: Compiled by the authors.

Notes: C: Conventional index; P: Participatory index; → one-sided causality; ↔ two-sided causality influence each other's investment decisions. Therefore, there is huge potential for improving the participative fund management strategies by using various innovative financial products based on Shariah rules in the world. It is a fact that the Muslim population in the world represents approximately one-fourth of the total population size. However, less than 1% of the share of financial products to which this investor segment may be interested in total financial assets is Shariah compliant. The establishment of Shariah complaint financial markets is not easy and there are some critical issues such as valuation of assets and funding cost management (PwC, 2009, pp. 4–5). It is a strict rule that Shariah boards should elevate costs of such financial products. This rule brings the necessity of asset screening closely. Currently, there is a scale problem in participative funds. In other words, there is a lack of liquidity in some instruments. In time when the participatory finance sector matures in the world, experts and fund management professionals will solve these issues. In this respect, financial institutions should review their current approach to their clients and renew their approach as the participatory finance sector develops.

There is a fast expanding investor profile in Islamic regions of the world. Especially, the Gulf Cooperation Council (GCC) countries and Malaysia are the key market players in the global Takaful market. In addition, Turkey, Indonesia, India and Pakistan have great potential markets. After the global financial crisis, there is a rise in the Shariah complaint products in the global financial markets based on political reasons.

5. CONCLUSION

In this work, the existence of volatility spillover between conventional stock index and participation index is analysed based on the indexes in Turkish Capital Markets, namely BIST-30, against Katılım-30 Participation Indexes. The DECO methodology is applied to the daily data for the period July 2014–October 2018. There is a strong correlation between BIST-30 and Katılım-30. There exists volatility spillover between them. Conditional covariances and conditional correlations have the same pattern that indicates that their responses to shocks are also similar. They are affected by the same shocks. There is a short memory character for these indexes since d parameters of the series are not significant.

Considering the Shariah rules, we expect to see different investor behaviours for Katılım-30 and BIST-30. However, they give the impression to be the same investors. In this respect, the investor profile in Turkish Capital Markets seems to be dominated by the conventional investors who are aiming to maximise their profit by utilising new instruments such as Katılım-30.

DECO model provides a considerable simplification in modelling time varying conditional covariance matrices for returns of an arbitrary number of assets. The equicorrelation presumption can be applied to decrease noise and enhance portfolio selection procedures, and it is a simplifying presumption that arises by nature in a wide range of financial contexts.

6. NEXT STEPS

This work may be expanded in various ways. This study may be expanded by taking asymmetric effects into consideration. In addition, causal relations between Islamic and conventional indices may be investigated. Besides, by comparing the relations between Islamic stock indices and fundamental risk factors and macroeconomic variables, the responses of Islamic indices to these factors and the responses of conventional indices to the same factors may be compared. These relations may be discussed on an industrial basis in further studies.

REFERENCES

Ajmi, A. N., Hammoudeh, S., Nguyen, D. K., & Sarafrazi, S. (2014). How strong are the causal relationships between islamic and conventional finance systems? Evidence from linear and nonlinear tests. *Journal of International Financial Markets, Institutions & Money, 28*, 213–227.

Albaity, M., & Ahmad, R. (2011). Return performance, leverage effect, and volatility spillover in Islamic stock indices evidence from DJIMI, FTSEGII and KLSI. *Investment Management and Financial Innovations, 8*(3), 161–171.

Al-Khazali, O., Lean, H. H., & Samet, A. (2014). Do Islamic stock indexes outperform conventional stock indexes? A stochastic dominance approach. *Pacific-Basin Finance Journal, 28*, 29–46.

Aydin, N. (2012). Time value of money. In G. Sevil & M. Başar (Eds.), *Financial management-I*, T. C. Anadolu University Pub. No 2577 (pp. 56–83). Eskişehir: Anadolu University.

Beck, S., Demirguc-Kunt, A., & Merrouche, Q., (2013). Islamic vs. conventional banking: Business model, efficiency and stability. *Journal of Banking Finance, 37*, 433–447.

Buğan, M. F. (2016). Islamic stock indices. In S. Erdoğan, A. Gedikli, & D. Ç. Yıldırım (Eds.), *Islamic economy and finance* (pp. 249–272). Kocaeli: Umuttepe Publishing.

Celik, I., Ozdemir, A., & Gulbahar, S. D. (2018). Return and volatility spillover between Islamic stock indices: An application of multivarite VAR-EGARCH on developed and emerging markets. *Bulletin of Accounting and Finance Reviews, 1*(2), 89–100.

Clements, A., Scott, A., & Silvennoinen, A., (2014). *On the benefits of equicorrelation for portfolio allocation*. NCER Working Paper Series No. 99. Retrieved from http://www.ncer.edu.au/papers/documents/WP99.pdf.

Conrad, C. (2010). Non-negativity conditions for the hyperbolic GARCH model. *Journal of Econometrics, 157*, 441–457.

Dania, A., & Malhotra, D. K. (2013). An empirical examination of the dynamic linkages of faith-based socially responsible investing. *The Journal of Wealth Management, 16*(1), 65–79.

Davidson, J. (2004). Moment and memory properties of linear conditional heteroscedasticity models, and a new model. *Journal of Business & Economic Statistics, 22*, 16–29.

Dewandaru, G., Bacha, O. I., Masih., A. M. M., & Masih, R. (2015). Risk-return characteristics of Islamic equity indices: Multi-timescales analysis. *Journal of Multinational Financial Management, 29*, 115–138.

Dickey, D. A., & Fuller, W. A. (1979). Distribution of estimators for autoregressive time series with a unit root. *Journal of the American Statistical Association, 74*, 427–431

Engle, R. F. (1982). Autoregressive conditional heteroskedasticity with estimates of the variance of United Kingdom inflation. *Econometrica, 50*, 987–1007.

Engle, R. F. (2002). Dynamic conditional correlation: A simple class of multivariate generalized autoregressive conditional heteroskedasticity models. *Journal of Business and Economic Statistics, 20*, 339–350.

Engle, R. F., & Kelly, B. (2012). Dynamic equicorrelation. *Journal of Business & Economic Statistics, 30*(2), 212–228.

Engle, R. F., & Sheppard, K. (2005). *Theoretical and empirical properties of dynamic conditional correlation multivariate GARCH*. Working Paper. Oxford University.

Gebka, B., & Serwa, D. (2007). Intra- and inter-regional spillovers between emerging capital markets around the world. *Research in International Business and Finance, 21*(2007), 203–221.

Granger, C. W. J. (1969). Investigating causal relations by econometric models and cross-spectral methods. *Econometrica, 37*, 424–459.

Hammoudeh, S., Mensi, W., Reboredo, J. C., & Nguyen, D. K. (2014). Dynamic dependence of the global Islamic equity index with global conventional equity market indices and risk factors. *Pacific-Basin Finance Journal, 30*(C), 189–206.

Hayat, R., & Kraussl, R., (2011). Risk and return characteristics of Islamic equity funds. *Emerging Markets Review, 12*, 189–203.

ICD-Thomson Reuters. (2018). Islamic finance development report-2018. Retrieved from https:// repository.salaamgateway.com/images/iep/galleries/documents/20181125124744259232831. pdf. Accessed on January 8, 2019.

Jawadi, F., Jawadi, N., & Louhichi, W. (2014). Conventional and Islamic stock price performance: An empirical investigation. *International Economics, 137*, 73–87.

Kılıç, Y., & Buğan, M. F. (2016). Are Islamic equity markets "Safe Havens"? Testing the contagion effect using DCC-GARCH. *International Journal of Academic Research in Accounting, Finance and Management Sciences, 6*(4), 167–176.

Kwiatkowski, D., Phillips, P. C. B., Schmidt, P., & Shin, Y. (1992). Testing the null hypothesis of stationarity against the alternative of a unit root. *Journal of Econometrics, 54*, 159–178.

Majdoub, J., & Mansour, W. (2014). Islamic equity market integration and volatility spillover between emerging and US stock markets. *The North American Journal of Economics and Finance, 29*, 452–470.

Majdoub, J., & Sassi, S. B. (2017). Volatility spillover and hedging effectiveness among China and emerging Asian Islamic equity indexes. *Emerging Markets Review, 31*, 16–31.

Masih, M., Kamil, N. K. M., & Bacha, O. I. (2018). Issues in Islamic equities: A literature survey. *Emerging Markets Finance and Trade, 54*(1), 1–26.

Mensi, W., Hammoudeh, S., Sensoy, A., & Yoon, S. M. (2016). Analysing dynamic linkages and hedging strategies between Islamic and conventional sector equity indexes. *Applied Economics, 49*(25), 2456–2479.

Milly, M., & Sultan, J. (2012). *Portfolio diversification during financial crisis: Analysis of faith based investment strategies. Building bridges across the financial communities: The global financial crisis, social responsibility, and faith-based finance* (pp. 334–352). Harvard Law School, Islamic Finance Project,.

Mulyadi, M. S. (2009). *Volatility spillover in Indonesia, USA, and Japan capital market.* MPRA Paper No. 16914. Munich Personal RePEc Archive.

Muyi, L., Li, W. K., & Li, G. (2014). A new hyperbolic GARCH model. Retrieved from https://pdfs. semanticscholar.org/efa6/682ba7e61f69a8941f22320a1630763652ff.pdf

Nazlioglu, S., Hammoudeh, S., & Gupta, R. (2015). Volatility transmission between Islamic and conventional equity markets: Evidence from causality-in-variance test. *Applied Economics, 47*(46), 1–16.

PwC. (2009). Shariah-compliant funds: A whole new world of investment. Retrieved from https://www. pwc.com/gx/en/financial-services/islamic-finance-programme/assets/shariah-compliant-funds. pdf

Rejeb, A. B. (2016). *Volatility spillover between Islamic and conventional stock markets: Evidence from quantile regression analysis.* MPRA Paper No. 73302, 1–44.

Saadaoui, A., & Boujelbene, Y. (2015). Volatility transmission between Dow Jones stock index and emerging Islamic stock index: Case of subprime financial crises. *Emerging Markets Journal, 5*(1), 40–49.

Shahzad, S. J. H., Ferrer, R., Ballester, L., & Umar, Z. (2017). Risk transmission between Islamic and conventional stock markets: A return and volatility spillover analysis. *International Review of Financial Analysis, 52*, 9–26.

Umar, Z., (2017). Islamic vs conventional equities in a strategic asset allocation framework. *Pacific-Basin Finance Journal, 42*, 1–10.

Wiener, N. (1956). The theory of prediction. In E. F. Beckenback (Ed.), *The theory of prediction* (Chap. 8 pp. 165–190.). New York, NY: McGraw-Hill.

CHAPTER 2

BANKRUPTCY RISK PREDICTION IN ASSURING THE FINANCIAL PERFORMANCE OF ROMANIAN INDUSTRIAL COMPANIES

Olimpia Livia Preda Buzgurescu and Negru Elena

ABSTRACT

Introduction – *The Romanian industry was one of the most important traditional branches and in the context of the integration of the country into the European Union, the Romanian industry has made progress in the development of several types of industrial branches, attracting in this sector investors with foreign capital that have determined economic growth by branch having a major impact on the achievement of gross domestic product. The progress and sustainable development of a country is interdependent on both macroeconomic and microeconomic development, and the development of a branch of the economy leads to the creation of a stable environment for attracting new investors and implicitly to the upward evolution of the economy by branch.*

Purpose – *This article identifies models of bankruptcy risk analysis that have as variables relevant performance indicators for examining the bankruptcy risk of Romanian industrial companies so that it is verified how predictable and significant it is to avoid their potential bankruptcy.*

Methodology – *By using performance indicators such as liquidity, profitability and insolvency, the analysis aims to be a benchmark for the Romanian industrial companies' research in terms of bankruptcy risk, but also the accuracy of the models chosen to diagnose a potential bankruptcy.*

Contemporary Issues in Business, Economics and Finance
Contemporary Studies in Economic and Financial Analysis, Volume 104, 19–28
Copyright © 2020 by Emerald Publishing Limited
ISSN: 1569-3759/doi:10.1108/S1569-375920200000104003

Findings – *There was highlighted a strong relationship between the economic and financial indicators and the Z score functions.*

Keywords: Risk; performance; bankruptcy; industry; indicators; Romanian companies; Bucharest Stock Exchange; case study; Altman model; Conan & Holder model

JEL Classification: G23; O12; C12

1. INTRODUCTION

This article examines the role of bankruptcy prediction on the basis of discriminatory analysis in ensuring the financial performance of Romanian companies in the industrial branch. So, bankruptcy risk analysis models are identified that have as variables performance indicators relevant to the assessment of the economic and financial situation of the selected firms in the analysed sample in order to take the best decisions in the managerial risk situations.

Bankruptcy risk analysis is of interest to a wide range of stakeholders, such as creditors, suppliers, employees, shareholders and stock investors who are directly interested in taking decisions based on the likelihood of firms going bankrupt. In this regard, methods of assessing the risk of permanent bankruptcy have been developed.

The anticipation of the bankruptcy risk allows the premature identification of the causes and disturbing factors affecting the firm's activity, errors in the management of the enterprise and the adoption of appropriate measures for their elimination or reduction.

The prediction of bankruptcy and the understanding of the causes of economic failure are based on financial considerations. Bankruptcy involves direct costs of legal fees, fees of accountants and lawyers, bailiffs, but they are reduced compared to the losses incurred by investors (shareholders and creditors) due to the decrease in the company's value and its impossibility to repay debts and pay interest on them. At the same time, bankruptcy also entails indirect costs, such as losses for managers, employees, financial institutions, country, which in turn can reach considerable dimensions. All these costs justify efforts to identify the causes of bankruptcy and its prediction.

Also we can answer questions such as: What is the most relevant prediction model of bankruptcy risk? Can financial performance be ensured through the prediction of bankruptcy risk?

The hypothesis from which we started to realise the article refers to the existing relation between the financial performance indicators and the bankruptcy risk prediction for the companies in the industrial branch listed on the Bucharest Stock Exchange, thus emerging the hypothesis according to which there is a direct and a significant correlation between indicators of economic and financial performance (economic profitability rate, financial profitability rate, operating profit, net profit, turnover index) and bankruptcy risk prediction. This hypothesis will be verified and analysed on the basis of a study at the level of 11 companies in the Romanian industrial branch listed on the Bucharest Stock Exchange.

2. LITERATURE REVIEW

Bankruptcy is one of the biggest threats to companies and arises as a result of the company's inability to honour its payments on time. This concept is found in various areas such as literature, law, technology and economics.

The study of the problem of bankruptcy risk allowed the design of prediction models, useful both for economic theory and for practical activity. Among the evaluation methods recommended by the literature for bankruptcy risk assessment, it has been found that statistical methods are the most used in practice and provide the most relevant results.

Statistical methods provide an improvement in empirical methods for determining bankruptcy risk. Statistical methods are also divided into one-dimensional methods and multidimensional methods. The multidimensional approach implies, in fact, the classification of a set of *n* subjects, respectively, of enterprises, belonging to a particular sample and which are characterised by *m* variables (e.g., rates). In terms of risk analysis, discriminatory analysis is essential and was created by E.I. Altman.

In the literature, discriminatory analysis is most often used, on the basis of which numerous tools and models for analysing and predicting bankruptcy of enterprises have been developed. The most common such models are the Z-scores, which involve a linear combination of a set of financial ratios considered to be representative of the disparity of failed firms by non-food firms.

On the one hand, the author M. Niculescu (2005) defined an enterprise in difficulty according to the following criteria:

- insolvency – available assets did not allow debts to be settled;
- over-indebtedness – the high level of debt made it difficult to pay off debts; and
- existence of facts that compromised the continuity of the exploitation activity.

On the other hand, Szathmary-Miclea (2003) distinguished between the notion of bankruptcy and the bankruptcy risk, considering that the bankruptcy represented the probability that a debtor (trader, industrialist, banker) for some reason at some point would go bankrupt, instead bankruptcy referred to a state of affairs.

As an evolution over time, we are exemplifying some predictive bankruptcy risk models based on discriminatory analysis. In 1966, following a study of a sample of 79 bankruptcies and 79 non-food firms, Beaver (1966) published in Empirical Research in Accounting: Selected Studies, Supplement to *Journal of Accounting Research*, No.4, 'Financial ratios as predictors of failure', a forecasted bankruptcy risk model based on five financial ratios.

Altman (1968) analysed the activity in the period 1946–1965, of 33 industrial companies with financial problems and 33 firms smoothly in terms of 22 indicators and created a model based on five rates considered which he published with comments in 1968 in 'Financial ratios, discriminant analysis and the prediction of corporate bankruptcy'. Since this model was applicable only to listed companies, the author replaced the indicator that was related to market value and recalculated the weight of all indicators. To extend the application of the model to other business areas (not only in the industry), he reconsidered the score function and retained four rates.

J. Argenti (1976) analysed the bankruptcy risk and found out that the financial indicators did not have the same value; they varied from one case to another. Conan and Holder (1979) published a model based on research findings on a sample of 95 industrial companies (1970–1975). The authors also collaborated on the development of specific models for other fields of activity. Keasey and Watson (1991) showed in 1987, through the study of 73 failed firms and 73 non-bankruptcy firms, that the inclusion of non-financial variables increased the prediction power of the model.

In Romania there was also interest in the development of a tool for prediction models of bankruptcy risk for banks and companies. Gheorghe Bailesteanu (2005), based on the Altman, Argenti, Conan and Holder models, proposed in 1998 for Romanian companies a model consisting of four variables: current liquidity, debt service coverage, customer loan rotation rate and profit rate. I. Anghel (2002) proposed a score for the Romanian economy, starting from a sample of 276 companies belonging to 12 branches of the economy, which were divided into 60% healthy companies and 40% bankruptcy. Then, by applying the discriminatory analysis, four financial ratios and a constant were retained. D. Circiumaru (2013) elaborated in 2007, taking as a sample 152 industrial companies listed on the Stock Exchange, for the construction of the model, six financial rates with discriminatory power were retained.

In 2012, D. Circiumaru developed another model, taking into account the financial bankruptcy connotation instead of the legal one, so diagnosing the financial difficulties of a firm with a high probability of achieving net loss for consecutive years and with a high probability of going bankrupt in the future, triggered an alarm before the traditional score functions, built on legal bankruptcy.

For the construction of the score function, 18 financial ratios were tested. Applying the discriminatory analysis, four financial ratios have been retained as having the highest discriminating power, and the accessibility of entry data and the ease with which a company is ranked among bankrupt firms. In 2014, an econometric prediction model was developed by Brédart, which showed a prediction accuracy of more than 80%, using three correlated financial ratios as variables (2014).

Another study on the effect of financial rates in bankruptcy prediction was conducted by Alkhatib and Bzour (2011) for companies in Jordan using the Altman and Kida models. Industrial and non-financial services companies for the years 1990–2006 were analysed. The model that outlined the possibility of bankruptcy in the analysed years was the Altman model with an average prediction capacity of 93.8% compared to the average of the Kida model of 69%.

Also, in the article 'Financial Failure Estimation of Companies in BIST Tourism Index by Altman Model and its Effect on Market Prices' (Karaca & Özen, 2017), the tourism sector companies listed on the Istanbul Stock Exchange with the Altman Z-score model were analysed in period 2009–2016 in order to show the evolution of the negative effects of the tourism sector in Turkey on the financial failures of the listed companies. The results showed that the problems occurred in the period 2015–2016 increased the risk of bankruptcy of tourism companies.

The article named 'Predicting financially distressed small- and medium-sized enterprises in Malaysia' pointed out the factors that might predict financially distressed for small and medium-sized enterprises. The companies were part of manufacturing sector. Using logic regression, it was found out that debt ratio, current ratio, short-term liabilities to total liabilities, return on assets, sales to total assets and net income to share capital were important factors in predicting bankruptcy. Also, the research showed that young companies were more likely to fail than established firms and that the larger the size of the company, the greater the probability that the enterprise will have financial problems.

We can draw the conclusion on the prediction of bankruptcy risk and, at the same time, we can increase the prediction capacity of the developed score functions to announce the bankruptcy risk, being also a sensitive area in which the specialists have proposed to investigate, develop and improve the prediction of a mathematical model that answers questions such as:

- 'What is the probability of the company going bankrupt or not?'
- 'How predictable and easy to apply by stakeholders is the model?'

3. RESEARCH METHODOLOGY

Among the score functions developed in the foreign and Romanian literature, useful in predicting the bankruptcy risk and for testing the predictive capacity of the score functions, a statistical study was carried out on a sample of 11 companies from the Romanian industrial branch listed on the Stock Exchange Bucharest, for the period 2015–2017. Although the analysis included only Romanian companies, foreign score functions have been used, due to their relevance to economies other than those for which they were developed. For the case study, three score functions were chosen (Altman, 1968; Circiumaru, 2013; Conan & Holder, 1979). From a multitude of models for bankruptcy risk analysis, we chose three models for comparing results, namely the Altman model because it represents the original model based on which the bankruptcy risk analysis was developed. The Circiumaru model is relevant to the selected sample, as it was developed for the Romanian companies. The Conan and Holder model was selected because the characteristics of this model are close to those of the Romanian companies.

3.1. Data and Methodology Description

The 1968 Altman model was developed on the basis of a representative sample of 66 businesses, of which 33 companies were healthy and 33 firms had financial difficulties. For the construction of the model, 22 financial ratios were tested, of which 5 were retained as having significant discriminating power. The Altman's score function in 1968 had the following form:

$$Z = 1.2\,X_1 + 1.4\,X_2 + 3.3\,X_3 + 0.6\,X_4 + 1.0\,X_5$$

where X_1 = Working capital/total assets; X_2 = Retained earnings/total assets; X_3 = Earnings before interest and taxes/total assets; X_4 = Market v alue of equity/book value of total debt; and X_5 = Sales/total assets.

The ranges of values of the function are:

- if $Z < 1.81$ – the firm is bankrupt;
- if $1.81 < Z \leq 2.90$ – the company is in distress;
- if $Z > 2.90$ – the company might be considered economically healthy.

Analysing the companies with financial difficulties, Altman identified five phases of bankruptcy in an enterprise:

- the emergence of first signs of financial difficulties (slight decrease in profitability, turnover, reduction in cash availability) but ignored by the company's management;
- the clear manifestation of financial difficulties, which are not followed by the adoption of resolution measures in the hope that they will disappear on their own;
- the strong deterioration of the financial situation, the disturbing factors affecting the entire activity of the firm;
- the collapse or the inability of management to take adequate measures to remedy the situation;
- intervention, either by recovery measures or by declaring bankruptcy.

Conan and Holder have developed several score functions, differentiated on the sectors of activity of the studied companies, namely the industrial domain, the wholesale trade sector and the transport sector. For industrial companies, the score function is as follows: $Z = 0.24\ X_1 + 0.22\ X_2 + 0.16\ X_3 - 0.78\ X_4 - 0.10\ X_5$

where X_1 = Gross operating surplus/total debts; X_2 = Long-term capital/total capital; X_3 = (Cash + Receivables)/total assets; X_4 = Financial charges/turnover; and X_5 = Personnel expenses/value added.

According to this function, the companies enterprises can fall into one of the following categories:

- good situation, when $Z > 0.9$ and the probability of failure is less than 30%;
- caution, when $0.04 \leq Z < 0.09$ and the probability of bankruptcy is between 30% and 65%; and
- danger, when $Z < 0.04$ and the probability of bankruptcy is more than 65%.

The Circiumaru model (2013) brought novelty to the consideration of bankruptcy instead of the legal one for companies that had a net loss of at least two years out of the four analysed before the legal insolvency proceedings are triggered, by the will of the creditors. The calculated score function has four highest financial rates and is as follows:

$$Z = 0.041\ R_1 + 0.055\ R_2 + 0.924\ R_3 + 0.493\ R_4 + 0.249$$

where R_1 = Total debt ratio (total debt/total capital); R_2 = Financial return rate (net profit/equity); R_3 = Economic return rate (operating profit/total assets); and R_4 = Permanent fixed capital ratio (permanent fixed capital/total capital).

According to this score, companies can fall into one of the following categories:

- $Z < 0.506$ – firms have financial difficulties.
- $0.506 < Z < 0.546$ – uncertainty area.
- $Z > 0.546$ – firms are healthy.

In order to test the predictive capacity of the selected scores, Altman (1968), Connan and Holder (1979), and Circiumaru (2013), a statistical study will be carried out on a number of 11 chosen Romanian companies listed on the Bucharest Stock Exchange in the industrial branch for the period 2015–2017.

3.2. Case Study

Based on the financial statements for the years covered by the study and the financial ratios applicable to the score functions, the bankruptcy risk prediction for the 11 companies in the Romanian industrial branch will be determined: Tmk Artrom, Alum Tulcea, Alro SA (industry of aluminium processing); Turbomecanica (aeronautical industry); OMV Petrom, Transgaz (petroleum industry); Transelectrica (energy industry); Rompetrol Well Services, Dafora (oil and gas extraction industry); Altur (industry of manufacture of machine parts); and Bucovina SA Scheia (food industry).

First, the financial institutions, banks, shipping and construction companies on the Bucharest Stock Exchange were not taken into account for the present research. The 11 Romanian companies represent 13% of the total of the remaining companies (83). These companies are part of the most important domains of activity and were randomly selected.

The study will determine the possibility of testing the hypothesis according to which score functions can predict the occurrence of bankruptcy, correlated with the gradual degradation of the financial rate and, implicitly, the calculated score for each function. The results of the score functions calculated based on the three methods are described in Table 1.

For TMK Artrom, the Altman Score values for the entire timeframe analysed showed that the situation of the company could be considered economically good ($Z > 2.90$). Also, Conan and Holder scores highlighted a good financial situation recorded by the company over the three years under review, with the lowest bankruptcy risk ($Z > 0.09$), although in 2016 and 2017 the likelihood of bankruptcy risk was over 30%. According to the Circiumaru model, the economic entity had in all years taken into account a financial situation without difficulty.

For Alum Tulcea, the Conan and Holder and Circiumaru models best described the poor financial situation in the three years in correlation with economic and financial ratios such as total indebtedness, net profit and constantly employed capital. According to the Circiumaru model, in 2015 the company was

Table 1. Values of Score Functions for the Analysed Companies.

The Name of Company	Altman (1968)			Conan and Holder			Circiumaru (2012)		
	2015	2016	2017	2015	2016	2017	2015	2016	2017
TMK Artrom	23.64	23.07	20.68	0.10	0.09	0.09	0.67	0.60	0.57
Alum Tulcea	985.85	512.89	397.21	−0.01	−0.14	0.05	0.52	0.48	4.85
Turbomecanica	4.19	6.32	6.27	−0.03	0.06	0.13	0.70	0.76	0.80
OMV Petrom	14.30	22.07	24.48	216.91	112.78	87.28	0.65	0.71	0.75
Transgaz	2.06	2.26	2.31	1.62	0.79	0.69	0.82	0.84	0.83
Transelectrica	13.93	15.74	18.63	0.26	0.25	0.18	0.69	0.67	0.63
Alro SA	8.18	7.45	7.26	73.66	−81.13	1.10	0.57	0.72	0.68
Rompetrol Well Services	63.24	45.83	39.64	−0.65	0.04	0.25	0.49	0.65	0.71
Dafora	0.01	−0.75	9.75	−0.72	−0.68	0.45	−0.57	−0.66	1.33
Altur	34.89	36.18	37.82	0.03	0.05	−0.10	0.60	0.63	0.62
Bucovina SA Scheia	1.84	1.64	1.59	0.03	−0.01	−0.11	0.19	0.15	0.01

Source: Calculated by the authors.

in the uncertainty area, and in the coming years it would be experiencing great financial difficulties. In this case, the Altman function did not render the company's financial reality.

The Turbomecanica firm, which is part of the aeronautical industry, had overall a good situation financial according to the values Z calculated using methods of predicting risk of bankruptcy, although in 2015 the probability of bankruptcy was high, greater than 65% according to the model Conan and Holder.

A company with excellent results according to economic indicators and score functions is OMV Petrom, which had a tremendously good financial situation for the period 2015–2017, this being reflected by the functions calculated using the three chosen models. For Transgaz, the coefficients for the Z function of the Conan and Holder and Circiumaru models showed a good financial situation compared to the Altman model, which stated that the firm had a difficult situation ($Z < 2.90$) in the years under review.

For Transelectrica, all score points indicated the same thing, namely that this company had a good and healthy financial situation over the 3 years analysed without encountering any economic difficulties in this respect. This was also supported by the company's financial indicators.

Scoring functions based on the three different methods of bankruptcy risk assessment showed differences between them. Thus, for Alro SA, the Altman model showed that the company did not face financial difficulties, with Z-score higher than 2.90. In the same way, according to the Circiumaru model, this firm was in a financially safe area. But a better rendering of economic reality is given by the Conan and Holder function, according to which the company was in the bankruptcy area in 2016 and recovered in the next year, reaching the value of the Z function of 1.10, which meant it succeeded to overcome bankruptcy.

According to the Altman model, Rompetrol Well Services recorded a good financial situation in the period under review, but the score had a slight downward trend due to the increase in current assets. The score functions of Conan and Holder and Circiumaru showed in 2015 a high likelihood of bankruptcy. Also, the two methods of assessing bankruptcy point out that in the following years the situation had improved considerably.

The economic and financial situation and the calculated scores indicated a very high probability of bankruptcy for Dafora in the first two years analysed under all bankruptcy risk assessment models. But the following year, it could be appreciated that the company had emerged from the risk area, having a better evolution, as demonstrated by the profitability rates.

At Altur, the three models revealed a different situation, so the Altman and Circiumaru score functions put the company out of the uncertainty. The Conan and Holder model showed financial difficulties, in 2015 the company was in danger of bankruptcy, in 2016 there was a slight recovery and 2017 was a year under a probability of bankruptcy risk. It should be noted that there has been a significant decrease in turnover from year to year, so that the deterioration of the financial situation was also evidenced by the economic profitability rate, which had a constant depreciation, the company's profitability was deficient with a poor efficiency of the activity. The same results can be observed with regard to the rate of financial return, as a conclusion can be appreciated a poor efficiency in the use of equity and the risk must be assumed by the shareholders.

At Bucovina SA Scheia, the economic and financial situation and the scores calculated on the basis of the chosen methods indicated a very high probability of insolvency. So, in all three years of analysis there was no good development of the financial situation. Therefore, the Altman score placed Bucovina SA Scheia in the uncertainty zone, with some financial difficulties ($Z < 1.81$). The Conan and Holder and Circiumaru models showed an imminent bankruptcy risk through the calculated scores, the company going on a loss in the three years under review, unable to recover its economic situation.

In this way, the three rating models for bankruptcy risk can fit financial statements of companies based on financial and economic indicators in the three areas: uncertainty, risk, uncertainty area and bankruptcy.

Based on the rating analysis of the 11 companies included in the sample, eight companies were identified that recorded values of the score functions that placed companies outside the uncertainty area, thus determining a good financial situation reflected in the positive evolution of performance indicators. Thus, the heterogeneity of the models is observed in the assessment of the financial situation of the companies.

4. CONCLUSION

From the analysis we can estimate the heterogeneity of the models in the diagnosis of the bankruptcy risk prediction of the companies, out of the 11 companies included in the study – nine companies are outside any bankruptcy risk having a positive evolution and a good financial situation given by the performance indicators, and two companies were in a situation of financial difficulty and a high probability of bankruptcy risk in all three years under review.

The scores calculated using the three models had a fairly accurate assessment of the situation that the 11 companies surveyed crossed the three years of analysis.

The depreciation of the financial situation of Dafora and Bucovina SA Scheia in the period of time analysed 2015–2017 was highlighted both in the deterioration of profitability indicators and other performance indicators as well as in the scores obtained for each function that indicated a bankruptcy risk prediction. From this point of view, the score functions used in the study, even if they did not predominantly have financial ratios reflecting profitability, had a similar prediction of the financial situation, but the best risk assessment could not be identified. But on the other hand, it was shown that the rating functions created for other economies indicated the real situation of the Romanian companies.

At the same time, the influence of financial indicators on the Z-score functions was demonstrated, being a relationship of dependence between them and the results of the functions. Thus, the financial position of the companies is influenced by the liquidity and solvency indicators, therefore the score functions may vary depending on the component elements.

Therefore, the case study demonstrated the previously announced hypothesis that there is a relationship between the economic and financial performance indicators, namely those of solvency and liquidity, on the basis of which are calculated the scores of the bankruptcy risk assessment methods, which are of particular importance for company management so that it takes the right decisions to prevent financial difficulties.

REFERENCES

Abdullah, N. A. H, Ahmad, A. H., Zainudin, N., & Rus, R. M. (2019). Predicting financially distressed small- and medium-sized enterprises in Malaysia. *Global Business Review*, *20*(3), 627–639.

Alkhatib, K., & Al Bzour, A. E. (2011). Predicting corporate bankruptcy of Jordanian listed companies: Using Altman and Kida models. *International Journal of Business and Management*, *6*(3), 208–215.

Altman, E. I. (1968). Financial ratios, discriminant analysis, and the prediction of corporate bankruptcy. *Journal of Finance*, *23*(September), 589–609.

Anghel, I. (2002). *Bankruptcy. Radiography and prediction*. Bucharest: Economica Publishing House.

Argenti, J. (1976). *Corporate collapse: The causes and the symptoms*. Maidenhead: McGraw-Hill.

Bailesteanu, G. (2005). *Diagnosis, risk and efficiency in business*. Timişoara: Mirton Publishing House.

Beaver, W. H. (1966). *Financial ratios as predictors of failure*. Blackwell Publishing. Empirical Research in Accounting-Selected Studies. *Journal of Accounting Research*, *4*, 71–111.

Bredart, X. (2014). Bankruptcy prediction model: The case of the United States. *International Journal of Economics and Finance*, *6*(3), 1–7.

Circiumaru, D. (2013). *Risk analysis of the company*. Craiova: Universitaria Publishing House.

Conan, D., & Holder, M. (1979). *Variables explicatives de performances et controle de gestion dans les P.M.I.*, These d'Etat, CERG, Université Paris Dauphine.

Karaca, S., & Özen, E. (2017). Financial failure estimation of companies in BIST tourism index by Altman model and its effect on market prices. *Broad Research in Accounting, Negotiation, and Distribution*, *8*(2), 11–23.

Keasey, K., & Watson, R. (1991). Financial distress prediction models: A review of their usefulness. *British Journal of Management*, *2*, 89–102.

Niculescu, M. (2005). *Financial diagnosis*. Bucureşti: Economica Publishing House.

Szathmary-Miclea, C. (2003). *Risk assessment and management in small and medium-sized enterprises*. Timişoara: West University Press.

CHAPTER 3

THE EFFECTS OF FEMALE EMPLOYMENT ON ECONOMIC GROWTH: AN APPLICATION OF PANEL DATA ON THE MEMBER COUNTRIES OF THE ORGANISATION OF ISLAMIC COOPERATION

Nurgül Emine Barin, Sabriye Kundak and Vildan Saba Cenikli

ABSTRACT

Introduction – *Female employment and policies are an important aspect of growth and development. Inadequate utilisation of female labour force within the national economy reflects in economic and social indicators especially in developing countries. Women's self-development, active participation in labour markets, and social and economic opportunities are the main factors in the development of countries. This study attempts to research the effects of female work force participation in the member countries of the Organisation of Islamic Cooperation (OIC) on economic growth in time period between 2004 and 2016. The countries were selected among the countries that have high and middle human development index according to Human Development Report in 2017.*

Contemporary Issues in Business, Economics and Finance
Contemporary Studies in Economic and Financial Analysis, Volume 104, 29–44
Copyright © 2020 by Emerald Publishing Limited
All rights of reproduction in any form reserved
ISSN: 1569-3759/doi:10.1108/S1569-375920200000104004

Purpose – *In this chapter, it is aimed to support the employment of female labour force and to show its share in development and growth in the member countries of the OIC. The aspect differs from similar studies to address the issue in term of Islamic countries.*

Methodology – *While analysing the impact of female employment on growth, the panel data analysis method and fixed and random effect model were used.*

Findings – *It has been found that female employment has a positive impact on economic growth for the selected OIC countries.*

Keywords: Female workforce; growth; employment; panel data analysing; economic growth; female employment

JEL classification: J16; F43; C33

1. INTRODUCTION

The removal of barriers to women's participation in working life became a necessity in the modern global economy. There is a widespread belief in Islamic countries that there are reservations about the participation of women in working life within the framework of Islamic rules. The purpose of the study is to eliminate this prejudice by investigating how much the effect of women's employment on growth in Islamic countries.

Many studies confirm the positive relation between overall growth and women's employment share (Goldin, 1986; Lofstrom, 2009; Sehrawat & Giri, 2017; Taymaz, 2010; Tsani, Paroussos, Fragiadakis, Charalambidis, & Capros, 2013; Verick, 2018; Zeren & Savrul, 2017). In a study published in 2013, GDP in OECD countries could increase 12% with more gender-balanced economy (OECD, 2013, January). The McKinsey Global Institute (2015) reported that exterminating gender differentiation in the working place will annex a forecasted $12 trillion to the world GDP by 2025.

When we look at the issue legally, it is emphasised in many international documents that labour force participation is a right for both sexes, the necessity of equal opportunities for participation in employment.

In the ILO Report published in 2019, the difference in employment rates between men and women has decreased by less than two points in the last 27 years. In 2018, women rated point 26% lower in employment than men. This result contradicts the findings of the ILO-Gallup 2017 global report on people's views on women's participation in paid work. The Report reveals that 70% of women prefer to have a job instead of staying at home, and men agree (ILO Report, 2019).

It is seen that the participation of the female labour force to employment is of great importance in all sectors, be it economically, legally and socially.

The impact of the employment of female labour force on economic growth is examined from the point of view of Organisation of Islamic Cooperation (OIC) member countries. The organisation was established in Jeddah, Saudi Arabia on 25 September 1969 and has 57 members. In the Human Development Index Report 2017, the countries subject to the study are the OIC member countries with high and middle-high human development index level.[1]

2. LITERATURE REVIEW

Increasing awareness of women's employment changes leads many researchers to examine women's issues socially, politically and economically through statistical and applied studies for various countries or country groups. Among the first studies to examine the economic participation of women in the labour force were Mincer's (1962) and Cain's (1966) studies on the married women's employment.

Tansel (2002) analysed the link between the attendance of women in the labour force and growth in 67 provinces in Turkey. As a result, labour force accession positively affected economic growth.

Özer and Biçerli (2003) analysed female workforce in Turkish rural and urban areas between 1988 and 2001 with panel data analysis. Wages of women, inflation and growth rate had no direct impact of factors such as the unemployment rate. They explained the reason for this situation as the social status of women in society and family and their inability to go beyond their traditional roles.

Baliamoune-lutz and McGilivray (2007) examined the correlation between growth and female labour force participation rates in Sub-Saharan African and Arab countries. As a result of the study, it was revealed that there is a negative link between female labour force accession and growth in the mentioned countries.

Klasen and Lamanna (2009) examined the extent to which differences in education levels and employment effected economic growth, in their studies covering the years between 1960 and 2000, and determined that gender differences in employment and education significantly reduced economic growth.

Luci (2009) analysis for 184 countries between 1965 and 2004 based on the panel data's result is that female labour force participation has a positive impact on growth, but the impact of growth on female labour force participation is not clear.

Lee, Lim, and Hwang (2012) analysed the relationship between fertility, women's employment and economic growth using data from 8 East Asian and 15 EU countries between 1980 and 2008. As a result of the study, they found that the changes in the employment and fertility rates of women affected the growth rates in EU countries by 15% and this effect was higher than the effect in East Asian countries (10%).

Er (2012) researched the impact of female employment on economic growth for 187 countries for the period between 1998 and 2008. As a result of the study, it was revealed that the increase in female employment increment economic growth.

Kasa and Alptekin (2015), 2000–2013 for between women's educational situation in Turkey according to their impact on labour force and economic growth participation, have investigated using VAR model. They concluded that unqualified women and women who entered the labour market after vocational training made a significant contribution to growth, irrespective of their level of education.

Lenchman and Kaur (2015) studied the correlation between economic growth female and labour force participation rates for 162 countries in the 1990 and 2012 period by using the panel data analysis method. The countries in the analysis were separated into four income groups, from low-income to high-income. They found that there is a correlation between economic growth and female labour force participation rates in country groups.

Heathcotea, Storeslettenb, and Violante (2017), in their studies examining the impact of the increment in female labour supply on the US economic performance between 1967 and 2002, concluded that half of the increase per capita earnings in the United States may be due to the growth in the female labour supply.

Dücan (2017) investigated the impact of female labour force participation on GDP in OECD countries, using panel data analysis. According to the determinations, the increase in female/male labour force participation rates in OECD countries has a negative effect on GDP growth and this effect is higher for G7 countries compared to other OECD countries.

Serel and Özdemir (2017) examined women's employment from a wide perspective. In Turkey's 2000: 1-2013: 4 period the relationship between real GDP, female unemployment, women's employment variables are analyzed. In the study the regression method was applied.According to the results of the study, the increase in female employment affects the real GDP positively.

Alshammari and Al Rakhis (2017) examined the effect of gender inequality on economic growth in the Arab region for the period 1990–2014. The findings found no evidence that gender inequality in education and labour inequality in the Arab region had a negative impact on economic growth. The result of the study shows that the main factors that drive economic growth in the Arab region are capital accumulation as well as population accumulation.

Karoui and Feki (2018) panel model investigated the effects of gender inequality on economic growth in Africa using generalised method of moments (GMM). The results show that there is a negative and significant relationship between economic growth (GDP) and gender inequality index.

In E. N. Appiah's (2018) study, from 1975 to 2015, he used panel data from World Development Indicators to support his assumption and examined the effect of women's labour force participation on economic growth. He determined that the effect of women's labour force participation on economic growth would have a positive impact on economic progress in developing countries, including sub-Saharan countries.

Pata (2018) studied the relationship between women's employment and economic growth for the 1988–2015 period for Turkey and his analysis with symmetric and asymmetric causality tests revealed that female employment in the service sector positively affects economic growth.

Karlılar and Kıral (2019) tested the existence of a U-shaped relationship between economic growth and female labour force participation rate by GMM panel data analysis. Using the World Bank data between 1996 and 2017, they analysed 48 high-income, 46 upper-middle income, 41 lower-middle-income and 27 low-income countries. It is concluded that U-shaped femininity hypothesis is valid for high-income countries and upper-middle-income countries. Analysis results for lower-middle income countries and low-income countries reject the validity of the *U*-shaped femininity hypothesis and an inverse *U*-shaped relationship emerges. In other words, it is concluded that women's labour force participation increases while income increases, but labour force participation decreases despite the increase in income after a certain point.

3. METHODOLOGY

When the problems faced by men and women in social and economic life are examined, one can see that there are more obstacles that women are forced to overcome. This leads to the emergence of gender differences.

Table 1 presents the general labour force participation rate and the female labour force participation rate of selected OIC countries between 1995 and 2018. In general, it is not possible to talk about the same labour force participation of female labour force as male labour force.

On the other hand; many economists agree that high employment rates alone do not mean that women are employed with better and equal conditions. Export-oriented, labour-intensive production has created unprotected and pre-carious working conditions for most women (Bahramitash & Esfahani, 2016). This shows that women have various social, economic and cultural barriers at the point of entering working life. There are significant differences between the estimated earned income and wage equality for similar work between male and female labour (Albar, 2019; Ceylan-Ataman, 2019).

When the labour force participation rates in selected OIC countries analysed in the study are examined, the labour force participation rates of men are higher in the majority of countries. More than half of the women do not participate in the labour force (Fig. 1).

It would not be correct to explain the low labour force participation rates of women with the preventive attitude of Islamic law. It is stated in many studies that there are no provisions in Islamic law that prevent women from working. Bahramitash and Esfahani (2016), Middle East and North Africa (MENA region) in their work, stressed that there are no Islamic laws directly preventing women from engaging in economic activities. And that it is difficult to explain the scarcity of women's economic activities by Islamic rules. Kuzgun and Sevim (2004) in their study of 67 women and 37 men found that traditional gender roles were more effective than religious orientations. Yıldırım (2008) also emphasises that in terms of Islamic law, it clearly shows that there are no obstacles for women who want to start a business.

At the same time, Gouda and Potrafke (2016), in their studies using women's rights indicators and cross-country variations, have argued that differentiation against women is more evident in countries where Islamic law applies. Many studies are found in the same direction. Tzannatos (1999) concludes that religion is more effective than most standard economic variables in explaining gender differences in labour force participation. Baliamoune-Lutz and McGillivray (2009), in the study of the impact of gender inequality on literacy in sub-Saharan African and Arab countries, argued that culture instead of religion should be used in empirical studies.

Table 1. Human Development Data (1995–2018): Labour Force Participation Rate and Labour Force Participation Rate (Female) for Selected OIC Countries.

HDI Rank 2018	Country	1995		2000		2005		2010		2011	
		LFPR	LFPR Female	LFPR	LFPR Female	LFPR	LFPR Female	LFPR	LFPR Female	LFPR	LFPR Female
69	Albania	73.9	53.8	73.6	51.8	67.9	48.1	63.0	45.7	64.4	47.1
82	Algeria	77.7	11.8	74.7	11.9	71.8	12.8	70.1	14.4	69.5	15.2
87	Azerbaijan	72.0	56.3	70.7	56.3	68.4	57.7	67.5	60.2	67.4	60.8
45	Bahrain	87.7	31.7	86.7	34.8	86.2	38.9	87.4	43.8	86.7	43.0
43	Brunei Darussalam	80.7	50.4	79.9	55.8	77.6	56.2	75.3	56.9	75.0	57.2
165	Côte d'Ivoire	82.7	48.4	80.9	48.4	76.9	48.3	72.3	48.2	71.3	48.1
116	Egypt	72.2	21.0	72.6	19.9	73.0	20.2	75.7	22.6	75.9	22.0
65	Iran (Islamic Republic of)	76.0	10.5	73.7	13.9	74.3	19.4	70.0	16.0	69.9	15.3
50	Kazakhstan	78.3	65.4	77.1	65.6	75.3	64.4	75.9	65.4	75.9	65.4
57	Kuwait	83.8	47.5	82.4	49.6	82.7	49.0	84.5	53.6	84.9	54.5
122	Kyrgyzstan	73.8	56.1	73.9	55.2	76.1	54.1	76.6	52.2	77.1	52.6
93	Lebanon	68.8	19.7	69.6	20.5	70.7	20.4	67.9	22.0	68.4	22.3
61	Malaysia	78.2	44.9	78.2	44.7	77.5	44.0	76.2	43.5	76.7	45.0
121	Morocco	78.8	23.9	77.5	24.9	76.1	26.5	75.6	25.6	75.5	25.5
152	Pakistan	83.2	12.5	83.7	16.1	82.3	18.4	80.1	21.7	79.8	22.1
41	Qatar	94.6	44.8	92.5	41.2	94.0	45.4	95.8	51.1	94.6	52.6
36	Saudi Arabia	77.3	14.9	75.6	16.1	74.0	17.7	74.4	18.2	75.3	19.6
125	Tajikistan	55.4	29.5	54.8	30.0	54.9	30.3	57.0	29.5	57.5	29.3
59	Turkey	77.5	30.8	72.6	26.3	70.1	23.3	69.6	27.0	70.5	28.3
35	United Arab Emirates	92.2	31.3	91.5	33.7	92.5	37.2	94.5	44.0	94.4	45.1

Source: Human Development Reports (2019), http://hdr.undp.org/en/data.
LFPR: Labour force participation rate.

2012		2013		2014		2015		2016		2017		2018	
LFPR	LFPR Female	LFPR	LFPR Female	LFPR	LFPR Female	LFPR	LFPR Female	LFPR	LFPR Female	LFPR	LFPR Female	LFPR	LFPR Female
66.1	48.8	62.7	44.7	63.9	44.8	65.2	47.7	65.1	47.5	65.0	47.3	64.9	47.2
68.9	16.2	70.2	16.9	67.4	15.3	67.4	15.2	67.5	15.0	67.6	14.9	67.4	14.9
67.6	61.1	68.0	61.3	68.4	61.9	68.7	62.5	69.7	63.0	70.1	63.3	69.7	63.1
86.9	43.2	87.0	43.4	87.1	43.6	87.0	43.8	87.0	44.0	87.1	44.4	87.3	44.5
74.6	57.4	74.1	57.6	73.6	57.8	73.1	58.0	72.6	58.2	72.0	58.4	71.7	58.2
70.3	48.1	69.3	48.1	68.3	48.0	67.3	48.0	66.3	48.1	66.1	48.2	66.0	48.3
76.3	22.5	76.5	23.4	76.3	23.7	74.1	22.6	73.3	22.9	73.2	22.7	73.2	22.8
69.8	14.7	69.6	14.2	69.5	13.7	70.3	15.2	71.5	17.1	71.4	17.0	71.2	16.8
76.1	65.4	76.3	65.5	76.8	65.6	77.0	65.4	77.2	65.4	77.2	65.3	77.1	65.2
85.3	55.4	85.8	56.6	86.2	57.6	86.5	58.5	85.7	58.0	85.5	57.8	85.3	57.5
76.9	51.6	76.5	49.2	75.0	50.3	75.6	49.8	75.5	48.4	75.7	48.3	75.8	48.0
68.9	22.5	69.4	22.7	69.9	22.8	70.4	23.0	70.6	23.2	70.8	23.4	70.9	23.5
77.3	46.4	77.6	49.0	77.3	50.0	77.4	50.3	77.2	50.6	77.2	50.7	77.4	50.9
74.9	24.8	74.3	24.6	73.4	23.8	72.4	23.0	71.5	22.3	70.5	21.5	70.4	21.4
80.2	22.4	80.7	22.6	80.1	23.0	81.2	23.9	81.3	23.8	81.4	23.7	81.5	23.9
94.0	54.1	94.0	55.7	94.4	57.3	95.1	58.9	94.7	58.5	94.6	58.1	94.7	57.8
77.0	20.3	78.4	20.3	78.9	20.7	79.2	22.1	78.7	23.0	79.0	23.3	79.2	23.4
57.9	29.0	58.3	28.7	58.6	28.5	58.9	28.3	59.2	28.1	59.5	27.9	59.7	27.8
69.8	28.9	70.4	30.1	71.2	30.2	71.7	31.5	72.2	32.5	72.7	33.6	72.6	33.5
94.2	46.2	94.2	47.3	94.4	48.3	94.7	49.4	94.1	50.2	93.5	51.3	93.4	51.2

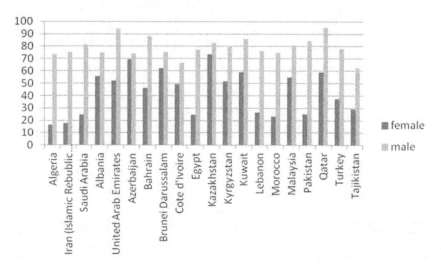

Fig. 1. Labour Force Participation (Female and Male) Index of Selected OIC Countries (2020). *Source*: Global Gender Gap Index 2020. World Economic Forum.

Pippa and Inglehart (2009), although they acknowledge the existence of gender inequality in orthodox societies, they concluded that Islamic societies were less supportive of gender equality. In their research, Luigi, Sapienza, and Zingales (2003) stated that all religions showed more conservative attitudes towards women, but the attitudes were much stronger for participants who defined themselves as Muslims. They also found that religious affiliation was associated with a range of economic behaviours that could affect growth (including power, laws, private property, markets and inequality). Braunstein (2014), while examining the relationship between gender inequality and economic growth, pointed out the impact of Islam on patriarchal preferences. The establishment and maintenance of patriarchal institutions lead to a higher cost of economic growth than measured by standard gender inequality variables. In the majority of Muslim countries, the low level of female employment is generally explained by the patriarchal social structure, while the differences between these countries and each other should not be ignored (Spierings, 2014). Therefore, male-dominated society structure negatively affects female labour force participation.

In this case, it would be a more appropriate approach to address the causes of both low female labour force participation rates and gender inequality in working life in terms of social and cultural attitudes in society. One of the statements posed in the World Values Surveys demonstrates the cultural perspective of society to women's work. The statement in question is: 'When jobs are scarce, men should have more right to a job than women'. Accordingly, a high percentage of respondents have negative cultural attitudes towards women's economic participation (Eastern Europe 34.1%, East Asia and Pacific 39.3%, European Union 17.1%, Africa 39.5%, Former Soviet Union 47.4%, Middle East and North Africa 69.4%, Latin America/ Caribbean 25.3%, North America 18.7%, Mena region comprising 61.3% of OCI countries, other developed countries 21.0%) (Bahramitash & Esfahani, 2016). It is also a fact that the general dominance of men over women reduces the employment of women, scientific studies show. The roles and duties assigned to women in the family and society (such as being a mother, being a spouse, providing elderly care, maintaining the order of the house) prevent women from entering the labour market (Spierings, 2014). These roles and tasks also lead to women's backwardness in education, social and political areas. The deprivation of women from educational opportunities, the lack of managerial opportunities, the wage differences between men and women in similar jobs, either completely distract women from the labour market, or lead them to struggle with barriers in working life.

4. MODEL AND DATA SET

The impact of female employment on economic growth was analysed with the panel data model. Economic growth was determined as a dependent variable and multiple modelling of different independent variables was performed and included in the analysis.

However, the following model, which gives the best estimation results, is determined as the econometric model of the study. In this context, the econometric model used in the study is expressed as follows.

$$\text{grw}_{it} = \alpha_0 + \beta_1 \text{fem}_{it} + \beta_2 \text{cap} + v_{it}$$

$i=1,......,28; t=1,....13$
i: the number of units and t: the time interval.

In practice, in order to test the validity of factors for the member countries of the Organisation for Islamic Cooperation, the grw variable represents the annual growth rate of GDP (%), the fem variable represents the ratio of female labour force participation rate to male labour force participation ratio and the cap variable represents the ratio of gross fixed capital formation to GDP.

As the fem variable increases, it is expected that fem coefficient will be positive as economic growth increases.

As with all-time series analysis, panel data analyses that perform both time and cross-sectional analysis together require variables to be sta ble so as not to cause false relationships between variables. In the study, common unit root processes were investigated with Levin, Lin and Chu test, panel unit root tests and unit root process with Im, Pesaran and Shin test for each unit. Steadiness in the series independent units was examined by the Generalised Dickey Fuller (ADF) unit root test method.

In Levin, Lin and Chu test, Im, Peseran and Shin test and ADF test, the hypotheses were established as follows:

H0. There is a general unit root in the series.

H1. There is no general unit root in the series

Table 2. Panel Unit Root Test Statistics Results.

| | Panel Unit Root Test Statistics Results | | | | | | | |
| | Fem | | Cap | | grw | | Cross | Number of |
	Statistic	p-Value	Statistic	p-Value	Statistic	p-value	Section	Observation
Method							20	200
Levin, Lin, & Chu, t-statistics	1.91	0.027	0.8	0.78	−6.79	0.000	20	200
Im, Peseran and Shin W-statistics	1.69	0.9546	0.64	0.739	−2.83	0.002	20	200
ADF-Fisher Ki-Kare	38.03	0.55	29.06	0.89	−70.08	0.002	20	200

As can be seen from Table 2, since the calculated p-values are smaller than the critical value of 0.05, the expression $H0$: There is a general unit root in the series is rejected. When each of the variables was examined individually, while the presence of unit root was not detected in the GRW variable, the presence of unit root was found in CAP and FEM variables. This situation does not constitute an obstacle to the study since static panel analysis will be implemented. There are three approaches in the prediction of the panel data model: pooled regression, fixed effects and random effects.

F-test is used to decide OLS or fixed effect model. Breusch–Pagan test is used to decide pooled or random effect model. If $H0$ is rejected in F-test and Breusch–Pagan test, LM test is used to decide fixed effect or random effect model.

In the analysis, the F-test decides whether to use the two-factor fixed effect model or OLS model. Hypotheses are expressed as follows:

$H0$: OLS model is appropriate and alternative hypothesis.

$H1$. Fixed effect model is appropriate are tested by F-test.

Hypothesis is rejected when F-statistic value$>$ F-table, that is, F-statistic is above the table value. This means that the coefficients of the dummy variables are different from each other. Therefore, in such a model, a two-factor fixed effect model is used, which includes individual and time effects. When Table 3 is examined, one can see that F-test probability value is 0.00001. The probability value of F-test is less than 0.05 and the $H0$ is therefore rejected at all levels of significance. Instead of pooled regression model, one can see that the fixed effects model is suitable.

Table 3. F-test Statistical Value.

| F-test Statistical Value | | | |
Impact Test	Statistics	df	Possibility
Horizontal section F	3.52	(12.245)	0.0001
Horizontal section Chi^2	41.41	12	0.0000

Table 4. Probability Value.

Test	Probability Value
LM1	0.0000
LM2	0.0000
LM	0.0000

In the second stage, Breusch–Pagan test is used to determine the appropriate model between the pooled model and the random regression model. The main hypotheses of the test are as follows:

H0. The pooled regression model is appropriate.

H1. The random effects regression model is appropriate.

Test results are given in Table 4.

According to the results of Table 4, one can see that the individual effects are random, the time effects are random and the individual and time effects are random.

At this stage of the study, the relationship between individual effects and explanatory variables (internality problem) is tested with the Hausman method. At the other stage of the analysis, the LM test (Breush–Pagan Multiplier) is performed to determine the type of individual effects and time effect (random or constant). As can be seen from Table 4, it was concluded that the *H0* was rejected because the LM>Chi-square statistic was less than 0.05 in the established models; the model could not be pooled.

In Table 5, Hausman test was performed and $Chi^2 = 14.87$ and Chi^2 probability value = 0.0006. Since this value was less than 0.05, *H0* was rejected and it was confirmed that there was an internality problem in the model. In this case, the analysis needs to be done with a fixed effects model. According to the hypotheses

H0. the random effects model is suitable.

H1. the fixed effects model is suitable, the fixed table is estimated by panel data analysis and the results are presented.

According to the results of Table 5, the probability value of Hausman test statistics was found to be 0.0006. Since this value is less than 0.01, *H0* is rejected for all significance levels. As a result of the analysis conducted within this scope, it was decided that the appropriate model would be a fixed effects model.

Table 5. Hausman Test Statistics Results.

Test Summary	Chikare Statistics	Chikare SD	Possibility
Horizontal section random	148.798	2	0.0006

Table 6. Coefficient, Standard Error, *t*-Statistic and Probability Results.

Variable	Coefficient	SE	*t*-Statistic	Prob.
C	−0.318113	1.342365	−0.236979	0.8129
FEM	0.104023	0.029782	3.492769	0.0006
CAP	0.094436	0.033777	2.795865	0.0056
R-squared	0.061076	Mean dependent var		4.946390
Adjusted *R*-squared	0.053769	SD dependent var		4.812879
SE of regression	4.681700	Akaike info criterion		5.936671
Sum squared resid	5633.007	Schwarz criterion		5.977756
Log likelihood	−768.7672	Hannan–Quinn criter.		5.953188
F-statistic	8.358718	Durbin–Watson stat		0.861673
Prob (*F*-statistic)	0.000304			

According to the results of Table 6, coefficient of the ratio of female labour force participation rate to male labour force participation is positive and statistically significant. One Unit increase in the ratio of female labour force participation rate to male labour force participation leads to a 0.10 unit increase in economic growth. Coefficient of the gross capital formation (%GDP) is positive and statistically significant. One unit increase in the gross capital formation (%GDP) leads to a 0.09 unit increase in economic growth.

5. CONCLUSIONS

According to the above results, as the ratio of female labour force participation rate to male labour force share increases, it is observed that.economic growth increases. Therefore, the female labour force participation ratio is expected to be positive. Coefficient of female labour force participation ratio to male labour force participation ratio is statistically significant and it was found positive, consistent with the studies in the literature.

The OIC's declaration in 2018 (Declaration of Ouagadougou at the end of the 7th Ministerial Conference on the Role of Women in the Development of Member States of the OIC) emphasised that stimulating the role of women in society is an important factor in the development of member states, and no country can achieve development by ignoring half the female population. According to the declaration, poverty, ignorance and limited access by women to production, resources and decision-making factors prevent women from taking part in the development of member states.

The impact of the share of female labour force participation rates on the male labour force participation rates in 20 Islamic cooperation member countries on economic growth was investigated. The study found that when the ratio of female labour force participation rate to male labour force participation rate increases, economic growth also increases. One unit increase in female labour force participation rate leads to 0.10 unit increase in economic growth. This shows that the participation of the dormant female labour force in the working life and the elimination of gender gap in education, social, political and economic fields will also contribute positively to economic growth.

In this context, increasing the share of women in employment is of great importance. In front of women, efforts to remove religious, traditional and social barriers should be increased. Although Islamic rules do not impose a clear ban on women's working life, there are studies showing that both patriarchal social structure and religious rules (misapplied by people) adversely affect female labour force participation (Dildar, 2015; Tailassane, 2019).

The tasks imposed on society by women (motherhood, childcare, elderly care, household chores) and walls built by social and religious rules make it difficult for her to enter working life. The number of children prevents women's participation in the labour force, which attaches importance to tradition and religion (Ucal & Günay, 2019).

Problems encountered in working life (low wages, discriminatory behaviours, informal employment) reduce productivity and contribution to economy. In particular, women in the backwardness of education makes participation in the labour force more difficult.

Women also have a great role in ensuring and increasing women's participation in the labour force. First of all, it should not be forgotten that the most effective concept in solving this problem is again women. In particular, the importance and priority of the women involved in decision-making mechanisms and the administrative units working in this field will be a social message.

It is also important that the legal regulations and the principles of the rule of law have the content to eliminate gender discrimination.

Women in employment in underdeveloped countries are generally employed in low-income agricultural and service sectors, home services and flexible employment. A significant proportion of women working in these areas are employed informally.

In this context, in order to provide women with better opportunities in labour force participation, firstly it is important to implement the following measures:

- Implementation of equality of opportunity in education with legal and social rules.
- Preventing the use of religious rules by institutions and individuals as a mechanism for gaining and protecting power.
- Elimination of inequalities of opportunity in social, political and legal decision-making mechanisms.
- Becoming conscious of that economic and social development can be achieved by transferring all the labour potential of the country to employment,
- Emphasising that both parents should be educated, productive and in solidarity in order to better educate future generations.
- Ensuring social solidarity in the fight against inequalities in social, political and economic life.
- Eliminating the negative effects of women's responsibility in the home (extending the kindergarten system, providing financial and moral support services, extending the period of paid leave).
- Adapting positive discrimination practices to changing and developing working conditions.

In this study, if equal opportunities are provided for women in labour force participation and employment in selected OIC member countries, in addition to the development in social and political fields, economic growth will be positively affected.

NOTE

1. The OIC member countries with high and middle-high human-development index level; Egypt, Albania, United Arab Emirates, Kuwait, Azerbaijan, Bahrain, Brunei Darussalam, Pakistan, Cote d'Ivoire, Algeria, Iran (Islamic Republic of), Kazakhstan, Kyrgyzstan, Lebanon, Morocco, Malaysia, Qatar, Turkey, Tajikistan and Saudi Arabia.

REFERENCES

Albar, B. Ö. (2019). Kadınlara Yönelik Ayrımcılık. *Sosyal Araştırmalar ve Davranış Bilimleri*, 5(8), 274–286.

Alshammari, N., & Al Rakhis, M. (2017). Impact of gender inequality on economic growth in the Arab region. *Research in Applied Economics*, 9(2), 18–31.

Appiah, E. N. (2018). Female labor force participation and economic growth in developing countries. *Global Journal of Human-Social Science: E Economics*, 18(2), 1–6.

Bahramitash, R., & Esfahani, H. S. (2016). Women's economic role in the MENA region: Growth and equality through female-owned SMEs. In R. Bahramitash & H. S. Esfahani (Eds.), *Political and socio-economic change in the Middle East and North Africa* (pp. 155–190). Basingstoke: Palgrave Macmillan

Baliamoune-lutz, M., & McGilivray, M. (2007). Gender inequality and growth in SubSaharan Africa and Arab countries. In African economic conference, 15–17 November, Ethiopia.

Baliamoune-Lutz, M., & McGillivray, M. (2009). Does gender inequality reduce growth in sub-Saharan African and Arab countries? *African Development Review*, 21(2), 224–242.

Braunstein, E. (2014). Patriarchy versus Islam: Gender and religion in economic growth. *Feminist Economics*, 20(4), 58–86.

Cain, G. G. (1966). *Married women in the labor force: An economic analysis*. Chicago, IL: University of Chicago Press.

Ceylan-Ataman, B. (2019). Küresel Ekonomide Cinsiyete Dayalı Ücret Eşitsizliği: Nedenler Ve Önlemler [Gender-based wage inequality in the global economy: Causes and measures]. In B. Ceylan-Ataman & G. Taşkıran (Eds.), *Recent evaluations on humanities and social sciences* (p. 11). London: IJOPEC Publication Ltd.

Dildar, Y. (2015). Patriarchal norms, religion, and female labor supply: Evidence from Turkey. *World Development*, 76, 40–61.

Dücan, E., & Polat, M. A. (2017). Kadın İstihdamının Ekonomik Büyümeye Etkisi: OECD Ülkeleri İçin Panel Veri Analizi. *Çanakkale University Journal of the Institute of Social Sciences*, 26(1), 155–170.

Er, Ş. (2012). Women indicators of economic growth: A panel data approach. *The Economic Research Guardian*, 2(1), 27-42.

Goldin, C. (1986). The female labor force and American economic growth, 1890–1980. In S. L. Engerman & R. E. Gallman (Eds.), *Long-term factors in American economic growth* (pp. 557–604). Chicago, IL: University of Chicago Press.

Gouda, M., & Potrafke, N. (2016). Gender equality in Muslim-majority countries. *Economic Systems*, 40(4), 683–698.

Heathcotea J., Storeslettenb K., & Violante G. L. (2017). The macroeconomics of the quiet revolution: Understanding the implications of the rise in women's participation for economic growth and inequality. *Research in Economics*, 71, 521–539.

Human Development Reports. (2019). Retrieved from http://hdr.undp.org/en/data

ILO Report. (2019). Retrieved from https://www.ilo.org/global/about-the-ilo/newsroom/news/WCMS_674816/lang--tr/index.htm. Accessed on July 15, 2019.

Karlılar, S., & Kıral, G. (2019). Kadın İşgücüne Katılımı ve Ekonomik Büyüme Arasındaki İlişki: Ülke Grupları İçin Panel Veri Analizi. *Third Sector Social Economic Review*, *54*(2), 935–948.

Karoui, K., & Feki, R. (2018). The effect of gender inequality on economic development: Case of African countries. *Journal of the Knowledge Economy*, *9*(1), 294–300.

Kasa, H., & Alptekin, V. (2015). Türkiye'de Kadın İşgücünün Büyümeye Etkisi. *Sosyal Bilimler Meslek Yüksekokulu Dergisi*, *18*(1), 1–23.

Klasen, S., & Lamanna, F. (2009). The impact of gender inequality in education and employment on economic growth: New evidence for a panel of countries. *Feminist Economics*, 15(3), 91–132.

Kuzgun, Y., & Sevim, S. A. (2004). Kadınların Çalışmasına Karşı Tutum ve Dini Yönelim Arasındaki İlişki, *Ankara University. Journal of Faculty of Educational Sciences*, *37*(1), 14–27.

Lee, J. H., Lim, E., & Hwang, J. (2012). Panel SVAR model of women's employment, fertility and economic growth: A comparative study of East Asian and EU countries. *The Social Science Journal*, *49*, 386–389.

Lenchman, E., & Kaur, H. (2015). Economic growth and female labor force participation-verifying the u-feminization hypothesis. New evidence for 162 countries over the period 1990–2012. *Economics and Sociology*, *8*(1), 246–257.

Lofstrom, Å. (2009). *Gender equality, economic growth and employment*. Stockholm: Swedish Ministry of Integration and Gender Equality.

Luci, A. (2009). Female labour market participation and economic growth. *International Journal of Innovation and Sustainable Development*, *4*(2), 97–108.

Luigi, G., Sapienza, P.,& Zingales, L. (2003). People's opium? Religion and economic attitudes. *Journal of Monetary Economics*, *50*(1), 225–282.

McKinsey Global Institute Report. (2015). Retrieved from https://www.mckinsey.com/featured-insights/employment-and-growth/how-advancing-womens-equality-can-add-12-trillion-to-global-growth

Mincer, J. (1962). *Labor force participation of married women: A study of labor supply. Aspects of labor economics*. National Bureau of Economic Research (pp. 63–105). Princeton, NJ: Princeton University Press.

OECD. (2013, January). *Gender dynamics: How can countries close the economic gender gap?* World Economic Forum Annual Meeting, Remarks by Angel Gurría, OECD Secretary-General Davos, Switzerland.

Özer, M., & Biçerli, K. (2003). Türkiye'de Kadın İşgücünün Panel Veri Analizi. Retrieved from https://earsiv.anadolu.edu.tr/xmlui/handle/11421/502

Pata, U. K. (2018). Türkiye'de Kadın İstihdamı ve Ekonomik Büyüme İlişkisi: Simetrik ve Asimetrik Nedensellik Testleri İle Sektörel Bir Analiz. *UİİD-IJEAS*, *21*, 135–150.

Pippa, N., & Inglehart, R. (2009). Islamic culture and democracy: Testing the 'clash of civilizations' thesis. In M. Sasaki (Ed.), *New frontiers in comparative sociology* (pp. 221–249). Leiden: Brill.

Sehrawat, M., & Giri, A. K. (2017). Does female human capital contribute to economic growth in India? An empirical investigation. *International Journal of Social Economics*, *44*(11), 1506–1521.

Serel, H., & Özdemir, B. S. (2017). Türkiye'de Kadın İstihdamı Ve Ekonomik Büyüme İlişkisi. *Yönetim ve Ekonomi Araştırmaları Dergisi*, *15*(3), 134–150.

Spierings, N. (2014). The influence of patriarchal norms, institutions, and household composition on women's employment in twenty-eight Muslim-majority countries. *Feminist Economics*, *20*(4), 87–112.

Tailassane, R. (2019). Women's rights and representation in Saudi Arabia, Iran, and Turkey: The patriarchal domination of religious interpretations. *International Relations Honors Papers*. 5. Retrieved from https://digitalcommons.ursinus.edu/int_hon/5. Accessed on March 2, 2020.

Tansel, A. (2002). *Economic development and female labor force participation in Turkey: Time-series evidence and cross-province estimates*. ERC Working Papers in Economics 01/05. Economic Research Center, Middle East Technical University

Taymaz, E. (2010). *Büyüme, İstihdam, Vasıflar ve Kadın İşgücü*. Ankara: DPT.

Tsani, S., Paroussos, L., Fragiadakis, C., Charalambidis, I., & Capros, P. (2013). Female labour force participation and economic growth in the South Mediterranean countries. *Economics Letters*, *120*(2), 323–328.

Tzannatos, Z. (1999). Women and labor market changes in the global economy: Growth helps, inequalities hurt and public policy matters. *World Development*, *27*(3), 551–569.

Ucal, M., & Günay, S. (2019). Female employment status: A survey analysis of selected member states of the Arab League. *Eurasian Economic Review, 9*(3), 373–394.

Verick, S. (2018). *Female labor force participation and development.* Bonn: IZA World of Labor.

Yıldırım, M. (2008). *İslam Hukukunda Kadının Çalışması.* National Symposium on Islam and Work Life. Retrieved from http://isamveri.org/pdfdrg/D179845/2005/2005_YILDIRIMM.pdf

Zeren, F., & Savrul, B. K. (2017). Kadınların işgücüne katılım oranı, ekonomik büyüme, işsizlik oranı ve kentleşme oranı arasındaki saklı koentegrasyon ilişkisinin araştırılması. *Yönetim Bilimleri Dergisi, 15*(30), 87–103.

CHAPTER 4

VOLATILITY SPILLOVER FROM OIL PRICES TO PRECIOUS METALS UNDER DIFFERENT REGIMES

Ayşegül Kirkpınar

ABSTRACT

Introduction – *Increases in prices of commodity markets may be associated with increased volatility in financial markets. That is why analysing time-varying co-movements of commodity prices can be of great importance for investors who take into consideration optimal asset allocation.*

Purpose – *The aim of this study is to investigate the volatility spillover from oil to precious metals under high-volatility and low-volatility regimes.*

Methodology – *The data covered daily closing prices of assets such as oil, palladium, and platinum for the period January 2010–December 2018. GARCH models were analysed in order to determine the most appropriate volatility structure, and it was determined that GARCH (1,1) model was the most suitable model for all commodities. Markov Switching model was used to analyse the volatility spillover from oil to precious metals.*

Findings – *According to the analyses, the results showed that there were volatility spillovers from oil to palladium and platinum in low-volatility regimes and from oil to platinum in high-volatility regimes. On the other hand, there was no volatility spillover from oil to palladium in high-volatility regimes. Investing into oil and palladium in the same portfolio can provide diversification benefits for investors in high-volatility regimes. On the other hand, investing into oil and palladium in the same portfolio may not provide diversification benefits for investors in low-volatility regimes. The findings of the analyses can be*

Contemporary Issues in Business, Economics and Finance
Contemporary Studies in Economic and Financial Analysis, Volume 104, 45–56
ISSN: 1569-3759/doi:10.1108/S1569-375920200000104005

beneficial for investors, market participants, and portfolio managers to make an
accurate portfolio management.

Keywords: Volatility spillover; Markov switching model; commodity
markets; precious metals; oil; portfolio management

JEL classifications: G11; G15; C22

1. INTRODUCTION

Developments in international policies and crises in international financial markets may increase the volatility in stock markets, derivatives, and international
bonds. In order to minimise the portfolio risks, investors make portfolio diversification using negative correlated assets with each other in the same portfolio.
The main purpose of this strategy is to reduce risk by diversifying the portfolio. The benefit of international portfolio diversification is to eliminate the
risks of investing in only one market. In this manner, the risk or volatility of
portfolio diminishes by diversifying in other markets' financial assets. While the
financial assets in the same market tend to move together, international assets
tend to lower movement when together. The theory of international diversification grounds in the study of Grubel (1968). Grubel (1968) extended the modern
portfolio theory of Markowitz (1959) and indicated that investors were likely to
reduce risk by holding international rather than individual assets. Later, Levy
and Sarnat (1970) demonstrated the fact that co-movements among different
national assets were low. That is why the correlation coefficient between the
financial assets (such as stocks, bonds, commodities, and more complicated
financial instruments, such as stock options or currency options) is an important issue of the international diversification theory. Even though the correlation coefficients between any two of these markets vary in time, they are always
far from unity. The low correlation between these markets indicates a successful risk diversification. Makridakis and Wheelwright (1974) and King, Sentana,
and Wadhwani (1994) found that international correlation was changeable over
time. In a similar vein, Longin and Solnik (1995) observed that international
correlation and covariance matrices were not stable over the period between
1960 and 1990, for seven stock markets, including Germany, France, England,
Canada, United States, Japan, and Switzerland. They stated that market volatility had changed dramatically during that period. These studies used unconditional correlations over periods by comparing conditional correlations with
time variance.

In the periods of uncertainty within the economy, commodities can be seen
as a safe haven against risk. Increases in prices of commodity markets may be
associated with increased volatility in financial markets. Especially after the 2008
global financial crisis, the risk spillover between these markets has increased.
Therefore, it may be crucial to examine the effects of volatility spillover among

commodities. This is why analysing time-varying co-movements of commodity prices can be of great importance for portfolio managers or investors who take into consideration optimal asset allocation.

Commodity markets can be divided into three main groups. These are energy assets, such as natural gas, gasoline, heating oil, and crude oil; precious and industrial assets, such as gold, silver, palladium, platinum, and copper; and finally agricultural assets, such as corn, wheat, cocoa, cotton, etc. It has generally been noted that precious metals like platinum, palladium, silver, and gold can be as safe havens in periods of financial crises.

Palladium is mainly used in the automobile industry and also in the production of white gold. Due to the increased automotive demand, palladium prices may increase due to the reduction in the supply of this metal. Besides, platinum and palladium are very close to each other in terms of their physical and chemical properties and they have similar usage areas. Therefore, their correlations can be generally very high. In addition to these metals, this study also considers crude oil. For many years, oil still has the highest share in the world's total energy consumption. It is used by many industries as the main input product for production as well as the so-called precious metals. That is why precious metals volatility may be affected negatively by an increase in oil prices (Hammoudeh & Yuan, 2008).

The aim of this study is to analyse volatility spillover from crude oil prices to the selected two precious metals such as palladium and platinum under different regimes using the Markov Switching model. This study takes into consideration two different regimes. These are the high-volatility (crises) regime and the low-volatility (tranquil) regime.

The study is organised as follows. Section 2 gives a brief literature review. Section 3 illustrates the methodology and data. Section 4 gives empirical results. Lastly, Section 5 presents concluding remarks.

2. LITERATURE REVIEW

There are various studies about analysing volatility spillover of different markets over time. Different methods were used to analyse volatility spillover in the literature. Nicola, Paceb, and Hernandez (2016), Malik and Ewing (2009), Mensi, Hammoudeh, Nguyen, and Yoon (2014), Kang, Mciver, and Yoon (2017), Sensoy (2013), and Haesen, Houweling, and Van Zundert (2017) used Multivariate GARCH models. On the other hand, there are some studies that analyse volatility spillover using Markov Switching model. Akkaya and Koy (2018) analysed regime switching behaviour in 11 equity markets. They used three regimes including recession regime, expansion regime, and moderate growth regime. They found the highest correlation among the indices in moderate growth regime whose volatility was lower than other regimes. They also concluded that the market's possibility of staying the longest in average was for moderate growth regime.

Chkili and Nguyen (2014) investigated the impact of stock markets of BRICS countries on exchange rates using MS-VAR model and two regimes such as a low- and high-volatility regimes. They found positive effects of stock markets on exchange rates in both regimes.

Chan, Treepongkaruna, Brooks, and Gray (2011) analysed relationship among Treasury bonds, the US stocks, commodities such as gold and oil, and real estate assets by implementing Markov Switching model and two regimes such as economic expansion and economic decline. Their results indicated the evidence of contagion among real estate, oil, and stocks.

Medhioub (2015) examined Markov Switching model in industrial production index and growth rates of Tunisia using three regimes such as high growth regime, a moderate growth regime, and a recession regime. He found that Tunisian business cycle performed well in the three regimes.

Furthermore, some studies used energy and precious metals to analyse volatility spillover between these markets. Antonakakis and Kizys (2015) examined the relation among palladium, platinum, silver, gold, and four exchange rates using the generalised VAR method of Diebold and Yilmaz (2012). Their results showed that in the period of global financial crisis, gold was the leader role as a net transmitting in commodities. They also added that after the global financial crisis, the return shocks of platinum, silver, and gold got weaker, whereas the net transmitting role of platinum, silver and gold got stronger.

Mensi et al. (2014) analysed volatility spillover between four oil markets and cereal markets (Wheat, Corn, Sorghum, Barley) using VAR DCC-GARCH and VAR-BEKK-GARCH models. They found strong relationships between these markets.

Nicola et al. (2016) investigated volatility spillover among food commodities, agricultural, and energy price returns using Multivariate DCC-GARCH and a rolling regression procedure. They found that agricultural and energy returns were highly correlated, and after 2007, stock market volatility was positively related with co-movement of returns of these markets.

Kang et al. (2017) also analysed volatility spillover among some commodity futures markets such as agriculture, precious metal, and oil using Multivariate DECO-GARCH model. Their results showed bidirectional volatility spillovers across commodity futures markets. These spillovers had a strong effect in the crisis period. They also found silver and gold were informative metals to other commodities.

Sensoy (2013) investigated volatility spillover among some precious metals such as gold, silver, platinum, and palladium using consistent dynamic conditional correlation. He found a strong correlation with each other.

Kirkulak-Uludağ and Lkhamazhapov (2014) analysed volatility spillover among palladium, platinum, gold, and silver by implementing DCC-MGARCH approach. They found strong correlation among precious metals. They also noted that because silver had a low correlation with other metals, it might be used as a diversification tool in a portfolio.

Balcilar, Hammoudeh, and Asaba (2015) examined the relationship among some precious metals, oil, and dollar exchange rate using Markov-switching VEC model. They confirmed low- and high-volatility regimes. They found gold was the most informative metal in high- and low-volatility regimes. Platinum and palladium were also the most informative metals in low-volatility regimes.

3. METHODOLOGY AND DATA

3.1. Methodology

The study seeks to analyse volatility spillover from crude oil prices to the selected two precious metals such as palladium and platinum under different regimes using Markov Switching model.

First, GARCH models were analysed in order to determine the most appropriate volatility structure. GARCH (*p*, *q*) model was developed by Bollerslev (1986). It is a model for modelling the dynamic structure of time-varying conditional variances. It can be viewed as follows:

$$e_t / \psi_{t-1} \sim N(0, h_t)$$

$$h_t = \alpha_0 + \sum_{i=1}^{q} \alpha_i e_{t-i}^2 + \sum_{i=1}^{p} \beta_i h_{t-i} = \alpha_0 + A(L)e_t^2 + B(L)h_t$$

ε_t presents stochastic process and ψ_t demonstrates information set in time *t*. In GARCH (*p*, *q*) model, conditional variance is expressed as a function of both time-delayed error terms and time-delayed conditional variances.

Secondly, Markov Switching models were adopted to analyse the volatility spillover from oil to precious metals in this study. This model with time-varying parameters reflects regime switching. This model was first implemented by Hamilton (1989). Markov Switching models can capture the business cycle asymmetries of assets (Medhioub, 2015). An autoregressive model of order *p* with first-order *K*-state Markov-switching mean and variance is shown in general as follows:

$$y_t = \mu_{s_t} + \beta_{s_t} y_{t-1} + \varepsilon_t$$

The transition probabilities between the states are derived from transition probabilities matrix of *p*.

$$p = \begin{bmatrix} p_{11} & p_{12} \cdots p_{1K} \\ p_{21} & p_{22} \cdots p_{1K} \end{bmatrix}$$

$$p_{ij} = \Pr\{S_t = j | S_{t-1} = i\}; \quad i, j = 1, 2, \ldots, K.$$

$$\sum_{j=1}^{K} = 1$$

$S_{Kt} = 1$ if $S_t = K$, and $S_{Kt} = 0$, otherwise.

3.2. Data

In this study, daily close spot prices of West Texas crude oil, palladium,, and platinum commodities were used. The period covered was that between 5 January 2010 and 12 December 2018, and consisted of 2,234 observations. The data about precious metals were obtained from Global Financial Data Database. The data regarding West Texas crude oil prices were collected from the official website of the US Energy Information Administration. E-Views and Ox Metrics programs were used.

Oil, palladium, and platinum indices are shown in Fig. 1. The prices of oil, palladium, and platinum decreased in 2016. After 2016, palladium increased faster, while oil showed a relatively slow increase. On the other hand, platinum decreased again after a small rise.

4. EMPIRICAL RESULTS

Table 1 depicts descriptive statistics of the returns of oil, palladium, and platinum series. According to Table 1, the lowest standard deviation was for platinum, whereas the highest standard deviation was for oil as viewed by its standard deviation (0.019). This fact may be due to the fact that oil is used by many industries as the main input for production as well as the precious metals. It has also the highest share in the world's total energy consumption. As for skewness and kurtosis, all series were negatively skewed and all series provided excess kurtosis. According to the Jarque-Bera test, oil, palladium, and platinum series rejected null hypothesis of normality with the significance level of 1%.

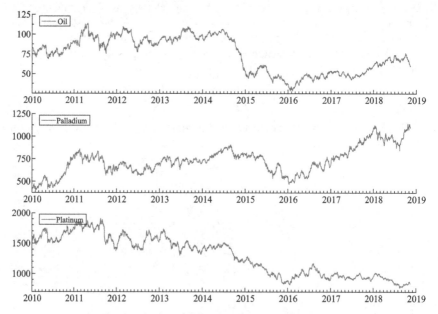

Fig. 1.   Series of Oil, Palladium, and Platinum.

Table 1.   Descriptive Statistics.

	Oil	Palladium	Platinum
Mean	−0.000138	0.000431	−0.000264
Median	0.000734	0.001137	0.000000
Maximum	0.093125	0.062894	0.044184
Minimum	−0.090379	−0.106325	−0.064518
SD	0.019340	0.017398	0.011908
Skewness	−0.026324	−0.422651	−0.248105
Kurtosis	4.911203	5.039003	4.339256
Jarque-Bera	340.2631	453.5086	189.8743
Probability	0.000000	0.000000	0.000000
Sum	−0.307548	0.962356	−0.589239

Table 2.   Correlation Matrix of the Returns of Oil, Palladium, and Platinum Series.

	Oil	Palladium	Platinum
Oil	1.000		
	–		
Palladium	0.3360***	1.000	
	(0.0000)	–	
Platinum	0.3048***	0.6450***	1.000
	(0.0000)	(0.0000)	–

Notes: *** shows the significance level at 1%. The values in parenthesis are p values.

Table 2 illustrates the correlation matrix of the returns of oil, palladium, and platinum series. Palladium and platinum have the highest positive correlation among them (64.50%) and they were followed by the positive correlation between oil and palladium (33.60%). The reason for the high correlation between palladium and platinum may be that they are used for the same industry, especially the automobile industry. As mentioned earlier, platinum and palladium are very close to each other in terms of their physical and chemical properties and they have similar usage areas. Therefore, their correlations can be generally very high. The lowest correlation in the group was for the relation between oil and platinum (30.48%). Due to the lowest correlation of platinum with oil, portfolio managers or investors may consider incorporating platinum in their portfolios as a hedge asset.

Before the models are created for volatility spillovers from crude oil prices to two precious metals such as palladium and platinum, it was examined the stationary of the series. That is why the analyses with non-stationary series lead to false regression problems and cause to mis-estimation of the relationship between the series. The Augmented Dickey Fuller (ADF) and Phillips–Perron unit root tests were applied to determine the time series properties of the oil, palladium, and platinum series. Table 3 shows ADF and Phillips–Perron unit root test results of the series such as oil, palladium, and platinum.

For all of the series, the presence of unit roots was rejected at the significance level of 1% as seen from Table 3. It means that all indices were stationary in accordance with the significance level at 1%.

Table 3.   Unit Root Tests of Oil, Palladium, and Platinum Series.

	Oil	Palladium	Platinum
ADF	−49.13113***	−44.42887***	−45.45330***
PP	−49.13093***	−44.43057***	−45.53271***

Notes: ADF, Dickey and Fuller (1979); PP, Phillips and Perron (1988). The *** represents the significance level at 1%.

After examining the unit root tests, GARCH models were analysed in order to determine the most appropriate volatility structure. As a result of that, it was determined that GARCH (1,1) model was the most suitable model for all commodities. When choosing this model, Akaike and Schwarz information criteria, the significance of coefficients, and assumptions of stationary were taken into consideration. Table 4 depicts the results of these information and the variance equations of GARCH (1,1) model for each series. According to this table, there was high-volatility for oil series with the significance level at 1% and this volatility was permanent with the significance level at 1%. As far as palladium was concerned, it was seen that the volatility of palladium was high in accordance with the significance level of 5% and the shocks in the palladium market were permanent at significance level of 1%. As for platinum, similarly, the volatility in the platinum market was high with the significance level at 5% and the shocks of this market were permanent at the significance level of 1%.

In summary, it can be stated that the volatilities of oil, palladium, and platinum series were high and the shocks in these series were permanent.

After the determination of the volatility structure for each series, Markov Switching model was used to analyse the volatility spillover from oil to palladium and platinum. Estimation results for Markov Switching model regarding volatility spillover from oil to palladium are shown in Table 5. According to Table 5, Sigma (1) represented high-volatility regime, whereas Sigma (0) represented low-volatility regime because Sigma (1) is bigger than Sigma (0). When

Table 4.   Results of GARCH (1,1) Model for Each Series.

	Oil	Palladium	Platinum
A	0.059535 (0.0009)***	0.080676 (0.0484)**	0.046147 (0.0188)**
B	0.935152 (0.0000) ***	0.881101 (0.0000) ***	0.925858 (0.0000) ***
Akaike	−5.234025	−5.349269	−6.060434
Schwarz	−5.200789	−5.298136	−6.022084
ARCH (1-2)	5.5585	1.7459	5.1390
Q (50)	35.7330	34.0817	33.8238
Alpha[1]+Beta[1]	0.99469	0.96178	0.97200

Notes: ***, ** show the significance levels at %1, %5, respectively. α presents ARCH parameter, whereas β represents GARCH parameter. The values in parenthesis are *p*-values.

Table 5.   Volatility Spillover from Oil to Palladium.

	Coefficient	SE	t-Value	t-Prob
CondOil(0)	0.129118	0.02519	5.12	0.000
CondOil(1)	0.226289	0.3036	0.745	0.456
Sigma(0)	7.44747e−005	1.382e−005	5.39	0.000
Sigma(1)	0.000176697	9.112e−006	19.4	0.000

the economy was in a low-volatility regime, there was volatility spillover from oil to palladium at a significance level of 1%. On the other hand, there was no volatility spillover from oil to palladium, when the economy was in a high-volatility regime.

As can be seen from Fig. 2, regime (0) represents high-volatility regime and regime (1) means low-volatility regime. The high-volatility regime generally represents a crises period for the oil and palladium series, whereas the low-volatility regime presents generally a tranquil period for these series.

Table 6 shows transition probabilities of regimes for oil and palladium. The transition probability of taking part in low-volatility regime (regime 0) was 0.49951, whereas the transition probability of taking part in high-volatility regime (regime 1) was 0.50049, indicating that both regimes were not permanent. According to these results, it can be stated that they may switch between themselves.

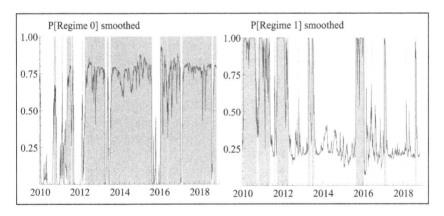

Fig. 2.   Smoothed Probabilities of Regimes for Oil and Palladium.

Table 6.   Transition Probabilities of Regimes for Oil and Palladium.

	Regime 0	Regime 1
Regime 0	0.49951	0.49951
Regime 1	0.50049	0.50049

Table 7. Volatility Spillover from Oil to Platinum.

	Coefficient	SE	*t*-Value	*t*-Prob
CondOil(0)	0.0642338	0.01003	6.41	0.000
CondOil(1)	0.0788990	0.009402	8.39	0.000
Sigma(0)	2.69832e−005	4.420e−006	6.10	0.000
Sigma(1)	4.46602e−005	7.261e−006	6.15	0.000

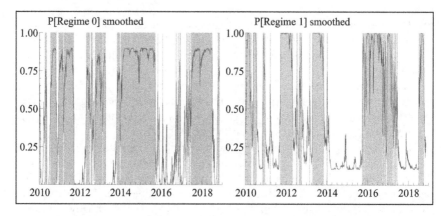

Fig. 3. Smoothed Probabilities of Regimes for Oil and Platinum.

Table 7 represents estimation results for Markov Switching model regarding volatility spillover from oil to platinum. Because Sigma (1) is bigger than Sigma (0), Sigma (1) represented a high-volatility regime and Sigma (0) represented a low-volatility regime. When an economy was both in a low- and high-volatility regimes, there was volatility spillover from oil to platinum at a significance level of 1%.

Fig. 3 illustrates smoothed probabilities of regimes for oil and platinum. The regime (0) represents high-volatility regime and the regime (1) means low-volatility regime and one can note the similar patterns for oil and palladium series.

Table 8 depicts transition probabilities of regimes for oil and platinum. Transition probability of low-volatility regime (regime 0) was 0.49976, whereas the transition probability of taking part in high-volatility regime (regime 1) was 0.50024, indicating that both regimes were not permanent. These findings are the same as the results of transition probabilities of regimes for oil and palladium series.

Table 8. Transition Probabilities of Regimes for Oil and Platinum.

	Regime 0	Regime 1
Regime 0	0.49976	0.49976
Regime 1	0.50024	0.50024

5. CONCLUSION

In this study, the author investigated the volatility spillover from oil to some precious metals such as palladium and platinum under high- and low-volatility regimes using Markov Switching model. The data covered from 5 January 2010, to 12 December 2018. As far as correlations of these series are concerned, palladium and platinum have the highest positive correlation among them. The reason for this may be the fact that they are used for the same industry, especially the automotive industry. Besides, platinum and palladium are also very close to each other in terms of their physical and chemical properties and they have similar usage areas. Therefore, their correlations can be generally very high. The lowest correlation in the group was for the relation between oil and platinum. Due to the lowest correlation of platinum with oil, investors may consider platinum in their portfolios as a hedge asset.

GARCH models were analysed in order to determine the most appropriate volatility structure for each series in the study. As a result of that, it was determined that GARCH (1,1) model was the most suitable model for all series. The volatilities of oil, palladium, and platinum series were high and the shocks in these series were permanent. According to the findings of the Markov Switching model, there were significant volatility spillovers from oil to palladium and platinum in low-volatility regimes and from oil to platinum in high-volatility regimes. There was no volatility spillover from oil to palladium in high-volatility regimes. These results of volatility spillovers are consistent with the studies of Balcilar et al. (2015) and Antonakakis and Kizys (2015), who found a relationship between oil and platinum in the literature.

These findings have significant policy implications for asset allocation and diversification. Investing into oil and palladium in the same portfolio may not provide diversification benefits for investors or portfolio managers in low-volatility regimes. On the other hand, investing into oil and palladium in the same portfolio can provide diversification benefits for investors in high-volatility regimes. Investing into oil and platinum in the same portfolio might not provide diversification benefits for investors or portfolio managers in both regimes. Investors of precious metals should watch oil prices carefully especially in relation to platinum prices because it can reflect sufficient information that may lead the changes in platinum prices.

REFERENCES

Akkaya, M., & Koy, A. (2018). Mutual switching behavior between high growth and low growth econo-mies' stock markets. *Journal of Business Research-Türk*, *10*(1), 45–60.

Antonakakis, N., & Kizys, R. (2015). Dynamic spillovers between commodity and currency markets. *International Review of Financial Analysis*, *41*, 303–319.

Balcilar, M., Hammoudeh, S., & Asaba, N.A.F. (2015). A regime-dependent assessment of the infor-mation transmission dynamics between oil prices, precious metal prices and exchange rates. *International Review of Economics and Finance*, *40*, 72–89.

Bollerslev, T. (1986). Generalized autoregressive conditional heteroscedasticity. *Journal of Econometrics*, *31*(3), 307–327.

Chan, K. F., Treepongkaruna, S., Brooks, R., & Gray, S. (2011). Asset market linkages: Evidence from financial, commodity and real estate assets. *Journal of Banking & Finance, 35*, 1415–1426.

Chkili, W., & Nguyen, D. K. (2014). Exchange rate movements and stock market returns in a regime-switching environment: Evidence for BRICS countries. *Research in International Business and Finance, 31*, 46–56.

Dickey, D. A., & Fuller, W. A. (1979). Distribution of the estimators for autoregressive time series with a unit root. *Journal of the American Statistical Association, 74*, 427–431.

Diebold, F. X., & Yilmaz, K. (2012). Better to give than to receive: Predictive directional measurement of volatility spillovers. *International Journal of Forecasting, 28*, 57–66.

Grubel, H. G. (1968). Internationally diversified portfolios: welfare gains and capital flows. *The American Economic Review, 58*(5), 1299–1314.

Haesen, D., Houweling, P., & Van Zundert, J. (2017). Momentum spillover from stocks to corporate bonds. *Journal of Banking & Finance, 79*, 28–41.

Hamilton J. D. (1989). A new approach to the economic analysis of nonstationary time series and the business cycle. *Econometrica, 57*(2), 357–384.

Hammoudeh, S., & Yuan, Y. (2008). Metal volatility in presence of oil and interest rate shocks. *Energy Economics, 30*(2), 606–620.

Kang, S. H., Mciver, R., & Yoon, S. M. (2017). Dynamic spillover effects among crude oil, precious metal, and agricultural commodity futures markets. *Energy Economics, 62*, 19–32.

King, M., Sentana, E., & Wadhwani, S. (1994). Volatility and the links between national stock markets. *Econometrica, 62*, 901–934

Kirkulak-Uludağ, B., & Lkhamazhapov, Z. (2014). Volatility dynamics of precious metals: Evidence from Russia. *Finance a úvěr-Czech Journal of Economics and Finance, 67*(4), 300–317.

Levy, H., & Sarnat, M. (1970). International diversification of investment portfolios. *The American Economic Review, 60*(4), 668–675.

Longin, F., & Solnik, B. (1995). Is the correlation in international equity returns constant: 1960–1990? *Journal of International Money and Finance, 14*(1), 3–26.

Makridakis, S. G., & Wheelwright, S. C. (1974). An analysis of the interrelationships among the major world stock exchanges. *Journal of Business Finance & Accounting, 1*(2), 195–215.

Malik, F., & Ewing, B. T. (2009). Volatility transmission between oil prices and equity sector returns. *International Review of Financial Analysis, 18*, 95–100.

Markowitz, H. (1959). *Efficient diversification of investments* (pp. 26–31). New York, NY: John Wiley and Sons.

Medhioub, I. (2015). A Markov switching three regime model of Tunisian business cycle. *American Journal of Economics, 5*(3), 394–403.

Mensi, W., Hammoudeh, S., Nguyen, D. K., & Yoon, S. M. (2014). Dynamic spillovers among major energy and cereal commodity prices. *Energy Economics, 43*, 225–243.

Nicola, F., Paceb, P., & Hernandez, M. A. (2016). Co-movement of major energy, agricultural, and food commodity price returns: A time-series assessment. *Energy Economics, 57*, 28–41.

Phillips, P. C. B., & Perron, P. (1988). Testing for a unit root in time series regressions. *Biometrika, 75*, 335–346.

Sensoy, A. (2013). Dynamic relationship between precious metals. *Resources Policy, 38*, 504–511.

CHAPTER 5

EXCHANGE RISK PERCEPTION AND EXCHANGE RISK MANAGEMENT: A REGIONAL APPLICATION IN TURKEY'S MANUFACTURING FIRMS

Serdar Ogel, Adem Boyukaslan and Semih Acikgozoglu

ABSTRACT

The present study aims to reveal knowledge, report on perception level and look at the evaluation of exchange rate risk management techniques of enterprises registered to Afyonkarahisar Chamber of Commerce and Industry. In order to achieve this, the authors conducted a study that included a field-survey and consisted of 223 enterprises that have foreign trade transactions in Afyonkarahisar city. The data that were used in the analysis had been collected via a survey and they were statistically evaluated by SPSS program.

Within the scope of the study, the authors investigated the determination of corporational identity of the sampled manufacturing enterprises, organisational structure of finance departments, determination of ownership structures of these enterprises, determination of foreign exchange risk perceptions, classification of exchange rate risks according to industry type and the determination of risk management instruments such as internal and external hedging strategies and information and usage levels of derivative instruments.

The most important result obtained in the study is that the majority of the companies, which operate in a competitive environment, are intensely exposed to foreign exchange risk but try to overcome the foreign exchange risk using

Contemporary Issues in Business, Economics and Finance
Contemporary Studies in Economic and Financial Analysis, Volume 104, 57–84
Copyright © 2020 by Emerald Publishing Limited
All rights of reproduction in any form reserved
ISSN: 1569-3759/doi:10.1108/S1569-375920200000104006

traditional internal firm-level hedging methods instead of well-reputed external hedging methods or derivative instruments. Firms declared to be out of knowledge – by any means – for derivative instruments as the main reason for not utilising a well-reputed external foreign exchange risk management techniques.

Keywords: Exchange rate risk; derivative instruments; hedging; currency; risk management; emerging economies; bakruptcy; financial failure

JEL classifications: G32; P45

1. INTRODUCTION

The financial markets' fluctuations are mainly considered as a source of risk, affecting individual investors, companies and national economies regardless of their development level. Particularly, the consensus among those, who have steered economic policies since the 1980s on the benefits of the liberalisation of financial markets, enabled the adoption of financial practices to allow free circulation of capital. However, being integrated to these practises, developing countries, which aim to realise their country's economic development faster, have encountered economic problems in that period and this beckoned the questions on the contribution of financial integrations to economic growth (Sever, Ozdemir, & Mizirik, 2010). Increased capital movements due to globalisation and the additional rapid movement of capital among economies paved the way for a more fragile economic structure. As a result of these enlargements, many financial problems that have risen today, the effects of the liberal economic order are intensely perceived, have exposed the enterprises confronted with uncertainties, as well as all other economic units.

Unexpected events, such as weak macroeconomic indicators, erroneous economic policies, insufficient financial infrastructure, moral risk and asymmetric information problem and misconduct of creditors and international financial institutions in the market, political assassination or terrorist attack, are accepted as the main problems causing exchange rate risks (Kibritcioglu, 2001). Therefore, it can be stated that economic fluctuations may be experienced due to various factors. In addition, the effects of these fluctuations on foreign exchange markets affect all enterprises significantly regardless of their small or large scale and it constitutes a risk factor.

In that regard, the post-1970 period, which commenced with the collapse of the Bretton Woods System, gained momentum with two oil crises and has been commemorated by many other financial crises. In this era, the increasing mobility of financial capital at an international level has brought financial crises into the agenda of the world economy with increasing frequency in both developed and developing countries (Delice, 2003). The financial crisis which have been experienced more recently in Mexico (1994), Asia (1997), Russia (1999), Argentina (2001), Turkey (2001) and finally the mortgage crisis in the USA (2008) are examples where one can perfectly understand the economic bottleneck all over the world. The experiences of these crises, which are now dominated by liberalisation of capital movements, have shown that governments' effectiveness on monetary policy, interest rates and exchange rates have significantly weakened. Remarkably, the countries that were deprived of capital had to keep their real interest rates above inflation in order to ensure the endurance of foreign capital inflows. However, intensely booming capital inflows generally led to an increase in imports of consumer goods and consequently the current account deficits have created fragile economies against capital movements (Seyidoglu, 2003).

Turkey had imposed a closed economic model based on fixed exchange rate regime withstanding import substitution until the 1980s. National economic structure has been successfully sustained with high growth rates in industrial production, until renowned 'radical economical decisions of 24 January 1980' which has been a landmark for the Turkey's economy. On this date, the country had switched on a new economical strategy based on financial liberalisation. In addition to the economic reforms and fiscal regulations, the governmental economic decisions focussed on outward growth system and followed an export-oriented industrialisation strategy. Brand new open economy models have brought many improvements in the economic life of the country, and foreign exchange transactions and capital movements have been extricated and full liberalisation of the economy has been achieved in 1989. During this period, the liberalisation of foreign exchange transactions and capital movements paved the way for banks to provide funds through borrowing from abroad (Ural, 2003). But although the openness of the economy and the easing of the capital movements have ensured, Turkey's economy has faced the financial crises on 5 April 1994, then in November 2000 and finally in February 2001 due to the lacking off-balancing policies, which could not be properly produced.

Covering the years from 2000 until 2019, the exchange rate changes in Turkey are depicted Fig. 1. During this period, the Turkish lira depreciated more than 10 times against the currencies defined as reserve money despite the withdrawal in

Fig. 1. Exchange Rate Fluctuations in Turkey (2000–2019).

the last six months, as visible in Fig. 1. In this regard, considered among one of the liberal and emerging market economies, Turkey will very likely suffer a new financial crisis stemming from exchange rate fluctuations in the upcoming periods sometimes as a result of it and sometimes as a reason for it. This economic condition forces enterprises that trade in different currencies to take financial measures and to manage exchange rate risks. Businesses that operate in developing countries, such as Turkey, are quite susceptible to fluctuations in exchange rates resulting from economic uncertainty, and this may result in a bankruptcy at the end if they cannot successfully manage the aforementioned risks. Therefore, financial risk management instruments become more important in fragile economies. However, assuming that exchange rate risk is a systematic risk, it is not possible to prevent the emergence of exchange rate crises in such economies through individual or institutional efforts and the management of exchange rate risk becomes more meaningful for firms.

The exchange rate risk was earlier defined as the probability of change in assets, resources and cash flows of firms due to unexpected changes in exchange rates in the future (Glaum, 1990). However, the exchange rate risk can also be explained as the emerging of negative effects of the upward or downward changes in foreign currencies' value compared to one national currency due to various reasons on the financial position of local firms (Aksu, 2016). Exchange rate risk occurs in foreign trade operations in foreign currency, in international transactions and in foreign investments (Yildiz & Ciftci, 2011). The main reason for the exchange rate risk arising from foreign trade operations is that receivables and payables are formed in different currencies and the amount of receivables and payables are different from each other (Karas & Celikkol, 2019).

However, the concept of hedging is mostly defined in financial risk management terminology as undertaking an opposing position process that eliminates the risk. In general, it is possible to indicate the products and methods used for hedging as internal and external exchange rate risk management techniques. Firms can utilise such methods like matching, netting, currency baskets, leading and lagging (setting the time of cash flows), diversification and selection of invoicing currency as internal hedging techniques within their organisational structure (Buker, Asikoglu, & Sevil, 2014). External hedging methods include financial instruments and strategies (namely derivative products) with a wide range of options available from outside the firms. These instruments are known as derivative products in this framework such as forwards, futures, options, swaps, and they are performed by means of contracts (Conkar & Ata, 2002). The use of derivative products contributes to the continuity of stability by ensuring depth to the financial markets at the macro level and it also provides the opportunity to manage risks arising from the uncertainty of the future at the level of firms. Nowadays, it is more important for firms to utilise derivative products as vital hedging techniques to reduce uncertainties in the financial markets and to make effective planning and predictions for the future to minimise unexpected financial misfortunes (Kaygusuzoglu, 2011). Therefore, analysing the ways in which the companies manage their currency risks would provide valuable information for the theoreticians and practitioners in understanding the exchange rate management problems encountered.

In many disciplines, especially in the social sciences, the first stage of the research process is to determine the research area and to reveal the population characteristics. Being descriptive and exploratory, the present study aims to determine how much the concept of exchange rate risk management is recognised and how frequently the hedging techniques are benefited by the Turkish manufacturing firms. In this context, first we present the results of similar studies in the literature and then reveal our findings according to our exploratory field study to define the area within the determined sample.

2. LITERATUR REVIEW

Sezer (1999), in his study on public companies in Kayseri city, Turkey, indicated that export companies follow exchange rate changes through banks. Additionally, 90% of the companies included in the study did not prefer derivative products to protect themselves from exchange rate changes and 80% of the enterprises did not use derivative products to hedge foreign exchange positions. The author reported that the mentioned 80% made balancing payment transactions in terms of time, amount and currency, and the firms preferred the re-pricing strategy of products/services by turning to marketing as a strategy of protection against exchange rate risk.

Allayannis and Ofek (2001) investigated the use of derivative instruments for hedging or speculative purposes with a sample of non-financial companies listed on S&P. The results showed that the companies reduced their exchange rate risks through derivative instruments as a hedging technique. Research findings also reported that the decision of utilising derivative instruments generally depended on external factors, such as foreign sales and foreign trade transactions.

Allayannis, Brown, and Klapper (2001) examined exchange rate risk management and the use of derivative instruments on 327 non-financial institutions in eight East Asian countries. The findings of the study showed that exchange rate risk management using derivative instruments had a positive effect on the efficiency of operating activities. On the other hand, the findings indicated that there was no significant relationship between the companies that use derivative instruments and those who do not.

Bradley and Moles (2002) investigated the impact of exchange rate movements on firm value and highlighted the international impact. In this context, the study emphasises that the use of financial instruments can provide effective risk management and it proposed strategic exchange rate management approaches against exchange rate changes. According to the findings, large-scale and publicly traded UK companies preferred strategic approaches to exchange rate risk. However, it was reported that operational techniques had increased and improved in order to avoid exchange rate risk in UK companies. One of the results of the study was that the number of enterprises selling their inputs with the same currency was high. However, accounting risk was not manageable by the enterprises. The authors also stated that these companies occasionally used repo, leasing, factoring, foreign currency options and forward transactions against financial risk.

In a survey conducted on 50 international trade companies in Denizli city, which is of one of the most important export centre of Turkey, Yildiran (2004) concluded that the companies thought exchange rate movements were frequently influenced by political developments in Turkey. The findings also unveiled that exchange rate risk has been shown as the most important risk type faced by enterprises. In addition, the companies considered the transaction risk as a kind of manageable risk. Accordingly, the firms would pick changing their production and marketing strategies as a first option to deal with the exchange rate risk.

Ozdemir (2005) used survey data collected from 60 manufacturing companies listed on the Istanbul Stock Exchange (ISE). While examining the hedging methods of the mentioned firms, the researcher additionally handled the other internal hedging types namely, transaction risk, economic risk and accounting risk. The findings of the study showed that enterprises were mainly affected by economic risk and transaction risk among the exchange rate risk. On the other hand, while using internal techniques to protect them from transaction risk, the firms did not prefer external techniques even though they had enough information. The researcher also reported that the companies applied to change marketing and financing strategies in order to minimise economic risk they were exposed to.

Kutukiz (2005) examined 120 tourism firms operating in Mugla city, Turkey, with data collected through questionnaires. The study examined foreign exchange risk perception of the companies and hedging methods before and after the financial crisis. According to the results, tourism companies saw interest and commodity price risk as the most important risk types before the 2001 financial crisis and they stressed exchange rate and interest risk as the most important risk type after the 2001 crisis. In addition, it was stated in the findings that before the 2001 crisis, companies tended to use foreign exchange currency instead of domestic currency against the changes in the exchange rate and after the 2001 crisis their income decreased despite the appreciation of the domestic currency and the increase in the occupancy rates. The authors highlighted that one of the most important findings in the study was that firms did not prefer derivative products to reduce exchange rate risk due to their lack of knowledge and also a lack of an organised stock market where these instruments could be traded.

Nazlı (2006) utilised data from a sample consisting of 51 firms that were registered on the Istanbul Chamber of Commerce and examined the exchange rate risk management, productivity and the knowledge level of decision-makers. Research results showed that decisions upon exchange rate risk techniques were usually taken by a staff with undergraduate and graduate degrees. The findings revealed that the companies preferred to make hedging transactions on a single foreign currency, whereas forward contracts were the main hedging technique among the external methods. However, the usage rates of the hedging techniques did not satisfied the researcher and the author finally suggested that exchange rate risk management was extremely necessary for the companies.

Ozen, Yolas, and Ozdemir (2006) selected manufacturing enterprises listed in Borsa Istanbul (BIST) as a sample. The results of the study showed that manufacturing firms were inadequate in policy making processes to reduce the exchange rate risk they were exposed to and due to the high exposure to export and import ratios, they were more affected by exchange rate changes. In addition, the companies confessed that they had lower information levels on these financial instruments and they therefore did not use alternative financial methods.

Aabo, Høg, and Kuhn (2010) investigated small- and medium-sized enterprises in Denmark and examined the derivative instruments and imports used in exchange rate risk management. The findings showed that there was significantly strong and negative relation between the derivative instruments and import. According to another finding in the study, companies tended to cover the exchange rate risk they were exposed to due to their foreign sales through imports.

Bayrakdaroglu, Sari, and Heybeli (2013) conducted a questionnaire on 58 manufacturing firms in Denizli city, Turkey, and investigated foreign exchange risk perceptions, foreign exchange risk management policies and the frequency of use of derivative instruments in the firms. The findings of the study indicated that these enterprises were intensely affected by the changes in exchange rates, whereas the use of derivative instruments was quite low. According to the findings, enterprises were quite reluctant to utilise hedging products even though derivative products were well known by these firms. Another finding of the study emphasised that large-scale companies preferred derivative products for speculative purposes rather than hedging reasons although derivative instruments were not generally preferred by firms.

Kandir, Karadeniz, and Erismis (2015) examined the firm sensitivity to exchange rate risk and used the data from eight tourism companies listed in ISE for the 2002–2010 period. According to the results, three companies stated that exchange rate risk was the most important risk type for them. On the other hand, the three enterprises declared that they were affected negatively by the exchange rate risk by having more open foreign exchange positions than the other tourism enterprises.

Ito, Koibuchi, Sato, and Shimizu (2016) examined the exposure of Japanese companies to exchange rate risk and investigated Japan firms' exchange rate risk management techniques. According to the results, which came from 227 companies on the Tokyo Stock Exchange, companies whose revenues depended on sales in foreign markets were exposed to greater exchange rate risk. Another result showed that companies with high US dollar (USD) transactions reduced the exchange rate risk using both financial and operational instruments together. Findings also showed that companies invoicing their sales in Yen were exposed to lower exchange rate risk. But the main finding of the study was that Japanese firms reduced the exchange rate risk using financial and operational instruments.

Doganay (2016) selected tobacco industry firms in Turkey to determine the exchange rate risk management approaches the firms used, exchange rate risk levels they are exposed to and the positions of enterprises to reduce the risk. The results of the study revealed that the enterprises in the tobacco sector aimed to protect themselves from exchange rate risk especially in export transactions. The researcher reported that there was no systematic management for exchange rate risk in a significant part of the tobacco industry. In addition, tobacco industry enterprises preferred internal techniques over financial instruments in order to mitigate exchange rate risk. The reason for this was attributed to the intense import transactions of these enterprises and the expectations of the exchange rate.

As one of the important results of the study, the preference of dollar-based foreign currency indexed loan for the firms as a foreign exchange risk management tool was noted.

Sezer and Canpolat (2017) studied the use of derivative products and deposits in foreign trade transactions in terms of managing the exchange rate risk in Turkish firms. The researchers drew attention to the lack of awareness and the low use of derivative products in Turkish firms despite the frequent use of derivative products in developed countries.

3. SAMPLE SELECTION, DATA COLLECTION AND METHODOLOGY

The aim of the present research has been to determine the risk perception level of the regional manufacturing firms regarding exchange rate management, to measure their attitudes for the type of risk they perceive and to reveal their approaches about the financial instruments in order to avoid exchange rate risk. The sample chosen for this study was the manufacturing enterprises operating in Afyonkarahisar city and which were registered to Afyonkarahisar Chamber of Commerce and Industry (ACCI). In this context, the study has also aimed to reveal the sectoral diversity of the companies operating with different currencies. The present study focuses on a field research and it has an exploratory identity about revealing the exchange rate management techniques of the enterprises registered with the ACCI.

The data used in the analyses were obtained from face-to-face interviews and surveys in enterprises registered with the ACCI. As of March 2018, the time when the fieldwork started, the number of enterprises with foreign trade transactions and registered to the ACCI was officially 302. Data from 228 enterprises were collected by a survey that was compiled from Ozdemir (2005) and Nazlı's (2006) past works. The data from five enterprises, whose discrepancies were seen as distorting the distribution with outlier values and also having missing responses, were excluded from the analyses. As a result, the sample of the study consisted of 223 enterprises (68.1% of all registered firms) and the data from a total of 223 enterprises were used in the final analysis. Consisting of multiple choice and open-ended survey statements, a questionnaire was directed to the participants of the industry members at provincial centre mostly in a five-point Likert Scale form. The obtained data were analysed using the IBM Statistical Package for the Social Sciences 20.0 Program.

The findings of the analyses are presented in the following section.

4. FINDINGS

In research conducted through surveys in the social sciences, reliability analysis is strongly proposed to determine the consistency of the expressions presented to the participants and the proximity of their assessments (Leech, Barrett, & Morgan, 2013). The most commonly used method for measuring intrinsic consistency is

Cronbach alpha value which shows the reliability coefficient of the scale. It is an acceptable value to have 0.5 in some sources although it is desirable that this value be at least 0.7 (Altunışık, Coşkun, Bayraktaroglu, & Yıldırım, 2007). According to the reliability analysis, the reliability value of the scale that is used in the study and the 34 expression of the foreign currency risk perception and foreign exchange risk management techniques were satisfactory ($N = 223$; $\alpha = 0.961$). In this context, it can be noted that the scale has a high degree of reliability.

As to the findings of the study, these are presented in two parts. The first includes descriptive statistics results reflecting the questions, such as general characteristics of the firms, financial transaction volumes, foreign trade information, how the financial decisions are taken and so on.

The second is the presentation of the main findings containing the type of financial transactions made by the manufacturing enterprises in order to protect their approaches and types for exchange rate risk management techniques and methods.

4.1. Descriptive Statistics Results

The sectoral distribution of the sampled manufacturing firms and the share of these sectors in the total sample are displayed in Table 1.

Among the companies participating in the survey, the majority of the enterprises are in the marble, stone, soil and mining sectors (186 firms, 83.4% of total) operating in the underground activities. This result is compatible with the economic sectoral activities of Afyonkarahisar province and districts according to the 2017 export report data officially released by ACCI. Following the marble, stone, soil and mining sector, food and tobacco industry firms came in second at 5.4% of the total.

Table 2 is exhibiting the information about the organisation and ownership structures involved in the study.

According to Table 2, which demonstrates the distribution of ownership structures of the sampled firms, 141 businesses are in limited company status (63.2%) while 48 business (21.5%) are joint-stock companies. Individual companies follow limited and joint-stock companies with a distribution of 15.2%. These results are an important in explaining our next findings regarding institutionalisation of these firms.

Table 1. Distribution and Percentages of Sampled Firms by Sectors.

Industry	Frequency	%
Marble, stone, soil, mining	186	83.4
Marble, stone, soil, mining	12	5.4
Weaving, apparel, leather, footwear	1	0.4
Forestry products and furniture	5	2.2
Paper and paper products, printing	2	0.9
Chemical, petroleum products, rubber and plastics	6	2.7
Metal	3	1.3
Metalware, machinery and equipment	4	1.8
Automotive industry	4	1.8
Total	223	100.0

Table 2.   Distribution and Percentages of Firms' Ownership Structures.

Ownership	Frequency	%	Total %
Joint-stock companies	48	21.5	21.5
Limited companies	141	63.2	84.8
Individual companies	34	15.2	100.0
Total	223	100.0	

Table 3.   Distribution of Firms According to Finance Department Existence.

Fin. Dept.	Frequency	%	Total %
Yes	146	65.5	65.5
No	77	34.5	100.0
Total	223	100.0	

Table 4.   Distribution of Financial Decisions and Risk Management
Decisions in Firms.

Decision Made by		Frequency	%	Total %
Valid	Company owner	95	42.6	67.4
	Company manager	39	17.5	95.0
	Accountant	6	2.7	99.3
	Bank and other financial institution referrals	1	0.4	100.0
	Total	141	63.2	
Missing	Unanswered	82	36.8	
Total		223	100.0	

The information on the organisational structure, stating whether companies have a financial department or not, is shown in Table 3.

The number of the firms which declared to having a finance department in their organisational structure is 146 (65.5% of the total). The number of businesses expressed the absence of a finance department is 77 (34.5%).

The distribution of responses for the people responsible for financial decisions and risk management decisions in the enterprise is shown in Table 4.

According to the findings of the participants who answered the statement on 'who gave financial decisions and risk management decisions', in 95 business (42.6% of total) financial decisions and risk management decisions are taken by the business owner. The number of respondents who expressed that financial decisions and risk management decisions were taken by the company's manager was 39 (17.5% of total). However, 82 respondents (36.8% of total) were hesitant to respond to this question.

The data obtained from participants regarding the education level of the decision-makers were presented in Table 5.

The majority of decision-makers, 120 participants (53.8%), had an undergraduate level of education. Next in line were executive managers with a graduate level of education with 49 participants (22%). The managers who have other levels of education are in third position with a total of 45 (20.2%).

Table 5. Distribution of the Education Level of Financial Decision-makers in Firms.

Education Level of the Decision-makers	Frequency	%	Total %
Graduate	49	22.0	22.0
Undergraduate	120	53.8	75.8
Other	45	20.2	96.0
Unanswered	9	4.0	100.0
Total	223	100.0	

Table 6. Distribution of Training Programmes for the Finance Department Staff.

	Never		Rarely		Occasionally		Often		Always		Total	
	Freq.	%	Freq.	%	Freq.	%	Freq.	%	Freq.	%	Freq.	%
Orientation	34	15.2	28	12.6	45	20.2	24	10.8	26	11.7	157	70.4
Domestic courses, seminars	36	16.1	32	14.3	39	17.5	34	15.2	9	4.0	150	67.3
International orientation training	83	37.2	12	5.4	27	12.1	23	10.3	4	1.8	149	66.8
Internal Orientation Training	44	19.7	25	11.2	28	12.6	39	17.5	16	7.2	152	68.2
No training	40	17.9	4	1.8	2	0.9	5	2.2	66	29.6	117	52.5

The distribution of the responses relating to questions to determine the opportunities for staff training is shown in Table 6.

The results of the participants who were asked retraining procedures after being hired to the finance department are as follows:

(a) The number of participants who said there had been *no* orientation training was 34 (15.2%), and the number who said that they had *rarely* been given orientation training was 28 (12.6%). The count of participants saying there had been an *occasional* orientation training was 45 (20.2%). Accordingly 24 participants (10.8%) who expressed the orientation training had been held *often* and 26 participants (11.7%) who stated that orientation training had been *always* organised.

The results relating to the training procedures in finance departments are as follows:

(b) As to the domestic courses or seminar-type training programmes, 36 participants (16.1%) stated that there had been *no* domestic courses, seminars, etc., held in their firms while there were 32 participants (14.3%) saying a course or seminar was *rarely* held. In addition, 39 participants (17.5%) expressed that there had been *occasional* training in their finance departments and 43 participants (19.2%) responded to the statements indicating that training was held *often* and *always*.

With reference to statements relating to internal trainings:

(c) Eighty-three participants (37.2%) declared that there had been *no* education abroad while 12 participants (5.4%) stated that there had been *rarely* been an international course or seminar for the finance staff. Some of the participants,

27 (12.1%) replied that international courses were *occasionally* held, while 27 participants (12.1%) responded that international training had been *often* and *always* held. The ratio of all participants to the total participants was 66.8%. While interpreting this response, the authors of the present chapter have concluded that participation to the fairs which were held abroad affected the answers given.

As to the replies relating to internal training:

(d) Forty participants (17.9%) stated that *no* internal training was provided while 25 participants (11.2%) stated that internal training had *rarely* been arranged. Twenty-eight participants (12.6%) replied that there had been *occasionally* internal training. However, 39 participants (17.5%) agreed with statements like *often* while 16 participants (7.2%) replied as *always*. The ratio of all respondents to the total participants for internal training facilities is 682%.

As to the answers which concerned the internal orientation training held in the finance department:

(e) Forty participants (17.9%) replied that there had been *no* internal orientation programs in their firms, while 66 participants (29.6%) responded that a training study was *always* organised. The ratio of all respondents to the total participants was 52.5%.

Following the assessments of the information obtained about the characteristic of manufacturing enterprises and the determination of the financial decision-makers, the participants were asked to respond the statements relating to currency types, currency transactions, payables–receivables volumes over currencies they used and the findings are presented in Table 7.

When the responses relating to the exchange types were evaluated, the results showed that the USD was the most common currency type in enterprises' foreign trade transactions. One hundred and ninety-four participants (87%) declared that they frequently preferred the USD in foreign trade transactions in the multi-selection option statement given. The European Union currency Unit (EUR) was in second place with 26%. Another remarkable finding in the table is that Ruble, Yuan, Sterlin and other currencies were almost never preferred in foreign trade transactions by businesses.

The information for the annual receivables and payables of manufacturing enterprises in foreign currency are displayed in Tables 8 and 9.

Table 7.   Distribution of Traded Currency Types.[a]

Currency Types	Never		Rarely		Occasionally		Much		Very Much		Total	
	Freq.	%	Freq.	%	Freq.	%	Freq.	%	Freq.	%	Freq.	%
EUR	82	36.8	31	13.9	52	23.3	34	15.2	24	10.8	223	100
USD	4	1.8	6	2.7	19	8.5	39	17.5	155	69.5	223	100
RUBLE	219	98.2	3	1.3	–	–	–	–	1	0.4	223	100
YUAN	214	96.0	3	1.3	6	2.7	–	–	–	–	223	100
STERLIN	214	96.0	9	4.0	–	–	–	–	–	–	223	100
Other	223	100,	–	–	–	–	–	–	–	–	223	100

Note: [a]Multi-selection.

Table 8. Distribution of Currency Collections (Annual Trading Volumes).

Annual Trade Volume	Frequency	%	Total %
Under 1 million $ collections	124	55.6	55.6
Over 1 million $ collections	99	44.4	100.0
Total	223	100.0	

Table 9. Distribution of Currency Payments (Annual Trading Volumes).

Annual Trade Volume	Frequency	%	Total %
Under 1 million $ payments	151	67.7	68.3
Over 1 million $ payments	70	31.4	99.1
Total	221	99.1	99.1

Considering the collections of manufacturing enterprises in USD, the number of enterprises that have been collecting under 1 million USD per year was 124 (55.6%) while the number of enterprises which had annual receivables over $1 million USD was 99 (44.4%).

Considering the payments in USD of manufacturing enterprises sampled, the number of enterprises that have been collecting under 1 million USD per year was 151 (67.7%), while the number of enterprises whose annual payments were over 1 million USD was 70 (31.4%). One of the reasons for the payments under 1 million USD was due to the fact that the vast majority of businesses participating in the research were from the marble and mining sectors, whose input costs were as Turkish lira.

4.2. Statistics and Findings on Exchange Rate Risk Techniques and Exchange Risk Management

Following the evaluation of the overall characteristics and general information on the enterprises, the findings on determining the exchange rate risk perceptions of manufacturing enterprises will first be presented in this section. In this context, Tables 10 and 11 demonstrate the findings of how enterprises perceive the risk of exchange rate.

Table 10. Distribution of the Exposed Exchange Rate Risk for Firms Compared by Other Kind of Risk Factors.

		Frequency	%	Total %
Valid	Very much	77	34.5	35.2
	Much	86	38.6	74.4
	Partly	43	19.3	94.1
	Rarely	6	2.7	96.8
	Never	7	3.1	100.0
	Total	219	98.2	
Invalid	System	4	1.8	
Total		223	100.0	

Table 11.   Distribution of Exchange Rate Risk Types Exposed by Firms.

	Strongly Unimportant		Unimportant		Neither Important or Unimportant		Important		Strongly Important		Total	
	Freq.	%	Freq.	%	Freq.	%	Freq.	%	Freq.	%	Freq.	%
The changes in the TL or currency value affect our costs and sales directly/ indirectly, and therefore we are faced with the risk of losing our market share	7	3.1	8	3.6	15	6.7	89	39.9	98	43.9	217	97.3
Risk of changing rates in the terms of our buying and selling contracts	8	3.6	11	4.9	22	9.9	96	43.0	80	35.9	217	97.3
The risk of changes in the currencies at the end of the accounting period, as we record the records of transactions we have made in local currency	5	2.2	18	8.1	28	12.6	98	43.9	63	28.3	212	95.1

According to the risks exposed by the firms, the representatives declared that foreign exchange rate risk extremely affected firms. 163 participants replied that the exchange rate risk *very much* and *much* affected the business facilitates and this number constituted the 74.4% of respondents. In light of the findings, it is concluded from the responses that the exchange rate risk was more intensely perceived by enterprises than other risk groups.

After determining which level of exchange rate risk was perceived against other risk groups, the statements that followed asked the participants to determine which exchange rate risks they were exposed to in their firms. The results are shown in Table 11.

The number of enterprises which chose the statement including 'the market share losses will arise with changes in the exchange rate' as *important* and *very important* is 187 (83.8%). However, the number of the firms that chose the statement including 'risk of changing rates in the terms and date of their purchasing and

Table 12. Distribution of the Firm Strategies to Reduce the Exchange Rate Risk.

		Frequency	%	Total %
Valid	Benefit from financial institutions in accordance with the strategies set by the company's manager or owners	165	74.0	83.8
	Benefit from financial institutions in accordance with the strategies set by the Finance Department	32	14.3	100.0
	Total	197	88.3	
Missing		26	11.7	
Total		223	100.0	

selling contracts' as *important* and *very important* was 176 (% 78.9). The number of enterprises that chose 'the risk of being exposed as a result of accounting operations' as *important* or *very important* was 161 (72.2%). It is clear from Table 11 that the companies participating in the research were being intensely affected by the specified exchange rate risk types.

The answers to the statement of exchange rate risk strategies pursued by the manufacturing enterprises to reduce the risk of exchange rate are shown in Table 12.

According to the findings, the number of businesses which are trying to reduce the risk of exchange by referring to financial institutions was 165 (74.0%). The number of firms which preferred to reduce the risk of exchange through the presence of a finance department instead was 32 (14.3%). The number of informants who left the question unanswered was 26 (11.7%). These findings are evaluated in relation to the ownership structure of the enterprises, and one can conclude that the decisions about the advice or consultancy services taken from financial institutions were primarily made by business owners or managers.

The responses that relate the preference level of the internal methods that are used to reduce the exchange rate risk are exhibited in Table 13.

As to the responses for the preferred internal hedging techniques used in order to manage the risk of exchange rate for the sampled manufacturing enterprises one notes that the number of enterprises that manage the risk of exchange through matching the same currency for the receivables and payables was 147 (65.9%). The number of those who had not paid their credit and payments in the same currency was 24 (10.8%). According to these data, it can be concluded that the enterprises in the study were trying to reduce the rate of exchange risk by trading mostly through the same currency (matching).

The number of enterprises attempting to manage the risk of exchange by anticipating possible changes in the exchange rates – trying to extend payment term or trying to make early payment when currency tends to increase – was 96 (43%). The number of participants who expressed that they try to anticipate changes in currency rates, and depending on that, they request an extension or make an early payment was 55 (%24.7). Fifty-eight (26%) of the enterprises stated that they preferred this technique at a moderate level.

According to Table 13, 126 (56.5%) firms stated that they did not have a different type of currency or have a small amount of different currency types within the business in order to reduce the risk. The number of enterprises that try to avoid the exchange rate risk by having different currency types was just 37 (16.5%).

Table 13. Distribution of the Internal Methods to Reduce the Exchange Rate Risk.

	Never		Rarely		Partly		Much		Very Much		Total	
	Freq.	%	Freq.	%	Freq.	%	Freq.	%	Freq.	%	Freq.	%
We are trying to get the currency and payments through a single currency	10	4.5	14	6.3	44	19.7	75	33.6	72	32.3	215	96.4
We are attempting to manage the risk of exchange by anticipating possible changes in the exchange rates when currency tends to decline we try to extend payment term or when currency tends to increase we tend to make early payment	20	9.0	35	15.7	58	26.0	58	26.0	38	17.0	209	93.7
We hold a portfolio of different currencies	84	37.7	42	18.8	44	19.7	32	14.3	5	2.2	207	92.8
we ensure the execution of foreign exchange risk management from one hand by establishing sales centres in our overseas markets	77	34.5	21	9.4	30	13.5	45	20.2	32	14.3	205	91.9
We store the import price amounts from the spot market and keep it in the currency account until the payment is due	88	39.5	25	11.2	42	18.8	30	13.5	20	9.0	205	91.9

By establishing sales centres in overseas markets to protect against the exchange rate risk, those firms who prefer the single-hand execution of foreign exchange risk management, was of 77 (34.5%).

'Saving the import revenue amounts in the currency account from the spot market until meets the maturity of the loan' is an internal risk management technique which is used to manage exchange rate risk and the number of the firms that adopted this technique was 50 (22.5%) participants. On the other hand, 88 (39.5%) of the enterprises expressed that they did not adopt this technique in any way.

Table 14. Distribution of Contracts Usage Based in BIST Derivative Market.

		Frequency	%
Valid	Yes	58	26.0
	No	157	70.4
	Total	215	96.4
Missing	Unanswered	8	3.6
Total		223	100.0

Table 15. Distribution of the Reasons for Not Using Future and Option Contracts.

		Frequency	%	Total %
Valid	Lack of knowledge	89	39.9	58.6
	High risk	24	10.8	74.3
	High cost	16	7.2	84.9
	Other	23	10.3	100.0
	Total	152	68.2	
Missing	Unanswered	71	31.8	
Total		223	100.0	

Table 14 exhibits the responses of the companies' hedging contract usage in BIST Derivative Market (VIOP).

When evaluating the participants' preference for future or option contracts through the derivative markets, the results showed that 157 (70.4%) businesses did not prefer either future or option contracts in the markets, whereas 58 (26%) of the participants declared to use future and option contracts.

Table 15 demonstrates the distribution of responses including the reasons for the firms not to use future and option contracts in the markets.

When looking at the reasons why firms do not participate in future and option contracts in the markets, it is observed that enterprises had insufficient knowledge about the contracts. This can be observed from the 89 (58.6%) respondents out of the 152 participants who said that the firms fell short of sufficient knowledge to use future and option contracts. This finding can be regarded as one of the most noteworthy results of our study. In addition, 71 (31.8%) of the participants avoided responding to this question.

Table 16 exhibits the results compiled from the responses of the participants containing the statements regarding which methods were primarily preferred as an external technique (hedging) in order to reduce the foreign exchange rate risk.

As to the firms' preference of external methods (hedging) to manage the exchange risk, one can observe from the results that firms tended not to prefer external hedging techniques. When the external methods were assessed separately in the form of financial derivative instruments, the number of those who did not prefer forward transactions was 146 (65.5%) and the number of those who did not prefer future transactions was 144 (64.6%). In addition, the number of those who did not prefer option transactions was 120 (53.8%), whereas the number of those who did not prefer swap operations was 153 (68.6%). These findings are

Table 16.   Distribution of Preferred External Hedging Techniques to Reduce
Exchange Rate Risk.

	Never Used		Little Used		Sometimes Used		Much Used		Very Much Used		Total	
	Freq.	%	Freq.	%	Freq.	%	Freq.	%	Freq.	%	Freq.	%
Forward	146	65.5	17	7.6	30	13.5	9	4.0	11	4.9	213	95.5
Future	144	64.6	15	6.7	39	17.5	15	6.7	-	-	213	95.5
Option	120	53.8	17	7.6	33	14.8	26	11.7	17	7.6	213	95.5
Swap	153	68.6	16	7.2	23	10.3	14	6.3	7	3.1	213	95.5

also among the remarkable results obtained in the study. In this context, it can be noted that the sampled enterprises were generally against external exchange risk management techniques.

At this point, when considering the business types and the parties which use swap transactions in Turkey, the answers for 'I use more' and 'I use too much' for the statements regarding swap contracts was about 10 % of all respondents. This can be attributed to the fact that they did not have much knowledge about these methods.

After determining which of the external methods existed in the firms and which of them were preferred/not preferred for managing the exchange rate risk, the other statements directed to the respondents aimed to reveal their assessments/perceptions about these techniques.

Tables 17–20 present the distributions of responses concerning the participants' considerations of external hedging techniques. In this manner, Table 17 exhibits the results for the respondents' assessments on the forward transactions while Table 18 demonstrates the future contracts assessments of the informants. Similarly, Table 19 shows the evaluation of participants on option contracts, whereas swap contracts evaluations are included in Table 20.

As to the responses on how forward transactions are evaluated by the firms, the majority of respondents, 137 (61.4%), declared that they had no opinion about the following derivative statement: *forward agreements cannot be found in the desired amounts of contracts.* Another statement presented on forward transactions was that related to *the failure to reverse (terminate) before maturity.* Again, the majority, 145 of respondents, (65%) were neutral on this subject. The statement relating to *no forward exchange at any time* garnered a neutral response from 151 participants (67.7%).

With reference to the statement *the fact that it can be done with a wide variety of currency types,* 132 (59.3%) of the participants said that they had no idea. One of the features of forward transactions was reflected in the phrase *mutual interoperability with banks.* Again, 142 of the respondents (63.7%) gave a neutral answer. Likewise, for the phrase *the determination of contract futures between the desired dates,* 139 (62.3%) participants responded in the neutral. One hundred and fifty (67.3%) participants when replying to the statement *do not have to obligation to possession of a guarantee to enterprises* said that 'we have no idea about it'.

Future contracts are a type of contract that needs to be done through organised markets due to qualifications and therefore must be used by an intermediary

Table 17. Distribution of Firms' Assessments upon Forward Contracts.

	Strongly Unimportant		Unimportant		Neither Important or Unimportant		Important		Strongly Important		Total	
	Freq.	%	Freq.	%	Freq.	%	Freq.	%	Freq.	%	Freq.	%
No contract for desired amounts	27	12.1	17	7.6	137	61.4	40	17.9	2	0.9	223	100.0
Not find possible contract to reverse (terminate) before maturity	26	11.7	2	0.9	145	65.0	47	21.1	3	1.3	223	100.0
No forward rates when requested	26	11.7	2	0.9	151	67.7	29	13.0	15	6.7	223	100.0
Being made with a wide variety of currency types	31	13.9	15	6.7	132	59.2	40	17.9	5	2.2	223	100.0
To be made mutually with banks	25	11.2	1	0.4	142	63.7	50	22.4	5	2.2	223	100.0
Contract terms can be made between the desired dates	25	11.2	6	2.7	139	62.3	36	16.1	17	7.6	223	100.0
Lack of collateral obligations in enterprises	24	10.8	2	0.9	150	67.3	26	11.7	21	9.4	223	100.0

institution. When the responses were examined on how future transactions were assessed by the sampled businesses, the conclusions are as follows: 122 of the participants (54.7%) replied that they had no idea to the statement *transactions on well-organized exchanges*, whereas 130 (58.3%) respondents answered in the same manner to the statement regarding *it is difficult for companies to enter the future markets.* Similarly, 139 participants (62.3%) responded neutrally to the statement 'it is possible to close the position by reversing the contract due to the possibility of closure'.

Out of the sampled respondents, 130 (58.3%) answered they have no idea to the statement 'the ability to close the position by reversing the contract before it is due date', whereas 127 (57%) of the respondents replied in the same manner to the statement 'due to the fact that the costs are not fully known until the transaction date and the cost is very high'. Additionally, 154 (69.1%) respondents declared to having no idea on the statement 'future contracts can only be made in certain maturities'.

Table 18. Distribution of Firms' Assessments upon Future Contracts.

	Strongly Unimportant		Unimportant		Neither Important or Unimportant		Important		Strongly Important		Total	
	Freq.	%	Freq.	%	Freq.	%	Freq.	%	Freq.	%	Freq.	%
Making transactions on well-organised exchange market	29	13.0	3	1.3	122	54.7	64	28.7	5	2.2	223	100.0
It is easier for the company to enter these markets than in other markets	28	12.6	5	2.2	130	58.3	34	15.2	26	11.7	223	100.0
The standard of contract sizes and terms	28	12.6	12	5.4	132	59.2	28	12.6	23	10.3	223	100.0
The ability to close the position by reversing the contract before it is due date	22	9.9	3	1.3	139	62.3	44	19.7	15	6.7	223	100.0
Due to the fact that the costs are not fully known until the transaction date and the cost is very high	23	10.3	44	11.8	130	58.3	27	12.1	39	117.5	223	100.0
It is difficult to follow profit/loss accounts due to daily execution of transactions	24	10.8	77	33.1	127	57.0	32	14.3	33	14.8	223	100.0
Future agreements can only be made in certain terms	24	10.8	11	4.9	154	69.1	14	6.3	20	9.0	223	100.0

An option contract is a kind of process that gives to the paying party the right to withdraw from the contract before the maturity or at the end of the date but is essentially based on the same basically fundamental logic similar to the forward and future contracts. As to the results on how the option transactions were assessed by the firms, the findings were similar to those for forwards and futures. One hundred and twelve (50.2%) participants replied that they had no idea regarding the statement 'the ease of not using the option in the absence of expectations', while 124 (55.6%) respondents answered they had no knowledge as to 'it's easy to terminate the contract at any time on the American type option'.

The statement relating to the 'non-refundability of the premiums deposited at the beginning of the transaction and therefore the high cost of the process' was met with a lack of knowledge by 121 participants (54.3%) indicating 'they had no

Table 19. Distribution of Firms' Assessments upon Option Contracts.

	Strongly Unimportant		Unimportant		Neither Important or Unimportant		Important		Strongly Important		Total	
	Freq.	%	Freq.	%	Freq.	%	Freq.	%	Freq.	%	Freq.	%
Easy to non-use option if expectations are not fulfilled	26	11.7	3	1.3	112	50.2	47	21.1	35	15.7	223	100.0
Easy to terminate contract at any time in the American type option	23	10.3	1	0.4	124	55.6	44	19.7	31	13.9	223	100.0
Excess costs due to non-refundable premiums deposited at the beginning of the transaction	31	13.9	5	22.2	1,121	54.3	40	17.9	26	11.7	2,223	100.0
Non-using the option before term in the European type option	33	14.8	1	00.4	1,131	58.7	32	14.3	26	11.7	2,223	100.0

idea' on this feature, while 131 (58.7%) participants responded in the same manner to the phrase 'not to use the option before maturity in the European type option'.

The statements relating to SWAP contracts have been intentionally directed to participants in order to determine their financial knowledge level on this financial tool, even though this technique is *not* used as a hedging instrument in the non-banking sectors considering the exchange rate risk management. When the results on how SWAP transactions were evaluated by the firms, the findings are presented as follows. The level of knowledge on SWAP contracts was noted to be very low among respondents. With reference to the statement relating to 'the ease and quickness of operation and the lack of bureaucracy' 123 (55.2%) participants said 'we had no idea about it' while to the statement 'the increase of credit opportunities in international markets with swap transactions' 135 (60.5%) participants said 'we had no idea about it'. Similarly, the number of participants responding in the same way to the statement 'swap transactions with relatively less risk' was 123 (55.2%) indicating as 'they had no idea' and, in addition, 134 (60.1%) respondents replied in a similar manner for the statement 'with swap transactions, international debts can be paid in the desired currency'.

The same lack of knowledge was noted for the statement of 'unable to get swap quotes at any time' for 155 (69.5%) participants, 'withdrawal from the financial intermediary institutions needed for swap' for 158 (70.9%) participants and also 'height of swap cost' for 153 (68.6%) respondents.

Table 20. Distribution of Firms' Assessments upon SWAP Contracts.

	Strongly Unimportant		Unimportant		Neither Important or Unimportant		Important		Strongly Important		Total	
	Freq.	%	Freq.	%	Freq.	%	Freq.	%	Freq.	%	Freq.	%
The process is very easy and quick, the bureaucracy is less	26	11.7	8	3.6	123	55.2	39	17.5	27	12.1	223	100.0
Increased credit opportunities in international markets due to Swap	33	14.8	11	4.9	135	60.5	14	6.3	30	13.5	223	100.0
The risk is relatively less	29	13.0	4	1.8	123	55.2	28	12.6	39	17.5	223	100.0
International debts can be paid in the desired currency due to Swap	19	8.5	10	4.5	134	60.1	37	16.6	23	10.3	223	100.0
Unable to retrieve the swap quota at any time	22	9.9	12	5.4	155	69.5	28	12.6	6	2.7	223	100.0
Lack of financial intermediary institutions required for Swap	23	10.3	8	3.6	158	70.9	29	13.0	5	2.2	223	100.0
Expensive Swap cost	24	10.8	3	1.3	153	68.6	30	13.5	13	5.8	223	100.0

The participants' responses as to which financial institutions they preferred collaborating with to manage the exchange rate risk are located in Table 21.

From Table 21, one can note that commercial banks (total 167 responses, 74.9%) emerged as the most popular traded financial institutions. Participation banks (116 respondents, 53.4% of total) appeared to be the second option for firms although indicating the frequency of the transactions as 'neither much or less'. On the other hand, 154 participants (69.1%) stated that they did not have any preference in choosing the brokerage agencies.

Although this result created a supposition that forward transactions were fulfilled by the firms, this is actually due to the firms' preference to work with banks at a local basis and they request the banks to act as mediator for internal hedging transactions.

The sampled manufacturing firms have been requested to review the industry in which they operate within a number of different expression statements. Table 22 exhibits the responses given by the businesses in assessing their sector.

Table 21. Distribution of Companies' Preferred Financial Institutions by the Firms to Trade in Exchange Rate Risk Management.

	Very Less		Less		Neither Much or Less		Much		Very Much		Total	
	Freq.	%	Freq.	%	Freq.	%	Freq.	%	Freq.	%	Freq.	%
Commercial Banks	9	4.0	1	0.4	46	20.6	70	31.4	97	43.5	223	100.0
Participation Banks	28	12.6	2	0.9	119	53.4	48	21.5	26	11.7	223	100.0
Brokerage Agency	42	18.8	8	3.6	154	69.1	3	1.3	16	7.2	223	100.0

The sampled firms have been requested to review their sectors in the perspective of training opportunities and levels offered by the personnel in charge of exchange rate risk management. The results are located in Table 22. One can note that 171 (76.7%) of the participants felt that the education of personal was compatible with the work to be carried out in the exchange risk management and the work to be done by staff was important.

One hundred and thirty-two (59.2%) of the respondents felt that staff in charge of risk management who were well equipped with adequate training were sufficient to eliminate the exchange risk. Another 64 (28.7%) participants expressed no opinion.

In the study, the number of participants evaluating the education level of the staff in exchange rate risk management as *important* or *very important* for enterprises was 165 (74%). Forty-five participants (20.2%) did not express their opinion about the issue.

The number of enterprises that respond to the expression of a positive relationship between the education level of the staff in charge of the risk management and the success of the exchange rate risk management for enterprises was 163 (73.1%) in total. Forty-seven businesses (21.1%) stated that they had no idea about this statement.

Participants were also requested to assess the necessity of exchange rate risk management training for every business according to Turkey's economic conditions. In this respect, the number of participants who felt the need for exchange rate risk management training for each firm was 161 (72.2%). The number of respondents who expressed no opinion was 54 (24.2%).

In another statement, participants were asked whether the exchange rate risk management techniques could be applied to the current legislation in Turkey. From the table one can note that 32 (14.3%) participants assessed the statement as 'not applicable' while 90 (40.4%) had no idea. The total number of enterprises which found this to be applicable was 75 (33.7%).

Companies were additionally requested to review exchange rate risk management in their sectors. The given responses are exhibited in Table 23.

One hundred and twelve (50.2%) of the companies evaluated the other firms in the sector as successful in exchange rate risk management while 102 (45.7%) assessed the other firms having *not succeeded*. In addition, nine businesses left the question unanswered.

Table 22. Distribution of the Sectoral Assessment in Which They Operate.

	Strongly Unimportant		Unimportant		Neither Important or Unimportant		Important		Strongly Important		Total	
	Freq.	%	Freq.	%	Freq.	%	Freq.	%	Freq.	%	Freq.	%
The education of personnel employed in exchange rate risk management and his work is compatible with each other	7	3.1	8	3.6	37	16.6	114	51.1	57	25.6	223	100.0
The education level of the personnel employed in the exchange rate risk management is sufficient to eliminate the exchange rate risks	25	11.2	2	0.9	64	28.7	116	52.0	16	7.2	223	100.0
The education level of the staff at the exchange rate risk management is important for businesses	4	1.8	9	4.0	45	20.2	102	45.7	63	28.3	223	100.0
There is a positive relationship between the education of the personnel employed by the exchange rate risk management and the achievements of the enterprises in exchange rate risk management	12	5.4	1	0.4	47	21.1	104	46.6	59	26.5	223	100.0
In consideration of Turkey's economic conditions, exchange rate risk management is required for every business that trades with currency	6	2.7	2	0.9	54	24.2	85	38.1	76	34.1	223	100.0
Exchange rate risk management techniques can be applied according to current legislation in Turkey	32	14.3	26	11.7	90	40.4	45	20.2	30	13.5	223	100.0

Table 23. Distribution of Companies by Evaluating Exchange Rate Risk
Management for Other Enterprises in the Sector.

		Freq.	%	Total %
Valid	Yes	112	50.2	52.3
	No	102	45.7	100.0
	Total	214	96.0	
Missing	Unanswered	9	4.0	
Total		223	100.0	

5. CONCLUSION AND FUTURE RESEARCH DIRECTIONS

In the late part of the twentieth century, the free movement of goods and cap-ital became easier with the removal of the barriers to international trade and, in that way, financial liberalisation has begun to dominate the world economy. Nevertheless while simple trade of goods and capital facilitated international trade and transactions, changes in the values of different currencies of the national econ-omies against other countries' economies have emerged as a problem. Changes in the local currencies value, which bring out exchange rate risk, have led businesses, which are the lifeblood of the national economies, to seek ways to be less affected by these value changes. In today's business world, by effectively managing the exchange rate risk, businesses can protect and increase business income from main operational activities, reduce the uncertainties arising from foreign trade transac-tions and increase the firm's profitability and business value.

Present research was initially carried out to determine which measures were taken by firms and which methods and techniques were utilised by firms that were exposed to foreign exchange risk to manage the foreign currency risk. It also aimed to reveal the knowledge level of firms. Within the scope of the study, the authors included 203 manufacturing firms that were directly involved in foreign exchange risk due to having foreign trade activities in Afyonkarahisar city.

According to the sample characteristics, the enterprises were mainly consti-tuted from the industry of marble, stone, soil and mining sector and as to the ownership structures of manufacturing enterprises, mostly were limited compa-nies. The financial decision-makers in the enterprises were mainly business own-ers and seldom mid-level finance staff although most of the businesses declared to have a finance department. Considering the organisational structure of the sampled firms, the reality is that the most firms were SMEs. However, the finan-cial decisions were mostly taken through the accounting unit and it made us think that the separation between the accounting and finance department was still not possible. The education levels of financial decision-makers reached undergradu-ate and graduate levels in the study. When this result was evaluated in relation to the financial decision-makers' qualifications, we conclude that there is a sig-nificant lack of corporate governance abilities within our sampled firms. When the two results, the lack of organisation of the accounting or finance unit and the education level of financial decision-makers are considered together, it can be concluded that the lack of a finance department and the low education of business owners or managers lead them to stay away from taking part in a regular market transactions where a small effort could help them avoid exchange rate risk. Although there was a positive relationship between the education level of the personnel assigned in the management of exchange rate risk and the success of enterprises in exchange rate risk management and even though the findings showed that the education level of financial decision-makers was high, it is noted in the study that these financial decisions did not force enterprises to engage in any activity in order to avoid exchange rate risk.

Another important result of the present study emerged from the answers given to the statements about the financial training of the finance department staff. The participants stated that orientation training was organised after the recruitment of financial personnel in most of the enterprises, but there was no consistent program for the continuity of the trainings. This finding also supports the answers about other internal training. Thus, it could be concluded from the responses of enterprises that internal trainings are not continuous even though there is an effort to organise them. However, the frequency of the 'I have no idea' answers shows that the business habits of the past continue and the firms still are not aware of the requirements for well-trained staff in this field. Besides, although businesses are considering the international activities, such as overseas trips and fairs, as international training program these do not contribute financially to the firms. In this sense, we can indicate that there is a lack of perception among the manufacturing enterprises in the sample in terms of training, development and recognition of new products and tools in terms of finance.

As to the other findings, the most traded currency is the USD ($) among the firms that have foreign transactions. In addition, enterprises consider the changes in exchange rates as the most important source of exchange risk and they are intensely concerning of the risk of losing market shares as a result of the changes in exchange rates that affect the cost and sales. At this point, the companies declared to prefer classical internal risk management methods in order to manage the exchange rate risk. The responses of the companies for the recognition and utilising of derivative instruments showed that they did not have any idea about hedging products. Likewise, as a reason for not preferring derivative products, the enterprises came up with the rationale that they did have no information about derivative products. These main findings indicate that hedging techniques and derivative instruments were not generally recognised by the sampled manufacturing firms and derivative instruments were not considered as alternative tools due to insufficient financial knowledge in the exchange rate risk management processes.

To conclude, it is possible to emphasise that exchange rate risk is a systematic risk type in today's economic system and that the risk management becomes more and more important, especially for developing economies such as Turkey, from the smallest to the largest ones. Because of the changes in the exchange rate, depending on the direction of the fluctuation, sometimes foreign currency is needed, although this may lead to firms confronting with the high costs. In this respect, classical internal hedging methods may be insufficient and may cause high cost transactions for the businesses. Consequently, there appears to be a strong inclination for firms to use alternative hedging products because these instruments make it easier for businesses to reduce the exchange risks with lower collaterals and leveraged transactions.

When the results are assessed, the findings showed that the firms had no knowledge of derivative instruments and therefore the manufacturing firms in Afyonkarahisar city could not complete their institutionalisation.

Based on the above results, the authors of the present study suggest that a joint-effort structure is a vital requirement for the training programs in exchange rate risk management techniques with the coordinated works of corporations such as Turkey Chambers of Commerce and Industry, BIST Derivative Markets (VIOP) and universities. One could increase the knowledge level of enterprises about risk management methods and derivative instruments in this way. In this context, the study initially proposes to conduct field analyses for all regions in Turkey and then to develop appropriate applied training programs regarding the level of knowledge determined in enterprises. The study also emphasises the urgent need of financial units operating with a high level of knowledge in business organisations in order to establish more efficient management of business and country resources.

6. ACKNOWLEDGMENT

This study was funded by Scientific Research Coordination Unit of Afyon Kocatepe University with the project number of 17.IIBF.01.

REFERENCES

Aabo, T., Høg, E., & Kuhn, J. (2010). Integrated foreign exchange risk management: The role of import in medium-sized manufacturing firms. *Journal of Multinational Financial Management*, *20*(4–5), 235–250.

Aksu, D. (2016). İmalat sektöründe kur riskinin birincil ve ikincil etkileri ve kur riskine karşı çözüm önerileri. *Journal of Accounting & Finance*, *71*, 149–164.

Allayannis, G., & Ofek, E. (2001). Exchange rate exposure, hedging and the use of foreign currency derivatives. *Journal of International Money and Finance*, *20*(2), 273–296.

Allayannis, G., Brown, G. W., & Klapper, L. (2001). *Exchange rate risk management: Evidence from East Asia* (Vol. 2606). Washington, DC: World Bank.

Altunışık, R., Coşkun, R., Bayraktaroglu, S., & Yıldırım, E. (2007). *Sosyal bilimlerde araştırma yöntemleri: SPSS Uygulamalı*. Sakarya: Sakarya Yayıncılık.

Bayrakdaroglu, A., Sari, B., & Heybeli, B. (2013). İşletmelerin finansal risk yönetiminde türev ürün kullanımlarına ilişkin bir saha araştırması: Denizli ili örneği. *Muhasebe ve Finansman Dergisi*, *57*, 57–88.

Bradley, K., & Moles, P. (2002). Managing strategic exchange rate exposures: Evidence from UK firms. *Managerial Finance*, *28*(11), 28–42.

Buker, S., Asikoglu, R., & Sevil, G. (2014). *Finansal yönetim* (p. 523). Ankara: Sözkesen Matbaacılık.

Conkar, K., & Ata, H. A., (2002). Riskten korunma aracı olarak türev ürünlerin gelişmiş ülkeler ve Türkiye'de kullanımı. *Afyon Kocatepe Üniversitesi, İ.İ.B.F. Dergisi IV*(2), 1–17.

Delice, G. (2003). Finansal krizler: teorik ve tarihsel bir perspektif. *Erciyes Üniversitesi İktisadi ve İdari Bilimler Fakültesi Dergisi*, *20*, 57–81.

Doganay, M. (2016). Döviz kuru riski yönetimine sektörel bir yaklaşım. *Uluslararası Kültürel ve Sosyal Araştırmalar Dergisi (UKSAD)*, *2*(Special Issue-1), 149–164.

Glaum, M. (1990). Strategic management of exchange rate risk. *Long Range Planning*, *4*(23), 65–72.

Ito, T., Koibuchi, S., Sato, K., & Shimizu, J. (2016). Exchange rate exposure and risk management: The case of Japanese exporting firms. *Journal of the Japanese and International Economies*, *41*, 17–29.

Kandir, S. Y., Karadeniz, E., & Erismis, A. (2015). The exchange rate risk of Turkish tourism firms. *The Journal of Hospitality Financial Management*, *23*(1), 63–71.

Karas, G., & Celikkol, H. (2019). Foreign trade and hedging of exchange rate risk: Analysis of TR33 region in Turkey. *Finance and Accounting*, *1*, 89–103.

Kaygusuzoglu, M. (2011). Finansal türev ürünlerden forward sözleşmeleri ve muhasebe işlemleri. *Atatürk Üniversitesi İktisadi ve İdari Bilimler Dergisi*, *25*(2), 137–149.

Kibritcioglu, A. (2001). Türkiye'de ekonomik krizler ve hükümetler, 1969–2001. *Yeni Türkiye Dergisi Ekonomik Kriz Özel Sayısı*, *7*(41), 174–182.

Kutukiz, D. (2005). Turizm sektöründe döviz riski ve korunma yöntemleri. *Muhasebe ve Finansman Dergisi*, *28*, 198–207.

Leech, N. L., Barrett, K. C., & Morgan, G. A. (2013). *SPSS for intermediate statistics: Use and interpretation*. London: Routledge.

Nazlı, A. T. (2006). *Döviz kuru riski yönetim tekniklerinin Türkiye'de uygulanabilirliği ve uygulayıcıların eğitiminin önemi*. Gazi Üniversitesi, Eğitim Bilimleri Enstitüsü, Yüksek Lisans Tezi.

Ozdemir, L. M. (2005). *İşletmelerde döviz kuru riskinden korunma (hedging) yöntemleri: IMKB'de işlem gören imalat işletmeleri üzerine bir araştırma*. Afyon Kocatepe Üniversitesi, Sosyal Bilimler Enstitüsü, Yüksek Lisans Tezi.

Ozen, E., Yolas, S., & ve Ozdemir, L. (2006). İMKB'de imalat işletmelerinin döviz kuru riskinden korunma düzeylerine ilişkin bir araştırma, *5. Orta Anadolu İşletmecilik Kongresi*, Gaziosmanpaşa Üniversitesi (pp. 241–249).

Sever, E., Ozdemir, Z., & Mizirik, Z. (2010). Finansal globalleşme, krizler ve ekonomik büyüme: Yükselen piyasa ekonomileri örneğinde bir inceleme. *Akademik Araştırmalar ve Çalışmalar Dergisi (AKAD)*, *2*(3), 45–64.

Seyidoglu, H. (2003). Uluslararası mali krizler, IMF politikaları, az gelişmiş ülkeler, Türkiye ve dönüşüm ekonomileri. *Dogus University Journal*, *4*(2), 141–156.

Sezer, S. (1999). Döviz kuru riskine karşı firmaların duyarlılığı: Kayseri örneği. (Basılmamış Yüksek Lisans Tezi) Erciyes Üniversitesi Sosyal Bilimler Enstitüsü, Aralık.

Sezer, S., & Canpolat, K. (2017). Firma mevduatları ve dış ticaret açısından kur riskinin yönetilmesinde türev ürünlerin kullanımı. *Paradoks Ekonomi, Sosyoloji ve Politika Dergisi*, *13*(1), 29–46.

Ural, M. (2003). Finansal Krizler ve Türkiye. *Dokuz Eylül Üniversitesi İktisadi ve İdari Bilimler Fakültesi Dergisi*, *18*(1), 11–28.

Yildiran, M. (2004). İhracat yapan işletmelerin kur riski yönetiminde yeni mali yöntemleri kullanım sıklığı üzerine bir inceleme. *Süleyman Demirel Üniversitesi İktisadi ve İdari Bilimler Fakültesi Dergisi*, *9*(2), 341–352.

Yildiz, R., & Ciftci, F. (2011). *Bankacılıkta ve dış ticarette döviz kuru riskine karşı korunma: hedging işlemleri*. Geliştirilmiş 2. Ankara: Detay Yayınları.

CHAPTER 6

DETERMINING THE RELATIONSHIP BETWEEN CAMLS VARIABLES AND PROFITABILITY: AN APPLICATION ON BANKS IN THE BIST BANK INDEX

Hasan Hüseyin Yildirim and Bahadir Ildokuz

ABSTRACT

Introduction – *The banking sector is one of the most important building blocks of the financial system. A failure in the banking sector can cause serious problems in a country's economy. In order for countries to achieve economic growth and development goals, the banking sector, which affects all sectors significantly, needs to be strong. Countries with a robust and reliable banking system have a high credit rating. As a result of this high credit rating, the interest of foreign capital in the country increases. Thus, the credit volume of banks expands and loans are provided at a more appropriate rate for investments. In this respect, the performance and profitability of banks are important. The CAMELS performance model is a valuation system used to determine the general status of banks. The CAMELS model consists of six components. According to this, C represents capital adequacy; A, asset quality; M, management adequacy; E, earnings; L, liquidity; and S, sensitivity to market risks.*

Purpose – *The purpose of this study is to demonstrate the effect of the CAMLS variables on the variable E.*

Contemporary Issues in Business, Economics and Finance
Contemporary Studies in Economic and Financial Analysis, Volume 104, 85–103
ISSN: 1569-3759/doi:10.1108/S1569-375920200000104017

Methodology – *In the implementation part of the study, the data of 11 banks in the BIST Bank Index between 2004 and 2018 were used. In the analysis part of the study, a panel data analysis method was used.*

Findings – *The capital adequacy (C), management adequacy (M) and liquidity (L) variables were effective on profitability. This study revealed the importance of the capital, management and liquidity variables, which are internal factors, in increasing the profitability of banks.*

Keywords: Banking sector; performance; CAMELS analysis; profitability; panel data analysis; Borsa İstanbul; regression analysis

JEL classifications: C23, G17, G21

1. INTRODUCTION

There is a wide range of financial methods and capital market instruments, starting from common stocks, bonds, forfeiting, factoring and financial leasing to Islamic banking instruments for meeting the financial needs of firms.

It is possible to categorise the financial markets in two main groups. The first group mainly depends on the banking sector, where financial intermediation takes place through the banks in the market, while in the second group, pension and investment funds are more dominant than other financial institutions.

For the sake of financial stability in countries such as Turkey, the banking sector needs to be financially solid and strong (Kartal, 2018).

Needless to say, those banks play an important role in financial systems for the industrial and economic development of both developed and developing countries (Reis, Kiliç, & Buğan, 2016). Financial intermediation, efficiency in allocation of capital through adjusting the optimum maturity and amount of the capital, providing financial support for the development of international trade, etc., can be listed as some of the benefits provided by banks in the financial system (Aydın et al., 2012).

As can be seen, the banking sector is one of the most significant participants of the domestic economy and financial system. Therefore, an efficient and financially strong banking system is a must for economic growth and financial stability. Recently, the banking system has participated in the stock and derivatives markets in addition to ordinary deposit and credit operations in order to increase market share and profitability (Sarıtaş, Uyar, & Gökçe, 2016).

According to the June 2018 banking regulation and supervision agency report, 34 deposit banks, 5 participation banks and 13 investment and development banks, in total, 52 banks have legal operations in Turkey. Furthermore, government banks have 3,892 branches, while domestic private banks have 4,029 and foreign banks have 3,677. Moreover, government banks employ 65,871 people while domestic private banks employ 74,662 and foreign banks employ 68,435. In addition, total asset size of the Turkish banking system is 3,672 billion TL according to the same report (Banking Regulation and Supervision Agency, 2018).

Table 1 presents the Turkish banking system asset size and the market share of deposit, participation and development banks.

Table 1. Turkish Banking Sector Asset Size and Share of Different Banking Groups.

Types	Asset Size			Deposit Size			Credit Size		
	2017 (Million TL)	2017 Share (%)	2016 Share (%)	2017 (Million TL)	2017 Share (%)	2016 Share (%)	2017 (Million TL)	2017 Share (%)	2016 Share (%)
Participation banks	160,136	4.9	4.9	105,310	6.1	5.6	106,733	5.0	4.8
Deposit banks	2,922,680	89.7	89.9	1,613,839	93.9	94.4	1,905,940	88.8	89.4
Development banks	175,002	5.4	5.2	–	–	–	132,807	6.2	5.7
Total	3,257,818	100	100	1,719,149	100	100	1,514,045	100	100

Source: Participation Banks Association of Turkey, TKBB, 2017, p. 89.

There is no a significant change in Table 1 between 2016 and 2017 in terms of asset, deposit and credit size. Yet, deposit banks dominate the banking sector compared with participation banks, which can also be interpreted as the great growth potential of participation banks.

Fig. 1 illustrates that total assets of the banking sector denominated in TL increased from 2014 to 2018 while total assets denominated in USD did not change significantly. Likewise, total deposits of the banking sector followed a similar path with total assets, as can be seen in Fig. 2.

Fig. 3 shows the ratios of interest earnings to total assets, interest expense to total assets and finally net interest income to total assets. The net interest income to total assets ratio between 2014 and 2018 was around 3% while the interest income to total assets ratio rose from 6% to 9% in four years.

The financial system in Turkey primarily depends on the banking sector. According to the 5411 banking code, deposit banks represent the banks and their branches operating in Turkey in addition to the branches of foreign banks operating in Turkey which accept deposits to be able to give credit to firms. The only difference between deposit banks and participation banks is the way of accepting deposits and financing firms which, with the latter, is done through the methods of Islamic finance according to the same legislation. However, investment and development banks do not have permission to collect deposits, yet are able to give credit or perform certain tasks that are specified through laws and legislations.

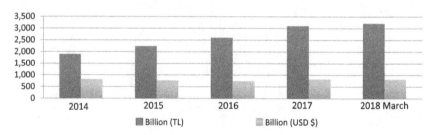

Fig. 1. Total Assets (2014–2018). *Source*: Banking Regulation and Supervision Agency (2018).

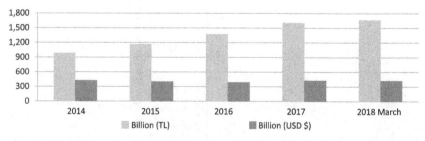

Fig. 2. Total Deposits (2014–2018). *Source*: Banking Regulation and Supervision Agency (2018).

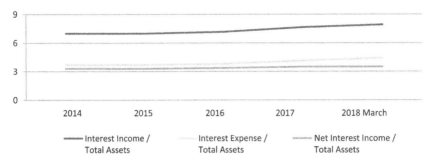

Fig. 3. Interest Income/Total Assets (%), Interest Expense/Total Assets (%), and Net Interest Income/Total Assets (%). *Source*: Banking Regulation and Supervision Agency (2018).

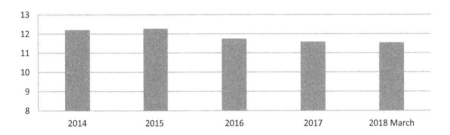

Fig. 4. Number of Branches (Thousand). *Source*: The Banks Association of Turkey (2018).

Fig. 4 shows the number of branches in the Turkish banking sector. As can be seen, there has been a fall in the number of branches since 2015. There are a couple of reasons behind this fact. First of all, increased competition in the banking sector led to cost-cutting policies and therefore to closing unprofitable branches. Another reason is the technological improvements which allow customers to do banking transactions through internet banking. Accordingly, the number of total banking sector employees shows a similar trend to the number of branches, as can be seen in Fig. 5.

A solid banking sector plays a crucial role in economic performance. Therefore, regulation of the sector and measurement of its performance are significantly important for the domestic economy (Çağıl & Mukhtarov, 2014). Similar to other firms, banks aim to make profits and the profitability of banks is in return nothing more than the performance of bank management.

2. CONTENT OF CAMELS VARIABLES

Ratio analysis helps to measure data regarding the performance of operations such as liquidity and profitability. CAMELS analysis is one of the most frequently used performance measurement methods to evaluate the borrowing performance

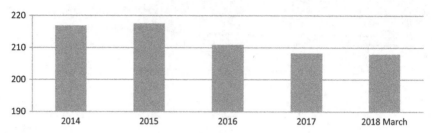

Fig. 5. Number of Employees (Thousand). *Source*: The Banks Association of Turkey (2018).

of banks (Islamoglu, 2013, p. 391). It is a rating system accepted by the regulatory and supervision authorities of USA and is used while auditing commercial banks with a risk-based approach.

CAMELS is a combination of the six factors that are used to evaluate the performance of banks. These factors are capital adequacy, asset quality, management adequacy, earnings, liquidity and finally sensitivity to market risk, and their abbreviations are C, A, M, E, L and S, respectively. Initially, there was a 5-factor system (CAMEL). However, since 1997, sensitivity to market risk (S) has also been used to measure the performance of banks (Sakarya, 2010).

C (Capital) Capital adequacy: Capital adequacy is a significant tool to measure the optimum amount of capital that a bank needs in case of the occurrence of unexpected risks and uncertainties (Kandemir & Arıcı, 2013).

A (Asset) Asset quality: In addition to off-balance sheet operations, credit risk arising from not only the investment portfolio but also other credit activities, quality of fixed assets and other assets of banks are investigated through the asset quality tool. Moreover, ability of the management to define, measure, monitor and control credit risk is also assessed through the asset quality tool (Kılıç & Fettahoğlu, 2005).

M (Management) Management quality: The bank management not only defines, measures, monitors and controls the operating risks arising from operations but also ensures bank activities operate effectively in accordance with both internal and external regulations and legislations (Sakarya, 2010).

E (Earnings) Earnings status: One of the prerequisites for banks to carry out their activities in a healthy way is profitability. Thus, earnings are an indispensable part of the profitability of banks (Karaçor et al., 2017).

L (Liquidity) Liquidity status: Liquid assets should match short-term liabilities and unexpected cash outflows. Therefore, fund management is crucial for determining the liquidity of banks (Karaçor et al., 2017).

S (Sensitivity) Sensitivity to market risk: Sensitivity to market risk measures the risk level that banks are exposed to such as changes in interest rates, exchange rates, price level of goods and stocks because of operating in that specific market.

Table 2 illustrates the components of CAMELS analysis and the ratios used for those components. However, different ratios have also been used for CAMELS components in the literature. Therefore, this chapter chooses widely used ratios and provides the reference sources in Table 2.

Table 2. Tools of CAMELS Analysis.

Abbreviation	Components	Ratios for Components
C	Capital adequacy	• *Capital adequacy ratio* (Altemur, Karaca, & Güvemli, 2018; Arıçelik. 2010: Gündoğdu, 2017; Karaçor, Mangir, Kodaz, & Kartal. 2017; Kaya. 2001; Sakarya, 2010) • *Equity/total assets* (Altemur et al., 2018; Çağıl & Mukhtarov, 2014; Ege, Topaloğlu, & Karakozak. 2015; Gümüş & Nalbantoğlu, 2015; Gündoğdu, 2017; Kandemir & Arıcı, 2013; Karaçor et al., 2017) • *(Equity –fixed assets)/total assets* (Altemur et al., 2018; Arıçelik, 2010; Çağıl & Mukhtarov, 2014; Ege et al., 2015; Kandemir & Arıcı, 2013)
A	Asset quality	• *Non-performing loans/total credit* (Arıçelik, 2010; Ege et al., 2015; Gündoğdu, 2017; Kandemir & Arıcı, 2013; Karaçor et al., 2017; Kaya, 2001; Sakarya, 2010) • *Total credit/total assets* (Altemur et al., 2018; Arıçelik, 2010; Çağıl & Mukhtarov, 2014; Ege et al., 2015; Gündoğdu, 2017; Kandemir & Arıcı, 2013; Karaçor et al., 2017; Sakarya, 2010) • *Total credit/total deposits* (Altemur et al., 2018; Çağıl & Mukhtarov, 2014; Ege et al., 2015; Karaçor et al., 2017; Sakarya, 2010) • *Fixed assets/total assets* (Altemur et al., 2018; Arıçelik, 2010; Çağıl & Mukhtarov, 2014; Gümüş & Nalbantoğlu, 2015; Kandemir & Arıcı, 2013; Karaçor et al., 2017; Kaya, 2001; Sakarya, 2010)
M	Management quality	• *Operating expenses/total assets* (Gündoğdu, 2017; Karaçor et al., 2017; Sakarya, 2010) • *Net profits per branch* (Altemur et al., 2018; Arıçelik. 2010; Çağıl & Mukhtarov, 2014; Gündoğdu, 2017; Kandemir & Arıcı, 2013; Karaçor et al., 2017; Sakarya, 2010) • *Total deposits/total assets* (Altemur et al., 2018)
E	Earnings	• *Net profit/total assets* (Arıçelik, 2010; Çağıl & Mukhtarov, 2014; Ege et al., 2015; Gümüş & Nalbantoğlu, 2015; Gündoğdu, 2017; Kandemir & Arıcı, 2013; Karaçor et al., 2017; Kaya, 2001; Sakarya, 2010) • *Net profit/total equity* (Arıçelik, 2010; Çağıl & Mukhtarov, 2014; Ege et al., 2015; Gümüş & Nalbantoğlu, 2015; Gündoğdu, 2017; Kandemir & Arıcı, 2013; Karaçor et al., 2017; Kaya, 2001; Sakarya, 2010) • *Profit before tax/total assets* (Ege et al., 2015; Gündoğdu, 2017; Kandemir & Arıcı, 2013; Karaçor et al., 2017; Kaya, 2001; Sakarya, 2010)
L	Liquidity	• *Total income/total expenses* (Ege et al., 2015; Gündoğdu, 2017; Karaçor et al., 2017; Kaya, 2001; Sakarya, 2010) • *Liquid assets/total assets* (Altemur et al., 2018; Çağıl & Mukhtarov, 2014; Ege et al., 2015; Gümüş & Nalbantoğlu, 2015; Gündoğdu, 2017; Karaçor et al., 2017; Kaya, 2001; Sakarya, 2010) • *Liquid assets/short-term liabilities* (Altemur et al., 2018; Ege et al., 2015; Gündoğdu, 2017; Karaçor et al., 2017; Sakarya, 2010)
S	Sensitivity to market risk	• *Foreign currency assets/foreign currency liabilities* (Altemur et al., 2018; Arıçelik, 2010; Ege et al., 2015; Gümüş & Nalbantoğlu, 2015; Gündoğdu, 2017; Kandemir & Arıcı, 2013; Kaya, 2001; Sakarya, 2010) • *FX position/total equity* (Ege et al., 2015; Kandemir & Arıcı, 2013; Karaçor et al., 2017; Kaya, 2001; Sakarya, 2010)

3. LITERATURE RESEARCH

Banks meeting the financial needs of the real sector have an important place for economies globally. *Which factors are effective on the performance and profitability of these crucial institutions?* is a question that has also been the focus of researchers. In these terms, there are a lot of published studies on the subject of profitability performance analysis of banks. Some of these studies cover the banks in a specific country while the others focus on the banks of several countries. In the following, some of the research studies using CAMELS variables and the banking industry are stated.

Saunders and Schumacher (2000) aimed to figure out the determiners of the net interest margin of 614 banks operating in seven developed economies using data between the years 1988 and 1995. According to the results, macro interest rate volatility was found to have a significant impact on banks' net interest margin.

Kaya (2001) applied the CAMELS analysis, a tool for remote monitoring and on-site supervision, to the Turkish banking industry between 1997 and 2000. It was stated that the grades based on CAMELS analysis results deteriorated in 2000 compared to 1997. Banks were grouped by their total assets. In 1997, small banks regarding their total assets achieved better CAMELS grades than the others. On the contrary, in 2000 banks having larger total assets gained the advantage in terms of CAMELS grades. In addition, the relation between the CAMELS grades of the banks and their situation of being taken over by the Savings Deposit Insurance Fund (SDIF) was investigated. In these research studies, non-parametric tests were carried out in order to figure out the differentiation of the banks' CAMELS performance and it was stated that the difference between 2000 and 1997 stems from the banks which had been taken over by the SDIF.

Ersoy (2003) analysed the performance of privately owned commercial banks before and after being taken over by the SDIF according to the CAMELS model and compared these results with the performance of the ones which were not taken over by the SDIF. It was concluded that the banks taken over by the SDIF performed worse than others and some of those which obtained 4 as a compound CAMELS grade had been carrying high risks before being taken over by the SDIF.

In the research carried out by Kılıç and Fettahoğlu (2005), an attempt was made to reveal the financial situation or performance of Turkish banking industry between 2002 and 2004 by CAMELS analysis. According to the outcomes of the research, it was stated that CAMELS analysis is optimistically regarded in terms of its power of foresight on the Turkish banking industry and can be developed as an early warning system.

According to Pasiouras and Kosmidou (2007) in their research across 15 EU countries, it was stated that equity ratio, yearly inflation, stock market capitalisation/GDP ratio and stock market capitalisation/total assets of deposit banks ratio positively affected the average return on assets (ROA). On the contrary, the costs/revenues ratio, liquidity ratio, total asset size, maturity level of the banking industry and GDP growth rate negatively affected the average ROA.

Bepari and Mollik (2008) used CAMELS analysis in order to figure out the financial situation of the banking industry of Bangladesh and identify the problematic banks, and they concluded that it was essential that the problematic ones should be kept under supervision.

Ata (2009) analysed the financials of 25 deposit banks in the period 2002–2007. He analysed the effects of the variables on profitability and he added the financials of the banks as internal variables and macro-economic variables as external variables into his model. He concluded that the internal variables are more dominant on the profitability than the external ones. Also, total assets, loans/deposits ratio and total assets of the banking industry/GDP ratio had a positive effect on profitability; on the other hand, cost ratio, capital requirement ratio and NPL ratio had a negative impact on profitability.

Bumin (2009) classified the banks with respect to their functions and their owners' equity structure based on the data between 2002 and 2008. Reforms that were realised aligned with the 'banking industry restructuring programme' started in 2001 were effective on the profitability increase of the banking industry. This study verifies the effectiveness of the programme and foresees a decrease in profitability in 2008 as well.

Sakarya (2010) analysed and compared the performance of the domestic- and foreign-owned capital banks whose stocks were traded on the Istanbul Stock Exchange (ISE) according to the CAMELS rating system. He pointed out that the domestic-owned banks performed better in terms of profitability.

Sangmi and Nazir (2010) used CAMELS analysis in order to determine the financial situation of several banks operating in northern India based on the data between 2001 and 2005. As a result, banks covered in the study were financially in a good condition.

Taşkın (2011) aimed to find the internal and external factors that affect the performance of commercial banks based on the data between 1995 and 2000. In the study, panel data analysis was used and as the performance indicators, ratios composed of ROA, net interest margin and return on equity (ROE) were used. In this regard, an attempt was made to analyse how and in which direction the macro- and micro-economic factors were effective. As a result, micro-economic factors were effective on bank performance.

İskenderoğlu, Karadeniz, and Atioğlu (2012) studied the effects of equity structure, growth and total assets decisions on profitability. In this regard, quarterly reported financials between 2004 and 2009 of 13 banks whose shares were traded on the ISE were analysed by the GMM method. As a result, it was stated that bank profitability was sustainable, that decisions on the ratios regarding owners' equity structure affected profitability negatively and that, on the other hand, growth rates and the volume of total assets had a positive effect on profitability.

Sarıtaş and Saray (2012) used profitability performance ratio analysis on the Turkish banking industry over the period 2002–2009. Restructuring the banking industry programme was accepted as a step of the 'Transition to a Strong Economy Programme' in 2001 by the government in order to rehabilitate the economy which was negatively affected by the crisis. Thus, the period 2002–2009 was analysed. In the light of all these results, during the years from 2002 to 2009, profitability was increased except in 2008 due to the global economic crisis.

Kandemir and Arıcı (2013) studied the performance of banks operating in Turkey during the years 2001–2010. In this study, they grouped the deposit banks as state-owned, privately owned and foreign-owned and they used the CAMELS model to make a comparative analysis. As a result, after the 2001 banking crisis, deposit banks gained high capital requirement ratios and liquidity ratios. Thus, banks operated very carefully and cautiously against these types of crisis.

Abdullayev (2013) applied the CAMELS analysis to the Turkish banking industry for the years between 2005 and 2008. According to his analysis, from 2005 to 2008, the CAMELS grade of the deposit banks was ameliorated. In addition, the highest average CAMELS grade was observed in 2008.

Demirel, Atakişi, and Abacioğlu (2013) classified banks as state-owned, privately owned and foreign-owned deposit banks and then compared their operating ratios and profit indicators using time series and panel data analysis methods. Ratios that are classified under profitability like ROA and net interest margin and ratios like other operating expenses/total assets constitute the criteria of this study. As a result, state-owned banks were more efficient than privately owned and foreign-owned ones, whereas privately owned banks were more profitable than the others.

Riaz (2013) aimed to analyse the macro-economic parameters and bank-specific internal factors that influenced the profitability of 32 commercial banks in the period 2006–2010 in Pakistan. In the study, ROA and ROE were determined as the dependent variables. In this study, in which regression analysis was used, it was stated that credit risk, operating efficiency and GDP ratio affected ROA positively, while CPI and interest rate affected ROA negatively. As for ROE, total loans/total assets, deposits/total assets, GDP growth ratio and growth variables affected ROE positively, whereas credit risk, operating efficiency, interest rate and CPI affected ROE negatively.

Yılmaz (2013) analysed the performance of banks in nine developing countries including Turkey in terms of profitability, ROA and net interest margin by measuring the effective factors with the help of panel data analysis. As a result, liquidity, operational expenses and capitalisaton, inflation and total asset size had a significant effect on ROA.

Çağıl and Mukhtarov (2014) analysed the performance of domestic and foreign banks operating in Azerbaijan in the period 2007–2010 using the CAMELS rating system. As a result, domestic banks performed worse than foreign ones.

Kiganda (2014) aimed to analyse the macro-economic factors effective on the profitability of banks between 2008 and 2012 in Kenya. In this study, ROA was chosen as the dependent variable, whereas GDP, inflation and foreign currency rates were the independent variables. The OLS method was used and according to the findings of this study, GDP, inflation and currency rates did not have a significant effect on the profitability of the banks that could benefit only from the owners' equity between 2008 and 2012.

Ege et al. (2015) studied a comparative analysis of government, private and foreign banks by the CAMELS method based on the data from 2002 to 2010. In the light of the results of the study, in terms of capital requirement, market risk sensitivity and management adequacy, government deposit banks, in terms of profitability, private deposit banks and in terms of asset quality and liquidity, foreign deposit banks were in a better condition with respect to the other bank groups.

Sarıtaş et al. (2016) studied the internal and external factors that affected the profits of banks operating in Turkey between the years 2002 and 2013. In addition, how effective the 2008 global economic crisis was on profitability levels was included in the study as well. According to the analysis outcomes, the 2008 crisis was not effective on ROA but had a negative effect in the following years.

Reis et al. (2016) tested internal and external factors affecting profitability with panel data analysis using net interest margin and ROA' in order to figure out the determiners of profitability in the Turkish banking industry. According to the findings, internal variables such as leverage ratio, loan/deposit ratio and market capitalisation had a meaningful relationship with external variables such as GDP and bank profitability.

Karaçor et al. (2017) comparatively analysed the performance of banks operating in Turkey between the years 2003 and 2015 using the CAMELS model. As a result of his analysis, private banks had a positive outlook in terms of capital adequacy, management quality and asset quality, whereas they were in an unfavourable position in terms of revenue and liquidity. On the other hand, it was stated that state-owned banks were more sensitive to market risks than privately owned banks.

4. DATA AND METHOD

It is possible to group factors that affect the profitability of banks in two groups: internal (firm-specific factors) and external (macro-economic factors and structure of the financial market) factors (Gunter, Krenn, & Sigmund, 2013). Factors included in the financial statements of a firm are listed under the group of internal factors while factors that influence the performance of all banks such as economic conditions, legislations and regulations are recorded as external factors. However, those factors vary depending on the geographic location, country and financial system according to the literature (Doyran, 2013; Reis et al., 2016). Profitability gives information about whether the profit is appropriate according to the volume of net sales, equity and net working capital used for production. This study focuses on the internal factors and specifically, the CAMELS ratios while determining the profitability of banks. According to the model used in this chapter, the components of CAMLS represent independent variables while component E (Earnings) stands for the dependent variable, as shown in Fig. 6.

Profitability is the value of the profit of an enterprise over the assets, equity and net sales used in production. There are various ratios used in financial theory to measure the profitability of enterprises. Within the scope of this study, ROE and ROA are chosen among the alternative ratios that measure profitability. The ROE measures the profit obtained from the money invested in the firm by shareholders and shows the performance of the entity as a whole (Aydın et al., 2014, p. 115). The main interest of the bank owners is the return on their investments as well. This information can be obtained through the ROE ratio, which is a measure of profitability (Şıklar, 2004).

ROE is calculated by dividing the net profit after tax by equity. It is expressed as follows (Van Horne & Wachowıcz, 1995, p. 142):

$$ROE = Net\ Profit/Equity$$

The ROA ratio is used as another method to measure profitability. This ratio shows how effective an entity uses its assets, in other words, how much return is

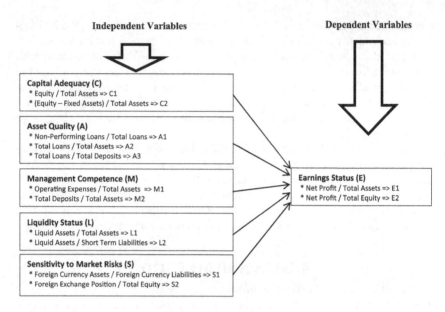

Fig. 6. Research Model.

generated from its assets. The shareholders of the bank may use the ROA ratio, which is a measure of profitability, in order to see whether the bank they own is well managed or not (Şıklar, 2004, p. 264). The ROA ratio is calculated as follows (Peterson, 1994, p. 119):

$$ROA = Net\ Profit/Total\ Assets$$

This study uses the annual data of 11 banks that are included in the BIST Bank Index from 2004 to 2018.

Two models are addressed in this study. In Model 1, the dependent variable is the ROA whereas in Model 2 the dependent variable is the ROE. The first of the following equations belongs to Model 1, whereas Eq. (2) represents Model 2:

$$E1_{it} = \beta_0 + \beta_1 C1_{it} + \beta_2 C2_{it} + \beta_3 A1_{it} + \beta_4 A2_{it} + \beta_5 A3_{it} + \beta_6 M1_{it}$$
$$+ \beta_7 M2_{it} + \beta_8 M2_{it} + \beta_9 L1_{it} + \beta_{10} L2_{it} + \beta_{11} S1_{it} + \beta_{12} S2_{it} + u_{it}$$

(Model 1)

$$E2_{it} = \beta_0 + \beta_1 C1_{it} + \beta_2 C2_{it} + \beta_3 A1_{it} + \beta_4 A2_{it} + \beta_5 A3_{it} + \beta_6 M1_{it}$$
$$+ \beta_7 M2_{it} + \beta_8 M2_{it} + \beta_9 L1_{it} + \beta_{10} L2_{it} + \beta_{11} S1_{it} + \beta_{12} S2_{it} + u_{it}$$

(Model 2)

4.1. Research Findings

Table 3 shows the descriptive test statistics of the variables. The average value of the dependent variable E1 is 1.7%, and its standard deviation is 1%, while the average ROE E2 is 15.2% and its standard deviation is 8.8%. The average value of the independent variable C1 (Equity/Total Assets), which is the variable selected for capital adequacy, is 11.4%, and the average value of C2 (Equities-Fixed Assets/Total Assets) is 9.7%. The average value of the independent variable selected for asset quality, A1 (Non-Performing Loans/Total Loans), is 4.4%, while the average value of A2 (Total Loans/Total Assets) is 59.2% and the average value of A3 (Total Loans/Total Deposits) is 96.3%. The average value of the independent variable selected for management adequacy, M1 (Operating Expenses/Total Assets), is 2.9%, and the average value of M2 (Total Deposits/Total Assets) is 63%. The average value of the independent variable selected for liquidity status, L1 (Liquid Assets/Total Assets), is 9.8%, whereas the average value of L2 (Liquid Assets/Short-Term Liabilities) is 11%. The average value of the independent variable selected for sensitivity to market risks, S1 (Foreign Currency Assets/Foreign Currency Liabilities), is 89.4%, and the average value of S2 (Total FX Position/Equity) is –36.8%.

Table 4 shows the correlation matrix of the variables used in the analysis. Ninety-five-percent positive correlation is found between the dependent variables E1 (ROA) and E2 (ROE). According to the correlation matrix, the dependent variable E1 has a positive correlation with the independent variables C1, C2, M2, and the correlation coefficients are 22%, 34% and 16%, respectively. However, there is a negative relationship between the dependent variable E1 and the independent variables A1, A2, A3, M1, L1, L2, S1 and S2, and the correlation coefficients are –11%, –18%, –27%, –32% 30, –29%, –4% and –2%, respectively. According to the correlation matrix, the dependent variable E2 has a positive correlation with the independent variables C2 and M2, and the correlation coefficients are 10% and 23%, respectively. However, there is a negative relationship between the dependent variable E2 and the independent variables C1, A1, A2, A3, M1, L1, L2, S1 and S2, and the correlation coefficients are –1%, –8%, –15%, –27%, –30%, –23%, –23%, –1% and –2%, respectively.

Table 3. Descriptive Statistical Values of Variables.

Symbol	Average	Median	Maximum	Minimum	SD
E1	0.017	0.017	0.049	−0.064	0.010
E2	0.152	0.154	0.404	−0.496	0.088
C1	0.114	0.114	0.219	0.067	0.024
C2	0.097	0.098	0.186	0.017	0.024
A1	0.044	0.041	0.281	0.005	0.031
A2	0.592	0.616	0.765	0.169	0.106
A3	0.963	0.983	2.272	0.223	0.239
M1	0.029	0.025	0.145	0.008	0.014
M2	0.630	0.611	0.876	0.261	0.090
L1	0.098	0.098	0.264	0.006	0.041
L2	0.110	0.113	0.286	0.007	0.044
S1	0.894	0.920	1.105	0.544	0.134
S2	−0.368	−0.251	0.397	−1.740	0.482

Table 4. Correlation Matrix of Variables.

	E1	E2	C1	C2	A1	A2	A3	M1	M2	L1	L2	S1	S2
E1	1												
E2	0.95	1											
C1	0.22	−0.01	1										
C2	0.34	0.10	0.88	1									
A1	−0.11	−0.08	0.05	−0.10	1								
A2	−0.18	−0.15	−0.14	0.01	−0.47	1							
A3	−0.27	−0.27	−0.14	0.05	−0.48	0.68	1						
M1	−0.32	−0.30	0.08	−0.16	0.26	−0.13	−0.24	1					
M2	0.16	0.23	−0.02	−0.16	0.34	−0.03	−0.69	0.26	1				
L1	−0.30	−0.23	−0.48	−0.27	−0.25	0.39	0.46	−0.39	−0.26	1			
L2	−0.29	−0.23	−0.43	−0.23	−0.25	0.40	0.47	−0.40	−0.27	0.99	1		
S1	−0.04	−0.01	−0.12	−0.12	−0.17	−0.16	−0.23	−0.26	0.17	0.07	0.06	1	
S2	−0.02	−0.02	−0.01	−0.04	−0.08	−0.19	−0.36	−0.14	0.31	−0.03	−0.04	0.92	1

Table 5. Unit Root Test Results of Variables.

Variables	Levin, Lin, and Chu t^*		ADF		PP	
	Statistic	Prob	Statistic	Prob	Statistic	Prob
E1	4.3831	0.001	115.697	0.001	148.112	0.001
E2	16.5042	0.001	109.728	0.001	156.866	0.001
C1	−17.6632	0.001	141.962	0.001	137.466	0.001
C2	−25.7357	0.001	131.434	0.001	132.501	0.001
A1	−5.9635	0.001	68.3577	0.001	95.5444	0.001
A2	−6.9766	0.001	80.2493	0.001	108.838	0.001
A3	−6.5885	0.001	66.8460	0.001	79.7059	0.001
M1	−4.13696	0.001	41.7218	0.001	10.6417	0.001
M2	−10.1623	0.001	96.5247	0.001	168.222	0.001
L1	−29.1188	0.001	116.943	0.001	196.369	0.001
L2	−24.6727	0.001	118.188	0.001	198.625	0.001
S1	−11.5229	0.001	109.740	0.001	209.842	0.001
S2	−11.4358	0.001	92.3991	0.001	108.934	0.001

Moreover, E1 has a positive correlation with C1 (22%), while E2 has a negative correlation with C1 (1%). The correlation signs and correlation coefficients of the other independent variables, except for C1, are similar.

The next step of this chapter was the regression analysis, which was performed according to the model indicated in Fig. 6.

Before the regression analysis, it should be checked whether the series are stationary. As in the time series, it is desirable for the series to be stationary in panel data analysis (Sarıkovanlık, Koy, Akkaya, Yıldırım, & Kantar,, 2019, p. 185). If econometric analyses are performed with non-stationary (unit root-containing) series, the problem of spurious regression is likely to arise (Sevüktekin & Nargeleçekenler, 2010). Thus, yearly change in all variables is taken into account before the unit root test.

Table 5 shows the unit root test results of the values of percentage changes of the variables compared to the previous year. According to the Levin, Lin & Chu,

Table 6.   Regression Analysis Results of Model 1.

Dependent Variable: E1
Sample (adjusted): 2005–2018
Periods included: 14
Cross-sections included: 11
Total panel (balanced) observations: 154

Variable	Coefficient	SE	t-Statistic	Prob.
C	0.548894	0.138308	3.968625	0.0001
C1	**−2.685771**	**1.284608**	**−2.090733**	**0.0383**
C2	**2.686649**	**0.703098**	**3.821160**	**0.0002**
A1	0.267263	0.316771	0.843711	0.4002
A2	−3.354422	2.316747	−1.447902	0.1498
A3	3.254287	2.317186	1.404413	0.1624
M1	**7.791519**	**0.523567**	**14.88160**	**0.0000**
M2	**4.670500**	**2.069107**	**2.257254**	**0.0255**
L1	**12.41505**	**2.295276**	**5.408957**	**0.0000**
L2	**−13.28612**	**2.459116**	**−5.402804**	**0.0000**
S1	0.800587	1.216581	0.658063	0.5116
S2	−0.008360	0.009697	−0.862195	0.3900
R-squared	0.724338	Mean dependent var		0.185589
Adjusted R-squared	0.702984	SD dependent var		2.532819
SE of regression	1.380365	Akaike info criterion		3.557291
Sum squared resid	270.5677	Schwarz criterion		3.793937
Log likelihood	−261.9114	Hannan-Quinn criter.		3.653416
F-statistic	33.92038	Durbin-Watson stat		1.660999
Prob(F-statistic)	0.000000			

ADF and PP unit root test results, probability values are less than 5% and therefore, all variables are stationary.

In the next stage, regression analysis was performed with stationary series for Model 1 and Model 2. Table 6 shows the regression test results of Model 1.

According to the results, C1 (Equity/Total Assets) and L2 (Liquid Assets/Short-Term Liabilities) are statistically significant since the probability value is lower than 0.05, and thus, these variables affect the ROA negatively. Furthermore, the C2 ((Equity-Fixed Assets)/Total Assets), M1 (Operating Expenses/Total Assets) and M2 (Total Deposits/Total Assets), and L1 (Liquid Assets/Total Assets) and L2 (Liquid Assets/Short-Term Liabilities) variables are statistically significant, as the probability values are smaller than 0.05, which indicates that these variables affect the ROA positively. Finally, variables A1, A2, A3, S1 and S2 have no effect on the ROA, as their probability values are higher than 0.05.

According to the regression test results in Table 7, the variables C1 (Equity/Total Assets) and L2 (Liquid Assets/Short-Term Liabilities) are statistically significant since the probability values are lower than 0.05, and these variables affect the ROE negatively. Moreover, variables C2 ((Equity-Fixed Assets)/Total Assets), M1 (Operating Expenses/Total Assets) and M2 (Total Deposits/Total Assets), and L1 (Liquid Assets/Total Assets) and L2 (Liquid Assets/Short-Term Liabilities) are statistically

Table 7. Model 2 Regression Analysis Results.

Dependent Variable: E2
Sample (adjusted): 2005–2018
Periods included: 14
Cross-sections included: 11
Total panel (balanced) observations: 154

Variable	Coefficient	SE	t-Statistic	Prob.
C	0.626591	0.152875	4.098722	0.0001
C1	−3.282300	1.419901	−2.311640	0.0222
C2	2.912964	0.777147	3.748278	0.0003
A1	0.224282	0.350133	0.640563	0.5228
A2	−3.737568	2.560744	−1.459564	0.1466
A3	3.288027	2.561229	1.283769	0.2013
M1	8.591386	0.578709	14.84578	0.0000
M2	4.932935	2.287023	2.156924	0.0327
L1	13.63296	2.537012	5.373629	0.0000
L2	−14.57692	2.718107	−5.362896	0.0000
S1	0.670978	1.344710	0.498976	0.6186
S2	−0.009608	0.010718	−0.896434	0.3715
R-squared	0.725874	Mean dependent var		0.208546
Adjusted R-squared	0.704639	S.D. dependent var		2.807403
SE of regression	1.525743	Akaike info criterion		3.757559
Sum squared resid	330.5607	Schwarz criterion		3.994205
Log likelihood	−277.3320	Hannan-Quinn criter.		3.853684
F-statistic	34.18273	Durbin-Watson stat		1.656520
Prob(F-statistic)	0.000000			

significant and affect the ROE positively. Lastly, the variables A1, A2, A3, S1 and S2 have no effect on the ROE because the probability values are higher than 0.05.

The results obtained from Model 1 in Table 6 are very similar to the results of Model 2 in Table 7. The independent variables affecting the ROA and ROE are similar. It can easily be said that the variables of asset quality and market risks do not significantly affect the dependent variables for both models.

5. CONCLUSIONS AND RECOMMENDATIONS

Profitability is an important output for the continuity of activities and sustainable growth of banks due to intense competition. In this study, internal factors of banks such as capital adequacy, asset quality, management adequacy, liquidity status and sensitivity to market risks, and the effects of those factors on ROA and ROE were investigated.

According to the results of this study, capital adequacy, management adequacy and liquidity status have a significant effect on the ROA and ROE ratios of banks. However, asset quality and sensitivity to market risks do not have a significant effect on the ratios mentioned above.

Furthermore, C1 (Equity/Total Assets) and L2 (Liquid Assets/Short-Term Liabilities) affect the ROA and ROE ratios negatively. These findings are similar to those of Pasiouras and Kosmidou (2007) and Yılmaz (2013) in the literature. In addition, variables C2, M1, M2, L1 and L2 affect ROA and ROE in a positive way. Also, these findings are similar to those of Ata (2009) and Karaçor et al. (2017) in the literature.

ROA and ROE, also known as Dupont profitability, are considered to be an important output while measuring the profitability of banks as a measure of banks' profitability. As can be seen from the test results, the ratios of C1 and L2 should be reduced in order to increase not only ROA but also ROE. However, the capital adequacy variable, C2 ((Equity-Fixed Assets)/Total Assets), the management adequacy variables, M1 (Operating Expenses/Total Assets) and M2 (Total Deposits/Total Assets) and the liquidity variables, L1 (Liquid Assets/Total) and L2 (Liquid Assets/Short-Term Liabilities) should be increased in order to raise profits according to Model 1 and Model 2.

The findings of this chapter are in accordance with the previous studies in the literature. It will be beneficial for further studies on this topic to expand the time period and increase the variables used in this chapter.

REFERENCES

Abdullayev, M. (2013). Türk Bankacılık Sektöründe Dezenflasyon Sürecinde CAMELS Analizi [CAMELS analysis of the Turkish banking sector in the disinflation period], *Dumlupınar University-Journal of Social Sciences*, *37*, 97–112.

Altemur, N., Karaca, S. S., & Güvemli, B. (2018). Türkiye'deki Yabancı Sermayeli Bankaların CAMELS Analizi İle Performanslarının Ölçülmesi [Evaluation of foreign capital banks' performance in Turkey by CAMELS analysis]. *Journal of International Management, Educational and Economics Perspectives*, *6*(1), 57–65.

Arıçelik, G. (2010). *Ticari bankalarda performans ölçümü: CAMELS analizine dayalı bir inceleme [Performance measurement at commercial banks: A survey based on CAMELS analysis]*. Ph.D. thesis, Dokuz Eylül University-Institute of Social Sciences, İzmir.

Ata, H. A. (2009). Kriz Sonrası Türkiye'de Mevduat Bankaları Kârlılığına Etki Eden Faktörler/Factors affecting deposit banks' profitability in Turkey after the crisis. *Dokuz Eylül University-Business Faculty Journal*, *10*(2), 137–151.

Aydın, N., Başar, M., & Çoşkun, M. (2014). *Finansal Yönetim [Financial Management]*. Ankara: Detay Publication.

Aydın, N., Delikanlı, İ. U., Çabukel, R., Erdal, L., Erdal, F., & Ergeç, E. H. (2012). *Bankacılık ve Sigortacılığa Giriş [Introduction to banking and insurance]*. Eskişehir: Anadolu University Publication.

Banking Regulation and Supervision Agency. (2018). Main indicators of Turkish banking sector. Retrieved from www.bddk.org.tr, İstanbul.

Bepari, M. K., & Mollik, A. (2008). Banking system in Bangladesh: stable or vulnerable? A macroprudential assessment. *Journal of Business Administration*, *34*, 3–4.

Bumin, M. (2009). Türk Bankacılık Sektörünün Kârlılık Analizi [Profitability analysis of the Turkish banking sector: 2002–2008]. *Maliye Finans Yazıları*, *23*(84), 39–60.

Çağıl, G., & Mukhtarov, S. (2014). Azerbaycan Ticari Bankacılık Sektörünün CAMELS Yöntemi İle Performans Analizi [Performance analysis of the commercial banking sector of Azerbaijan by CAMELS method]. *Öneri Dergisi*, *11*(41), 77–94.

Demirel, E., Atakişi, A., & Abacıoğlu, S. (2013). Bankacılık Faaliyet Oranlarının Panel Veri Analizi: Türkiye'deki Kamu, Özel ve Yabancı Sermayeli Bankaların Durumu [Panel data analyzes of banking operational ratios: The case of state, private and foreign owned banks in Turkey]. *The Journal of Accounting and Finance*, *59*, 101–112.

Doyran, M. A. (2013). Net interest margins and firm performance in developing countries: Evidence from Argentine commercial banks. *Management Research Review*, 720–742.

Ege, İ., Topaloğlu, E. E., & Karakozak, Ö. (2015). CAMELS Performans Değerleme Modeli: Türkiye'deki Mevduat Bankaları Üzerine Ampirik Bir Uygulama/The CAMELS performance evaluation model: An empirical implementation on deposit banks in Turkey. *Ömer Halis Demir University – Academic Review of Economics and Administrative Sciences*, *8*(4), 109–126.

Ersoy, E. (2003). CAMELS Derecelendirme Sistemine göre TMSF'ye Devredilen ve Devredilmeyen Bankaların Karşılaştırmalı Analizi, *Active Bankacılık ve Finans Dergisi*, 32, 66–72.

Gümüş, F. B., & Nalbantoğlu, Ö. (2015). Türk Bankacılık Sektörünün CAMELS Analizi Yöntemiyle 2002-2013 Yılları Arasında Performans Analizi [Performance analysis of Turkish banking sector with CAMELS analysis between the years 2002–2013]. *Afyon Kocatepe University-Journal of Economics and Administrative Sciences*, *17*(2), 83–106.

Gündoğdu, A. (2017). Türkiye'de Mevduat Bankalarının CAMELS Analizi [The CAMELS analysis of Turkish deposit banks]. *Journal of Banking and Financial Research (BAFAD)*, *4*(2), 26–43.

Gunter, U., Krenn, G., & Sigmund, M. (2013). Macro-economic, market and bank-specific determinants of the net interest margin in Austria. *Financial Stability*, *25*, 87–101.

İskenderoğlu, Ö., Karadeniz, E., & Atioğlu, E. (2012). Türk bankacılık sektöründe büyüme, büyüklük ve sermaye yapısı kararlarının karlılığa etkisinin analizi [The effects of growth, size and capital structure decisions on profitability in the Turkish banking sector]. *Eskişehir Osmangazi University-Journal of Economics and Administrative Sciences*, *7*(1), 291–311.

Islamoglu, M. (2013). Bankalarda Aktif Pasif Yönetimi (16. Bölüm) [Asset and Liability Management in Banks (Chapter 16)], Editor: Kaya, F., Bankacılık; Giriş ve İlkeleri/Banking; introduction and principles (2nd ed.), Beta Publications, Istanbul.

Kandemir, T., & Arıcı, N. D. (2013). Mevduat Bankalarında CAMELS Performans Değerleme Modeli Üzerine Karşılaştırmalı Bir Çalışma (2001-2010) [A comparative study on the CAMELS performance evaluation model in deposit banks (2001–2010)]. *Suleyman Demirel University-The Journal of Faculty of Economics and Administrative Sciences*, *18*(1), 61–87.

Karaçor, Z. Ö., Mangir, F., Kodaz, Ş. S., & Kartal, M. (2017). Kamusal ve Özel Sermayeli Bankaların CAMELS Performans Analizi: Türkiye Örneği [CAMELS performance analysis of public and private banks: The example of Turkey]. *Istanbul Gelisim University-Journal of Social Sciences*, *4*(2), 47–65.

Kartal, M. T. (2018, August 5–27). Bankaların Finans Sektöründeki Önemi [Importance of banks in the finance sector]. *Finansal İktisat [Financial Economics]*. Retrieved from https://ssrn.com/abstract=3232801

Kaya, Y. T. (2001). *Türk Bankacılık Sektöründe CAMELS Analizi [CAMELS analysis for the Turkish banking sector, banking regulation and supervision agency]*. MSPD Working Reports, No: 2001/6, Banking Regulation And Supervision Agency, Ankara.

Kiganda, E. O. (2014). Effect of macroeconomic factors on commercial banks profitability in Kenya: Case of equity bank limited. *Journal of Economics and Sustainable Development*, *2*, 46–56.

Kılıç, Ç., & Fettahoğlu, A. (2005). Türk Bankacılık Sektörünün CAMELS Analizi ile Değerlendirilmesi/ Evaluation of Turkish banking sector with CAMELS analysis, In 9th national finance symposium proceedings, Nevşehir, September 29–30 (pp. 89–128).

Participation Banks Association of Turkey. (2017). Participation Banks 2017 Annual Report, Istanbul, Turkey. Retrieved from http://www.tkbb.org.tr

Pasiouras, F., & Kosmidou, K. (2007). Factors influencing the profitability of domestic and foreign commercial banks in the European Union. *Research in International Business and Finance*, *21*(2), 222–237.

Peterson, P. (1994). *Financial management and analysis*. New York, NY: McGraw Hill.

Reis, Ş. G., Kiliç, Y., & Buğan, M. F. (2016). Banka Karlılığını Etkileyen Faktörler: Türkiye Örneğİ [Factors that affect bank profitability: The case of Turkey]. *The Journal of Accounting and Finance*, *72*, 21–36.

Riaz, S. (2013). Profitability determinants of commercial banks in Pakistan. In Proceedings of 6th international business and social sciences research conference, January 3–4, Dubai.

Sakarya, Ş. (2010). CAMELS Derecelendirme Sistemine Göre İMKB'deki Yerli Ve Yabancı Sermayeli Bankaların Karşılaştırmalı Analizi [Comparative analysis of domestic and foreign capital banks in Istanbul stock exchange as per CAMELS rating system]. *Journal of Academic Research and Studies* Prof. dr. Alaeddin YAVAŞÇA Special Issue - June 2010, 7–21.

Sangmi, M. D., & Nazir, T. (2010). Analyzing financial performance of commercial banks in India: An application of CAMELS model. *Pakistan Journal of Commerce and Social Sciences*, 4(1), 40–55.

Sarıkovanlık, V., Koy, A., Akkaya, M., Yıldırım, H. H., & Kantar, L. (2019). *Finans Biliminde Ekonometri Uygulamaları*. Ankara: Seçkin Publishing.

Sarıtaş, H., & Saray, C. (2012). Türk Bankacılık Sektörünün Kârlılık Performansının Analizi [Analysis of profitability performance of Turkish banking sector]. *Pamukkale University-Journal of Social Sciences Institute, 11*, 23–37.

Sarıtaş, H., Uyar, S. K., & Gökçe, A. (2016). Banka Karlılığı Ile Finansal Oranlar Ve Makroekonomik Değişkenler Arasındaki Ilişkilerin Sistem Dinamik Panel Veri Modeli Ile Analizi: Türkiye Araştırması [The analysis of banks's profitability with financial ratios and macroeconomics variables based on system dynamic panel data model: Research on Turkey]. *Eskişehir Osmangazi University-Journal of Economics and Administrative Sciences, 11*, 87–108.

Saunders, A., & Schumacher, L. (2000). The determinants of bank interest margins: An international study. *Journal of International Money and Finance*, 19(6), 813–832.

Sevüktekin, M., & Nargeleçekenler, M. (2010). *Ekonometrik Zaman Serileri Analizi Eviews Uygulamalı* (3rd ed). İstanbul: Nobel Publishing.

Şıklar, I. (2004). *Financial economics*. Eskişehir: Anadolu University Publishing.

Taşkın, F. D. (2011). Türkiye'de Ticari Bankaların Performansını Etkileyen Faktörler [The factors affecting the performance of the Turkish commercial banks]. *Ege Academic Review, 11*(2), 289–298.

The Banks Association of Turkey. (2018). Banking Sector in Turkey (March 2014–2018), İstanbul. Retrieved from www.tbb.org.tr.

Van Horne, J., & Wachowıcz, J. M. (1995). *Fundamentals of financial management*. Englewood Cliffs, NJ: Prentice Hall International Editions.

Yılmaz, A. A. (2013). Profitability of banking system: Evidence from emerging markets. In WEI international academic conference proceedings, Antalya.

CHAPTER 7

THE INTERACTION BETWEEN CUSTOMER EXPERIENCE, SATISFACTION AND POSITIVE WORD OF MOUTH: A STUDY ON CITY MARKETING IN AFYONKARAHISAR

Alparslan Özmen and İlkin Yaran Ögel

ABSTRACT

Introduction – *Today, just like the goods and services, cities may provide a context for marketing activities. In this way, through the right marketing strategies and activities, cities can turn into brands, as well. Starting from this fact, it can be readily thought that cities can also be experienced as well as goods and/or services and some behaviours such as satisfaction and positive word of mouth can emerge, as a result of the experience.*

Purpose – *In this sense, the authors attempted to examine the interplay between experience, satisfaction and positive word of mouth within the context of city marketing.*

Methodology – *The authors designed the study as a causal research. The sample of the study was reached through convenience sampling method. Data were collected via survey method. The data compiled for the study were analysed with Model 4 in Hayes Macro Process Models.*

Contemporary Issues in Business, Economics and Finance
Contemporary Studies in Economic and Financial Analysis, Volume 104, 105–121
Copyright © 2020 by Emerald Publishing Limited
All rights of reproduction in any form reserved
ISSN: 1569-3759/doi:10.1108/S1569-375920200000104007

Findings – *The findings of the study displayed an interaction between experience, satisfaction and positive word of mouth regarding a city. Additionally, it presented the mediator role of satisfaction on the relationship between experience and positive word of mouth. In this respect, it is thought that by emphasising the importance of experience regarding the city and showing the importance of measuring satisfaction level of visitors, the findings of the study are expected to contribute to the activities of local governments which want to promote their cities.*

Keywords: Experience; satisfaction; positive word of mouth; city marketing; city branding; city promotion; Afyonkarahisar; Hayes Macro Process

JEL classification: M31; M39

1. INTRODUCTION

In a globalising world, marketing activities are not limited with only goods and services. Ideas, person(s), countries, places and many other phenomena can be a subject of marketing activities (Kotler & Armstrong, 2010). Recent years, besides goods and services, the interests towards these phenomena have been incrementally enhanced. Among these phenomena, particularly researches on marketing of places, countries and cities have shown remarkable increase. The reason behind the increase in the interest towards city marketing can be explained by the potential of countries, regions, cities and places to be the subject of marketing activities and even their potentials to turn into brands.

Branding is a way to be valuable in the eyes of consumers and preferable for target consumers. So, this makes any product to be sold more and profitable. Initiated by this argument, it can be readily concluded that in order to increase the number of visitors, draw the attention of investors and gain much more profit, cities should be promoted to be a brand. For that reason, todays, just like the companies, cities have started to use the marketing strategies effectively in order to create added value; to make them as attraction centre; to create more liveable places and happier visitors, investors and residents.

Particularly as the economic competition increases, cities have been turned into goods that are marketed aggressively to attract the attention of people who want either to visit the cities or to make investment in these cities. Additionally, rapid changes in global economy, problems occurred with urban development and increase in the need for local financial sources enforce cities use efficient marketing strategies and programs (Langer, 2000). As a result, recent years, the successful campaigns carried out for the promotion of cities and all of these campaigns have revealed the effect of positive image on creating financial value for the cities (Asworth & Voogd, 1990). The use of right marketing strategies has an important role in this success because right marketing strategies differentiate the one city from the others and by increasing positive word-of-mouth communication regarding the city. So, it leads to an increase from the number of visitors to be visited the city to income per capita of the residents living in the city (Altunbaş, 2007).

Nevertheless, increasing the number of visitors and investors is not an easy task for local governments. Particularly, when the extent of the competition among the cities in drawing the attention of visitors and investors is taken into consideration, it can be readily concluded that local governments have to find some novel ways to promote their cities. For that reason, to create an identity and strong, unique, favourable image regarding a city and to provide a better positioning for it, the collaboration between its local government and marketing managers has increased day by day. Thus, new marketing trends used in marketing of goods and services have also be adopted for marketing of cities and places. For instance, recent years, in order to promote the products and services, creating an experience for them is becoming much more critical because good experience regarding the marketing offerings creates more satisfied consumers (Chinomona, 2013), which in turn, increases in the positive word-of-mouth behaviour regarding the offerings. When the lifetime value of consumers is considered, a good experience regarding a marketing offering that leads to satisfaction and positive word of mouth is more likely to influence the consumers' next purchases for the offerings (Kotler & Armstrong, 2010). For that reason, creating an experience for consumers is regarded as a way to differentiate marketing offerings from the others and to position them better in the minds of consumers.

Recent years, in order to promote the cities and to attract the attention of visitors, experiencing a city in a sensual, emotional and behavioural way has more emphasised, as well. Today, local governments of the cities spend too much time, effort and money to either create or promote something else that can be experienced by the visitors they did in the past because if the consumers leave the city with good experiences, they are more likely to leave the city as a satisfied consumers and so engage in positive word-of-mouth behaviour. This is critical to create happy visitors, increase the number of new visitors and make a city as an attraction centre. Nevertheless, although there is a huge amount of research on city marketing in relevant literature, there is no any study on the role of experiencing a city on satisfaction of the visitors and so their positive word-of-mouth communication tendency regarding the city. Initiated from this fact, this study attempts to examine the interaction between experiencing a city, satisfaction from that city, and positive word-of-mouth communication behaviours of visitors regarding that city within the context of Afyonkarahisar. Afyonkarahisar was particularly chosen for this study because it is one of the well-known tourism destinations of Turkey and the world in terms of hot spring and thermal pools, delicious products like sujuk and buffalo milk cream that have geographical indications and historical sites belonging from Phrygians to Turkish war of independence. In this context, Afyonkarahisar can be regarded as a city which can be experienced through five senses. Additionally, in terms of marble and natural stone potential, Afyonkarahisar is also one of the well-known cities of Turkey in the world. Having all these in mind, the findings of the study are expected to contribute to local governments in structuring their future road maps to make Afyonkarahisar a brand in terms of tourism and trade. Moreover, it is expected to contribute to brand experience and city marketing literature.

2. LITERATURE REVIEW

2.1. City Marketing

The concept of city marketing has appeared due to the change in the perspective of people to places (Kotler, Asplund, Rein, & Heider, 1999, p. 160). In this process, it is understood that cities can be the issue of marketing activities, and using marketing and its tools, cities can also be promoted to attract the attention of investors and visitors. Particularly in recent years, local governments have started to need city marketing more than they needed in the past because successful city marketing provides several advantages to the cities. For instance, successful city marketing could draw the tourists and visitors to the city; draw the job opportunities from the other cities to the city; help local producers to maintain and develop their current works, grow their small businesses, export their products abroad and so expand into new markets; and finally increase the population of the city and provide its distribution in itself (Deffner & Liouris, 2005). Having all these advantages in mind, city marketing can be regarded as more important in terms of creating added value for its residents, local producers, investors, tourists and local governments.

City marketing is defined as the process of selling and re-constructing the image of city and so to make it attractive to local economic enterprises, visitors, locals and inhabitants of that city (Aksoylu, 2013). Hence, city marketing always requires use and coordination of marketing tools to create presentation of the city, to communicate with the others, to create distribution channels and to provide change. As seen its definition, activities, organisations, institutions and process are the main phenomena of the city marketing. These activities, organisations and processes are all about using and carrying out the marketing tools like marketing research, market segmentation, product development, selling and promotion, establishing marketing mix and branding (Braun, 2008).

In order to enhance the awareness of the cities, to attract the attention of visitors and investors, and to promote the inner richness of the cities like local tastes and cultural heritage, marketing and marketing tools have turned into very critical instruments. Today, increase in the number of events organised for promoting the cities indicates the extent of the competition among the cities (Braun, 2008). However, in order to create and maintain a success in marketing of the city, understanding the expectations of the target groups and creating a right perception towards the city to make them satisfied are a must (Deffner & Liouris, 2005; Kavaratzis & Ashwort, 2007).

City marketing is not limited with only marketing of the inner and outer assets of a city but also it includes the re-definition and creation of the image of the city. Just like the image of the brand, city image is all about how the customers see a city and what they keep in their minds about the city. Accordingly, while an individual is travelling around a city, the way how they experience the city through their five senses paves the way for creation of the image of the city. For that reason, city marketing is not only focussed on selling of the city just like selling a product, but it also concentrates on the creating positive image for the city. Having all these in mind, it is required to see city marketing as a goal for featuring the potential of the city and making local residents benefit from this promoted potential (Deffner & Liouris, 2005).

Additionally, city marketing should be accepted as a strategic decision. Depending upon the belief that investments prompt the economic recovery, city marketing is seen as a strategic process in which the real or imaginary value of the cities is promoted to foreign investors and visitors. Moreover, since city marketing is also related to some strategic issues like development of society and economy and creating a job, city marketing activities should be strategically planned and maintained (Nel & Binns, 2002). In this context, in putting city marketing into practice, it is required to gain the trust and support of all public.

Cities, which want to increase their competition advantages and attract the attention of several parties, need an urban planning which is prepared and applied in a right way (Deffner & Liouris, 2005). In carrying out the city marketing, functions, people and organisations have a strategic role (Braun, 2008). In this respect, Braun (2008) divides the customers who potentially play a role in city marketing into four categories in general. These customers are potential inhabitants and locals, potential businesses, potential visitors and potential investors.

Among these customer categories, particularly understanding potential visitors and their perception, attitudes and behaviours towards city marketing mix is extremely important because satisfied visitors are more likely to contribute to promotion of the cities through positive word-of-mouth communication. Thus, in order to attract the attention of new visitors and make visitors leave the city in a satisfied way, understanding how they experience the city that they visit is a must. In this context, since the cities have a potential to turn into brands, brand experience can be used to examine the experience of visitors regarding a city.

2.2. Brand Experience

Brand experience can be defined as feelings, sensations, cognitions and behavioural responses evoked by brand-related stimuli like brand design, brand identity, package, promotion and so on (Brakus, Schmitt, & Zarantonello, 2009). On the basis of this definition, the extents of brand experience are divided into sensory, affective, intellectual and behavioural extents. In this context, in order to understand how a visitor experiences a city, it will be better to examine his or her sensory, affective, intellectual and behavioural responses towards the city while he or she is travelling around the city.

Lee and Kang (2012) suggested that brand experience is extremely critical in terms of marketing practices. They specifically indicated that brand experience considerably changes and develops the quality of relationship between customers and brands, positively. Accordingly, the experiences created for customers regarding a city like bringing a city-originated delicious taste into the forefront, creating visit areas in which the moments regarding the history of the city animated or giving emphasis to promotion of a source of the city such as thermal tourism influence the way how the visitors experience the city and so whether they leave the city in a satisfied way.

Shamim and Butt (2013) present the direct and indirect effects of brand experience on several important concepts in branding literature. In this context, when the experience is examined within the context of city marketing, it is normal to think that experiencing a city can influence several attitudes and behaviours of visitors towards the cities that they visit. For instance, satisfaction is one of the most important behaviours that can potentially occur after experiencing a city in a positive way.

2.3. Satisfaction

If the expectation of a customer matches with the performance of a marketing offering, it is possible to mention about satisfied customer (Kotler & Armstrong, 2010). Accordingly, if visitors leave a city as their expectations from the city are met, they will be turn into satisfied visitors. In this context, it is expected that the more the customers are satisfied, the more they influence the number of new visitors by engaging in positive word-of-mouth communication.

2.4. Positive Word-of-Mouth Communication

The role of interpersonal communication which is known as word of mouth is significantly effective in consumers' buying behaviours (De Matos & Rossi, 2008). The good experience obtained from using a specific product or brand is always positively transferred to the others. Nevertheless, if the consumers are not satisfied from the product or brand that they used, word-of-mouth communication can be negative. When the cities are accepted as either a brand or phenomenon that is experienced, it is normal to expect that individual who positively experience a city and get satisfaction from that city will potentially carry out positive word-of-mouth communication behaviour.

2.5. Theoretical Framework of the Study

This study examines the concepts, which are mostly used in marketing literature, such as experience, satisfaction and positive word of mouth within the context of city marketing. When the relevant literature is reviewed, it can be readily seen that experience created for a product increases satisfaction and positive word-of-mouth communication towards the product. Initiated by these findings, it can be assumed that experience created for a city can also influence satisfaction towards the city and positive word-of-mouth communication regarding the city. Additionally, it is not wrong to expect a positive relationship between satisfaction and positive word-of-mouth communication because the visitors who left the city in a satisfied way are more likely to communicate about the city positively with their close and distant relatives. Finally, it is assumed that the satisfaction of visitors towards a city has a mediating role in the relationship between experiencing the city and positive word-of-mouth communication regarding the city because being satisfied from the city can also be highly effective on the positive word-of-mouth communication of the visitors about the city as well as experience do. When the relationships to be examined in the study are taken into consideration,

Fig. 1.   Model of the Study.

four hypotheses are developed to test the given relationships. These hypotheses are given below. The model of the study developed on the basis of hypothesis is also given in Fig. 1.

H$_1$: Experiencing a city positively and significantly effects the satisfaction towards the city.

H$_2$: Satisfaction towards a city positively and significantly effects the positive word-of-mouth communication regarding the city.

H$_3$: Experiencing a city positively and significantly effects the positive word-of-mouth communication regarding the city.

H$_4$: Satisfaction towards a city has a mediating role on the relationship between experiencing the city and positive word-of-mouth communication regarding the city.

3. METHODOLOGY

3.1. Sampling Method and Data Collection

As stated before, the interaction between experience, satisfaction and positive word of mouth is examined within the context of Afyonkarahisar as one of the tourism destinations of Turkey. In order to test a model, it is better to use homogenous sample groups that have little differences in terms of variables such as socio-demographic, income and so on (Erdem et al., 2006). In this respect, university students were selected as the sample group for the study because they are frequently considered as a homogenous group. Additionally, when their potential of experiencing a city was taken into consideration, university students were seen as an appropriate sample group to collect data for this study. Initiated from these facts, the population of the study was determined as university students studying at Faculty of Economics and Administrative Sciences in Afyon Kocatepe University. Accordingly, the sample of the study was derived from the junior and senior students of Faculty of Economics and Administrative Sciences of Afyon Kocatepe University when the time that they spent in Afyonkarahisar was taken into account compared to the freshmen and sophomores studying at this faculty.

After determining sample group, sample size was determined for the study. Sample size must be 10 times of the item number and it must not be less than 200 (Kline, 2011). Additionally, when the population size is approximately 10,000,000, sample size should be at least 384 (Sekaran, 2003). Since the number of university students studying at the Faculty of Economics and Administrative Science of Afyon Kocatepe University is less than 10,000,000, 384 could be accepted as enough sample size for the study. Nevertheless, in order to reach an accurate sample size, sample size was calculated by taking standard deviation 1, significance level 0.05 and sampling error 0.1. Hence, on the basis of these indicators, sample size was determined as 340 for the study. When the several limitations like time and budget were taken into account, convenience sampling method was adopted to reach the determined sample size. Through this sampling method, it was reached to 384 students.

A face-to-face survey method was used in the study to collect data. The data were collected in time period between 1 October 2018 and 28 December 2018. Since the 11 of the 384 questionnaires were not fulfilled completely, they were excluded from the study. Hence, the number of questionnaire used in the study was determined as 373. The demographic characteristics of the respondents were given in Table 1.

The questionnaire used in the study consisted of four main parts. The first part of the questionnaire included questions for collecting demographic data. The second, third and last parts of the questionnaire included items regarding scales of experience, satisfaction and positive word of mouth, respectively. In order to measure experience, the scale with 12 items which was developed by Brakus et al. (2009); in order to measure satisfaction towards experience, the scale with three items which was used by Maxham and Netemeyer (2002); and finally in order to measure positive word of mouth, the scale with three items which was used by Alexandrov, Lilly, and Babakus (2013) were adapted to the study. To measure the items in the scales, a 5-point Likert-type scale was employed with the indicators ranging between '1= Strongly Disagree', '2=Disagree', '3= Neither Disagree nor Agree', '4 = Agree' and '5 = Strongly Agree'.

3.2. Analysis and Findings

3.2.1. Results of Reliability and Validity Tests of Scales Used in the Study

In order to determine the variables in the scale accurately, initially exploratory factor analysis was performed. In this context, in order to understand whether the collected data were appropriate for factor analysis, Kaiser–Mayer–Olkin (KMO) and Bartlett's tests were initially conducted for each scale used in the study and so their factor structures were detected. The values of KMO and Barlett's tests and other results of analysis of measurement tools were displayed in Table 2.

As seen in Table 2, three factors were determined for experience scale. These three factors were sensory/affective, behavioural and intellectual as similar with what the Brakus et al. (2009) suggested. Additionally, 1 factor was found for satisfaction scale and 1 factor was found for positive word-of-mouth scale. When the KMO values of scales used in the study were checked, it was seen that none of the variables had KMO values less than 0.50. Hence, exploratory factor analysis was performed together with all of the variables. As a result of exploratory factor analysis, KMO Measure of Sampling Adequacy Test value was found as 0.936.

Table 1. Demographic Characteristics of the Respondents.

	Demographic Characteristics	Frequency	%
Age	19	2	0.5
	20	55	14.7
	21	96	25.7
	22	122	32.7
	23	59	15.8
	24	24	6.4
	25	10	2.7
	26	4	1.1
	27	–	–
	28	1	0.3
	Total	373	100
Gender	Female	213	57.1
	Male	160	42.9
	Total	373	100
Department	Economics	46	12.3
	Business Administration	117	31.4
	International Finance and Trade	129	34.6
	Public Finance	40	10.7
	Business Administration (English)	18	4.8
	Public Administration	23	6.2
	Total	373	100
Class	Junior	181	48.5
	senior	192	51.5
	Total	373	100
Income	1,000–2,999TL	171	45.8
	3,000–4,999TL	126	33.8
	5,000–6,999TL	47	12.6
	7,000–8,999TL	13	3.5
	9,000–10,999TL	7	1.9
	11,000–12,999TL	1	0.3
	13,000–14,999TL	1	0.3
	15,000–16,999TL	3	0.8
	17,000–18,999TL	4	1.1
	Total	373	100

Table 2. Results of Analysis of Measurement Tools.

	Experience	Satisfaction	Positive Word-of-Mouth
KMO measure of sampling adequacy	0.957	0.750	0.756
Bartlett's test of sphericity	$\chi^2 = 3459.038$	$\chi^2 = 650.527$	$\chi^2 = 811.716$
	df: 153 p: 0.000	df: 3 p: 0.000	df: 3 p: 0.000
Number of factors according to factor loadings	3 Factors	1 Factor	1 Factor
Total variance explained	76%	82.61%	85.958%

Since the value obtained was higher than 0.90, it was concluded that suitability of data structure was perfect for factor analysis with respect to sampling adequacy (Şencan, 2005). Using principal component analysis and varimax rotation technique, factors were reduced in the study. Since factor loadings were above 0.50, all of the factors were selected (Costa-Font & Gil, 2009). According to the results of exploratory factor analysis, 3 factors and 18 items, whose eigen values were above 1, and, which explained the 71.486% of the total variance, were found. The results of exploratory factor analysis were presented in Table 3.

Later, in order to verify the factor structures used in the study, confirmatory factor analysis was conducted via Lisrel 8.70 statistical program. Confirmatory factor analysis is used to test the relationship between observed variables and latent variables that are measured via observed variables (İlhan & Çetin, 2014, p. 29). Initially, goodness-of-fit indices that present the fit between data in confirmatory factor analysis and factor structure were examined. In order to understand model fit, it is required to check several goodness-of-fit indices (Hair, Anderson, Tatham, & Black, 1998). The goodness-of-fit indices and their recommended values are given in Table 4.

Initially, χ^2/df ratio that presents the sample size adequacy was checked. The ratio of χ^2/df was found as 1.86 ($\chi^2 = 223.53$ df= 120 $p= 0.000$) and it was seen that χ^2/df ratio was within the acceptable fit criteria. The other goodness-of-fit indices such as AGFI (0.91), NNFI (0.99), NFI (0.99), IFI (0.99), RFI (0.99), CFI (0.99), SRMR (0.026) and RMR (0.057) were found within perfect fit criteria but GFI (0.94) and RMSEA (0.052) values were found in acceptable fit criteria. Having all these in mind, it was concluded that measurement values had a good fit with the measurement model (Hair, Black, Babin, & Anderson, 2013, p. 630; Tabachnick & Fidell, 2013, p. 739).

Table 3.   Results of Exploratory Factor Analysis.

Items	Factors		
	Experience	Satisfaction	Positive Word-of-Mouth
Sensory1	0.708		
Sensory2	0.699		
Sensory3	0.665		
Affective1	0.700		
Affective2	0.639		
Affective3	0.705		
Behaviour1	0.692		
Behaviour2	0.653		
Behaviour3	0.742		
Intellectual1	0.747		
Intellectual2	0.742		
Intellectual3	0.642		
Satisfaction1		0.749	
Satisfaction2		0.718	
Satisfaction3		0.812	
PWOM1			0.832
PWOM2			0.826
PWOM3			0.846
% of Variance explained	35.835	17.791	17.860
Cumulative variance explained (%)	35.835	53.626	71.486
KMO measure of sampling adequacy: 0.960			
Bartlett's test $\chi^2 = 5457.539$ df: 153 p: 0.000			

Table 4.   Goodness-of-Fit Indices and Their Recommended Values.

Fit Indices	Perfect Fit Indices Criteria	Acceptable Fit Indices Criteria	Findings	Results
χ^2/df[a]	$0 \leq \chi^2/df \leq 2$	$2 \leq \chi^2/df \leq 3$	1.86	Perfect fit
AGFI[b]	$0.90 \leq AGFI \leq 1.00$	$0.85 \leq AGFI \leq 0.90$	0.91	Perfect fit
GFI[c]	$0.95 \leq GFI \leq 1.00$	$0.90 \leq GFI \leq 95$	0.94	Acceptable fit
CFI[c]	$0.95 \leq CFI \leq 1.00$	$0.90 \leq CFI \leq 0.95$	0.99	Perfect fit
NFI[c]	$0.95 \leq NFI \leq 1.00$	$0.90 \leq NFI \leq 0.95$	0.99	Perfect fit
NNFI[c]	$0.95 \leq NNFI \leq 1.00$	$0.90 \leq NNFI \leq 0.95$	0.99	Perfect fit
RFI[c]	$0.95 \leq RFI \leq 1.00$	$0.90 \leq RFI \leq 0.95$	0.99	Perfect fit
IFI[c]	$0.95 \leq IFI \leq 1.00$	$0.90 \leq IFI \leq 0.95$	0.99	Perfect fit
RMSEA[d]	$0.00 \leq RMSEA \leq 0.05$	$0.05 \leq RMSEA \leq 0.08$	0.052	Acceptable fit
SRMR[d]	$0.00 \leq SRMR \leq 0.05$	$0.05 \leq SRMR \leq 0.10$	0.026	Perfect fit
RMR[e]	$0 \leq RMR \leq 0.05$	$0 \leq RMR \leq 1$	0.032	Perfect fit

[a]Kline (2011).
[b]Schermelleh-Engel and Moosbrugger (2003).
[c]Baumgartner and Homburg (1996), Bentler (1980), Bentler and Bonett (1980), Marsh, Hau, Artelt, Baumert, and Peschar (2006).
[d]Browne and Cudeck (1993).
[e]Golob (2003).

Results of confirmatory factor analysis and reliability test were displayed in Table 5. According to confirmatory factor analysis results, standardised parameter values between observed and latent variables ranged between 0.76 and 0.91. Thus, since there were no values less than 0.50 and all values were statistically significant ($p \leq 0.05$), all the values were included into the study (Hair et al., 2013, p. 617). Additionally, all t-values were found as statistically significant ($t > 1, 96$). The values of composite reliability (CR) which ranged between 0.80 and 0.92 showed that there was a good construct reliability (Fornell & Vlarcker, 1981). Moreover, the CR values were above the all average variance extracted (AVE) values and it showed that convergent validity was supported (Anderson & Gerbing, 1988; Bagozzi, Yi, & Philips, 1991; Chau, 1997; Fornell & Vlarcker, 1981; Hair et al., 2013). AVE values calculated for satisfaction and positive word of mouth were 0.58 and 0.70, respectively but the value calculated for experience was 0.48. Although, AVE value should be at least 0.50, the value less than 0.5 can be still accepted because according to Fornell and Vlarcker (1981), while the AVE value is less than 0.5, if the CR is higher than 0.6, the convergent validity of the construct could be still accepted as adequate. So, the AVE value less than 0.50 could not be regarded as the problem for the study.

Additionally, Cronbach α coefficient was calculated as 0.949 for experience; 0.894 for satisfaction and 0.918 for positive word of mouth. Since all Cronbach α coefficients were above 0.70 as a rule of thumb, it was concluded that the model was highly reliable (Nunally, 1978). Moreover, total Cronbach α coefficient of the scale was measured as 0.930 and it was seen one more time that the model was highly reliable. The results regarding confirmatory factor analysis and reliability test are presented in Table 5.

Table 5. Results of Confirmatory Factor Analysis and Reliability Test.

Factors		Standardised Loadings	*t*-values	Alpha Coefficient	CR	AVE	Mean	SD
Experience				0.949	0.92	0.48		
Sensory experience	Sensory1	0.80	18.35				2.9008	1.25438
	Sensory2	0.88	21.17				2.7480	1.22289
	Sensory3	0.78	17.48				2.8338	1.25905
Affective experience	Affective1	0.85	20.17				2.7989	1.17079
	Affective2	0.81	18.69				2.8740	1.21712
	Affective3	0.84	19.79				2.7105	1.16251
Behavioural Experience	Behaviour1	0.79	17.60				3.3244	1.14740
	Behaviour2	0.76	16.82				3.4665	0.97389
	Behaviour3	0.84	19.42				3.0536	1.11795
Intellectual experience	Intellectual1	0.84	19.64				2.7534	1.07926
	Intellectual2	0.83	19.03				3.0456	1.11469
	Intellectual3	0.79	17.87				2.8767	1.08797
Satisfaction				0.894	0.80	0.58		
Satisfaction	Satisfaction1	0.85	19.78				3.1019	1.09756
	Satisfaction2	0.90	21.85				3.0751	1.22683
	Satisfaction3	0.82	18.99				2.9437	1.10937
Positive word of mouth				0.918	0.87	0.70		
Positive word of mouth	PWOM1	0.85	20.19				3.3861	0.99516
	PWOM2	0.90	22.07				2.3056	1.04619
	PWOM3	0.91	22.20				3.3190	1.04346

Finally, in order to detect whether there was a probability of common method bias, Harman's single-factor test was adopted (Podsakoff & Organ, 1986). Hence, all variables were loaded on a single-factor and confirmatory factor analysis was re-performed (Podsakoff, Mackenzie, Lee, & Podsakoff, 2003). According to the results of repeated confirmatory factor analysis, a weak fit between data and factor structure was detected (χ^2(d.f 135) = 1,153.74; p = 0.00; AGFI = 0.68; GFI = 0.74; RMSEA = 0.142). Thus, it was concluded that common method bias was not a problem for the study.

3.2.2. Analysis of Model

The mediating role of satisfaction on the relationship between experience and positive word of mouth was tested via Hayes Macro Process Model 4 using SPSS statistical software program. Questionnaire items were included into the hypothesis testing by calculating arithmetic mean that represented each factor. In order to analyse the hypotheses of the study, regression analysis with four steps which is based on Baron and Kenny's (1986) model was used. The conditions suggested by Baron and Kenny (1986) for mediation effects are: (a) there is a significant relationship between independent variable and mediator variable; (b) there is a significant relationship between mediating variable and dependent variable; (c) there is a significant relationship between independent variable and dependent variable; and (d) when analysing the effect of mediating variable statistically, the significant existing relationship between independent variable and dependent variable as observed in the first condition should be zero and found as statistically insignificant. This condition indicates the full mediation effect. The results of mediation effect are given in Table 6.

According to Table 6, it was found that there was a partial mediating role of satisfaction towards a city. On the basis of the first step of the regression test of Baron and Kenny (1986), it was found that experience which was determined as an independent variable significantly increases (76%) satisfaction which was determined as the mediating variable and the 58% of the change in satisfaction (R^2) could be explained by experience. Initiated by the second step, it was seen that satisfaction significantly increases (approximately 29%) positive word-of-mouth communication which was the dependent variable of the study and 47% of the change in positive word-of-mouth behaviour could be explained by satisfaction. On the basis of the third step, in which mediating variable is kept under control and regression analysis is performed to test the relationship between independent and dependent variable without mediating variable, it was found that experience significantly increases (66%) positive word-of-mouth communication. Finally, when the mediating variable satisfaction was included into the regression analysis, the effect of experience on positive word-of-mouth communication decreases from 66% to 43% but it has still significantly affected the positive word-of-mouth communication.

Table 6.   Test Results of Mediation Effect.

Mediation Model (Baron & Kenny, 1986; Hayes Process 3.2)					
Direct Effects	Standardised Coefficients	SE	*t*	*P*	Model R^2
Satisfaction (dependent variable)					
Constant	0.4996	0.1167	4.2830	0.000	
Experience (independent variable)	0.7641	0.0378	22.8168	0.000	0.5839
Positive word of mouth (dependent variable)					
Constant	1.1983	0.1239	9.6706	0.000	
Experience (independent variable)	0.4339	0.0607	7.3861	0.000	
Satisfaction (mediator variable)	0.2932	0.0538	4.9911	0.000	0.4687
Positive word of mouth (dependent variable)					
Constant	1.3325	0.1248	10.6779	0.000	
Experience (independent variable)	0.6580	0.0404	16.8288	0.000	0.4329
Total effect	0.6580	0.0404	16.8288	0.000	
Direct effect	0.4339	0.0607	7.3861	0.000	
Indirect effect	Effect	BootStandard	BootLLCI	BootULCI	
	0.2204	Error 0.0542	0.1163	0.3308	

If the effect of independent variable on dependent variable decreases and also becomes insignificant when the mediating variable is included into the relationship, it is possible to mention about full mediating relationship. However, while the total effect is 0.66, the direct effect decreases to 0.43 when the mediating variable satisfaction was included into the model. In this context, according to analysis, the partial mediating role of satisfaction was observed in the model. Additionally, since the range between BootLLCI and BootULCI did not include zero value, the role of mediating variable was accepted as statistically significant. The model of the study is given in Fig. 2. The results of the hypotheses are presented in Table 7.

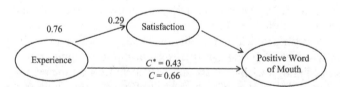

Fig. 2.   The Model of the Study. *Notes*: C^* = Direct Effect (The Effect Occurred, When the Mediator Variable Was Controlled); C = Total Effect (The Relationship between Independent and Dependent Variable without Mediator Variable); Indirect Effect: 0.2204**CI [0.1163, 0.3308].

Table 7. Results of the Hypotheses.

Hypotheses	Standardised Coefficients	t-Value	p-value	Hypothesis Condition
H_1. Experience → Satisfaction	0.76	22.8268	0.000	Accepted
H_2. Satisfaction → PWOM	0.29	4.911	0.000	Accepted
H_3. Experience → PWOM	0.66	16.8828	0.000	Accepted
H_4. Experience → Satisfaction → PWOM	0.43	7.3861	0.000	Accepted

4. CONCLUSIONS

4.1. Theoretical Implications

Today, countries and cities are increasingly becoming a brand. Initiated from this fact, brand experience, brand satisfaction and positive word-of-mouth behaviour occurred towards a brand can also occur towards cities within the context of city marketing. This study attempts to examine whether experiencing a city in a sensual, affective, behavioural and intellectual way just like experiencing a brand can influence satisfaction and positive word-of-mouth behaviour of visitors towards the city. The findings of the study indicate that experiencing Afyonkarahisar significantly and positively influence the satisfaction towards the city. Additionally, it was found that experiencing Afyonkarahisar also significantly and positively influences the positive word-of-mouth communication about Afyonkarahisar. When the satisfaction effect on positive word of mouth was examined, it was detected that satisfaction towards Afyonkarahisar effects the positive word-of-mouth communication regarding the city significantly and positively. In this context, whether satisfaction towards the city has a mediator role between the experience and positive word-of-mouth communication was checked. As a result, it was observed that satisfaction towards Afyonkarahisar has a mediating role between the relationship between experiencing the city and positive word-of-mouth behaviour of the visitors. Here, it can be readily concluded that not only creating experience for a visitor but also creating a satisfied visitor is required to create positive word-of-mouth behaviour which is essential to make the city as an attraction centre.

4.2. Practical Implications

If a city attracts the attention of visitors, this case provides several benefits to the city. For instance, local economy can be strengthened; infrastructure of the city can be developed; financial sources can be created for local governments; population can increase; and craftsman, little artisan and businessmen of the city can increase their networks to sell more products in different markets. For that reason, particularly local administrations have started to benefit from marketing knowledge to promote their cities and attract the attention of new visitors.

In order to perform the marketing activities in a more conscious and systematic way, local administrations have increasingly collaborated with the universities in their cities. In this respect, it is expected that the findings of the study will guide the strategies of local governments that want to promote their cities. The results of the study emphasised the importance of increasing sensory, affective, behavioural and intellectual experiences regarding a city to create satisfied visitors and to increase positive word-of-mouth communication regarding the city which can considerably influence the number of visitors. Besides experience, whether the visitors leave the city in a satisfied way, influences their positive word-of-mouth communication behaviour regarding the city. These findings highlight that local administrations should understand what the visitors expect from the city; they should know what they experience in the city and they should measure whether experiencing a city leads to satisfaction or not because happy visitors are one of the best communication and promotion tools of the cities.

REFERENCES

Aksoylu, S. (2013). The effects of the city marketing and branding activities on tourism: The case of Eskişehir. *Idealkent, 4*(8), 150–169.
Alexandrov, A., Lilly, B., & Babakus, E. (2013). The effects of social-and self-motives on the intentions to share positive and negative word of mouth. *Journal of the Academy of Marketing Science, 41*(5), 531–546.
Altunbaş, H. (2007). Marketing Communication and City Marketing: "Branding of Cities". *Selçuk İletişim, 4*(4), 156–162.
Anderson, J., & Gerbing, D. (1988). Structural equation modelling in practice: A review and recommended two-step approach. *Psychological Bulletin, 103*(3), 411–423.
Asworth, G. J., & Voogd, H. (1990). *Selling the city: Marketing approaches in public sector urban planning*. London: UK: Belhaven Press.
Bagozzi, R., Yi, Y., & Philips, L. (1991). Assessing construct validity in organisational research. *Administrative Science Quarterly, 36*(3), 421–458.
Baron, R., & Kenny, D. (1986). The moderator-mediator variable distinction in social psychological research: Conceptual, strategic, and statistical considerations. *Journal of Personality and Social Psychology, 51*(6), 1173–1182.
Baumgartner, H., & Homburg, C. (1996). Applications of structural equation modeling in marketing and consumer research: A review. *International Journal of Research in Marketing, 13*(2), 139–161.
Bentler, P. M. (1980). Multivariate analysis with latent variables: Causal modeling. *Annual Review of Psychology, 31*, 419–456.
Bentler, P. M., & Bonett, D. G. (1980). Significance tests and goodness of fit in the analysis of covariance structures. *Psychological Bulletin, 88*, 588–606.
Brakus, J. J., Schmitt, B. H., & Zarantonello, L. (2009). Brand experience: What is it? How is it measured? Does it affect loyalty? *Journal of Marketing, 73*(3), 52–68.
Braun, E. E. (2008). *City marketing: Towards an integrated approach*. ERIM Ph.D. Series Research in Management. Erasmus Research Institute of Management.
Browne, M. W., & Cudeck, R. (1993). Alternative ways of assessing model fit. In K. A. Bollen & J. S. Long (Eds.), *Testing structural equation models* (pp. 136–162). Beverly Hills, CA: Sage.
Chau, P. (1997). Re-examining a model for evaluating information centre success using a structural equation modelling approach. *Decision Science, 28*(2), 309–334.
Chinomona, R. (2013). The influence of brand experience on brand satisfaction, trust and attachment in South Africa. *International Business & Economics Research Journal (IBER), 12*(10), 1303–1316.
Costa-Font, M., & Gil, J. M. (2009). Structural equation modelling of consumer acceptance of genetically modified (GM) food in the Mediterranean Europe: A cross country study. *Food Quality and Preference, 20*(6), 399–409.
De Matos, C. A., & Rossi, C .A. V. (2008). Word-of-mouth communications in marketing: A meta-analytic review of the antecedents and moderators. *Journal of the Academy of Marketing Science, 36*(4), 578–596.

Deffner, A., & Liouris, C. (2005). City marketing – A significant planning tool for urban development in a globalised economy. In 45th Congress of the European Regional Science Association, August 23–27 (pp. 1–21).

Erdem, T., Swait, J., & Valenzuela, A. (2006). Brands As Signals: A Cross-Country Validation Study. *Journal of Marketing. 70*(1), 34–49.

Fornell, C., & Vlarcker, D. F. (1981). Evaluating structural equation models with unobservable variables and measurement error. *Journal of Marketing Research, 18*(1), 39–50.

Golob, T. F. (2003). Structural equation modeling for travel behavior research. *Transportation Research Part B, 37*, 1–25.

Hair, J. F., Anderson, R. E., Tatham, R. L., & Black, W. C. (1998). *Multivariate data analysis.* Englewood Cliffs, NJ: Prentice Hall.

Hair, J. F., Black, W., Babin, B., & Anderson, R. (2013). *Multivariate data analysis* (Pearson New International Edition). New York, NY: Pearson Education Limited.

İlhan, M., & Çetin, B. (2014). Comparing the Analysis Results of the Structural Equation Models (SEM) Conducted Using LISREL and AMOS. *Journal of Measurement and Evaluation in Education and Psychology, 5*(2), 26–42.

Kavaratzis, M., & Ashwort, G. J. (2007). Partners in coffeeshops, canals and commerce: Marketing the city of Amsterdam. *Cities, 24*(1), 16–25.

Kline, R. B. (2011). *Principles and practice of structural equation modeling.* New York, NY: The Guilford Press.

Kotler, P., & Armstrong, G. (2010). *Principles of marketing.* New York, NY: Pearson Education.

Kotler, P., Asplund, C., Rein, I., & Heider, D. (1999). *Marketing places Europe: Attracting investments, industries, residents and visitors to European cities, communities, regions and nations.* London: Pearson Education.

Langer, R. (2000). Place images and place marketing. *Department of Intercultural Communication and Management, Copenhagen Business School*, 1–31.

Lee, H. J., & Kang, M. S. (2012). The effect of brand experience on brand relationship quality. *Academy of Marketing Studies Journal, 16*(1), 87–98.

Marsh, H. W., Hau, K. T., Artelt, C., Baumert, J., & Peschar, J. L. (2006). OECD's brief self-report measure of educational psychology's most useful affective constructs: Cross-cultural, psychometric comparisons across 25 countries. *International Journal of Testing, 6*(4), 311–360.

Maxham, J. G., III., & Netemeyer, R. G. (2002). A longitudinal study of complaining customers' evaluations of multiple service failures and recovery efforts. *Journal of Marketing, 66*(4), 57–71.

Nel, E., & Binns, T. (2002). Place marketing, tourism promotion, and community based local economic development in post-Apartheid South Africa: The case of still bay—The "bay of sleeping beauty". *Urban Affairs Review, 38*(2), 184–208.

Nunally, J. C. (1978). *Psychometric theory.* New York, NY: McGraw-Hill.

Podsakoff, P. M., Mackenzie, S. B., Lee, J. Y., & Podsakoff, N. P. (2003). Common method biases in behavioral research: A critical review of the literature and recommended remedies. *Journal of Applied Psychology, 88*(5), 879–903.

Podsakoff, P. M., & Organ, D. W. (1986). Self-reports in organizational research: Problems and prospects. *Journal of Management, 12*(4), 531–544.

Schermelleh-Engel, K., & Moosbrugger, H. (2003). Evaluating the fit of structural equation models: Tests of significance and descriptive goodness-of-fit measures. *Methods of Psychological Research Online, 8*(2), 23–74.

Sekaran, U. (2003). Research methods for business: A skill building approach (4th ed.). New York, NY: John Wiley.

Şencan, H. (2005). *The realiability and validity in social and behavioral measurement.* Ankara: Seçkin Yayınları.

Shamim, A., & Mohsin Butt, M. (2013). A critical model of brand experience consequences. *Asia Pacific Journal of Marketing and Logistics, 25*(1), 102–117.

Tabachnick, B. G., & Fidell, L. S. (2013). *Using multivariate statistics.* New York, NY: Pearson Education.

CHAPTER 8

THE CROWDSOURCING CONCEPT AS A NEW MEDIA APPLICATION

Sevil Bektaş Durmuş

ABSTRACT

Introduction – *In the twenty-first century, which is the age of communication and information, the time and space concepts have changed with new media technologies and changes have occurred in habits and ways of doing business using the Internet. In this respect, crowdsourcing concept comes first among the new applications with which internet users can share content. The crowdsourcing, which may be understood as 'mass-based work' or 'crowded resource', consists of a combination of 'crowd' and 'source', and refers to the use of a great number of human societies to do a common work. The crowdsourcing concept, used commonly as of the 2000s for different purposes, is included in the literature as a concept showing the power of crowds. It is a method in which communication and internet technologies are used with efficacy in the advertising and marketing fields.*

Purpose – *The objective of the present study is to determine the pros and cons of the crowdsourcing concept through new media applications in the form of critical evaluations by examining sample case studies that use the crowdsourcing concept, which is becoming widespread in Turkey and in the whole world in recent years.*

Methodology – *In this study, the 'Case (Sample Event) Study Analysis', which is one of the qualitative research methods and which is a methodological approach that includes examining how the crowdsourcing system works in-depth, will be used.*

Contemporary Issues in Business, Economics and Finance
Contemporary Studies in Economic and Financial Analysis, Volume 104, 123–134
Copyright © 2020 by Emerald Publishing Limited
All rights of reproduction in any form reserved
ISSN: 1569-3759/doi:10.1108/S1569-375920200000104008

Findings – *Crowdsourcing is becoming a worldwide business model and allows anyone with free time and an internet connection to contribute to economic productivity. This study has discussed the importance of crowdsourcing for companies in contextual terms and has made predictions on how to make this concept become a better model in which fields.*

Keywords: New media; crowdsourcing concept; the power of crowds; mass-based work; crowdsourcing applications; new communication technologies; crowdcollaboration

1. INTRODUCTION

With the help of the new communication technologies, firstly, information sharing became common, and over time, Web 2.0 applications created a virtual environment in which people can express their feelings and thoughts freely based on sharing and discussion; and users thus became active content producers.

The Internet and associated technologies, which are considered as the inventions of the twenty-first century, changed communication processes. The fact that information and communication technologies (ICT) develop at a fast pace makes changes in social life inevitable. The utopian viewpoints, which argue that these changes are for the benefit of societies and the whole world, claim that the society that will emerge after industrial society will be based on knowledge. According to them, this society will emerge following evolution in information and will be called 'Information Society', or as defined by Alvin Toffler, 'Third Wave Civilization' (Sabuncuoğlu & Vural, 2008).

New web technologies, which have enabled time and space-free communication and the interaction characteristics of new media by acquiring functionality in social networks, gave birth to new ways of doing business not only for users but also for companies. In the information society where new communication technologies are the defining factors, virtual environments in which sharing and interaction are possible emerged. These virtual environments, which are called 'social media', provide individuals with opportunities in doing business as well as socialisation. One of these new internet-based business models is the crowdsourcing application.

Crowdsourcing, which is translated into Turkish as 'a mass-sourced study', appeared before us as an online, diffused problem-solving and production model in recent years. Crowdsourcing allows masses to form common values and to create content that is presented to the audience by the audience themselves. In the first part of this study, the new communication technologies and new media concepts will be dealt with, and their characteristics will be discussed. In the second part, the crowdsourcing will be explained as a new concept that has become common in the whole world, and that has come to the agenda in recent years; and in the last part, the crowdsourcing model will be evaluated in terms of sample events.

2. INTERNET TECHNOLOGIES AND NEW MEDIA

In our present day, communication technologies are developing at a fast pace, and the most important invention indicating the new phenomenon is, undoubtedly, the Internet. The basis of the new media is the Internet and Internet technologies. The Internet concept is at the very heart of the reflection of the technological developments on the media, which is called as the transition from the analogue media to the new media. The birth of the Internet dates back to the Cold War period. After the Soviet Union sent the satellite, Sputnik, to space in 1957, the US Government sought ways to protect military communications, especially in case of nuclear war. The system, which was developed for military research in the United States, was opened for the use of civil society by having the name 'the Internet' in the 1990s (Geray, 2003). With a general definition, the Internet is defined as a world-wide and constantly growing network in which many computer systems are interconnected in the whole world (Sayımer, 2008).

The Internet, which, according to some people in the literature, is defined as the 'International Network', and to some, 'Internetwork', or 'inter-network communication network', is a system, which has transformed millions of people into an interactive system, and the world into a global community or a global village (Gençer, 2015). With the help of the Internet and Internet technologies, people become socialised, have easy access to information and sources, and maybe informed about the developments in the world immediately. The 'global village' concept that was used by Mc Luhan, in which technology is the defining power, shows that the Internet is the most important means of communication in this information age.

The Internet is expressed by the development of web technologies. The Web is an interconnected system providing access to hypertext documents on the Internet. This network system, which is called 'WWW' (i.e. World Wide Web), is also called 'Web 1.0' because it is the first stage of the Web.

In the Web 1.0 period, the communication tool of the user was through e-mail and provided a stereo-typed web design. In time, the Web 2.0 technology to which a large number of users contributed was introduced by Darcy DiNucci with the development of technology. This new term, that is, the Web 2.0, is the expression showing the evolution of the Internet hosting the interaction characteristics that forms the basis of the new media with Web 2.0 technology.

As seen in Fig. 1, every new development in Internet technologies has added new virtual spheres to our lives. It has become possible to feel the technological developments in many fields from journalism to marketing with the social media and user-oriented networks that were made possible with Web 2.0 technologies. Social media is a group of Internet-based applications that are established on the ideological and technological bases of Web 2.0 allowing the creation and modification by the user. The social media concept, which is the result of Web 2.0 technologies and user-based content formation, is a structure providing the opportunity to create and share content (Pelenk & Sert, 2015, p. 99). Social networks and online communities entered our daily lives with the social media concept and social networking sites in the 2000s. In general, the foundations of social media were established with the opening of the 'world wide web' to the public.

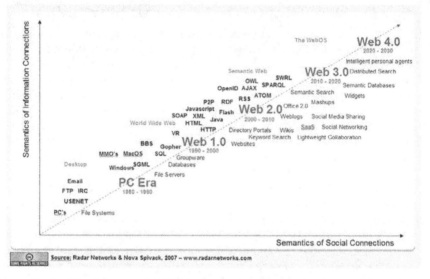

Fig. 1.   Development of the Web. *Source*: http://novaspivack.typepad.com/
RadarNetworksTowardsAWebOS.jpg.

The sixdegrees.com, which was the first-known social network, was faced by users
in 1998, and new popular networks offering bidirectional communication with
Web 2.0 technology emerged in 2004.

Web-based social networks are online communities in which participants can
establish relations and share sources with other users on the web. Social network
sites, with the simplest sense, are areas that allow users to establish online profiles or personal web pages and develop online social networks. Social network
sites allow people to form virtual media and serve the mass phenomenon. Firstly,
social networks unite people and create a virtual medium. Although not as it is
the case in the traditional sense, social networking sites also offer a different market medium and a new marketing communication channel (Akar, 2010). Today,
there are many examples showing that companies that are active in social network
sites in online communities have achieved success. For this reason, applications
that are specific to crowdsourcing, which make use of the power of masses and
which was made possible with the internet technologies, are becoming common.

The emergence of the 'new' media concept, which established the basis for the
traditional media being called the 'old' media, dates back to 1970s, when we first
met digital technologies. Although the new media dated back to the emergence
of digital technologies in the 1970s, it was shaped with the development of web
technologies, and therefore, with the development of digital technologies. In this
context, Binark (2014) defined new media as 'the computers, the Internet, mobile
phones, game consoles, iPod or palm database recorders and communicators'; in
other words, all these digital technologies are becoming increasingly a part of the
body because of a number of requirements of social life.

Because of the unpreventable nature of the Internet, newspapers, radios, and other traditional media moved to the Internet in the post-1990 period, and in this way, new communication tools which were called 'the new media' emerged (Asanova, 2018).

There are many definitions in the literature about the new media. In this context, Lievrouw considered the new media as the combination of material works of human communication processes, human practices, and social arrangements, and expressed the new communication technologies by schematising their difference from other media forms (Fig. 2).

With this scheme, Lievrouw stated that the new media is differentiated from the other media in four ways. The new communication technologies are continuously recombining and are dynamically network based in terms of their designs and usage. When considered in terms of social consequences, today, people use the new media extensively everywhere and in an interactive manner As the power of communication and interaction increases, so does the speed of distribution of technology, and in this context, it is emphasised that social media has the rate and nature that is specific to it. For example, although it took 38 years for the radio to reach 50 million users on a worldwide scale, it took 13 years for the television. Twitter alone reached a number of 50 million users within nine months (Kara, 2003). When the number of media channels reaching users is considered, it is seen that the most important distinction between the new media and the traditional one is the access and speed.

Lister (2010), with his approach that overlapped with the 'network community' concept, explained the combining term of 'the new media' by referring to various changes in media production, distribution, and usage. These changes are technological, textual, traditional, and cultural characteristics. As of the mid-1980s, a number of concepts defining the basic characteristics of the new media field have been described as a whole, which are the fixtures of the new media as the digital, interactive, hypertextual, virtual, and network-based characteristics (Yengin, 2015) (Fig. 3).

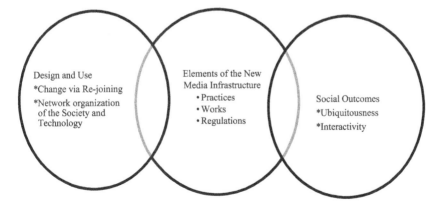

Fig. 2. Definition of the New Media. *Source*: Lievrouw (2016).

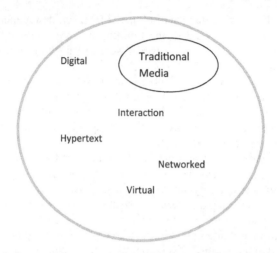

Fig. 3.   New Media Set. *Source*: Yengin (2014, p. 140).

With the simplest form, the new media set hosts the traditional one and is considered as the complementary element for each other. The characteristics of making the new media are digital, interaction, hypertext, network-based, and virtual elements. The most important point that must be considered here is the position of the traditional media in the set. The traditional media is included in the new media set and is distinguished only with other new media features in this set. This set shows that communication technologies are developing and continuing by including the old one (Yengin, 2015).

Despite the structure of the new media, which provides instant, fast, and simultaneous access to the information enabling interaction, there are also several opinions against the new media in the literature. The most striking criticism about the new media is that there is an inequality in terms of access to the Internet because of the fact that not everyone has the same speed and proportion in this respect. According to Kellner (2004), another criticism is the insecurity of the Internet-based new media-channel information. In this context, it is argued that the debates that are shared on the Internet are not based on the thinking process (Tekvar, 2016, p. 65).

In this respect, there is a new structure, which not only allows its users to access information but also to generate the contents on their own. User-based contents, which enable the formation of this new structure, are also defined as the contents of the Internet medium that are produced by the end-users. User-based contents allow people to access the information, which is not possible to find elsewhere. Since the language of these contents is similar to that of someone who is not professional and looks like themselves, people feel sincerer and more trustworthy. Right at this point, marketers learn and apply this new language (İşlek, 2002). In this respect, the crowdsourcing concept, in which the content production is carried out jointly with the users, will be discussed in the scope of the new media application.

3. THE CROWDSOURCING CONCEPT AS A NEW MEDIA APPLICATION AND ITS CHARACTERISTICS

The new media technologies, which influence the lives of everyone from producers to consumers, and which is called the 'alternative media', open new user-oriented concepts for discussion with each passing day. The crowdsourcing concept is the most prominent one among these new applications, which brought great success all over the world.

In actual fact, the emergence of community resources moves parallel to the human network. By 2005, it was seen that the number of young people who produced contents on the Internet was higher than the number of those who consumed (read/used) contents on the Internet, which meant that a new technology was created to share the contents produced and to keep people informed about these contents, and it really happened. The splendid emergence of the technologies that are called social networks or social media today overlapped with this period. As a matter of fact, the technology that was needed for this, and the examples that were not much different from the social networks that were famous in those years existed very long ago; however, the time for it had not yet come and was waiting for its turn. While this transformation was experienced in the social lives of individuals, it also influenced the way of doing business and business models (Seker, 2015, http://ybsansiklopedi.com/).

In our present day, people have started to do many practices online and have become both the content producer and the target mass of this content with applications like crowdsourcing, etc. The crowdsourcing is often used in marketing and advertising fields as well as in citizen journalism, which is a collective practice today (Yengin, 2015, p. 91).

The word 'crowdsourcing' is derived from the English word 'crowd' and 'source'. When it is translated into Turkish, it is translated as 'mass source' or 'crowded source'. The crowdsourcing concept was firstly used by Jeff Howe and Mark Robinson in 2016 and was defined as the business model, which employs creative solutions of a disorganised individual network as a result of a new, web-based, and open call for proposals (Daren C. Brabham, 2008).

Although it became widespread with the discovery of the Internet, the first crowdsourcing/mass source example was the 'Longitude Award' of the British Government in 1714 in exchange for designing a product that would determine longitude for ships (Gupta & Sharma, 2013, pp. 14–20).

Crowdsourcing means the crowds that have replaced the traditional workforce, which has accomplished the work that was once accomplished by professionals. This model, which is becoming more and more widely adopted all over the world, allows anyone who has a little free time, a desire to learn, and an Internet connection to contribute to economic productivity.

The common point of the definitions about crowdsourcing is the inclusion of a 'crowd' or a 'group' for a common purpose, like innovation, problem-solving, or efficiency. Since the crowdsourcing application is supported by new technologies, social media and Web 2.0, it may be carried out in many industries (crowdsourcingweek.com, 2019).

Howe (2008), who was among those who first used the crowdsourcing concept, which is defined as a mass source work, foresaw the following definition for this term:

If we are to define it simply, crowdsourcing means that a company or organisation takes a function, which was once carried out by its employees formerly, and outsources it with an open call (usually quite large) from among a network of people. This participation may be in the form of open production (if the business is carried out with cooperation). However, the main point is that this is an open call format, and consists of many potential employees.

Although there is no comprehensive implementation framework as crowdsourcing is relatively a new concept, it is possible to examine the processes that are involved in mass-sourcing applications by dividing them into four main areas, which are (Ghezzi et al., 2017):

1. The mass-based meeting management that covers the operations that are carried out by the intermediary that is called 'Meeting Management'.
2. The human management carried out to attract and motivate individual participants, including the strategies that are adopted by meeting managers.
3. Knowledge management, which is about how to organise and how to establish communities.
4. The technologies intended for mass-source use that are mostly used by ICT and software tools that are used to manage mass-sourced operations.

Crowdsourcing works are carried out in the form of activities which aim to find solutions with the masses to support a subject or a project, which is a collective practice, the masses providing funds to support a project, or in the form of asking for opinions from the masses during a product research stage. For this reason, an emotional bond is created between the brand and the target audience by involving the masses in business processes. Brabham divided the mass source models that were realised by masses into four groups (Table 1).

Table 1. Crowdsourcing Models.

Type	Process	Types of Problems
Discovery and management of knowledge	Revealing and compiling information in order to bring it for a common use in the organisation	Problems collecting, editing, and reporting information
Publication research approach	Solution of empirical problems	Experimentally provable problems such as scientific problems
Creative production approach by users	Creation of creative ideas by the crowd and choosing among them	Topics such as product design and aesthetics
Utilising distributed human intelligence	Analysing large amounts of information	Cases that human intelligence is more effective than computer applications

Source: Brabham (2011, p. 6).

Crowdsourcing, which makes use of the power of the masses, has three basic descriptive elements. According to Saxton, these are crowd, outsourcing, and social web. The use of crowdsourcing, on the other hand, is defined as the intersection point of these three elements (as seen in Fig. 4). Right at this point, there is a need for an interface provider for mass source use (Altunışık, 2017).

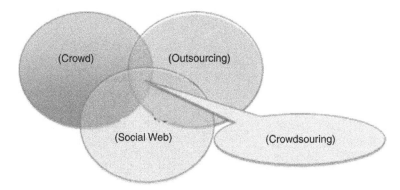

Fig. 4. Basic Elements of CS (Saxton et al., 2009). *Source*: Altunışık (2017).

It is possible to argue that there are two basic reasons for using the crowd-sourcing model. The first one is enabling the potential customer to produce his/her own products in production activities by making use of the power of the crowds; the second one is that these communities contribute to the sales of these products produced by themselves. For this reason, today, many companies use crowdsourcing as an Internet-based application model.

4. CROWDSOURCING WORKING SAMPLES

Crowdsourcing is an application that makes itself more preferable for companies in terms of its providing a voluntary workforce with zero costs. In our present day, it is observed that companies, which provide this voluntary community, have achieved sustainable success and reputation. The best method for the purpose of understanding how crowdsourcing works is to look at the most successful examples, which have been carried out in some industries. The first one of these examples is the 'Threadless.com' Company, which is a web-based T-shirt company sustaining its design process in mass-sourced fashion for T-shirts with an ongoing online competition.

Threadless is an application where people have the right to vote on designs or submit designs after they sign up with a valid e-mail. Community members download one of the templates of Adobe Flash or Adobe Photoshop, follow the outlines for image quality and the number of colours, then reload their designs to Threadless, and then vote between one to five for the purpose of presenting their designs on the Threadless website with the option 'I would buy'. In this way, new designs are presented to the community. Then this process continues like this; the designs are kept subject to voting for two weeks; and the ones that receive the most votes are selected and printed by Threadless employees and submitted to the Threadless website at the end of these two weeks. Although they are custom-designed T-shirts, the prices are usually around $15 or $10 during peak sales. The only reason why this is so is the low design costs. Successful designers earn $1,500 in cash and Threadless T-shirts and gift certificates worth $500. In addition to these, Threadless also manages a street team (for promotional purposes) and rewards its members for directing people to their website for sales, or for presenting their photos taken while wearing their Threadless T-shirt .

Another application that uses crowdsourcing is the 'iStockphoto' website. The iStockphoto.com is a web-based, franchise-free selling archive photos, animations, and video clips. For the purpose of becoming a photographer in iStockphoto, you must fill in an online form, submit a certificate to prove your identity, and upload three photos, which will be reviewed and approved by iStockphoto employees. Independently from the contents of the photographs, under normal conditions, the applicants are accepted as photographers on the website if the photos are technically flawless. In this context, photographers can upload their photos under various keywords to the site to be stored. The customers who seek general archive photos to use on their websites, in brochures, or in business presentations, etc., start to buy the images they desire by purchasing credits ($1 each credit) . Some photographers, who visit the online community more often, and who undertake the duty of reviewing the database of the website and the works of the applicants can earn up to 40% over the works sold by signing a special privilege agreement with iStockphoto (Mack, 2006, p. 17). iStockphoto has led to the development of an active artist community maintaining its presence producing increasingly better products at no additional costs in addition to overcoming its competitors. Like Threadless, the online community of iStockphoto consists of amateurs as well as professionals working in this field and creates a new industry by depending on the power of the crowds.

Threadless and iStockphoto have tried mass-sourced working applications in other businesses, which work with classic global business models, which use mass-sourced work methods on a full-time basis as well as some other businesses that work on the classical global company models. Converse, which is a shoe brand, published commercials of its customers at ConverseGallery.com, and there are companies like JetBlue, Sony, and Chrysler that aim to reach technology-specialist consumers, who will virally distribute the 'user-generated contents' (i.e. advertising) on the Web (Bosman, 2006, pp. 13–16).

Crowdsourcing is not an easy duty, as creating and maintaining a community requires more difficult processes on the Internet. When the company applies correct 'recipes', and when it works in agreement with its community, the result will be a highly effective production form.

5. RESULT

The developments experienced in communication technologies affected business life, political life, and economic activities as well as daily routines. With the Internet, a new commercial understanding period began offering 7/24 communication in business life (Karahisar & Kuyucu, 2013, p. 13).

The innovations that were brought by the Internet created changes not only in the communicational field but also in many other fields like science, entertainment, commerce, education, marketing, etc. These changes gave birth to new concepts that are specific to the new media. Crowdsourcing, which is one of these new applications, has been used widely in the marketing field as it is seen in the examples, and it is also used in applications like citizen journalism and blog journalism, which reflect the changing journalism concept.

Wikipedia is given as an example as another popular mass resource application, which may be considered as a crowdsourcing application. The establishing powers behind this online encyclopaedia that may generally be edited by the public decided that they would use the resources, passion, and time of their audience to create content instead of developing the contents of a whole website. As a result, Wikipedia became one of the most comprehensive encyclopaedia sources on a global scale. For this reason, Wikipedia became one of the most important examples of mass source work.

Threadless and iStockphoto, which are included in this study as new mass-sourced applications, provide a viewpoint of a problem-solving model, which may be applied to several industries that may resolve daily and highly complex tasks. The Crowdsourcing working model is used not only as a fashion word that is derived from Web 2.0 but also as a problem-solving method that is different from the traditional ways of doing business.

In our present day, the crowdsourcing model, which is preferred by companies, has advantages as well as disadvantages that are related to its application. One of these disadvantages is related to the faces that do not exist in the mass. Today, there are countries with no or limited internet access. Critics say that only the masses having internet access being included in a business model do not fully reflect the target audience.

According to Wiggins and Crowston (2011), another critique about the concept is that although crowdsourcing is defined as open participation of the masses in the production process, it is a 'sick' concept. Because it is not clear who the masses are in crowdsourcing. This unclear identity makes the implementation of the process also debatable. This situation brings with it the problems of transparency and reliability for the companies cooperating with the masses (Yeğen, 2015).

The magical world of the twenty-first century 'new' has caused changes not only in the media but also in the habits of ways of doing business. It may be argued that a connected world in which participation and access are considered at the forefront and people at the centre are waiting for us. In today's world, where speed and technology are defining elements, open innovation, mass use, crowdsourcing, and similar applications, which allow the masses to obtain mutual benefits, will play key roles in the success of companies. Today, crowdsourcing is an important application that brings success and contributes to the literature in that it shows the globalisation of the labour force, the economic value created by amateur class, and how crowds are converted into labour. In the new economic order, in which new communication technologies serve as the driving forces, the technical knowledge of professionals will be replaced by the creative ideas of amateurs.

REFERENCES

Akar, E. (2010). Social networking websites as a type of virtual communities: The functioning of it as a marketing communication channel. *Anadolu University, Social Sciences Journal*, *10*(1), 107–122.

Altunışık, R. (2017). Crowdsourcing (CS) as a data collection platform: A literature review over the case of Mechanical Turk and an evaluation. *International Management and Economy and Business Management Journal* (ICMEB17 Special Edition, pp. 975–982).

Asanova, A. (2018). The developmental process of the new media. In S. Gezgin (Ed.), *Communication in digital age* (pp. 187–194). Istanbul: Eğitim Publishing.

Binark, M. (2014). *Research methods and techniques in new media studies*. Istanbul: Ayrıntı Publishing.

Bosman, J. (2006). Chevy tries a Write-Your-Own-Ad approach, and the potshots fly, *New York Times* (4 April). http://www.nytimes.com.

Brabham, D. C. (2008). *Crowdsourcing as a model for problem solving*. Salt Lake City, UT: University of Utah.

Brabham, D. C. (2011). Crowdsourcing: a model for leveraging online communities. In T. Yazıcı (Trans.) "Crowdfunding" as the supporter of the amateur innovation: A review on "coincidence" site. *Global Media Journal TR Edition*, *9*(17) Fall. Retrieved from http://dbrabham.wordpress.com/sourcing

Crowdsourcing.week.com. (2019). What's crowdsourcing. Retrieved from https://crowdsourcingweek.com/what-is-crowdsourcing/. Accessed on July 10, 2019.

Gençer, Y. (2015). Organization in social media networking: Reflections of digital activism into social transformation. *E-Journal of Intermedia*, 505–522.

Geray, H. (2003). *New media policies in communication and technology, international compilation order*. Ankara: Utopya Publishing.

Ghezzi, A., Gabelloni, D., Martini, A., & Natalicchio, A. (2017). Crowdsourcing: A review and suggestions for future research. *International Journal of Management Reviews* , 1–57. DOI: 10.1111/ijmr.12135.

Gupta, D. K., & Sharma, V. (2013). In T. Yazıcı (Trans.). "Crowdfunding" as the supporter of the amateur innovation: A review on "coincidence" site. *Global Media Journal TR Edition*, *9*(17 Fall).

Howe, J. (2008). In G. Aksoy (Trans.), *How can crowdsourcing shape the future of a job?* Istanbul: Koç Sistem Publishing.

İşlek, M. (2012). *The effects of social media on consumer behaviors: A study on social media users in Turkey*. Post-Graduate Thesis Karamanoğlu Mehmetbey University, Karaman.

Kara, T. (2013). *Social media industry* (p. 49). Istanbul: Beta Publishing.

Karahisar, T., & Kuyucu, M. (2013). *New communication technologies and new media*. Istanbul: Zinde Publishing.

Lievrouw, L. A. (2016). In I. S. Temizalp (Trans.), *Alternative and Activist New Media* (pp. 24–25). Istanbul: Kafka Publishing.

Lister, (2010). In I. D. Yengin (Trans.) (2015, January). The opportunities of the new media: Semantic web. *The Turkish Online Journal of Design, Art and Communication – TOJDAC*, *5*(1). Retrieved from http://tojdac.org/ tojdac/VOLUME5-ISSUE1_files/tojdac_v05i104.pdf. Accessed on July 9, 2019.

Mack, S. (2006). Faces in the crowd: Interview series Part I. *Crowdsourcing: Tracking the rise of the amateur* (weblog, November 14). In D. C. Brabham (Trans.), *Crowdsourcing as a model for problem solving*. Salt Lake City, UT: University of Utah.

Pelenk, A., & Sert, N. (2015). *Digital public relations concept and tools*. Istanbul: Derin Publishing.

Sabuncuoğlu, A., & Vural, A. B. (2008). Information communication technologies and Utopian perspective. *Selçuk Communication Journal*, *5*(3), 5–19.

Sayımer, İ. (2008). *Public relations in virtual realm*. Istanbul: Beta Publishing.

Seker, S. E. (2015). Crowdsourcing, YBS encyclopedia, v.2, is.2 (pp. 1–5). Retrieved from http://ybsansiklopedi.com/. Accessed on July 11, 2019.

Tekvar, S. O. (2016). *New media new public relations*. Ankara: Karınca Publishing.

Yeğen, C. (2015). The "Crowdfunding" and "FonlaBeni" examples as a crowdsourced system developing with communication technologies. In E. Saka, A. Sayan, & V. Görgülü (Eds.), *New media works III* (pp. 87–112). Istanbul: Taşmektep Publishing.

Yengin, D. (2014). *New media and…* Istanbul: Anahtar Kitaplar Publishing.

Yengin, D. (2015, January). The opportunities of the new media: Semantic web. *The Turkish Online Journal of Design, Art and Communication – TOJDAC*, *5*(1). Retrieved from http://tojdac.org/ tojdac/VOLUME5-ISSUE1_files/tojdac_v05i104.pdf. Accessed on July 9, 2019.

CHAPTER 9

A FIELD STUDY OF THE EFFECT OF MOTIVATION FACTORS ON PERFORMANCE OF THE SALESPERSON

Umut Eroğlu and İbrahim Kiray

ABSTRACT

Introduction: – *Together with the increasing competition between businesses each day, the sales and marketing process of products and services have become increasingly difficult. For this reason, sales have become a marketing activity with an ever-growing importance to businesses. The performance of salespeople who undertake this challenge on behalf of the business is highly valuable for firms. Many researches have noted that there is a relationship between the performance of salesperson and motivation. The purpose of motivation in sales literature is to direct salespeople to exert more effort in reaching sales-oriented goals and aims. In order to ensure this, many businesses use various motivation tools/factors.*

Purpose – *The aim of this study is to analyse the effect of motivation factors on performance of salesperson.*

Methodology – *Quantitative research method was used in the study. A questionnaire was prepared with this aim in mind and administered to 315 employees working as salesperson in Çanakkale and Bursa provinces.*

Findings – *The findings from the analysis of the data show that the five dimensions namely satisfaction, image, relations, knowledge of product and service*

Contemporary Issues in Business, Economics and Finance
Contemporary Studies in Economic and Financial Analysis, Volume 104, 135–150
Copyright © 2020 by Emerald Publishing Limited
All rights of reproduction in any form reserved
ISSN: 1569-3759/doi:10.1108/S1569-375920200000104009

and advertisement related to motivation factors have a significant effect on the task performance of the salesperson.

Keywords: Sales; salesperson; motivation; motivation factors; task performance; contextual performance; knowledge of product and service; satisfaction

1. INTRODUCTION

In recent years, businesses have been striving to supply their products and services efficiently and effectively in order to have a competitive advantage in the mist of globalisation. Sales activities are among the main sources of income required for companies to maintain their activities and increase their productivity. However, the dimension of sales activities is continuously changing and becoming increasingly difficult due to the increase in the variety of the market and variance in customer demands and expectations as a result of the effect of global conditions. This change has made salespeople, who act as a bridge between the business and the customer, and are considered to have significant impacts on the market share of the business, the key employees of the business. Many businesses fail to offer or to effectively use motivation factors/tools to motivate their employees and ensure that they perform well. Sales literature indicates that motivation is an important determinant of the performance of salespersons (Badovick, Farrand, & Peter, 1993; Weitz, Sujan, & Sujan, 1986). The researches of Churchill, Ford, Steven, and Walker (1985) have put forth that motivation is an important determinant of the performance of salespersons. Brown and Peterson (1994) have offered empirical arguments regarding the positive impact of motivation on sales performance.

In this regard, the purpose of this study is to analyse the effect of motivation factors on the performance of salespersons. Looking at the research about motivation, this is mainly concerned with employee motivation while this study is original and important in that there is no research analysing the factors affecting the performance of salespersons. In this study, the literature is related to motivation factors and performance of salespersons that helps to explain motivation. Afterwards, the purpose, significance, method, population and limitations of the research, its model and hypotheses were explained, data obtained were analysed and findings were presented and interpreted. Finally, the results obtained in the research were revealed and suggestions were made for future studies.

2. THEORETICAL FRAMEWORK AND LITERATURE

In general terms, motivation is defined as taking action in order to fulfil a physiological or psychological deficiency (Luthans, 1992). In sales management, motivation refers to salespeople's desire and willingness to expend effort (Fu, 2015). It is highly important to know the factors affecting the performance of salespeople in order to be able to develop sales management activities and to increase the competitive advantage of the organisation (Roman & Rodríguez, 2015). In this context, a review of the main theories of motivation is particularly relevant in order to better understand the factors motivating the sales force (Ferreira, 2017).

2.1. Motivation Theories

The relevant theories about motivation in the literature are divided into two groups, namely 'Content' and 'Process' theories. The content theories prioritise intrinsic factors while process theories prioritise extrinsic factors (Önen & Kanayran, 2015). In other words, content theories focussed on satisfying the needs of employees while process theories put emphasis on the cognitive processes that take place within the minds of people and influence their behaviour (Jalagat, 2018). Process theories seek answers as to how an individual exhibiting a certain behaviour can be encouraged to perform or not repeat this behaviour again (Koçel, 2007). The advocates of content theories argue that individuals are satisfied only when some of their values and needs are fulfilled by organisations (Küçüközkan, 2015). In contrast to content theories, process theories look at the importance of personal differences in motivation (Eren, 2006).

2.2. Motivation Factors

The motivating factors are those that could motivate employees to improve on their work performance (Eshun & Duah, 2011). General motivation factors with different order of importance ascertained with various researches are grouped in three categories, namely economic factors, psycho-social factors and organisational/managerial factors (Şimşek, Çelik, & Akgemci, 2014; Tüz & Sabuncuoğlu, 2005). Motivation factors do not compete with each other, but they are mutually complementary (Robbins & Judge, 2012). Organisations can also utilise various tools in order to ensure motivation of salespeople. Main tools in the literature are sales promotion opportunities, sales competitions and sales meetings (Buciuniene & Skudiene, 2009; Çabuk, 2012).

2.3. Task Performance and Contextual Performance

The total business performance of an organisation is the sum of the individual performance of the employees. This performance can be said to have a multidimensional structure (Bağcı & Bursalı, 2015). In general, two different performance dimensions, namely task performance and contextual performance, are addressed in theories and practice (Borman & Motowidlo, 1997; Jawahar & Carr, 2007). Employees' doing their tasks means that they exhibit a good performance; however, they can display better performance when they enrich this performance with such attitudes as adaption to work environment and helping colleagues and complying with the rules of the organisation. For this reason, business performance is analysed as two different dimensions of performance (Aslan & Aytolan, 2017).

Task performance refers to the goods, services or ideas put forward for the accomplishment of the task and the achievement of the purpose in a way that meets the predetermined criteria within the task (Bağcı & Bursalı, 2015). According to another definition, task performance depicts job-related fixed duties and responsibilities that make a job differed from others (Jawahar & Carr, 2007). Such factors as clear and comprehensible job description, moral values, favourable working environment and professional competency are highly effective in achieving effective and high task performance.

Contextual performance is defined as the voluntary (cooperation and assistance with the employees of the organisation) attitudes excluded from the scope of task performance and not being part of the employee (Borman & Motowidlo, 1997). In a wider context, contextual performance denotes the works that enrich the organisational, the psychological and social atmosphere of the working environment in addition to the activities that fulfil the technical central function of the organisation (Ünlü & Yürür, 2011). Accordingly, it can be stated that task performance is related to fulfilling the determined tasks while contextual performance is about the voluntary behaviors that will yield benefit to the success of the organisation (Onay, 2011). Scotter and Motowidlo (1994) emphasise that supervisors take into account the contextual performance in overall performance evaluation and it is an important indicator denoting to what extent the employees get benefit in addition to task performance.

2.4. The Relation between Motivation and Performance of Salesperson

The relation between motivation and performance of salespersons was analysed by various researchers in the literature. Sales literature indicates that motivation is an important determinant of the performance of salespersons (Badovick et al., 1993; Weitz et al., 1986).

Research by Churchill et al. (1985) confirms the general inclination that motivation is an important determinant of the performance of salespersons. Brown and Peterson (1994) have offered empirical arguments regarding the positive impact of motivation on sales performance which is regarded as the salesperson's effort of doing her/his job. More specifically, Hultink and Atuahene-Gima (2000) have presented empirical evidence about the existence of a relation between sales performance of a new product and motivation.

Mallin and Ragland (2017) have conducted a research on the effect of the behaviours of sales managers (reward, coercive) on the motivation and performance of salespersons and the research findings indicate that sales managers can impact the performance of salesperson by using coercive and legitimate power. Fu (2015) has reached empirical findings on the fact that sales training may add value to improving sales performance and it provides positive contribution to the motivation of salespersons by enhancing organisational effectiveness. Ferreira (2017) has analysed the impact of motivational factors on sales teams. According to the findings of the research, it has been determined that the most effective intrinsic factors that best explain sales teams' motivation are personal goals and skills acquired, while extrinsic factors that best explain motivation in this context are trust in the company and transparency and loyalty in interactions with bosses. Talukder and Jan (2017) has presented that the factors of motivation are related to the performance of salespeople.

3. METHOD

3.1. Research Population and Data Collection

The research population is composed of the salespeople of the companies operating in the provinces of Çanakkale and Bursa. The sample group is composed of

315 salespeople working in Çanakkale and Bursa obtained through snowball and convenience sampling methods.

- It is assumed that the salespeople participating in the questionnaire give sincere and correct answers to the questions in the form.
- The research was conducted on salespeople and managers working in furniture, clothing, communication, cosmetics, food, technology, banking and pharmaceutical sectors in the provinces of Çanakkale and Bursa.

3.2. Scales Used in the Research

The questionnaire compiled from the literature was used as the data collection tool in the research (Appendix). The questionnaire form is composed of two parts.

Forty-nine items in the first part were compiled with the opinions of experts from the studies of Goodman and Daniel (1999), Jawahar and Carr (2007), Basir, Zamberi, and Kitchen (2010), William (2010), Şenol (2011), Miao and Evans (2013), Ünal (2016), Kilungu (2016), Talukder and Jan (2017).

A 5-point Likert scale was used for the items of the questionnaire and it denotes that 1: strongly disagree, 2: disagree, 3: neutral, 4: agree, 5: strongly agree.

There are 10 items in the second part of the questionnaire in order to determine the demographic characteristics of salespeople who participate in the questionnaire. These items are related to gender, marital status, age, educational background, duration of service in the profession, number of employees in the firm, number of salespeople in the firm, duration of service in the current job, the sector and position in the firm.

3.3. Research Model and Hypotheses

The research model is seen in Fig. 1. The hypotheses constructed among the variables related to the impact of motivation factors on the motivation and performance of salespeople are given in Fig. 1.

H_{1a}. Satisfaction of salesperson from the job has a positive impact on task performance.

H_{1b}. Satisfaction of salesperson from the job has a positive impact on contextual performance.

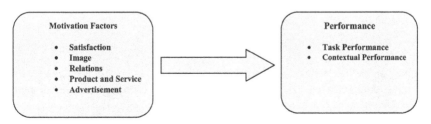

Fig 1. Research Model.

H_{2a}. The opinion of the salesperson about the image of the organisation has a positive impact on task performance.

H_{2b}. The opinion of the salesperson about the image of the organisation has a positive impact on contextual performance.

H_{3a}. The relationship of the salesperson with colleagues has a positive impact on task performance.

H_{3b}. The relationship of the salesperson with colleagues has a positive impact on contextual performance.

H_{4a}. The knowledge of the salesperson about the products and services s/he sells has a positive impact on task performance.

H_{4b}. The knowledge of the salesperson about the products and services s/he sells has a positive impact on contextual performance.

H_{5a}. The opinion of the salesperson about the advertisement activities of the organisation has a positive impact on task performance.

H_{5b}. The opinion of the salesperson about the advertisement activities of the organisation has a positive impact on contextual performance.

4. DATA ANALYSIS AND FINDINGS

In evaluating the findings obtained from the study, SPSS (Statistical Package for Social Sciences) for Windows 22.0 was used for statistical analyses. Factor analysis was applied by ascertaining seven dimensions for Likert-scaled questions. Factor analysis was performed for scales and the validity of the scale was revealed, Cronbach's alpha coefficient was calculated for the reliability of dimensions and general reliability. Correlation analysis was used to determine the relationships between scales and Regression analysis was used to test hypotheses.

This part of the research includes the findings obtained from the data analysis and the interpretations related to these findings. The results of factor analysis regarding the scales in the research and the reliability values indicating the consistency of the scales are given in the research. And then, the results of regression analysis performed to test hypotheses are given. Finally, Correlation coefficients among the variables are included.

4.1. Results of the Factor Analysis

Factor analysis is defined as multivariate statistics that aims to discover and find fewer significant new variables (dimensions/factors) by bringing together many interrelated variables (Büyüköztürk, 2002).

Factor analysis was used in the research in order to determine the dimensions of the scales related to the motivation factors and business performance.

According to the results of Factor analysis, 13 items were excluded from the scale. Kaiser–Meyer–Olkin (KMO) test was applied to determine whether the sample size was appropriate for factor analysis and the value about motivation factors was calculated as 0.926 (Table 1) while the value belonging to the performance scale was found as 0.850 (Table 2). These values mean that the sample size is appropriate and sufficient to perform a factor analysis (the value should be higher than 0.60). Since the Bartlett's test value, which determines whether there is a relation among the variables to perform a Factor analysis, is lower than 0.05, the fact that have a significant relation between the variables is observed in Sig. values in Tables 1 and 2.

4.2. Reliability Analyses

A reliability analysis was conducted to measure the reliability of data collected through the scale and Cronbach's alpha values were calculated. According to the alpha coefficient, the reliability level of a scale can be interpreted in line with the below ranges: (Kalaycı, 2010).

- If $0 <$ Alpha <0.40, the scale is not reliable.
- If $0.40 <$ Alpha <0.60, the reliability of the scale is low.
- If $0.60 <$ Alpha < 0.80, the scale is quite reliable.
- If $0.80 <$ Alpha < 1.00, the scale is highly reliable.

The questions in the survey were interrelated and divided into seven dimensions, each dimension was given a name:

1st Dimension: The satisfaction of the salesperson from the job.
2nd Dimension: The opinion of the salesperson about the image of the organisation.
3rd Dimension: The relationships of the salesperson with colleagues.
4th Dimension: The knowledge of the salesperson about the products and services s/he sells.
5th Dimension: The opinion of the salesperson about the advertisement activities of the organisation.
6th Dimension: Task performance.
7th Dimension: Contextual performance.

The alpha values obtained following the reliability analysis are indicated in Table 3.

According to the Table 3, the satisfaction of the salesperson from the job (0.926), the opinion of the salesperson about the image of the organisation (0.859) and the relationships of the salesperson with colleagues (0.814) among the motivation factors are highly reliable. Among the dimensions related to motivation factors, the opinion of the salesperson about the advertisement activities of the organisation (0.799) and the knowledge of the salesperson about the products and services s/he sells (0.687) are quite reliable. The general reliability coefficient

Table 1. Factor Analysis and Factor Loads Regarding Motivation Factors.

Items	Factor Loads
Dimension 1 Satisfaction	
23. Seniors pay attention to the learning and development process of their employees.	0.750
22. Employees are offered ways and opportunities for their career development.	0.746
24. Promotions and appointments are performed fairly.	0.745
21. Training opportunities are offered for the professional, personal and career development of employees.	0.700
25. Social activities (picnics, sport activities, trips, etc.) are organised for the development of relations between employees and increasing their morale and motivation.	0.689
12. Managers responsible for sales operations display positive attitudes and behaviours to employees.	0.666
11. The top management of the company attaches importance to the employees responsible for sales activities.	0.659
20. Achievements and the employees displaying high performance are appreciated and rewarded.	0.658
18. Wages and social benefits are at a level to compete with similar companies in the sector.	0.658
19. Employee performances are assessed in line with specific criteria and measurable targets.	0.586
26. Working hours and durations do not disrupt the work and life balance.	0.568
27. The company pays importance to occupational health and safety and takes the required measures.	0.513
Dimension 2 Image	
1. The company has a good image in the eyes of the society.	0.839
2. Sales potential of the products and/or services sold by the company is high.	0.732
3. This company is stronger than its competitors.	0.715
4. This company is a recommended place to work.	0.601
5. It is a company that fulfils its responsibilities towards society and the environment.	0.577
17. Satisfaction level of the company's customers is high.	0.471
Dimension 3 Relationships with Colleagues	
14. Colleagues work together in a harmonious and cooperative way.	0.851
15. Colleagues support each other's learning and development processes.	0.788
13. Effective and good relations exist among colleagues.	0.776
16. Relations between departments are good and support the sales activities.	0.543
Dimension 4 Products and Services	
9. I have knowledge about the production processes of the company's products or services.	0.816
8. I have knowledge about the features of the company's products or services.	0.642
10. Opportunities are provided for participation in the processes related to the development of the company's products and services.	0.489
Dimension 5 Advertisement	
7. Impressive promotions, banners, videos, web-based applications are available to communicate information about the products or services to customers.	0.648
6. The company places great importance on advertising activities and promotes effective advertising.	0.639
Total explained variance	64.952
KMO sample adequacy measure	0.926
Bartlett's test of sphericity Approx. Chi-square	5,144.879
Sig.	0.000

Table 2. Factor Analysis and Factor Loads Regarding Performance Scale.

Items	Factor Loads
Dimension 6 Task Performance	
29. I perform well in my work by doing my duties as expected.	0.858
30. I do my job with the fewest errors possible.	0.858
28. I successfully complete the sales targets for my job.	0.733
31. I always do my work, which must be completed on a given date, on time or before the time comes.	0.698
32. I reach the targets related to customer satisfaction, loyalty and engagement.	0.525
Dimension 7 Contextual Performance	
34. I defend my organisation when others outside the organisation criticise it.	0.830
35. I am proud of representing my organisation in the society.	0.810
33. I defend my organisation when other employees criticise it.	0.800
36. I encourage potential users to use my organisation's products and services.	0.797
Total explained variance	64.387
KMO Sample adequacy measure	0.850
Bartlett's test of sphericity Approx. Chi-square	1,294.409
Sig.	0.000

Table 3. Reliability Coefficients of the Scales.

	Cronbach's Alpha	Number of Questions
Dimension 1: The satisfaction of salesperson from the job	0.926	12
Dimension 2: The opinion of salesperson about the image of the organisation	0.859	6
Dimension 3: The relationships of salesperson with colleagues	0.814	4
Dimension 4: The knowledge of salesperson about the products and services s/he sells	0.687	3
Dimension 5: The opinion of salesperson about the advertisement activities of the organisation	0.799	2
General motivation factors	0.943	27
Dimension 6: Task performance	0.812	5
Dimension 7: Contextual performance	0.863	4
General performance	0.866	9

belonging to the scale of motivation factors (0.943) is highly reliable. Regarding performance scale, task performance (0.863) and contextual performance (0.863) are highly reliable. General reliability coefficient concerning the performance scale (0.866) is highly reliable.

4.3. Correlation Analysis Regarding the Variables

A correlation analysis was conducted to see the relations among the variables. The correlations belonging to the relations among the variables are indicated in Table 4.

Positive and statistically significant ($p < 0.01$) relations are observed among all variables (Table 4). Analysing the correlations among the variables used in the

Table 4.   Correlation Coefficients of the Variables.

Variables	1	2	3	4	5	6	7
1 Satisfaction	1						
2 Image	0.659**	1					
3 Relations	0.538**	0.470**	1				
4 Product and service	0.578**	0.518**	0.413**	1			
5 Advertisement	0.483**	0.563**	0.286**	0.375**	1		
6 Task performance	0.317	0.389	0.356	0.262	0.296	1	
7 Contextual performance	0.429	0.409	0.325	0.364	0.238	0.533	1

Note: **Correlation is significant at the 0.01 level (two-tailed).

research, it is observed that correlation coefficients are generally at low and moderate values. In particular, a high level of relation ($r = 0.659$) is observed between satisfaction and opinion about the image.

4.4. Test of Hypotheses and Regression Analyses

A regression analysis was performed to test the hypotheses in the research. The results of the regression analysis are observed in Table 5.

As a result of the analysis of the regression model created to show the effect of motivation factors on task performance, the model is observed to be statistically significant ($F = 15.255$; $p < 0.01$).

According to the results of the analysis (Table 5), satisfaction is observed not to have a significant impact on task performance ($\beta = -0.013$, $p > 0.05$). Image is seen to have a positive and significant effect on task performance ($\beta = 0.223$, $p < 0.05$). The relations with colleagues are observed to have a positively significant impact on task performance ($\beta = 0.024$, $p < 0.01$). It is seen that the knowledge of products and services does not have a significant effect on task performance ($\beta = 0.024$, $p > 0.05$). The opinion of the salesperson about the advertisement activities is seen not to have a significant effect on task performance ($\beta = 0.105$, $p > 0.05$).

Table 5.   Regression Analysis on the Relation between Motivation Factors and Task Performance.

Independent Variables	Standardised Coefficients	t	p
	Beta		
Satisfaction	−0.013	−0.163	0.870
Image	0.223	2.961	0.003
Relations with colleagues	0.218	3.530	0.000
Product and service	0.024	0.378	0.705
Advertisement	0.105	1.669	0.096

Notes: $F = 15.255$; R-square $= 0.189$; Sig. $= 0.00$.
Dependent Variable: Task Performance.

Table 6. Regression Analysis of the Relation between Motivation Factors and Contextual Performance.

Independent Variables	Standardised Coefficients	t	p
	Beta		
Satisfaction	0.201	2.663	0.008
Image	0.192	2.597	0.010
Relations with colleagues	0.085	1.406	0.161
Product and service	0.128	2.025	0.044
Advertisement	−0.039	−0.637	0.525

$F = 18.410$; R-square $= 0.230$; Sig. $= 0.00$.
Dependent Variable: Contextual Performance.

Accordingly, the variables of satisfaction, image, relations with colleagues, product and service and advertisement in the model explain 15% of the task performance. So, H_{2a} and H_{3a} hypotheses were supported. The hypotheses $H_{1a,}$ H_{4a} and H_{5a} were rejected.

As a result of the analysis of the regression model created to show the effect of motivation factors on contextual performance, the model is observed to be statistically significant ($F = 18.410$, $p < 0.01$).

According to the results of the analysis (Table 6), satisfaction is observed to have a positively significant effect on contextual performance ($\beta = 0.201$, $p < 0.01$). Accordingly, the higher the satisfaction, the higher the contextual performance level becomes. Image is seen to have a positive and significant effect on contextual performance ($\beta = 0.192$, $p < 0.05$). The relations with colleagues are observed not to have a significant impact on contextual performance ($\beta = 0.085$, $p > 0.05$). It is seen that the knowledge of products and services has a positively significant effect on contextual performance ($\beta = 0.128$, $p < 0.01$). The opinion of the salesperson about the advertisement activities is seen not to have a significant effect on contextual performance ($\beta = -0.039$, $p > 0.05$).

Accordingly, the variables of satisfaction, image, relations with colleagues, product and service and advertisement in the model explain 23% of the contextual performance. So, H_{1b}, H_{2b} and H_{4b} hypotheses were supported. The hypotheses H_{3b} and H_{5a} were rejected.

5. CONCLUSION

It is very important for salespeople to be motivated in order to be able to serve the purposes of the firm and reach the desired targets. It is highly valuable to know the motivation factors in sales literature and to be able to use them in favour of the firm in order to increase the motivation of salespersons.

For this reason, this study analyses the effect of motivation factors on the performance of salespersons. In this framework, a questionnaire study was conducted directed to the salespeople in the corporate firms in Çanakkale and Bursa provinces, by using a scale created following the literature review concerning motivation factors. Data obtained from the 315 salespeople who have participated in the research were analysed and answers were sought for the hypotheses which were created. After, the analysis results, factor analysis, reliability analysis, correlation coefficients between the variables and regression analyses were given.

From the analysis results, it is first observed that the dimensions of image and relations being among the dimensions related to motivation factors have a significant impact on the task performance of salespersons. Satisfaction, product and services and advertisement dimensions are observed not to have a significant effect on task performance. Accordingly, the position and value of the firm perceived by employees and the environment, good relationships of salespersons with colleagues, support given by each other during work processes help the salesperson to display good performance at work and build sustainable relations with customers.

Secondly, it is observed that satisfaction, image, product and service, being among the dimensions related to motivation factors, have a significant impact on contextual performance of salespersons. The dimensions of relations and advertisement are seen not to have a significant effect on contextual performance. Among the opportunities provided by the firm, satisfaction of salespersons, the firm's being respected by the environment and employees, firm's informing the salesperson about the manufacturing processes of the products and services and ensuring participation in these processes, this increases the contextual performance and promotes the loyalty of employees towards the institution they work for.

As a result of all these outcomes, firms and sales management should keep in mind these motivation factors if they expect the salespeople to reach better performance results under increased competition. A reasonable wage for salespeople, training, promotion and career opportunities in the firm, measurable goals of the enterprise, ensuring job security and social rights, giving importance to employees and showing a positive attitude, competitiveness of the firm with other firms, forming a ground for good friendship relations, providing information about products and services, providing training opportunities and valuing opinions will have a positive impact on the performance of salespeople and will benefit the company.

The motivation factors compiled from the literature were used in this study. The factors affecting the motivation of salespersons were discussed under five dimensions namely satisfaction, image, relations, product and service and advertisement. However, personal skills and personal traits of the salesperson can be among the factors affecting the motivation of the said salesperson. This study can be a guide for future studies and the dimensions can be addressed in a wider scope or discussed separately.

REFERENCES

Aslan, M., & Aytolan, Y. (2017). The Contextual Performance Scale for Nurses Who Work at Hospitals: Validity and Reliability. *Koç University Journal of Education and Research in Nursing, 14*(2), 104–111.

Badovick, G. J., Farrand, J. H., & Peter, F. K. (1993). Poor sales performers: Are they just poorly motivated? *Journal of Marketing Theory and Practice, 1*(3), 29–42.

Bağcı, Z., & Bursalı, Y. (2015). The Impact of Emotional Labor on Work Performance: An Empirical Research in Service Sector in Denizli. *Kafkas University Journal of the Faculty of Economics and Administrative Sciences, 6*(10), 69–90.

Basir, M. S., Zamberi, A., & Kitchen, P. J. (2010). The relationship between sales skills and salesperson performance: An empirical study in the Malaysia telecommunications company. *International Journal of Management and Marketing Research, 3*(1), 51–64.

Borman, W., & Motowidlo, S. (1997). Task performance and contextual performance: The meaning for personnel selection research. *Human Performance, 10*(2), 99–109.

Brown, S. P., & Peterson, R. (1994). The effect of effort on sales performance and job satisfaction. *The Journal of Marketing, 58*(2), 70–80.

Buciuniene, I., & Skudiene, V. (2009). Factors influencing salespeople motivation and relationship with the organization in B2b sector. *Engineering Economics, 64*(4), 79–80.

Büyüköztürk, Ş. (2002). Factor Analysis: Basic Concepts and Using To Development Scale. *Education Management in Theory and Practice, 32*(32), 470–483.

Çabuk, S. (2012). *Professional Sales Management*. Adana: Nobel Publishing.

Churchill, G. A., Ford, N., Steven, H., & Walker, O. (1985). The determinants of salesperson performance: A meta-analysis. *Journal of Marketing Research, 22*(2), 103–118.

Eren, E. (2006). *Organizational Behavior and Managerial Psychology* (9th ed.). İstanbul: Beta Publishing.

Eshun, C., & Duah, F. (2011). *Rewards as a motivation tool for employee performance.* Unpublished master dissertation, Blekinge Institute of Technology, School of Management, Blekinge.

Ferreira, T. S. (2017). Motivational factors in sales team management and their influence on individual performance. *Tourism & Management Studies, 13*(1), 60–65.

Fu, F. (2015). Motivate to improve salesforce performance: The sales training perspective. *Performance Improvement, 54*(4), 31–35.

Goodman, S. A., & Daniel J. S. (1999). Person–organization fit and contextual performance: Do shared values matter. *Journal of Vocational Behavior, 55*(2), 254–275.

Hultink, E. J., & Gima, K. A. (2000). The effect of sales force adoption on new product selling performance. *Journal of Product Innovation Management: An International Publication of the Product Development & Management Association, 17*(6), 435–450.

Jalagat, R., Jr. (2018). Job performance, job satisfaction, and motivation: A critical review of their relationship. *International Journal of Advances in Management and Economics, 5*(6), 36–43.

Jawahar, I. M., & Carr, D. (2007). Conscientiousness and contextual performance the compensatory effects of perceived organizational support and leader-member exchange. *Journal of Managerial Psychology, 22*(4), 330–349.

Kalaycı, Ş. (2010). *Spss Applied Multivariate Statistics Techniques*. Ankara: Asil Publishing.

Kilungu, K. M. (2016). *Salesforce motivation programs and performance of distributors of East African Breweries Limited in Mount Kenya region.* Unpublished master dissertation, University of Nairobi, Nairobi.

Koçel, T. (2007). *Business Management*. İstanbul: Arıkan Publishing.

Küçüközkan, Y. (2015). Leadership and Motivation Theories: Leadership and Motivation Theories: A theoretical Framework. *International Journal of Academic Management Sciences, 1*(2), 86–115.

Luthans, F. (1992). *Organizational behavior*. New York, NY: McGrawhill Inc.

Mallin, M., & Ragland, C. (2017). Power-base effects on salesperson motivation and performance: A contingency view. *Journal of Business-to-Business Marketing, 24*(2), 99–121.

Miao, C. F., & Evans, R. K. (2013). The interactive effects of sales control systems on salesperson performance: A job demands–resources perspective. *Journal of the Academy of Marketing Science, 41*(1), 73–90.

Onay, M. (2011). The Effect of Emotional Intelligence and Emotional Labor on Task Performance and Contextual Performance. *Ege Academic View*, *11*(4), 587–600.

Önen, M., & Kanayran, H. (2015). Leadership and Motivation: A Theoretical Evaluation. *Individual and Society Journal of Social Science*, *5*(10), 43–63.

Robbins, S. P., & Judge, T. (2012). In İ. Erdem (Ed. & Trans.), *Örgütsel Davranış*. İstanbul: Nobel Akademik Yayıncılık.

Roman, S., & Rodríguez, R. (2015). The influence of sales force technology use on outcome performance. *Journal of Business & Industrial Marketing*, *30*(6), 771–783.

Scotter, V. J., & Motowidlo, S. (1994). Evidence that task performance should be distinguished from contextual performance. *Journal of Applied Psychology*, *79*(4), 475–480.

Şenol, F. (2011). The effect of job security on the perception of external motivational tools: A study in hotel businesses. *Journal of Economic and Social Studies*, *1*(2), 33–60.

Şimşek, M. Ş., Çelik, A., & Akgemci, T. (2014). *Introduction to Behavioral Sciences and Behavior in Organizations*. Konya: Education Publishing.

Talukder, K. I., & Jan, M. T. (2017). Factors influencing sales peoples performance: A study of mobile service providers in Bangladesh. *Academy of Marketing Studies Journal*, *21*(2), 1–20.

Tüz, M., & Sabuncuoğlu, Z. (2005). *Organizational Psychology*. Bursa: Alfa Current Publishing.

Ünal, Ö. F. (2016). Employee Satisfaction In Service Sector: An Empirical Research On A Cargo Firm And Stationary Chain Stores Owned By A Grup Of Companies. *The International Journal Of Economic And Social Research*, *12*(1), 161–176.

Ünlü, O., & Yürür, S. (2011). The Relationship Among Emotional Labor, Emotional Exhaustion And Task/Contextual Performance: A Study With Service Industry Workers At Yalova. *Erciyes University Journal Of Faculty Of Economics And Administrative Sciences*, *37*, 183–207.

Weitz, B., Sujan, H., & Sujan, M. (1986). Knowledge, motivation, and adaptive behavior: A framework for improving selling effectiveness. *Journal of Marketing*, *50*(4), 174–191.

William, A. N. (2010). *Employee motivation and performance, business management*. Unpublished master dissertation, Mikkeli.

APPENDIX: QUESTIONNAIRE FORM

To Whom It May Concern,

The purpose of this research is to evaluate the motivation levels of the employees in sales teams, the factors affecting their motivation and the relations among the perceived performance levels. Your opinions shared will be kept confidential in line with the scientific ethics and they will be evaluated as a whole without disclosing the name of the company or person.

Thank you for your interest and contributions.

İbrahim KIRAY
Çanakkale Onsekiz Mart University
ibrahimkiray17@gmail.com

Asst. Prof. Umut EROĞLU
Çanakkale OnsekizMart University
umuteroglu@comu.edu.tr

Consider the status of your company and indicate to what extent you agree with the following statements.

1 = Strongly Disagree, 2 = Disagree, 3 = Neutral, 4 = Agree, 5 = Strongly Agree

1.	The company has a good image in the eyes of the society.	1	2	3	4	5
2.	Sales potential of the products and/or services sold by the company is high.	1	2	3	4	5
3.	This company is stronger than its competitors.	1	2	3	4	5
4.	This company is a recommended place to work.	1	2	3	4	5
5.	It is a company that fulfils its responsibilities towards society and the environment.	1	2	3	4	5
6.	The company places great importance on advertising activities and promotes effective advertising.	1	2	3	4	5
7.	Impressive promotions, banners, videos, web-based applications are available to communicate information about the products or services to customers.	1	2	3	4	5
8.	I have knowledge about the features of the company's products or services.	1	2	3	4	5
9.	I have knowledge about the production processes of the company's products or services.	1	2	3	4	5
10.	Opportunities are provided for participation in the processes related to the development of the company's products and services.	1	2	3	4	5
11.	The top management of the company attaches importance to the employees responsible for sales activities.	1	2	3	4	5
12.	Managers responsible for sales operations display positive attitudes and behaviours to employees.	1	2	3	4	5
13.	Effective and good relations exist among colleagues.	1	2	3	4	5
14.	Colleagues work together in a harmonious and cooperative way.	1	2	3	4	5
15.	Colleagues support each other's learning and development processes.	1	2	3	4	5
16.	Relations between departments are good and support the sales activities.	1	2	3	4	5
17.	Satisfaction level of the company's customers is high.	1	2	3	4	5
18.	Wages and social benefits are at a level to compete with similar companies in the sector.	1	2	3	4	5
19.	Employee performances are assessed in line with specific criteria and measurable targets.	1	2	3	4	5

1 = Strongly Disagree, 2 = Disagree, 3 = Neutral, 4 = Agree, 5 = Strongly Agree

20 Achievements and the employees displaying high performance are appreciated and rewarded.	1	2	3	4	5
21. Training opportunities are offered for the professional, personal and career development of employees.	1	2	3	4	5
22. Employees are offered ways and opportunities for their career development.	1	2	3	4	5
23. Seniors pay attention to the learning and development process of their employees.	1	2	3	4	5
24. Promotions and appointments are performed fairly.	1	2	3	4	5
25. Social activities (picnics, sport activities, trips, etc.) are organised for the development of relations between employees and increasing their morale and motivation.	1	2	3	4	5
26. Working hours and durations do not disrupt the work and life balance.	1	2	3	4	5
27. The company pays importance to occupational health and safety and takes the required measures.	1	2	3	4	5

When you evaluate your own work as a worker in your sector, please answer how it performs in the following subjects.

1 = Strongly Disagree, 2 = Disagree, 3 = Neutral, 4 = Agree, 5 = Strongly Agree

28. I successfully complete the sales targets for my job.	1	2	3	4	5
29. I perform well in my work by doing my duties as expected.	1	2	3	4	5
30. I do my job with the fewest errors possible.	1	2	3	4	5
31. I always do my work, which must be completed on a given date, on time or before the time comes.	1	2	3	4	5
32. I reach the targets related to customer satisfaction, loyalty and engagement.	1	2	3	4	5
33. I defend my organisation when other employees criticise it.	1	2	3	4	5
34. I defend my organisation when others outside the organisation criticise it.	1	2	3	4	5
35. I am proud of representing my organisation in the society.	1	2	3	4	5
36. I encourage potential users to use my organisation's products and services.	1	2	3	4	5

Gender	❐ Male		❐ Female	
Marital status	❐ Married		❐ Single	
Age	❐ 24 and below	❐ 25–40	❐ 41–52	❐ 53 and above
Education	❐ High school and below	❐ College	❐ Undergraduate	❐ Graduate
Duration of service in the profession	❐ 0–5 years	❐ 6–10 years	❐ 11–15 years	❐ 16 and more
Number of employees in the company	❐ 1–9	❐ 10–49	❐ 50–249	❐ 250 and more

Number of salespeople in the company   (Indicate):..........................

How long have you been working in your current job?   (Indicate): ....

Your sector   Your position in the company

(Indicate)..............................   (Indicate) ....

CHAPTER 10

JOB SEARCH: PREDICTORS OF JOB SEARCH BEHAVIOUR OF HUMAN RESOURCES MANAGERS

Seda Mumlu Karanfil

ABSTRACT

Introduction – *The most basic rule of job search is job search behaviour. Job search behaviour is defined as the effort of the individual, time spent on various activities in order to find a job. In the current competitive labour market – the modern employment environment, where many employees who may have a temporary employment status, where the use of outsourcing is common practice, or where there are those who are under-employed, there is great importance in adopting a robust job search behaviour for job seekers. However, employees may have other factors that affect their job search behaviour. In Trusty, Allen, and Fabian (2019), various motivational categories were put forward. These seven different categories range from wanting to avoid undesirable situations in the workplace to finding better job search methods.*

Purpose – *This article seeks to explain the data related to this research; it will focus on combining positive psychological capital with seven different sources of motivation, as categorised in Trusty et al. (2019).*

Methodology – *The method that will be used for this article will consist of a semi-structured interviews, which were used as a vehicle to gather qualitative research and for data collection. The interview questions were prepared using the seven different categories of motivation as detailed by Trusty et al. (2019) and related literature to determine the job search behaviour of the employees.*

Contemporary Issues in Business, Economics and Finance
Contemporary Studies in Economic and Financial Analysis, Volume 104, 151–164
ISSN: 1569-3759/doi:10.1108/S1569-375920200000104010

Findings – *The findings will also include input from managers of human resources department employees, where job search behaviour was found to be high, indications suggest problems caused within the working environment, includes poor working relationships with colleagues and supervisors. Also the inability to optimise the skills of individuals and limited career progression opportunities are examples that effect job search behaviour and attitudes to work.*

Keywords: Job search behaviour; human resources employees; positive psychological capital; career; interview method; talent

JEL classifications: E24; J24; J64; M10

1. INTRODUCTION

Job search is a process in which individuals who are looking for a job, or who want to find a job with better opportunities, look for employment opportunities. Job search behaviour includes the time, effort and the various activities that individuals undertake to find work, whether they are working or not, they are spending time finding suitable work. From an economic point of view, it is a three-stage process: researching job opportunities, deciding whether or not to apply for a job and accepting or rejecting an offer. To look for a job, people may behave differently and try different strategies to help their search.

Today, newly graduated individuals who do not have a job, and those currently employed may be in job search behaviour. The primary factor that causes this job search behaviour for unemployed individuals is to find a good work opportunity, for working individuals it is to find a better job with better work conditions, to find a job more suited to their skills or for career progression. Employees' job search behaviours constitute a cost element for businesses, for this reason, employers are engaged in assessing an employee's loyalty, motivation, job satisfaction and other important factors. Human resources personnel primarily perform the duties of making employees and business owners content with the working environment thereby fulfilling the human resources functions and objectives of the organisation.

This article aims to examine the happiness of human resources personnel performing their duties, while trying to assess employee job satisfaction, meeting the needs of employees, determining whether or not they are seeking other employment while working, and if so, the reasons for this underlying behaviour. In line with this goal, the first part includes the theoretical framework related to job search and job search behaviour for working and non-working individuals. In the second part, the methodology for the research is explained, analysis of the research is given and results of the research are presented.

2. BUSINESS SEARCH BEHAVIOUR

Job search is a process for individuals who do not have a job, or who want to find a job with better opportunities. This process uses a number of elements and it may take a varying period of time to find work. This could be dependent on various factors, such as available opportunities, the job seekers intent, new job requirements, etc. The goal of job seekers is to find a find suitable work. A person with or without a job may choose different paths and strategies to find gainful employment.

This process can be successfully completed by finding a job, or it can be ended by the job seeker without finding a job (Gökkaya, Latif, & Uçkun, 2015, p. 26). Stigler (1961) was the first person to introduce the job search theory to research literature. Stigler (1961) addressed this concept in his study "The Economics of Information" (Stigler, 1961, p. 213). Job search behaviour is the time, effort spent on various job search activities that a person devotes to looking for work. Professional people should have the ability to perform these activities (Van Hooft, Born, Taris, & Van Der Flier, 2005, p. 135).

Job search behaviour first attracted the attention of economists in the 1970s and became a research topic. From an economic point of view, it is a three-stage process: researching job opportunities, deciding whether or not to apply for a job, and accepting or rejecting an offer (Mcfadyen & Thomas, 1997, p. 1464). The economic point of view is concerned with criteria such as the cost of job search and possible application fees (Güler, 2012, p. 11). After the 1980s, the job search process, which was initially investigated by behavioural scientists, was also examined psychologically. Evaluating the psycho-social point of view and the motivational reasons that lead people to look for new job opportunities (Güler, 2012, p. 11). Job search activities and strategies in Turkey have increased with the establishment of human resources and personnel management since the 1990s. The importance of the employee selection process has also increased during this time period (Gökkaya et al., 2015, p. 27).

Job search behaviour has been defined in different ways by different researchers. According to Osberg (1993), a job search analogy is that a fisherman has appropriate fishing conditions and continues to fish until he catches a big fish. In other words, it is defined as a dynamic process in which individuals have the purpose of finding a job that meets their needs (Saks, 2004, p. 457; Sun, Song, & Lim, 2013, p. 771; Wanberg, Glomb, Song, & Sorenson 2005, p. 411). Saks (2005) in his study refers to the purpose of job search; he states that the individual finds that this job search behaviour ends when they find a suitable job.

In the period when the economic models related to job search developed, the understanding that not only the unemployed, but also the people in work, may adopt job search behaviour. Today, in cases where the employee cannot adapt to their job environment or maybe underemployed in a job below their education and experience, then these individuals may consider leaving their jobs if they find a better opportunity. In addition, an employee's perception of job security may cause them to quit a job (Güler, 2012, p. 12).

An employee's concern about employability may be due to their perceived job insecurity (Trusty, Allen, & Fabian, 2019). Job insecurity is defined as the threat perceived by the employee concerning the continuity of his/her job in the future. High perception of job insecurity causes employees to worry about losing their jobs. However, as a result of the high perception of job insecurity, the employee's job satisfaction, job welfare, intention to quit and organisational citizenship behaviour can be negatively affected. In addition there is organisational impact caused by the effects of job insecurity, it causes physical and psychological health problems in the employee. In the study conducted by Yücel, Demirel, and Yücel (2013), it was concluded that there is a negative relationship between job search behaviour and job satisfaction (Yücel et al., 2013, p. 167). A different study was conducted by Sverke, Hellgren, and Näswall (2002) and the perception of job insecurity, job satisfaction, work commitment, organisational commitment, organisational trust, performance, intention to quit and physical, mental health problems revealed that there are a number of significant sideeffects caused by job insecurity (Sverke et al., 2002, p. 245).

Loss of a job due to employee's perception of job insecurity or because of different reasons also causes problems in the economic sense while causing varying physical and mental health problems. The consequences of these problems may cause anxiety of being unemployed. Unemployment anxiety has negative effect on employee productivity (Erer, 2011, p. 48). Another situation that creates anxiety in the employee is the decrease in material and spiritual satisfaction that they would have gained if they had remained in employment. The decrease in the material and spiritual satisfaction of the employee from the job causes the individual to experience psychological problems. Psychological problems are stress, anxiety and aggressive behaviours (Aytaç & Keser, 2002, p. 2). As a result, employees may have varying sources of motivation and therefore job search motivations differ from one person to another.

However, if the job search behaviour is realised because of the fear of being unemployed and the perception of job insecurity, it causes the employee to experience further issues. An employee who is trying to find a different job will have low loyalty to his job, his organisational citizenship behaviour may be adversely affected and their intention to quit will increase; this may also impact on employee productivity and performance. For this reason, it is important for enterprises to find the reasons that force their employees to look for other employment opportunities and to develop procedures and policies that can maximise employee retention.

3. JOB SEARCH BEHAVIOUR FOR EMPLOYEES AND NON-EMPLOYEES

Individuals in different segments of the labour force will engage in different forms of job search behaviours. Job search behaviour includes the time, effort and the activities that individual undertake in order to find work. After completing their educational learning, the individual is unemployed, looking for appropriate employment or they may be working in a temporary position or in gainful employment. The individual who is seeking employment may use many different ways of searching for a job.

The common goal of people looking for work and those unemployed after completing their education is to find relevant employment opportunities

(Rogelberg, 2007, p. 414). Individuals showing job search behaviour compare themselves with other unemployed people. They work, and their circumstances maybe different to unemployed people, but they are looking for a job in a different manner than the unemployed people.

The employee may have different sources of motivation other than just finding work (Güler, 2012, p. 13). Employee dissatisfaction or a lack of company commitment to the employees may cause alienation and an impetus to leave their job. A study of 1,386 people in the United States in 2016 revealed that 74% of employees showed job search behaviour (Jobvite, 2016; Trusty et al., 2019, p. 28). Employees also exhibit job search behaviour through qualitative changes experienced in the workplace. In particular, outsourcing, the increase in the number of employees with a temporary status, decreasing levels of management engagement and changing economic conditions force employees to look for other employment opportunities proactively (Direnzo & Greenhaus, 2011, p. 567).

Employees continue their job search behaviour, whether actively or passively. The reasons for job search behaviour vary from individual to individual. Some are due to wages, working conditions, a lack of job security, the work environment, their relationship with their manager or other colleagues, difficulties in the management of the company, the presence of temporary employees, not seeing themselves as compatible with the job, etc.. Trusty et al. (2019) identified seven different sources of motivation that affect job search behaviour of employees based on past studies. These seven different categories are avoiding unwanted situations in the workplace, finding a better job in line with their talents and skills, discovering employability within the labour market, obtaining a higher salary, meeting the needs of oneself and one's family, career progression and being influenced by others (Trusty et al., 2019, p. 29). If these seven different sources of motivation are recognised by corporations and measures are taken to assess and improve employee satisfaction, then the rate of employee turnover will decrease.

4. PURPOSE AND IMPORTANCE OF RESEARCH

Human resource management deals with human relationships in a very wide range: identifying the needs of employees, preparing job announcements, advertising them, choosing the appropriate people for the organisation and adapting them to the culture of the organisation, evaluating the performance of the employees, motivating them, organising training and development, providing the communication within the organisation, creating communication within the organisation creating the organisational climate (Doğan, 2011, p. 13). Human resources personnel perform these functions in enterprises and corporations.

Human resources personnel primarily perform the duties of making employees and business owners content with the work environment, fulfilling the human resources functions and meeting the objectives of the organisation. The aim of this study is to examine how happy and content the human resources personnel performing these functions are in meeting these objectives, whether they are seeking another job while working, and the reasons underlying this behaviour, if any, within the framework of the seven different sources of motivation.

The lack of studies concerning job search behaviour of employees and the job search behaviour of human resources personnel constitutes the importance of this research. This study is intended to contribute to the literature and subsequent studies in this context.

5. RESEARCH METHOD AND ANALYSIS

In this research, seven human resources personnel working in established firms in Istanbul and actively performing their human resources functions were interviewed. In these interviews, questions around job search motivation were asked to the employees through a series of research questions which has been prepared previously. In these interviews, people give subjective answers to questions as they saw appropriate.

The reason for choosing this interview method for this research was that the people in human resource departments have difficulty in identifying the issues that cause job search behaviour and that the personnel do not want to answer the questions because they may experience the anxiety of being unemployed. In this context, it is thought that reaching the human resources personnel with snowball sampling method is the most appropriate way (Yıldırım & Şimşek, 2005). In this study, seven human resources personnel were interviewed.

Interview questions were prepared by using methods detailed by Trusty, Allen, Fabian (2019) to determine predictors of job search behaviour based on the seven different categories of motivation in job search. The interview questions were arranged through a pilot study. The seven interviewees were asked seven questions in seven different categories about their job search behaviour while working, and detailed answers were obtained. During the interviews, participants were informed about the purpose of the research and interviews lasted between 20 and 30 minutes. The data obtained as a result of the research were then subjected to analysis (Özdemir, 2013, p. 264).

Content analysis is used to characterise the records and compare the data obtained from the interviews. The content from the interviews defined systematically and indexed to make it easier to use in further analysis. Content analysis consists of frequency and significance analysis. In this research, significance analysis was preferred. 'Meaningfulness analysis' refers to the selection of participant views that are regarded as being meaningful to the research (Altunışık, Coşkun, Bayraktaroğlu, & Yıldırım, 2007, p. 268). In this context, the most important and prominent expressions were identified, tabulated and evaluated (Özdemir, 2013, p. 264).

6. LIMITATIONS OF RESEARCH

This research is limited to human resources personnel in the province of Istanbul.

The reason for this limitation is the extent to which human resources personnel performing human resources functions strive for employee loyalty and motivation, motivate their business and seek a level of commitment to their business.

As a result, the research examined whether or not job search behaviour exists, and the motivation behind a job search, if any.

The research was limited to human resources personnel. Human resources functions are performed by human resources personnel. Human resource personnel strive for the satisfaction of other employees. But how satisfied are human resources personnel with their own roles when trying to please others?

6.1. Findings

Six of the participants were female, and one was male. Education levels are postgraduate level for all employees showing high levels of comprehension and understanding of the working environment. According to the research findings, there are predominantly female employees in the human resources department. There was no difference in job search behaviour according to gender. However, it may be appropriate to re-evaluate the study by interviewing more male employees (Table 1).

Table 1. Demographic Characteristics of the Participants.

	Age	Gender	Marital Status	Level of Education	Position
A	30	Woman	Married	Postgraduate	Hr Business Partner
B	34	Woman	Married	Postgraduate	Hr Business Partner
C	40	Woman	Married	Postgraduate	Hr Manager
D	44	Woman	Single	Postgraduate	Hr Manager
E	34	Woman	Married	Postgraduate	Hr Specialist
F	41	Man	Single	Postgraduate	Hr Business Partner
G	34	Woman	Married	Postgraduate	Personel Specialist

7. CONTENT ANALYSIS RELATED TO JOB SEARCH BEHAVIOR

While working in an HR Department, employees of both the human resources department and other company departments enter into job search behaviour for various reasons. In this research, the motivation of those working in the human resources department is investigated as to whether they undertaking job search behaviour; the findings are summarised as follows.

7.1. Unwanted Situations

Findings: Disagreement with a manager is one of the most important reasons for an employee to begin their job search within an organisation. Exposure to bullying and poor levels of communication with the manager are frequent complaints (Table 2).

Also where career advancement and progression is limited are other drivers that lead to the employee seeking other job opportunities. It must also be noted that while those employees who have problems caused by their manager may still be satisfied with the company, but they seek a new job to in order to be move away from their manager.

Table 2. Findings of Unwanted Situations.

Participants	Reponses	
A	I began my job search due to negativity in work environment. I was subjected to work place bullying by my manager	Problems with the manager
	The manager did not want to lose his position and loved to be the centre of attention. He was always being critical of our work. Other than his behaviour, I didn't have a problem at work. We worked long hours sometimes, but I knew this when I accepted the job and it didn't bother me	lead to job search behaviour
	However, although I was satisfied with my job, I left because of my manager. Actually, I left my manager, not my company	
B	I experienced difficulties at work, primarily disagreements, not feeling valued, but working hard. However, I believe that most of these problems are related to the person, not the institution. No matter in which company you work, similar challenges may appear occur	
C	Yes, I was looking for a job. One reason for this was the long working hours. Also, I can't fully call it bullying at work, but I have experienced intimidating behaviour from my manager. This reduced my motivation to the job	
	My manager specifically interviewed me, but I thought he was acting like this because of his own concerns about losing his position. I wanted to get promoted, but they did not respond to my request or my abilities. I then started to look for other work; this was primarily due to my managers attitude	
D	I looked for a job while working because as a manager I was being micro managed and constantly being asked to obey decision made by senior managers when then had limited understanding of the situation on the ground, managers were not able to accept different ideas and approaches and appeared to be working for their own goals. In addition, I had no spare time for myself or my family due to long working hours. So that's why I started my job search	
E	Bullying and long working hours at work made me unhappy. I also had communication problems with my manager. That's why I started looking for another job	Long working hours are contributing to job
F	Yes, I've . I had disputes with my manager	search
	My manager failed to delegate responsibility for work. I couldn't take ownership on any work as he was interfering with our daily tasks .... I felt like a piece of furniture and I saw myself as a puppet, acting according to the manager's wishes, working long hours for his personal satisfaction That's why decided to look for other work opportunities	behaviour
G	Yes, I have some work-based negativity. I was not happy with what I was doing; I did the same work tasks with no advancement or opportunities. My manager did not provide a new work opportunities or additional responsibilities. My manager says that it is not possible for me to move from my current position to a higher position. That's why I started to look for another job	

7.2. Talent and Skills

Findings: Individuals working in human resources departments think that they are working in jobs appropriate to their abilities and skills. However, in some cases, doing the same work continuously and not being given additional responsibility are seen as factors that cause job search behaviour (Table 3).

Table 3. Findings of Skills and Talent.

Participants	Answer	
A	I am suited for my current position	The fact that
B	I think it's appropriate; that more responsibility could be given to me	no additional
	Your motivation, job satisfaction and efforts to master the learning	responsibility is
	curve are high when you start a job. As you develop yourself	given according
	and your skills, your expectations change. In cases where these	to the skills of
	conditions were not met, I have changed jobs. That's why I'm	the employee
	usually looking for a new job	is related to
C	Where I work, my work fits my talents and skills. My job showcases	job search
	and develops my skills	behaviour
D	I have looked for another position. Apart from my duties in the	
	company I work in, I was also doing some additional/outside work	
	However, I wanted to do more human resources work with my	
	current employer. The company didn't offer any additional work	
	or responsibilities and I felt restricted that I couldn't practice	
	what I knew	
E	My work skills were appropriate	
F	I think my job is suitable for my talents and skills. But I was looking	
	for work in order to increase my skills levels. I thought I was not	
	able to fully utilise my skills with my current employer	
G	A person who fits my skills and abilities wants to do something	
	different after a while. I started looking for a new job that will	
	add to my need for professional development. Since my job is an	
	operational position doing the same tasks, it leads unhappiness	
	and boredom after a while	

7.3. Market Situation and Competitiveness

Findings: The job search behaviour related to the market situation and competitiveness is generally not undertaken by employees. However, sometimes employees engage in job search behaviour to determine their competitiveness and their value in the market (Table 4).

Table 4. Findings Regarding Market Situation and Competitiveness.

Participants	Answer	
A	I did not undertake job search behaviour based on market	Job search behaviour
	conditions. I'll look for work when I have a reason. Or if I	to explore market
	get an offer, I might accept it, if the terms of the offer are	situation and
	agreeable	competitiveness is
B	If I am not dissatisfied with the company or the work I never	often unrealised
	look for a job. I do not look for a job based on how my	
	skills are positioned in the labour market	
C	I didn't look for a job because of what my skills are worth in	
	the labour market. But the status of the business I work for	
	is important to me	
	The fact that my company is competitive and well known, adds	
	to my competitiveness. That's why I didn't look for other	
	work	
D	No, I didn't	

Table 4. (*Continued*)

Participants	Answer	
E	No, I didn't	In some cases, job
F	I was looking for a job to determine my worth and competitiveness	search behaviour can be performed
G	That's why I didn't look for other work	to explore
	However, if offers come to me, I evaluate them if they are for a good position. Otherwise, I do not	competitiveness

7.4. Salary Level

Findings: Employees state that their pay is at market level. For some people, there are other sources of motivation other than wages, while other employees state that they can accept a job offer that exceeds their salary or market conditions. The salary for a job is not seen as a major source of motivation (Table 5).

Table 5. Findings Related to Salary Level.

Participants	Answer	
A	I would like to have more money than the given market rate, but for this reason I did not seek a job	Most employees are paid at the
B	I'm getting paid a little higher than the market rate for my skills and abilities. This stems from the company's competitive advantage and my technical competencies. I've never looked for a job so far. At the exit interviews with other employees, the main reason why they quit was inadequate pay	market level. Therefore, they do not engage in job search behaviour
C	My salary is not in line with market conditions. When I look at my own skills and value, I think I can get a better wage. However, my source of job motivation is not dependant on my level of wage	
D	My salary was generally at market level	
E	I didn't look for a job because of wages. But my wages were at the market level. I didn't accept it when they offered me the same salary, but I would accept it if it were higher	
F	The salary I received was at the market level. I never worked under it the market pay levels and sometimes I even worked above the market level	
G	The fee I received is normal according to the market. I am involved in many projects, but I do think I am paid less. My manager says I'm paid over the market rate, but my perception is the opposite. I would change jobs because of wage levels	

7.5. Career Opportunities

Findings: Employees in the human resources department are engaged in job search behaviour to advance their careers. Employees are looking for a job with the desire to develop and acquire new skills, and to have a more responsibilities. However, the employees in the top position state that they are not satisfied with their jobs when they are working under their potential skill levels, and are therefore unhappy (Table 6).

Table 6. Findings of Career Opportunities.

Participants	Answer	
A	Where I work, our career progression routes are clear. Which criteria is required for which position is clearly stated	The lack of career paths,
	That's not why I'm looking for a job. I've never left work for my career before	lack of advancement
B	I look for work to advance my career. But I'm not searching right now	and lack of development
C	If the offer comes from a better company, I would accept the offer. We have certain career paths in my company, but I have no ambition for advancement	opportunities are among the reasons for job
D	Because I could not use my skills to their full potential and I did not have the opportunity to develop myself in the institution I worked in, I did started my job search behaviour	search
E	I looked for a job because I didn't have any career opportunities at my last place of work	
F	I look for work to advance my career. My career paths at the institution I worked for were clear. But I would have to wait 10 years to get to the top position. Loyalty at the business was high and those people above me would have to leave, so it was difficult for me to move forward	
G	I'm not happy with my career opportunities. The next position is managerial, but there are multiple people working in the same level. For this reason, it is not possible to move to a higher position between the team and the manager, in order not to alienate other employees. I've been in search of a job to advance my career	

7.6. Affected by Other People

Findings: If employees are unhappy in a business because of the work environment, career opportunities, the manager, a lack of salary or the departure of others from an unhappy environment, finding a better job in better places may influence those employees to search for a new job. However, some employees state that instead of being influenced by others, they focus on their own needs and undertake job search behaviour solely when they determine it is necessary (Table 7).

Table 7. Findings Related to Influence from Other Persons.

Participants	Answer	
A	I'm not affected by other people's job search behaviour. I'll look for a job if I'm not happy with my job. I have friends who changed two jobs in a month. I'm not as brave as they are	Other people are not very effective in
B	I was affected. For example, I am not satisfied. I do not see the results of what I do; I do not see enough value or appreciation of my efforts. I would like a top position, but I am restricted. I cannot agree with my manager or colleagues; therefore, the efforts of others affect me	job search
C	The job search behaviour of others affects me. A friend of mine who left work has entered a new job and is very happy there. I think I could find a better job and be happier if I left	

Table 7.   (*Continued*)

Participants	Answer
D	I'm not influenced by others
E	I'm not affected by anyone else
F	No one else affects me, but better conditions will affect me
G	One friend became the manager of the insurance company; another one has left. We are happy for them. The success of the outgoing people creates the idea that I can find a job somewhere else. I'm pretty impressed with them. That's why I'm looking for a new job

8. RESULT

While the individuals working in the human resources department perform their duties to promote employee loyalty, satisfaction and motivation, they can also experience difficulties in the workplace, that results in them looking for other work. The findings from the interviews indicate the majority of employees have problems with their managers. Some of these problems are due to limited opportunities for promotion, and some are caused by communication problems. Some executives leave their subordinates in the dark because of a fear of losing their position, therefore making promotion opportunities more difficult. Some are exposed to work-based bullying without a discernible reason.

Another important issue that causes job search behaviour while working is that employees work in jobs that are not in line with their abilities and skills. When people are not able to develop or fully utilise their skills, they may respond by seeking other career opportunities.

The majority of the interviewees received wages at the market level and therefore stated that although they did not look for other work, they would consider a new job with a company if a better offer was presented. Therefore, the lack of a wage policy at industry market levels (across companies) maybe a factor in the departure of talented employees. Businesses should therefore review their wage policies.

Another important factor in job search behaviour while working is the career opportunities offered by the business. People must have many sources of motivation in life. In this context, development, self-realisation, respect and status are important sources of motivation. In some cases, employees want to be promoted in order to improve themselves rather than for wages and social rights, or for career advancement.

As a result of the interviews, it is seen that the employees primarily look for a job because they believe that their career paths are closed. In addition, the fact that the two specialists in operational roles have been doing the same job continuously without being offered more responsibility creates problems for career development, so they adopt job search behaviours. Businesses should give more responsibility to the employees who carry out operational roles and ensure that they take part in other functions of the business. Otherwise, employees may leave their businesses when they find a better job opportunity.

Lastly, people sometimes experience problems in the environment in which they work, and they are exposed to the problems of others. For this reason, people leave the job and find other work making them more willing to engage in job search behaviour.

Today, human resources departments play a strategic role in providing a competitive advantage and increasing the efficiency of a business. The people who assume these strategic roles are the human resources department managers and employees. These employees carry out many functions, such as establishing the culture of the organisation, recruiting, training, measuring performance and determining wage policies. Employees are motivated or not for different reasons, depending on the size, structure and culture of the organisation.

In some instances, while the employee is happy with their work and conditions, they may feel unhappy due to the conflict caused by their manager. Sometimes career progression routes or wages levels do not satisfy employees. In this context, within the scope of this study, it is recommended that companies enrich their business in operational activity by attaching importance to the delegation of authority, determine their salaries scales slightly above market level while determining company's wage policy and support people's development by clearly determining career paths.

Finally, it has become a necessity to educate both managers and employees about communication and to take measures to combat work-based bullying.

REFERENCES

Altunışık, R., Coşkun, R., Bayraktaroğlu, S., & Yıldırım, E. (2007). *Sosyal bilimlerde araştırma yöntemleri spss uygulamalı* [Research methods in social sciences applied] (4th ed.). Sakarya: Sakarya publications.

Aytaç, S., & Keser, A. (2002). İşsizliğin çalışan birey üzerindeki etkisi: İşsizlik kaygısı [The effect of unemployment on the working individual: Unemployment anxiety]. *ISGUC The Journal of Industrial Relations and Human Resources, 4*(2).

Direnzo, M. S., & Greenhaus, J. H. (2011). Job search and voluntary turnover in a boundaryless world: A control theory perspective. *Academy of Management Review, 36*(3), 567–589.

Doğan, A. (2011), A research for surveying the effect of electronic human resources management practises on managers' satisfaction towards the human resources department. Unpublished doctoral dissertation (in Turkish). İstanbul University social sciences institute.

Erer, E. (2011). *Türkiye'de iş arama davranışını etkileyen faktörlerin belirlenmesi* [Determining the factors that affect the job search behavior in Turkey]. Doctoral dissertation, deü sosyal bilimleri enstitüsü [Deü social sciences institute].

Gökkaya, Ö., Latif, H., & Uçkun, G. (2015). İş arama sürecinde iş ilanı çözümlemesi ve iş arayan-iş ilanı uyumu [Job posting analysis and job seeker-job posting compliance in the job search process]. *Kastamonu üniversitesi iktisadi ve idari bilimler fakültesi dergisi* [*Journal of faculty of economics and administrative sciences of Kastamonu University*], *8*(2), 25–38.

Güler, Y. D. D. B. K. (2012). İş arama davranışı: Bütüncül psiko-sosyal bir yaklaşım [Job search behavior: A holistic psycho-social approach]. *ISGUC The Journal of Industrial Relations and Human Resources, 14*(2), 7–32.

Jobvite. (2016). Job seeker nation study 2016. Retrieved from http://www.jobvite.com/wp-content/uploads/2016/03/Jobvite_Jobseeker_Nation_2016. pdf. Accessed on March 15 2019.

Mcfadyen, R. G., & Thomas, J. P. (1997). Economic and psychological models of job search behavior of the unemployed. *Human Relations*, *50*(12), 1461–1484.

Osberg, L. (1993). Fishing in different pools: Job search strategies and job-finding success in Canada in the early 1980s. *Journal of Labour Economics*, *11*(2), 348–386.

Özdemir, Y. (2013), Marmara bölgesi'ndeki işletmelerin ik yöneticilerinin kariyer anlayışındaki değişime yönelik değerlendirmeleri [The evaluations of the two managers of the enterprises in the Marmara region regarding the change in the career understanding]. *Çukurova üniversitesi sosyal bilimler enstitüsü dergisi* [Çukurova University social sciences institute journal], *22*(1), 257–274.

Rogelberg, S. G. (2007), Job search. In S. G. Rogelberg (Ed.). *Encyclopedia of organizational psychology* (pp. 414–416). CA: Sage Publications.

Saks, A. M. (2004). Job search. *Encyclopedia of Applied Psychology*, *2*, 457.

Saks, A. M. (2005). Job search success: A review and integration of the predictors, behaviors, and out-comes. In S. D. Brown & R. W. Lent (Eds.), *Career development and counseling: Putting theory and research to work* (pp. 155–179). Hoboken, NJ: John Wiley & Sons Inc.

Stigler, J. G. (1961). The economics of information. *Journal of political economy*, *69*(3), 213–225.

Sun, S., Song, Z., & Lim, V. K. (2013). Dynamics of the job search process: Developing and testing a mediated moderation model. *Journal of Applied Psychology*, *98*(5), 771.

Sverke, M., Hellgren, J., & Näswall, K. (2002). No security: A meta-analysis and review of job insecurity and its consequences. *Journal of Occupational Health Psychology*, *7*(3), 242.

Trusty, J., Allen, D. G., & Fabian, F. (2019). Hunting while working: An expanded model of employed job search. *Human Resource Management Review*, *29*(1), 28–42.

Van Hooft, E. A., Born, M. P., Taris, T. W., & Van Der Flier, H. (2005). Predictors and outcomes of job search behavior: The moderating effects of gender and family situation. *Journal of Vocational Behavior*, *67*(2), 133–152.

Wanberg, C. R., Glomb, T. M., Song, Z., & Sorenson, S. (2005), Job-search persistence during unemployment: A 10-wave longitudinal study. *Journal of Applied Psychology*, *90*(3), 411.

Yıldırım, A., & Şimşek, H. (2005). Sosyal bilimlerde nitel araştırma yöntemleri. *Güncelleştirilmiş ve genişletilmiş* [Qualitative research methods in the social sciences] (5th ed.). Ankara: Seçkin publications.

Yücel, İ., Demirel, Y., & Yücel, İ. (2013). Mevcut iş alternatiflerinin iş tatmini ve işten ayrılma ilişkisi üzerine etkisi: "Başka bir yol daha olmalı!" [The impact of existing job alternatives on job satisfaction and turnover relationship: "There must be another way!"]. *Atatürk üniversitesi iktisadi ve idari bilimler dergisi [Journal of Atatürk University Economic and Administrative Sciences]*, *27*(2), 159–177.

CHAPTER 11

TAX AS A SOLUTION FOR CLIMATE CHANGE

Gamze Yıldız Şeren Kurular

ABSTRACT

Introduction – *As a financial instrument, tax has always been one of the policy support instruments that governments apply to solve problems. The issue of the environment, on the other hand, is a notion that has gained more importance over the past years and governments struggle to create solutions to environmental problems on the global scale. Climate change is one of the most important parts of this issue. Especially in our modern day, as a result of natural disasters, forest fires and landslides, climate change has become a field in which serious political measures should be taken. Although it has become necessary to implement tax as a tool to decrease carbon emissions and to open new fields for works with less carbon emission, the expected/desired results about carbon emissions have not been obtained throughout the world.*

Purpose – *The aim of this chapter is to examine carbon taxes, which are the tax applied against climate change, and to draw attention to the multiple policy approach in the face of global environmental problems.*

Methodology – *This chapter, in which qualitative research method is adopted, has descriptive elements. In this context, an evaluation has been put forward in the light of the data obtained from various reports and scientific articles.*

Findings – *Though tax is indeed considered as an effective political tool among the precautions to be taken, one-dimensional approach might bring along a deadlock in the solution of this problem. In order to improve this approach and the perception towards the environment across society, it is necessary to include other factors that can play an important role in this process such as non-governmental organisations. Consequently, in order to solve the environmental problems which have occurred as a*

Contemporary Issues in Business, Economics and Finance
Contemporary Studies in Economic and Financial Analysis, Volume 104, 165–178
ISSN: 1569-3759/doi:10.1108/S1569-375920200000104011

result of human activities, it is essential to minimise the destruction caused by these human activities (although it is not possible to restore it completely). Therefore, a multi-dimensional policy instead of a one-dimensional policy, an environmentally conscious society and state, and cooperation of policy actors on a global scale are basic elements which can play an important role in the solution of the problem.

Keywords: Environmental taxes; carbon emission; global public goods; financial solution; public finance; climate change

JEL classification: H2; H0; Q5

Putting a price on carbon pollution is the most powerful and effective way to reduce emissions.
Jim Yong Kim

Nothing is certain except for death and taxes.
Benjamin Franklin

1. INTRODUCTION

Fiscal policy uses its tools to intervene in the economy for various reasons and in different shapes and forms. The issue of the environment, which has externalities, is one of the reasons. The problems related to the environment, which is defined as a global public good, have been widely discussed in the tax literature, proposing a solution that comes from the public sector. Intervening in environmental problems through tax channels is possible either through incentives or through taxes for deterrence. Accordingly, since taxation on an environmentally damaging activity will constitute additional costs, it is expected that this activity will decrease. Government incentives related to the environment are also expected to increase in environmentally sensitive activities. Unfortunately, not everything is as easy as putting together sentences or models, and scenarios can change when the 'human' factor comes into play.

The aim of this chapter is to examine carbon taxes, which are taxes applied in relation to climate change, and to draw attention to a multi-policy approach to global environmental issues. This study, which includes descriptive elements, is divided into three main sections. In the first part, the meaning of climate change which causes environmental problems is examined on the basis of concept and scope. The second section contains details on how to use the tax instrument in the face of environmental problems. In the last section, is the author will examined whether it is possible to look at the miracles of the earth through taxes.

2. A GLOBAL GOOD, A GLOBAL PROBLEM: CLIMATE CHANGE

It is possible to deal with climate change from two main perspectives. One of them is that certain gases in the atmosphere are transparent to ultraviolet light, but also absorb infrared radiation. Although the most known of these gases is carbon dioxide, water vapour, methane, nitrogen oxide, chlorofluorocarbons and various other gases have the same properties. The energy from the sun is absorbed by the objects on the ground through ultraviolet light. During this heating process, objects release energy in the form of infrared radiation. Thus, carbon dioxide raises global temperatures around the world, just as glass keeps a greenhouse warm. Other gases together with carbon dioxide are therefore called greenhouse gases. The second perspective is the share of human activities at this point. According to this, fossil fuel use adds approximately 6 billion tons of carbon dioxide to the atmosphere, which indicates that emissions are the highest in industrialised countries (Mckibbin & Wilcoxen, 2002). China, for example, is the country that emits the most greenhouse gases, followed by the United States (Amadeo, 2019).

It is possible to consider the following factors among the reasons why carbon dioxide levels have risen to astronomical values since the industrial revolution (Ecotality):

- Increase in greenhouse gas emissions.
- Small pollution particles (aerosols).
- Solar radiation fluctuations.
- Volcanic eruptions.
- Changes in the amount of land and trees.

Controlling the amount of carbon emissions worldwide is the next step to be taken. However, the latest United Nations (UN) report indicates that it has not yet achieved its emission reduction targets. Restrictions on emissions are the main mechanisms of both the 1997 Kyoto Protocol and the 2016 Paris agreement (Gleckman, 2018). According to the international energy agency, more than one-third of the world's fossil fuel reserves should not be burned until 2050. Otherwise, the atmosphere will heat up by 2°C to a dangerous level (Amadeo, 2019). It can be said that climate change is the most important problem of today. The impact of climate change is global. These effects cover a wide range of factors, from weather conditions threatening food production to rising sea levels and risk of flooding (UN, 2019).

In the face of environmental problems, states intervene through two main policy instruments, namely financial and legal instruments which are also known as command and control instruments. Environmental taxes, emission or user fees, product taxes, emissions trading, refundable deposit systems and incentives are financial instruments. Legal instruments include pollution prohibitions, environmental standards, regulation of waste disposal, licensing practices and environmental impact assessment. The main objective of this study is to analyse the use the financial instruments in the face of environmental problems and to realise the cost to the producer (Mutlu, 2002). Tax law examines the tax relationship of both the state and individuals and institutions. Under this, the state has a taxation authority and taxes are one of the means of intervention in economic and social life. Therefore, taxes can dominate economic activities. However, the primary purpose of the taxes designed for the environment is to change human preferences rather than income (Organ & Çiftçi, 2013). The Kyoto Protocol prepared by the UN Framework Convention also envisages regulations to limit the gases causing climate change as a result of global warming. In particular, taxation of carbon dioxide emissions is included in this scope and it should be noted that the greenhouse effect is a global environmental problem. Countries go beyond their borders with carbon dioxide emissions, causing climate change (Mutlu, 2006). Undoubtedly, the ability to prevent (reduce) climate change is of global public interest. All people living in the world benefit from this situation, but if one person benefits, it does not mean that the benefit of another person will decrease. As a global public good, it is possible to see climate change as the grandfather of other public goods. Because no global public interest can stress the difficulty of mitigating climate change (Chander, 2017).

It is possible to examine public goods in two main divisions: global public goods and national public goods. Global public goods represent the benefits/harms spread between countries and regions. For example, nuclear disarmament can be considered in this context. Given the fact that a country has a nuclear weapon in its hands, and therefore the citizens of other countries live in fear, nuclear disarmament in this context is of global public interest. If countries have no nuclear weapons, everyone will fear less. Climate change is also a public good in this group and if it is controlled, it creates benefits for the whole world (Chander, 2017). The concept of global public goods came up in the work of the UN development programme in 1999; no one can be excluded from the benefit, it is spread to benefit countries, people and future generations, and it is a good for which there is no competition between individuals in consumption (Kaul, Grunberg, & Stern, 1999). Carbon taxes can also be categorised in two main groups, either nationally or globally. While national carbon taxes are unilateral to the borders of the country, an indirect tax is envisaged to be applied at global level. This necessitates tax harmonisation among countries (Vural, n.d.). For example, the Kyoto Protocol requires the reduction of greenhouse gas emissions to the prescribed targets in Organisation for Economic Cooperation and Development (OECD) and transition countries. Thus, it is aimed to protect global goods such as the ozone layer, the atmosphere and air quality by reducing carbon dioxide emissions and to finance global institutions that will protect the environment by increasing public revenues (Tekin & Vural, n.d.). Ensuring this, however, is not as easy as it seems. It can be said that the UN is ineffective in enforcing these policies on member States. Sovereignty maintains the independence of nation-states and citizens in the area, just as in other areas. Although pressure can be made, there is no forcing it on other states to contribute to the procurement of global public goods in this process. The fact that even one country is lacking in the fight against climate change makes the efforts incomplete. It is a slow and difficult process for all countries to reach an agreement. The agreement for world countries should balance the costs and benefits of mitigating climate change and ensure a fair process (Chander, 2017).

3. CARBON TAX SOLUTION AGAINST CLIMATE CHANGE

In the face of climate change, green taxes are the first financial solution that comes to mind and are basically based on two principles. These include tax increases and tax reductions. While increasing the taxes might discourage against environmental damaging activities or goods, tax incentives are applied for environmental benefits. In both cases, the traditional tax principles are taken into account, but in addition to these traditional principles, the environmental impact of tax is now becoming a principle to consider (Milne, 2007). The basis of carbon taxes originates from the Pigouvian taxes, introduced by Arthur C. Pigou. Accordingly, the amount of damage to the environment is related to the tax that is imposed. A. C. Pigou developed Alfred Marshall's concept of externalities. Thus, he introduced the idea of internalising the environmental pollution through taxation.[1] In this respect, the existence of externalities for public intervention is a basic reason. Therefore, he advocated taxation for negative externalities such as environmental pollution and subsidies for activities that create positive externalities. These are called Pigouvian taxes and subsidies. Pigouvian taxes are still seen today as an effective way to combat environmental pollution (The Library of Economics and Liberty). Carbon tax is also considered under the classification of a Pigouvian tax (a tax that will enable the internalisation of negative externalities in the price system). For this purpose, it puts a price on the non-market or social cost of non-environmental pollution of carbon emissions resulting from the use of fossil fuels – coal, oil and natural gas in energy production (Herber & Raga, 1995).

Carbon tax is a tax that is used in the face of global warming – climate change – which has negative effects on the environment and its aim is to reduce the amount of emissions causing this heating. This chain effect occurs as follows. The increase in greenhouse gas concentrations in the world atmosphere causes the whole world to warm up, causing climate change and trapping the heat. The most important of these gases is the carbon dioxide produced by the combustion of fossil fuels. Reducing greenhouse gas emissions is the most reliable way to limit or prevent such changes. A carbon tax on such emissions (often called a carbon tax, although it applies to a wider range of gases than carbon dioxide) is seen as a cost-effective option to reduce such emissions (Williams, 2016). The purpose of a carbon tax is to reflect the real cost of burning carbon and to enable companies and consumers to pay the external costs imposed on society. Carbon-rich fuels produce greenhouse gases when burned. Gases such as carbon dioxide and methane create global warming by heating the atmosphere. This tax is a Pigouvian tax because it brings back the cost of global warming to producers (Amadeo, 2019). Carbon tax can only be applied for this purpose under different names, such taxes on energy products can be called hidden carbon taxes (Vural, n.d.).

There are two types of carbon pricing. One of these is carbon taxes, and the other is emissions trading systems (ETS). At ETS, low-emission industries sell their permits to industries that generate larger emissions, so that the required emission reduction is expected. Carbon tax defines a tax rate on the carbon content of fossil fuels or greenhouse gas emissions. The tool selected may vary according to the economic and national conditions of a country (The World Bank). Government interventions in the face of climate change are also expected to encourage low carbon emissions. Carbon taxes are being discussed as a promising political intervention. In this context, in 1990, Finland was the first country to apply the carbon tax. Here, a small tax is imposed on fuels, including turbo, except for biofuels. Following Finland, Norway, Sweden and Denmark were other countries that introduced carbon taxes in 1991 and 1992. In 1999, Germany imposed an ecological tax on fuel, natural gas, gasoline and electricity used in residential heating. Japan, on the other hand, reduced the tax on vehicles that would lead to low pollution to promote the sale of environmentally friendly vehicles and also restructured energy taxes. The UK imposed a climate change tax of 15% on electricity costs in 2001 (see Table 1 for other country examples and detailed information). Other indirect ways of pricing carbon are the abolition of fossil fuel subsidies, regulations involving social carbon costs and fuel taxes. Today, 40 countries and more than 20 cities, states and provinces use carbon-pricing mechanisms (The World Bank).

Along with the process of globalisation, national tax systems have a structure based on indirect taxes. In this context, carbon tax and similar environmental taxes are important sources of income for nation-states (Vural, n.d.). In addition to being a source of income, carbon taxes are seen as good policy instruments in terms of quantity-based carbon-pricing regulation and command/control arrangements. It is also claimed to be the most powerful policy tool on sustainable development. Listed below are the reasons why carbon tax is supported by countries (Acosta, 2015):

• Allowing public revenue.
• Providing environmental effectiveness.
• Transparent and simple.
• Economic efficiency.
• Accurate costs.

A carbon tax is a charge on the combustion of carbon-based fuels such as coal, oil and greenhouse gases. The aim is to reduce the use of fossil fuels that damage the climate and cause global warming. At this point, carbon tax is seen as the only way to pay for the climate damage caused by the release of carbon dioxide in the atmosphere. The carbon tax set to a sufficiently high value rewards those who do not use these fuels economically. Therefore, it becomes an element that motivates the use of clean energy (CTC). The tax to be applied for greenhouse gas emissions needs to be handled in a broad context in terms of both efficiency and justice principles. For example, home heating systems, factories, airplanes, power plants and cars should have the same carbon price. But this also leads to the following challenges (Marron et al., 2015):

• Presence of greenhouse gases other than carbon dioxide.
• Difficulty in tracking emissions.
• There are multiple ways to generate carbon emissions.
• The need to extend credit for the purpose of removing carbon emissions from the atmosphere.

Consequently, according to the analysis, carbon tax encourages investments to be made for clean energy, as well as reducing carbon pollution. However, there are

Table 1. Selected Countries in Terms of Carbon Tax Rate/Revenue/Scope.[a]

Country	Tax Rate	Annual Income	Income Distribution	Scope
Finland (1990)	$40/metric tonne of CO_2	750 million dollars	Government budget; independent discounts on income taxes	Heat, electricity, transportation, heating fuels
Norway (1991)	$4–$69/metric ton of CO_2.	900 million dollars (1994 estimate)	Government budget	Mineral oil, gasoline, natural gas
Swedish (1991)	Standard rate: $168/metric ton of CO_2. Industry rate: $23.04/metric ton of CO_2	3.665 billion dollars	Initially the government budget. After 2000, income used to offset labour taxes	Fossil fuels for heating and motor fuels
Denmark (1992)	$31/metric tonne of CO_2	905 million dollars	Environmental subsidies and return to industry	Consumption of fossil fuels (exceptions)
United Kingdom (2001)	$0.0078/kWh for electricity; US $0.0027 for natural gas supplied by the natural gas company; $0.0175/kg for liquefied petroleum gas or other gaseous hydrocarbons supplied in liquid form; $0.0213/kg for fuel and solid fuel	1.191 billion dollars	Reductions in other taxes	Fossil fuels used to generate electricity
Switzerland (2008)	$68/metric tonne of CO_2	-	Climate-friendly building renovation funds; the rest were redistributed through the benefits system	Fossil fuels not used for energy or covered by EU ETS

Source: C2ES (2013) and Marron, Toder, and Austin (2015)'ten derlenerek yazar tarafından oluşturulmuştur.
[a]About how design can be made about a possible carbon tax in Turkey, see Bavbek (2016).

doubts as to how low-income communities will be affected by the carbon tax due to these positive characteristics as well as the negative impact it has on social welfare (Carbon Tax Forum; Chi, Ma, & Zhu, 2012). There are also disadvantages such as political resistance, uncertainty of benefit and difficulty in coordination (Yonah & Uhlmann, 2009).

4. CARBON TAXES AND MIRACLES FOR A BALANCED CLIMATE AND A LIVEABLE WORLD

The general analysis of carbon taxes suggests that carbon tax both reduces carbon pollution and encourages new investments in clean energy. However, some analysis reveals that such a carbon tax will not positively affect low-income communities (Carbon Tax Forum). For example, according to Williams (2016), a carbon tax to be introduced represents a cost-effective way to reduce greenhouse gas emissions. For developed countries, carbon taxes can contribute to the improvement of economic conditions by replacing taxes, such as labour taxes, and thus reducing unemployment rates. From the perspective of developing countries, carbon taxes can be used to finance poverty reduction measures. Accordingly, financial instruments to be implemented, both mitigate climate change and promote economic growth and development (UN, 2010).

Governments set a price to be paid for each ton of greenhouse gas emissions. Consumers and businesses will take steps to change their fuels/use new technologies to reduce their emissions and thus avoid paying taxes (C2ES). In addition, carbon taxes, which offer significant opportunities to address environmental externalities, can also leave governments in a difficult position, since carbon taxes may have undesirable effects on the income of certain population groups, as well as possible impacts on the competitiveness of firms (Acosta, 2015).

What can be seen in relation to carbon tax is that there are both positive and negative consequences. This study aims to present a more clear assessment under the title of opportunities and threats. In this context, Table 2 is presented from a comparative perspective

Unlike other pollution problems, climate change can result in inaction when it comes to winners. For example, increasing global warming for higher latitudes may cause some farmers to have a warmer and longer growing season. The United States is not convinced by the fact that the benefits of reducing emissions will outweigh the costs. In summary, climate change promotes inaction, as it is not fully understood (Sandler, 2001).

It is possible to list the proposals for the carbon taxes implemented/to be implemented, following both the opportunities and threats under consideration (Acosta, 2015; Steier, 2018):

- In order to realise the economic and social benefits of carbon taxes, policy support, such as recycling of income is required. For example, carbon tax revenues can be re-invested in environmental cleaning programmes, green energy and social aid.

- Strong leadership is needed to negotiate with some interest groups in the face of opposition to carbon taxes.
- The public should be informed about the social benefits of the tax in order to ensure the acceptability of the carbon tax.
- Although consensus is reached between public, private and non-governmental organisations (NGOs) in countries that accept carbon taxes today, the conflict of interests in this regard may lead to regional and global lobbying actions. Therefore, consensus on carbon tax is an important issue.

Taking into account the opportunities presented in Table 2 and following consistent policies against threats, a carbon tax may lead to a clean and efficient economy. However, it seems difficult to carry the carbon tax from the 'whiteboard' to real life since, in principle, a well-functioning tax that is not problematic may take another form in practice. It is possible to say that a real carbon tax will fall behind some ideals due to the design difficulties of the tax (Marron et al., 2015).

Table 2. Opportunities and Threats of Carbon Tax.

Opportunities	Threats
Increased carbon-based fuel costs can encourage companies to switch to clean energy (solar, wind, hydro-powered)	Almost no one regularly uses renewable energy in any way. Most supplies are provided by carbon-based fuels
The cost of using the carbon tax tool is more transparent than other quantitative emission targets	This may mean that the costs of taxes on carbon are paid by society
As carbon tax will increase the price of gasoline and electricity, consumers reduce greenhouse gas emissions because they use energy efficiently	It takes time for businesses and consumers to accept the tax. For example, carbon tax has been imposed in British Columbia for 10 years, but the majority do not support it.
Allows industries to find the most cost-effective ways to reduce carbon emissions, which is more preferable than regulations	It is difficult to know the actual cost of carbon emissions to be reflected on to future generations and the environment
A carbon tax can also boost economic growth. For example, Sweden's carbon tax has reduced its emissions by 23% in the last 25 years. In the same period, the economy grew by 55%	It can be difficult to measure how much carbon is produced, so it is difficult to know what level of carbon tax one will apply
A carbon tax can bring significant income	Can put a huge burden on the consumer and the economy
Tax revenue can be used to reimburse government agencies dealing with the impacts of climate change	Carbon taxes can cause tax evasion. For example, companies are trying to mask the actual pollution level. Alternatively, it can be outsourced to countries with less rigid tax systems. This situation also exports pollution to poor countries. Therefore, the carbon tax may need a global agreement
The cost of using the carbon tax tool is more transparent than other quantitative emission targets	
Even oil companies support carbon tax. Exxon Mobil, Shell and BP called for this tax, and BP's general manager pledged to reduce emissions	Carbon taxes can reduce profitability by not encouraging investments

Source: Amadeo (2019), Ayres (2019), Pettinger (2016), Litman (2010), and Aldy, Ley, and Parry (2010).

Naturally, proper design of taxes and a sufficient proportionality can play an important role in addressing environmental problems. Moreover, revenues from such taxes may also play a role in achieving fiscal consolidation and reducing other tax rates. In order for an environmental tax to be accepted by the public and be effective, the following elements should be considered (OECD, 2011):

- Transparency.
- Public information.
- Certainty.
- Combine taxes with other instruments in light of the cyclical environment, taking into account the impact of overlapping instruments.

When designing the carbon tax, it is necessary to realise how the tax revenue will be used and how the tax will be applied. At this point, the tax rate may remain high considering the price effect, and the tax rate may remain low when the price effect is not taken into consideration. Since environmental taxes are dependent on economic, social and political conditions, policy mixes should be considered together with environmental taxes and other instruments (Takeshi, Lee, & Rudolph, 2017). The main problem in carbon tax design is that it cannot be harmonised with other financial instruments to reduce greenhouse heating. This is important in order to avoid the deviations in production–consumption decisions and to ensure the comparability of tax rates of chlorofluorocarbons and fossil fuels (Poterba, 1991). Agreements about a harmonised tax system and existing carbon taxes should be designed by the relevant experts. In this context, a club can be established, including the developing countries, in cooperation with the World Economic Forum or the OECD. In order to facilitate tariffs for countries opposing the system, amended World Trade Organisation rules may be proposed, and tax may be gradually increased to reduce global emissions (Carattini, Kallbekken, & Orlov, 2019).

As stated at the beginning of the study, the 'human' factor plays a leading role in the social sciences. Another shortcoming of progress towards climate change/global warming is that most policy makers do not empathise with future generations and do not have enough foresight (Sandler, 2001). Scientists have the same view that climate changes cause undesirable adverse weather conditions such as floods, forest fires, heatwaves and droughts. Each of these situations led to some economic costs. These costs are payed for by the government, landlords and farmers, while energy companies that generate greenhouse gases do not pay for them (Amadeo, 2019). The work done by Hotunluoğlu and Tekeli (2007) is remarkable at this point. Accordingly, the effect of carbon tax was analysed in line with the econometric analysis conducted in 18 European countries. Contrary to the common belief, it was concluded that carbon tax is not sufficiently effective in reducing emissions. Although the most appropriate way to reduce emissions is seen as increasing the costs of coal burning, gas and oil, it is evident that many countries refrain from setting high prices since this is a politically difficult choice for countries. For example, the rise in energy prices in France and Europe has caused voters to react angrily, and as a result, efforts to raise carbon taxes have been shelved. For this reason, it is possible to state that carbon pricing has only a supportive role in the face of global warming (Plumer & Popovich, 2019).

Global industrial players are using their power to influence the design of carbon taxes in both developed and undeveloped countries. The focus here is on competitiveness, in other words, economic interests. Although they make up a small portion of the population, their claims are based on arguments such as reduced employment and price increases. Efforts to balance the power of a small number of enterprises and to make the public heard can be achieved by the involvement of NGOs in the decision-making process. At this point, institutional structures should be established that allow NGOs to take part in this discussion (Acosta, 2015).

Carattini et al. (2019) pointed out that it is possible to create a global tax on carbon. Accordingly, harmonisation of the carbon tax system seems to be the easiest way to create a global carbon price. In their survey, the participants were asked whether they would support a carbon tax to be applied, and the majority of the respondents stated that they would support the tax in scenarios of spending the income from the tax on climate projects and giving back to the people. More studies are needed on the support given to carbon taxes, especially in EMUs. This approach also necessitates a multiple point of view such as economic, psychological and political science. The most effective way of communicating the necessary information on the social, environmental and economic impacts of the carbon tax to be introduced should be determined. It is imperative to find out what the public thinks in order to set a global carbon price high enough to reduce emissions and to combat climate change (Carattini et al., 2019).

5. CONCLUSION

Climate change is a global environmental problem that can negatively affect the whole world today. The necessity of producing a global solution to the global environmental problem is obvious. It is necessary to control the amount of carbon emissions in the world, but in accordance with the UN reports, it cannot be achieved and the emission reduction targets have not been met yet.

This study aimed at examining carbon tax which is an environmental tax. The basic idea of carbon tax is that consumers and firms should turn to other alternatives if they do not want to pay too much tax. There are two alternatives. One of them is to turn to a different source of fuel and the other is to use new and environmentally sensitive technologies.

Preventing climate change with tax measures is certainly not a useless approach. However, it does not seem to make much sense by itself. People do not regularly use renewable energy, which means that the cost of tax is borne by society. However, in communities where people's environmental awareness is not developed, taxes can give the desired results only up to a certain point. At this point, public spots can be considered as an effective solution for society to develop environmentally sensitive approaches.

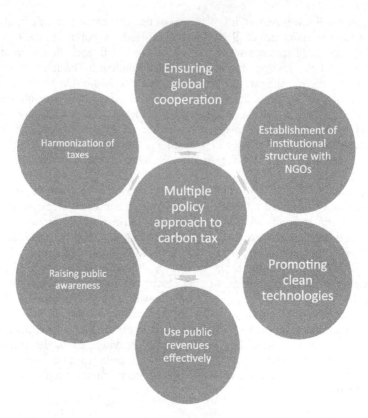

Fig. 1.   Multiple Policy Approach to Carbon Tax. *Source*: Created by Author.

Although it is not difficult to predict that actions that are not taken today will bring society to a worse predicament in the future, it is unfortunately not easy to develop a global solution. Although volunteerism is essential in the presentation of global public goods, if there is pressure, there is no coercion. The lack of effort of a single country in this process can frustrate the efforts put forward by others. Therefore, a global approach should be developed and every country should take serious steps to abide by this process. As a result, it is possible to reveal the following components in order to develop a global and multiple perspective on climate change as a global problem (Fig .1).

Although it is desirable to draw attention to the human factor, it should be remembered that, as can be seen from Fig. 1, other environmental taxes, such as carbon tax, may have many components and each component can affect the development of the process.

NOTE

1. For more information, see: Pigou (1920).

REFERENCES

Acosta, L. A. (2015). *Political economy in climate change mitigation: The case of carbon taxes.* Bonn: German Development Institute. Retrieved from http://www.practitioners-dialogue.de/files/assets/Klimainvestitionen/Downloads/Publications%20in%20cooperation%20with%20PDCI/DIE%20(2015)%20Case%20Stuy%20on%20Political%20Economy%20of%20Carbon%20Taxes.pdf. Accessed on April 18, 2019.

Aldy, J., Ley, E., & Parry, I. (2010). What is the role of carbon taxes in climate change mitigation? *The World Bank.* Retrieved from http://www1.worldbank.org/prem/PREMNotes/Note2_role_carbon_taxes.pdf. Accessed on April 10, 2019.

Amadeo, K. (2019). Carbon tax, its purpose, and how it works. *The Balance.* Retrieved from https://www.thebalance.com/carbon-tax-definition-how-it-works-4158043. Accessed on April 27, 2019.

Ayres, C. (2019). Advantages and disadvantages of carbon tax. *Vittana.* Retrieved from https://vittana.org/14-advantages-and-disadvantages-of-carbon-tax. Accessed on April 28, 2019.

Bavbek, G. (2016). *Design options for employing a carbon tax in Turkey.* EDAM Energy and Climate Change Climate Action Paper Series 2016/5. Retrieved from http://edam.org.tr/wp-content/uploads/2016/10/EDAM_CarbonTaxDesign_October2016-1.pdf. Accessed on April 18, 2019.

C2ES. (2013). Options and considerations for a Federal Carbon Tax. Retrieved from https://www.c2es.org/site/assets/uploads/2013/02/options-considerations-federal-carbon-tax.pdf. Accessed on April 20, 2019.

C2ES. (2019). Carbon tax. Retrieved from https://www.c2es.org/content/carbon-tax-basics/. Accessed on April 18, 2019.

Carattini, S., Kallbekken, S., & Orlov, A. (2019). How to win public support for a global carbon tax? *Nature, 565,* 289–291.

Carbon Tax Center (CTC). (2019). What's a carbon tax? Retrieved from https://www.carbontax.org/whats-a-carbon-tax/. Accessed on April 21, 2019.

Carbon Tax Forum. (2019). Recent carbon tax developments. Retrieved from https://www.carbontax-forum.com/on-co2. Accessed on April 18, 2019.

Chander, P. (2017). *Growing importance of global public goods: The case of climate change.* No. 174. RSIS, Singapore.

Chi, C., Ma, T., & Zhu, B. (2012). Towards a low-carbon economy: Coping with technological bifurcations with a carbon tax. *Energy Economics, 34,* 2081–2088.

Ecotality. (2019). Climate change report and how the advantages of solar energy can help global warming. Retrieved from https://ecotality.com/climate-change-report-how-advantages-of-solar-energy-help/. Accessed on April 20, 2019.

Gleckman, H. (2018, October). Bill Nordhaus, The Nobel Prize, and carbon taxes. *TaxVox.* Retrieved from https://www.taxpolicycenter.org/taxvox/bill-nordhaus-nobel-prize-and-carbon-taxes. Accessed on April 4, 2019.

Herber, B., & Raga, J. T. (1995). An International Carbon Tax to combat global warming: An economic and political analysis of the European Union proposal. *The American Journal of Economics and Sociology, 54*(3), 257–267. Retrieved from https://www.jstor.org/stable/pdf/3487089.pdf?refreqi d=excelsior%3Af133073f0fd64756a7aadfab61f880c1. Accessed on April 15, 2019.

Hotunluoğlu, H., & Tekeli, R. (2007). Analysis and Effects of Carbon Tax: Does Carbon Tax Reduce Emission? 107–125. Retrieved from Sosyoekonomi/2007-2/070206

Kaul, I., Grunberg, I., & Stern, A. M. (Eds.). (1999). *Global public goods: International cooperation in the 21st century.* New York, NY: Oxford University Press.

Litman, T. (2010). *Carbon taxes "Tax What You Burn, Not What You Earn".* Victoria: VTPI. Retrieved from https://www.vtpi.org/carbontax.pdf. Accessed on April 18, 2019.

Marron, D., & Toder, E., & Austin, L. (2015). *Taxing carbon: What, why, and how* (pp. 1–27). Washington, DC: Tax Policy Center. Retrieved from https://biotech.law.lsu.edu/blog/2000274-Taxing-Carbon-What-Why-and-How.pdf

Mckibbin, W. J., & Wilcoxen, P. J. (2002). The role of economics in climate change policy *Journal of Economic Perspectives, 16*(2), 107–129.

Milne, J. E. (2007). *Green taxes and climate change: Theory and reality,* Forum, CESifo DICE report. Retrieved from https://www.cesifo-group.de/DocDL/dicereport407-forum2.pdf. Accessed on April 15, 2019.

Mutlu, A. (2002). Environmental Economics, Policies, Practices and Turkey. Istanbul: Public Finance Research and Application Center.

Mutlu, A. (2006). Health Services and Environmental Pollution in the Context of Global Public Goods: Production, Financing and Management Problems. *Journal of Public Finance, 150*, 53–78.

OECD. (2011). Environmental taxation a guide for policy makers. Retrieved from https://www.oecd.org/env/tools-evaluation/48164926.pdf. Accessed on April 23, 2019.

Organ, İ., & Çiftçi, T. E. (2013). Carbon Tax. *Niğde University FEAS Journal, 6*(1), 81–95.

Pettinger, T. (2016). Carbon tax-advantages and disadvantages. Retrieved from https://www.economicshelp.org/blog/glossary/carbon-tax/. Accessed on April 28, 2019.

Pigou. A. C. (1920). *The economics of welfare*. London: Macmillan.

Plumer, B., & Popovich, N. (2019). These countries have prices on carbon. Are they working? *The New York Times*. Retrieved from https://www.nytimes.com/interactive/2019/04/02/climate/pricing-carbon-emissions.html. Accessed on April 18, 2019.

Poterba, J. M. (1991). *Tax policy to combat global warming: On designing a carbon tax* (pp. 1–40). NBER Working Paper No. 3649.

Sandler, T. (2001). *Understanding global public goods*. OECD Observer No 228. Retrieved from http://oecdobserver.org/news/fullstory.php/aid/540/Understanding_global_public_goods.html. Accessed on April 18, 2019.

Steier, G. (2018). The carbon tax vacuum and the debate about climate change impacts: Emission taxation of commodity crop production in food system regulation. *Pace Environmental Law Review, 35*(2), 345–374.

Takeshi, K., Lee, S., & Rudolph, S. (2017). *The Japanese carbon tax and the challenges to low-carbon policy cooperation in East Asia*. Graduate School of Economics discussion paper series, Discussion paper No. E-17-009. Kyoto University, Kyoto, Japan.

Tekin, A., & Vural, İ. Y. (n.d.). Global Kamusal Malların Finansman Aracı Olarak Global Vergi Önerileri (pp. 323–337). Retrieved from http://debis.deu.edu.tr/userweb//hilmi.coban/'%C3%B6devler/k%C3%BCresel%20%C4%B1s%C4%B1nma%20ve%20vergi/01global%20vergi%20%C3%B6nerileri.pdf. Accessed on April 20, 2019.

The Library of Economics and Liberty. (2019). Arthur Cecil Pigou. Retrieved from http://www.econlib.org/library/Enc/bios/Pigou.html. Accessed on April 20, 2019.

The World Bank. (2019). What is carbon pricing? Retrieved from http://www.worldbank.org/en/programs/pricing-carbon. Accessed on April 18, 2019.

UN. (2010). Tax cooperation on climate change, E/C.18/2010/CRP.12. Retrieved from https://static.un.org/esa/ffd/wp-content/uploads/2014/10/6STM_CRP12_Dr.pdf. Accessed on April 18, 2019.

UN. (2019). Climate Change, Retrieved from https://www.un.org/en/sections/issues-depth/climate-change/index.html. Accessed on April 18, 2019.

Vural, İ. Y. (n.d.). Karbon Vergilerinin Gelir Potansiyeli Ve Mevcut Uygulama. Retrieved from http://www.canaktan.org/ekoloji-cevre/karbon/uygulama.htm. Accessed on April 20, 2019.

Williams, R. C. (2016). *Environmental taxation*. Nber Working Paper Series, 22303, s.11, 1-39. Retrieved from http://www.nber.org/papers/w22303

Yonah, R. S. A., & Uhlmann, D. M. Combating global climate change: Why a carbon tax is a better response to global warming than cap and trade. *Stanford Environmental Law Journal, 28*(3), 3–50.

CHAPTER 12

COMMUNITY MEDIA, SUSTAINABILITY AND FEMALE-ORIENTED NGOs: THE CASE IN IZMIR

Asli Elgün

ABSTRACT

Introduction – *Community media was created as an alternative to the ever-globalising and rapidly monopolised media industry. This media is a unity that does not seek profit, voices the demands and problems of the community it serves, seeks the benefit of the public, and its creators are members of the community. It is seen as a tool for the development of democracy and pluralism, and to increase social impact. The sustainability of this tool has emerged as a debated topic in recent years. Community media can both serve as a tool for sustainable development and can be defined as a part of sustainable communication. The sustainability of community media is all about making the presence of the communicative tools of the community permanent and sustainable, or to insure the continuation of the community's channels of communication as a part of a specific strategy.*

Purpose – *In this chapter, the author will discuss the concepts of community media, sustainability and female-oriented non-governmental organisations (NGOs), and then attempt to explain the media usage habits and the factors that affect the sustainability of the preferred channels of the female-oriented NGOs in İzmir.*

Contemporary Issues in Business, Economics and Finance
Contemporary Studies in Economic and Financial Analysis, Volume 104, 179–191
ISSN: 1569-3759/doi:10.1108/S1569-375920200000104012

Methodology – *The study has been designed using a case study design based on qualitative research methods. Data have been collected via document analysis and in-depth face-to-face interviews. The data acquired were analysed descriptively.*

Findings – *Findings from the study show that the financial, content production-related, technical, and legal factors affect the sustainability of community media.*

Keywords: Community; community communication; community media; sustainability; NGOs; female-oriented non-governmental organisations; new media

JEL classifications: L31 – non-profit institutions; NGOs

1. INTRODUCTION

A community can be defined as a societal organisation gathered together to serve a common goal or agenda, and a political unity where the elements of compatriotism, autonomy, civil society, and collective identity are emphasised. Community communication (in the most general sense) encompasses all communicative work the community employs as an alternative to mass communication. One of the most important tools of this communication is community media. Community media, which has developed as an alternative to mainstream media in its content, forms, and means of distribution, can be described as the publications of individuals who have gathered together for a specific goal or purpose. The publications are independent on their finances and content, and represent the aim and goals of the community. Finances and content diverging from mainstream media are prerequisites in this context. The sustainability of community media becomes chief among the topics of discussion at this stage.

2. COMMUNITY MEDIA: THE TOOL OF COMMUNICATION OF THE COMMUNITY AND ITS SUSTAINABILITY

Community media is an alternative form of media and can be defined as 'non-profit media that is owned or accounted for by the community it serves' (Kern European Affairs (KEA), 2007, p. 5) This form of media seems to be important for citizens to be able to state their thoughts with open-access tools, create common meanings, and for the development of sharing and democracy. There are various definitions of the topic: Fuller (2007, p. 2) sees 'community communications/media as a concept referring to how individuals and organisations involve publics in participatory means of airing issues takes various forms, depending on time and place'. Carpentier, Lie, and Servaes (2003) on the other hand mention that community media is a part of civil media. Whereas Atton (2015) highlights that community media are able to construct realities that oppose the conventions and representations of the mainstream media.

Community media shows several common features within these definitions: Jankowski (2003) defined the characteristics of community media as:

1. Empowerment of the politically disenfranchised, shared, local ownership, 2. Local content, 3. Non-professional and volunteer ownership, 4. Electronic distribution, 5. Geographic distribution, and non-commercial finance structure, although they might also include sponsorship, advertising, and so forth. (Hatcher, 2012, p. 247)

Maslog, Navaro,Tabing, and Teodoro (1997, p. 3) cites the following characteristics of community media:

1. Owned and controlled by people in the community; 2. Usually smaller and low-cost; 3. Provides interactive two-way communication; 4. Non-profit and autonomous, therefore, non-commercial; 5. Has limited coverage or reach; 6. Utilises appropriate, indigenous materials and resources; 7. Reflects community needs and interests; 8. Its programs or content support community development.

As can be inferred from these properties, community media is a tool for disadvantaged groups to express themselves. It is seen as a tool that helps foster the concept of pluralism, the development of democracy, a process that creates social impact and change, is a part of information sharing for the benefit of the public, and allows the sustainable development goals to spread more effectively (Buckley, 2011; EPRA, 2017; KEA, 2007; Milan, 2009).

In this context, community media both serves as an intermediate for sustainable development and can be described as a part of sustainable communication. The sustainability of community media is about making the tools of communication of the community permanent, ensuring the community's continuity, or insuring the continuation of the community's channels of communication as a part of a specific strategy. Community media and its sustainability have come up in a meeting UNESCO held in Paris. Mixed definitions regarding the roles and aims of the community, the emergence of political and commercial agendas, failing to assure editorial control, and the lack of effective policies were listed as the factors that affected the sustainability of community media in this meeting (UNESCO, 2015), while the lack of access and licensing related policies oriented at publishers, problems related to accessing frequencies, technical impossibilities, community media being unable to afford the necessary costs, and the lack of specific subsidies/funds have been given as the factors that affect the sustainability of community media in another research by Mendel (2013).

3. THE DEVELOPMENT OF FEMALE-ORIENTED NON-GOVERNMENTAL ORGANISATIONS IN TURKEY

'Civil Society' is a complex term that is fairly widespread. In the most general sense 'civil society' is a term that is used to describe any manner of voluntary activity that benefits the public and is conducted in a non-profit manner by a person or community. Non-governmental organisations (NGOs) are structures that form the basis of societal change by serving as resources of concepts such as plurality, human rights, the supremacy of law, and the representation of disadvantaged groups, and have political, economic, cultural, and individual functions in society.

The development of civil society and NGOs in Turkey is different to that of the Western world. The Ottoman (Pre-Republic) national establishments, religious foundations, landed proprietors, and guilds are considered to be the starting point of civil society in that era. Civil society can be seen to have accelerated after 1980s in the Republic of Turkey, which has overcome many processes such as the one-party and multi-party systems, since its foundation (Yıldız, 2004). Changes in the constitution in the 1990s and the permission granted to privately owned radio and TV stations are also considered to be regulations that have contributed to the development of civil society (Özbudun, 1999; Özer, 2008). One of the main factors that have assured the vitalisation of civil society in Turkey is the women's movement. Sancar (2013) has classified the women's movement in Turkey into the following eras:

- Late modernisation and nationalisation feminism (1860–1930).
- The spread of the concept of modernising women's rights into the middle classes (1930–1965).
- The period of class-politics and social welfare (1968–1985).
- Independent radical feminism (1986–1995).
- The effects of global feminism and women's human rights post the Beijing World Conference of Women (1995–2000).
- Institutionalisation within the government alliances between women's organisations (2000–2005).
- Project feminism period (apolitical politisation) and the consolidation of women's rights in liberal democracies (2005–).

Women's rights-oriented NGOs have gained visibility in Turkey after the 1950s. Women's associations began being re-founded once more following the changes made to union law. The Women's People Party is re-founded alongside the Turkish branches of international associations such as the Soroptimists and the International Federation of University Women. The Progressive Women's Association was founded in 1975 and was followed by the foundation of the Democratic Women's Association, The Working Women's Union, and the Revolutionist Women's Association (Tekeli). A feminist movement that questioned male domination, potency, and power dominated after the 1980s (Koray, 1998). Female organisations that question patriarchy and gender politics formed within the feminist paradigm (Ecevit, 2004). We observe that female-oriented NGOs in Turkey have kept the issues of economic and cultural rights on their agenda, and have developed their own discourses. The word feminism ('feminizm' in Turkish) was first used in YAZKO (Writers and Translators Cooperative) in 1982, which was followed by the Women's Network Book Club in 1984, the first Feminist Weekend Days in 1989, and the first Women's Assembly (Tekeli, 1995). Leading female-oriented NGOs in Turkey in the 1990s included the Association for Supporting Contemporary Life, research centres for women's studies in İstanbul and Marmara universities, The Women's Library and Information Centre in İstanbul, the Purple Roof Women's Shelter Foundation, and the Association of Supporting and Educating Female Candidates (Tekeli). As Sancar (2013) has stated, NGO alliances have been prominent in women's movement in Turkey following the 2000s. A chief example of these alliances is the civil society formations in İzmir. Close to 100 women's rights associations are active in İzmir according to 2011 data. These associations and foundations are continuing the fight to assure women's rights as the components of various platforms and coalitions.

The next part of the study will address the media ownership of the female-oriented NGOs in Turkey which are classified as foundations under Turkish regulations and the factors affecting the sustainability of these media.

4. THE METHODOLOGY OF THE RESEARCH

The focal point of this study is constituted by the community media of NGOs in İzmir that focus on women and the sustainability of this media. This study aims to answer the questions:

RQ1 (Research Question 1). Which channels do the NGOs in İzmir that focus on women use?

RQ2. Why do they prefer these channels?

RQ3. What are the factors that affect the sustainability of the media they've used?

In order to find answers to the above questions, qualitative research methods and case study design, which is accepted as a pattern in the qualitative research process, were used in the study. The study was completed in two years. In order to obtain detailed and in-depth information on the subject, multiple sources of information were used.

Quantitative content analysis was used for the *RQ1*. Thus, the author tried to show the media ownership structure of female-oriented non-NGOs in İzmir. Then an inductive process was applied for *RQ2* and *RQ3*. Data were collected through in-depth interviews. Then data were coded, at the last stage the themes were created. After this process, the themes were compared with the literature and a descriptive analysis was performed. Data collection technique, sampling design, data analysis methods, and validity/reliability are explained in detail below.

5. DATA COLLECTION TECHNIQUES

Document analysis has been performed in the study to answer *RQ1* (Which channels do the NGOs in İzmir that focus on women use?)

> (Document analysis) encompasses the analysis of the written materials that contain information about the case or cases that are the subject of research. (Yıldırım & Şimşek, 2013, p. 217)

The media ownership of NGOs in İzmir that focus on women has been analysed both by asking the members/representatives of said NGOs and by online document analysis as a part of this study.

As for the relationship between RQ2 and RQ3 (why the NGOs that focus on women choose these channels and the relationship between media and sustainability), the study uses a qualitative process in accordance with the case study design. In-depth face-to-face interviews have been conducted and answers to these RQs were sought. The RQs were composed of open-ended questions that have been composed based on literature and aim to add to this literature by describing the topic.

6. SAMPLING DESIGN

Homogeneous sampling and criterion sampling have been used together as sampling methods in accordance with the aim and subject of the research.

To this aim:

As part of the document analysis: A female-focussed association that served as an umbrella organisation that represented 41 female-focused NGOs was included. The components of this association include the centre, foundations, associations, initiatives, and platforms. Only establishments that have the status of foundation or association were included, and only the İzmir branches of national and international organisations were included on a district-by-district basis. Fifteen foundations/associations that fit these criteria were included in the study. Ten of these foundations/associations are the İzmir branches of national/international foundations/associations, while the other five are categorised as foundations/associations based in İzmir.

As part of the in-depth interviews:

Representatives/members of associations and foundations based in İzmir that created content for three or more types of media were included in accordance with the results of the document analysis. Although situation analyses are intended to end when the study reaches a saturation of information, interviews conducted with five to six people were considered to be enough (Yıldırım & Şimşek, 2013, pp. 84–85). In this study, which has been designed according to the case study design, interviews were conducted with the members/representatives of seven establishments. The data were collected by meeting with the members/representatives at various times for two years as a part of a project.

7. DATA ANALYSIS METHODS

Another important matter in qualitative research is data analysis. Descriptive analysis and content analysis were used as techniques when analysing the data during the study.

According to Yıldırım and Şimşek (2013, pp. 256–257), there are four stages of descriptive analysis: First, a frame is formed based on the dimensions of the interview and/or observation; then, the data are read and sorted in accordance with this frame; the data are then described and directly supplemented by sources; finally, the cause and effect relationship between the findings is explained. Coding was performed for *RQ2* and *RQ3* and certain themes were discovered. These themes were compared to literature.

Another method of data analysis employed in qualitative studies is content analysis. Content analysis can include qualitative or quantitative processes. 'The quantification of qualitative data is: transforming written data obtained through interviews, observations or document analysis into numerical data through certain processes' (Yıldırım & Şimşek, 2013, p. 274). This study tries to identify which forms of media NGOs focused on women mainly use through quantitative analysis.

The names of the female-focused NGOs and their members/representatives have remained anonymous per their own requests while writing this report and were coded as participant organisation (*PO1–PO2–PO3–PO4–PO5–PO6–PO7–PO8–PO9–PO10–PO11–PO12–PO13–PO14–PO15*) for the establishments, and (*P1–P2–P3–P4–P5–P6–P7*) for the participants.

8. VALIDITY AND RELIABILITY

Certain precautions need to be taken to ensure validity and reliability in qualitative researches. Maxwell (2018, pp. 126–129) states that certain techniques such as, intense and sustained involvement, participant-affirmation, diversification, and comparison can be used for validity. The validity of data has been hopefully achieved in this study by sustained long-term (three years) involvement, participant-affirmation (*P2–P5–P6*), and meeting with members/representatives from different establishments to achieve a diverse range of data.

9. FINDINGS

1. Which channels do the NGOs in İzmir that focus on women use?

From the study and as a result of the coding, one could determine that the NGOs in İzmir that focus on women in the sample ($n = 15$) do not have any ownerships in traditional media channels (TV, radio, newspapers, magazines). It was discovered that establishments generally use new media channels for community communication. A distribution of new media channels categorised as social media and websites is shown in Table 1.

In this study, we have divided social media by the applications Facebook, Instagram, YouTube, and Twitter and investigated the account ownership of female-focused NGOs in the sample across these applications. It was identified that NGOs in İzmir that Focus on Women have a high rate of account ownership in Facebook compared to other applications (Fig. 1).

Table 1. New Media Ownership of NGOs That Focus on Women ($n = 15$).

New Media	Available	Unavailable	Total(n)
Associations/Foundations with Social Media Account	12	3	15
Associations/Foundations with Webpages	13	2	15

The document analysis that was performed has led to the identification of seven establishments among the NGOs in İzmir that focus on women that have three or more channels of media. This included both social media accounts and website ownership. The axis on Fig. 2 labelled with the code 'PO' shows the female-focused NGOs while the vertical axis shows media ownership numbers.

The study's findings on *RQ2* and *RQ3* (acquired as a result of the in-depth interviews) are as follows.

RQ2. Why do the NGOs in İzmir that focus on women choose these channels?

The document analysis has revealed that female-focused NGOs mainly own social media accounts and websites. The following questions were asked to the participants based on these data.

P2. I already use Facebook, so it seems simpler to do the work of the association through here.

P3. We don't really use our website as an association. Sure, we have one, but all our friends are already on Facebook. It's easier to reach them and organise through there. It's important that it's free, we're already doing this voluntarily, our financial resources are limited. We can reach more people through there.

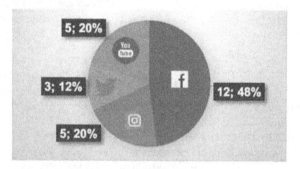

Fig. 1. Distribution of the Account Ownership of Female-focused NGOs in İzmir across Social Media Applications.

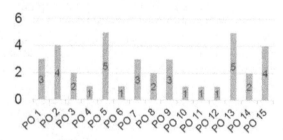

Fig. 2. Media Counts Belonging to Female-focused Associations/Foundations in İzmir.

P6. That's where the youth is, we can reach them free of charge, there are young women who follow us. That TV, radio stuff you talked about is too difficult. It's a matter of means.

As the answers reveal, the main reasons for the prevalence of social media can be concluded to be financial factors and the prevalence of these channels in the participants' own personal uses.

The findings regarding *RQ3* 'What are the factors that affect the sustainability of community media?' are as follows:

Four open-ended questions based on literature were asked during the in-depth face-to-face interviews in order to answer this RQ. The code-theme data analysis conducted in this frame yielded the following themes.

9.1. Finance Factor

The participants are of the opinion that financial problems are among the most important factors that negatively affect the sustainability of community media. The cost of creating a medium, creating related employment opportunities, and reaching the professionals that will create content for the medium is seen as an expensive activity for these NGOs that are trying to carry their activities with limited financial resources. The participants have identified their limited financial resources as the main reason they have gravitated to newer forms of media instead of traditional outlets. They have also added that the cost of creating and maintaining traditional media outlets is not feasible for associations and foundations carrying on with limited budgets, and that they usually elect to choose the newer, more cost-effective media outlets instead of traditional outlets.

The participants are of the opinion that new media outlets are advantageous both because their initial investment cost is low and because of their influence and popularity.

P1. It isn't really possible for us to reach communication outlets like tv, radio or newspapers because the financial resources of our association are limited. However, we are trying to make our voice heard through fields like Facebook or Instagram by our own means. These are free so we can deal with them.

P3. Of course, I would love it if we could have our own newspaper, but it isn't possible. We simply can't afford it.

This theme runs parallel with the literature, which states that community media often exists on the boundaries of economic sustainability. This is because community media is often a construct of disadvantaged groups who do not have much spending power and must procure their economic sustainability from financial sources outside the ordinary ones (advertisement, sponsorship, sales, etc.) (Buckley, 2011, p. 35). This in turn affects the sustainability of community media and causes these channels to be short-lived.

9.2. The Factor of Content Production

The participants have stated the process of content production to be one of the factors that affect sustainability. Although community media can make use of different financial structures, they still face difficulties in using these tools and produce content; and this affects the sustainability of the media. According to the participants, even if associations/foundations overcome the problem of accessing media, the sustainability of this media seems infeasible as they cannot regularly produce quality news/information.

They have listed the reasons for this phenomenon mainly as:

- Them lacking the know-how about the process of generating news for traditional media outlets.
- Them being unable to provide sustainable employment for people to master this field.
- That producing content for new forms of media is a new field for them, and they lack the necessary education in this field.

P2. We don't have someone in our association to run our social media, and us members can't really focus on this. We're usually busy with other work.

P7. We are sorely lacking in this field. There is a need for young volunteers who know this stuff. We can only do so much.

P3. I joined the association as a volunteer. I participate in many of the associations' activities and trainings, but we need to announce these from the right places in the right way. I don't know how to do this, or how to write things. It's not like sharing stuff on my own Facebook. You need to be more careful; you need the know-how.

The participants, aware of the importance of content creation, think that the content they produce should encompass not just the activities of the association/foundation, but must also transmit the aim of informing and educate their communities and then passing on the idea of societal gender equality to their target audiences in a qualitative and correct way.

9.3. Legal Factors

The participants agree that one of the factors regarding the sustainability and diversity of community media is the hardship of being a media owner in the eyes of the law. Both real people and legal entities (like companies, associations, or public institutions) can own periodical publications according to Turkish law. However, the participants view being able to have a periodical publication or own a media establishment in Turkey as a problem that requires the tackling of difficult legal procedures in addition to requiring a financial investment. Therefore, they usually don't elect to broadcast through traditional channels of mass media and instead use new media methods as the mode of communication for the community.

P1. I sometimes hesitate while writing captions underneath events. I don't even know why I hesitate, we're a legal association but I'm afraid I'll say the wrong thing.

P7. Even if we were to somehow come across some money as a foundation, there are so many procedures to this we don't know how to deal with them or even where to start. The process is difficult.

UNESCO has seen community media as one of the components of sustainability since the 2000s. It also stresses the importance of community media, which is seen as the means of communication of the communities of member countries, for legal renown. UNESCO encourages countries to legally acknowledge community media, be fair while granting access to licenses, and form plans and strategies to create sustainable financial resources (UNESCO, 2015).

9.4. Technical/Infrastructure Factors

Another factor that negatively affects sustainability which emerged during the interviews is that the community lacks technical resources. According to the participants, this may even sometimes mean that the community doesn't even have its own computer. Associations/Foundations hope to achieve the sustainability of their community media with the technical hardware and software resources of their volunteers.

P1. We don't even have a computer that belongs to the association. Everyone is trying to do something with their own resources. It's all we can do.

P5. We may want to create a simple poster for one of our events, but this gets very difficult sometimes. We run into problems like finding a computer or procuring a picture that could be related. It's not just this though, I don't know for certain what I should write, what sort of caption will generate the most interest.

The literature states that technical sustainability requires the selection of low-cost, easy-to-maintain, easily replaceable, and appropriate technological devices alongside technical support and 'know-how'. Community media that does not have reliable technical systems runs the risk of losing its audience, workers, and supporters (Buckley, 2011). Technical factors have become increasingly more important for the sustainability of community media as communication technologies keep evolving at an accelerating rate.

10. CONCLUSION

Findings show that that associations/foundations in İzmir that focus on women:

- Ensure community communications via new media methods.
- Mostly use Facebook as the social media outlet of choice.

- Do not have their own websites if they are an İzmir branch of a national/ international website, but are instead represented on a page in the websites of their umbrella organisations; and use social media.
- Choose these channels due to the insufficiency of financial resources, equipment, or information.

We have identified four factors that affect the sustainability of the community media of associations/foundations in İzmir that focus on women: Financial issues, content production, legal matters, and technology. The steps that should be taken to reduce/eliminate these factors can be listed as follows, based on extrapolations from literature analysis:

(a) *Financial Factors*: The financial factors that affect sustainability can be reduced via international funds, by developing strategies to increase voluntary support, or by cooperating with local authorities or other establishments with similar goals.

(b) *The Factor of Content Production:* Communities need activities such as cooperation with shareholders or educational establishments, or by meeting with members of the community for content management which can reduce the effects of this factor.

(c) *Legal Factors:* An interest group can be assembled by meeting with local or national authorities on the international legal renown of the community media.

(d) *Technical/Infrastructure Factors:* The technical abilities of the establishment can be improved by applying for support funds from international support foundations to improve the infrastructure of NGOs.

REFERENCES

Atton, C. (2015). *The Routledge companion to alternative and community media*. London: Routledge Publishing.

Buckley, S. (Ed.). (2011). *Community media: A good practice handbook*. Paris: UNESCO Publishing.

Carpentier, N., Lie, R., & Servaes, J. (2003). Community media: Muting the democratic discourse? *Continuum: Journal of Media & Cultural Studies, 17*(1), 51–68. http://dx.doi.org/10.1080/1030431022000049010

Creswell, J. (2012). *Qualitative inquiry and research design: Choosing among five approaches*. Thousand Oaks, CA: Sage Publishing.

Ecevit, Y. (2004). Important tools organization for women in the democratic development in Turkey. In Y. Ecevit (Ed.), *Women on Turkey and EU panel* (pp. 13–15). Istanbul: Bogazici University Publishing.

European Platform of Regulatory Authorities (EPRA). (2017). Community media sustainability. Retrieved from https://www.epra.org/news_items/community-media-sustainability-unesco-s-policy-series-targeting-broadcasting-regulators

Fuller, L. K. (2007). Introduction. In L. K. Fuller (Ed.), *Community media: International perspectives* (pp. 1–21). New York, NY: Palgrave Publishing.

Hatcher, J. A. (2012). Community journalism as an international phenomenon. In B. Reader & J. A. Hatcher (Eds.), *Foundations of community journalism* (pp. 241–255). Thousand Oaks, CA: Sage Publications.

Jankowski, N. (2003). Community media research: A quest for theoretically-grounded models. *Javnost – The Public*, *10*(1), 5–14. doi:10.1080/13183222.2003.11008818

Kern European Affairs. (2007). *The state of community media in the European Union*. Belçika: European Parliament's Committee on Culture and Education. Retrieved from http://www.europarl.europa.eu/RegData/etudes/etudes/join/2007/408943/IPOL-CULT_ET%282007%29408943_EN.pdf

Koray, M. (1998). Questions and problems of women's movement in Turkey. In A. B. Hacımirzaoğlu (Ed.), *Women and men in the 75th anniversary* (pp. 361–375). İstanbul: History Foundation Publishing.

Maslog, C. C., Navaro, N. L., Tabing, L. N., & Teodoro, L. V. (Eds.). (1997). *Communication for people power: An introduction to community communication*. Quezon City: UNESCO-TAMBULI Project.

Maxwell, J. A. (1996). Qualitative research design: An interactive approach. Thousand Oaks, CA: Sage Publishing.

Mendel, T. (2013). Tuning into development: International comparative survey of community broadcasting regulation. Retrieved from https://unesdoc.unesco.org/ark:/48223/pf0000224662

Milan, S. (2009). Four steps to community media as a development tool. *Development in Practise*, *19*, 589–609.

Özbudun, E. (1999). Civil society and democratic consolidation in Turkey. In E. Elisabeth Özdalga & S. Persson (Eds.), *Civil society, democracy and Islamic world* (pp. 112–121). İstanbul: History Foundation Publishing.

Özer, M. H. (2008). Economic and social functions of civil society organizations. *Electronic Journal of Social Sciences Journal*, *7*(26), 86–97.

Sancar, S. (2013). Politics of women's movement in Turkey: Historical context, political agenda and authenticity. In S. Sancar (Ed.), *Very short distance... 21 st Century feminist studies in Turkey* (pp. 61–120). İstanbul: Koç University Publishing.

Tekeli, Ş. (1995). *Women's in Turkey in 80s. Women from women's perspective in Turkey*. İstanbul: İletişim Publishing.

Tekeli, Ş. (2017). History of women's movement in Turkey. Retrieved from http://ka-der.org.tr/wp-content/uploads/2017/12/kadin-hareketinin-tarihi-sirin-tekeli.pdf

UNESCO. (2015). *International seminar on community media sustainability: Strengthening policies and funding*. Paris: UNESCO. Retrieved from http://www.unesco.org/new/en/communication-and-information/media-development/community-media/community-media-sustainability-strengthening-policies-and-funding/

Yıldırım, A., & Şimşek, H. (2013). *Qualitative methods in social sciences*. Ankara: Seçkin Publishing.

Ying, R. K. (2017). *Applications of case studies research*. (I. Günbayı, Trans.). Ankara: Nobel Akademic Publishing.

CHAPTER 13

THE EUROPEAN UNION'S FIGHT AGAINST DISCRIMINATION IN SPORTS

Nihan Akıncılar Köseoğlu

ABSTRACT

Introduction – *Since the entry into force of the Treaty of Lisbon (2009), sport has, for the first time, become a policy area of the European Union (EU).*

Purpose – *The aim of this chapter is to investigate the EU's anti-discrimination policy for sports.*

Methodology – *Firstly, all the agreements, regulations, directives, and court decisions regarding nondiscrimination in sports will be reviewed. Secondly, discriminative examples in different sport branches will be investigated. In fact, this research will examine discrimination in both professional and amateur sports, including discrimination towards men, women, and LGBTIQ+ persons. Thirdly, the bodies, institutions, or persons who are accused of any kind of discrimination in sports will be researched, including fans, officials of clubs and federations, referees, players, and sports media. Finally, recommendations will be presented for the development of an improved sports policy that is capable of increasing diversity and equal participation in European sports.*

Findings – *For many underlying reasons, which the author will try to address in this chapter, there is a tendency to ignore discrimination in sports. Although the EU has passed legislation specifically designed to prohibit discrimination in sport, neither the legal arrangements nor their applications in Member States serve to end any kind of discrimination in the realm of sports. Thus, this chapter will attempt to raise awareness of this crucial and unending problem.*

Contemporary Issues in Business, Economics and Finance
Contemporary Studies in Economic and Financial Analysis, Volume 104, 193–202
ISSN: 1569-3759/doi:10.1108/S1569-375920200000104013

Keywords: European Union; discrimination; European Union; discrimination; human rights; law; sports; European sports policy

1. INTRODUCTION

Before the Lisbon Treaty entered into force, the European Union (EU) had adopted an indirect sports policy, which concerned the protection of the Single European Market principles in the realm of sports. Just as the same with the other human rights categories, 'free movement of workers' was accepted as more important in terms of the players'/athletes' rights rather than the right to do sport freely. This can be understood from the decisions of the European Court of Justice. However, as a result of the Lisbon Treaty, sport has, for the first time, become a policy area of the EU, and therefore, in the literature, sports policy of the EU or of the Member and Candidate countries started to gain ground.

In this chapter, the EU's anti-discrimination policy for sports will be investigated, even though there are few resources on direct discrimination in sports. The report of the European Union Agency for Fundamental Rights (FRA) (2010) entitled 'Racism, ethnic discrimination, and exclusion of migrants and minorities in sport' emerges as the principal resource for this chapter. Moreover, Bradbury (2011) wrote in detail about the discrimination against minorities and women in European football. Many other books and journals alluding to indirect discrimination in sports have been consulted.

1.1. Anti-discrimination Law in Sports in the EU

In order to understand the anti-discrimination law in sports, all of the agreements, regulations, directives, court decisions, and decisions of other non-governmental or intergovernmental bodies and institutions regarding non-discrimination in sports will be reviewed.

Anti-discrimination law in Europe is based primarily on Article 14 of the European Convention on Human Rights (ECHR) (Council of Europe, 1950) and Article 21 of the EU Charter of Fundamental Rights (EU, 2000b). According to Article 14 (prohibition of discrimination) of the ECHR:

> the enjoyment of the rights and freedoms set forth in this Convention shall be secured without discrimination on any ground such as sex, race, colour, language, religion, political or other opinion, national or social origin, association with a national minority, property, birth or other status. (Council of Europe, 1950)

Article 21 (non-discrimination) of the EU Charter of Fundamental Rights states that:

> any discrimination based on any ground such as sex, race, colour, ethnic or social origin, genetic features, language, religion or belief, political or any other opinion, membership of a national minority, property, birth, disability, age or sexual orientation shall be prohibited. (EU, 2000b)

Moreover, Article 165 of the Treaty on the Functioning of the European Union (TFEU), states:

the Union shall contribute to the promotion of European sporting issues, while taking account of the specific nature of sport, its structures based on voluntary activity, and its social and educational function. (EU, 2012)

It argues that EU actions shall be aimed at:

developing the European dimension in sport, by promoting fairness and openness in sporting competitions and cooperation between bodies responsible for sports, and by protecting the physical and moral integrity of sportsmen and sportswomen, especially the youngest sportsmen and sportswomen. (EU, 2012)

After the entry into force of the Lisbon Treaty in December 2009, the EU Sport Ministers discussed EU sport policy in a formal meeting for the first time in May 2010 (DG for Culture and Education, 2010, p. 6).

Meanwhile, the Racial Equality Directive emphasises on the equal 'access to and supply of goods and services' which allow 'the participation of all persons irrespective of racial or ethnic origin' (EU, 2000a), in fitness clubs, swimming pools, or other sports facilities. Moreover, the European Commission's White Paper on Sport (2007) created an outline of EU sports policy. The European Parliament Resolution of 8 May 2008 on the 'White Paper on Sport' emphasised transforming the sporting arena into a workplace for players and athletes, free from discrimination and racism. Moreover, according to the Council of the EU Framework Decision on combating certain forms and expressions of racism and xenophobia by means of criminal law, 'each Member State shall take the measures necessary to ensure that the ... intentional conduct is punishable' (EU, 2008).

There are also several non-discrimination agreements between the EU and countries such as Ukraine, Armenia, and Morocco designed to protect third-country nationals with regard to 'working conditions, remuneration or dismissal as compared to its own nationals' of a Member State (Hannelin, 2016, p. 83).

Since 1976, when the Committee of Ministers adopted the European Sport for All Charter, the Council of Europe has in fact been the leading actor in European sports policy. With the European Sports Charter (1992), the Council of Europe began referring to anti-discrimination in the sporting arena. The EU also accepted the European Sports Charter as the primary document for the issues related to sport. In terms of anti-discrimination in sport, Article 4/1 of the Charter prohibits any discrimination in access to sports facilities and sports activities (Council of Europe, 2001). In 2000, the Council of Europe's Resolution on preventing racism, xenophobia, and intolerance in sport included the European Sport Ministers' concerns regarding 'recent outbreaks of racist behaviour at sport events'. The Istanbul Declaration (2004) also contributed to the intercultural dialogue in sports. In addition, ECRI's (European Commission against Racism and Intolerance) General Policy Recommendation No. 12 of the Council of Europe was adopted in December 2008 'on combating racism and racial discrimination in the field of sport'. It:

sets out a wide range of measures that the governments of Member States are advised to adopt in order to successfully combat racism and racial discrimination in the field of sport. (Council of Europe, 2008)

With regards to the United Nations, discrimination in sport was first touched upon in the preamble of the International Charter on Physical Education and Sport (1978). Moreover, the World Conference against Racism, Racial Discrimination, Xenophobia and Related Intolerance Declaration (2001) and the 'Global efforts for the total elimination of racism and the comprehensive implementation of and follow-up to the Durban Declaration and Programme of Action' Report (2014) invited Member States, international sports federations, and intergovernmental organisations to increase their efforts to fight against racism and discrimination in sport.

It is important here to mention that, of these above-mentioned documents referring to anti-discrimination in sport, only the Racial Equality Directive (2000) and the Council's Framework Decision on combating certain forms and expressions of racism and xenophobia by means of criminal law (2008) are binding. Other declarations, charters, recommendations, and resolutions remain nonbinding for all the Member States of the associated international organisation. Therefore, discriminative incidents in the sporting arena are continually encountered in Europe.

In addition to this anti-discrimination legislation, the decisions of the Court of Arbitration for Sport (CAS), the Court of Justice of the European Union (CJEU), and the European Court of Human Rights (ECtHR) regarding any kind of discrimination in sports are investigated. Unfortunately, no cases are found in the decisions of either the ECtHR or the CJEU under the direct title of 'discrimination in sports'. Nevertheless, there are many CAS cases under the title of 'discrimination in sports'; they are, however, primarily related to the testosterone threshold of female athletes. That is, court cases involving discrimination are focussing primarily on free movement of workers and anti-doping rules.

First, the Walrave judgement (1974), the then European Court of Justice (ECJ) concluded that 'the practice of sport is subject to Community law only in so far as it constitutes an economic activity' (European Court, 1974). Dona (1976) was the second important sports case of the ECJ, which stated that the free movement of workers principle outweighed the Italian football rules, which stipulated that only Italian nationals could play professional football (European Court, 1976). Third, the ECJ's ruling in the Bosman case (1995) illustrates that free movement of players and athletes outweighed any regulation regarding the realm of sports (European Court, 1995). That is, the transfer fee of Bosman, who was at the end of his contract, was contrary to the free movement of workers, according to the Court. In 2010, however, the Court decided, in the Bernard case (European Court, 2010), that training compensation demanded by the football club from the trained player was compatible with EU law (European Sports Law and Policy Bulletin, 1/2010, p. 13). Finally, the Lehtonen case concerned a Finnish basketball player who transferred to a Belgian team outside the transfer window for EU players but within the window for third-country players due to the deadlines, and he encountered disparate treatment as a result of this situation (European Court, 2000b). The Court decided according to Article 48 of the EC Treaty (Article 45 TFEU now) that such disparate treatment may be justified only if 'objective reasons concerning only sport as such or relating to differences between the position of players from a federation in the European zone and that of players from a federation not in that zone' exist (European Court, 2000a).

Although the CAS was established 'to deal with sports-related disputes, not matters of human rights' (Schwab, 2018, p. 219), it decides on the elimination of discrimination from sports. For instance, in the Dutee Chand case (2014), the CAS accepted that this Indian sprinter faced discrimination due to hyper-androgenism regulations of the International Association of Athletics Federations (CAS, 2018). There are also many other decisions of the CAS about doping events under the title of discrimination in sport.

Notwithstanding, there are several important institutions and bodies that fight against discrimination in sports, for example, Equality Bodies and National Human Rights Institutions (NHRIs), EU Agency for FRA, Football Against Racism in Europe (FARE), the Sport Unit as a sub-unit of the Directorate-General for Education and Culture (within the European Commission), sports federations, and sports clubs. Equality Bodies and NHRIs in Member States are also made responsible for combating racist and discriminatory activities in sports. Nevertheless, players and athletes are largely unaware of these bodies' jurisdiction for legal action. In 2000, UEFA and FARE collaborated to prepare the '10-Point Plan of Action for Professional Football Clubs' (UEFA, 2002). Meanwhile, 'FARE Action Week Against Racism', which has been held every October since 2000 and is observed in over 40 countries, attracts attention throughout Europe. In addition, 'Unite Against Racism in European Football', a collaboration between UEFA and FARE in 2003, effectively raised awareness of discrimination in football. Furthermore, the European Commission's Sport Unit has closely worked with UEFA and FARE. The DG for Education and Culture provided funding in 2008 for a television advertisement against racism in football; the advertisement was broadcasted during the 2008 UEFA European Football Championship (Euro 2008). Finally, UEFA's current 'Home-grown Player Rule' for more equal participation in football deserves attention. Quota regulations limiting the access of non-nationals to professional and amateur sports are balanced with the 'Home-grown Player Rule' so that European football becomes more balanced according to nationality/citizenship.

The World Players Association (WPA) was established in 2014:

> as an international federation of player and athlete associations and has affiliates that operate at the global, regional, and national levels as well as on a sport-specific and multi-sport basis. (Schwab, 2018, p. 223)

On 14 December 2017, the WPA released the Universal Declaration of Player Rights, which is the first example of internationally recognised human and labour rights of players and athletes, to protect players and athletes from ongoing and systemic human rights violations in sports (WPA, 2017). This declaration is expected to influence the European sports federations in a positive way, prompting them to prepare detailed rights and punishments in terms of the players' and athletes' human and labour rights.

When the statutes of the different sports federations are researched, the FRA (2010, p. 23) discovers that 12 sport branches (Football, Basketball, Volleyball, Handball, Ice Hockey, Speedway racing, Tennis, Cricket, Alpine skiing, Athletics, Hurling, Korfball) have anti-racism or anti-discrimination clauses in their statutes.

While the International Korfball Federation demands a written declaration from its members that promises anti-racism and non-discrimination:

> other federations merely state that racism and ethnic discrimination would not be tolerated in their sport or they stress that the practice of their sport is open to everyone without any racial, religious or other discriminating constraint. (FRA, 2010, pp. 22–23)

Only the European Cycling Union does not directly mention anti-racism or anti-discrimination; it mentions the equality of all sportsmen, though. Of these 13 sport branches, however, only FIFA establishes clear and detailed disciplinary regulations to apply in the case of any kind of discrimination in football. Also, the European Cricket Council has clear sanctions on racism and discrimination.

Finally, only 10 Member States in the EU have prepared special legislation on racism in sport: Belgium, Bulgaria, Cyprus, Czechia, France, Italy, Luxembourg, Portugal, Romania, and Spain (FRA, 2010, p. 40). Sanctions for racist incidents in sport vary from fines to imprisonment in those countries.

1.2. Discriminative Examples in Sports

The aim of this chapter is to investigate discriminative examples in different sport branches, such as football, basketball, volleyball, handball, boxing, athletics, table tennis, swimming, and rowing. Obvious discriminative, especially racist, examples, however, can be found only in football, where players of African origin face monkey calls, racist insults, and bananas thrown at them in the stadium by European football fans. Recent examples of racism witnessed during the UEFA Euro 2020 qualifying tournament will therefore be reviewed.

In the Germany–Serbia match in March 2019, İlkay Gündoğan and Leroy Sane, players belonging to Germany's national team experienced racist chants, whose perpetrators gave themselves up to the police after an investigation aimed at their arrest was launched (DW, 2019) (Deutsche Welle, 2019).

Moreover, the UEFA Control, Ethics and Disciplinary Body (CEDB) punished the Montenegrin national team after the UK-Montenegro match in March 2019, in which Danny Rose from the UK's national team was insulted (Diken, 2019).

In a report released in 2010, the FRA analysed the EU's 27 Member States (in 2010, therefore Croatia was excluded), searching for incidences of racism, discrimination, and exclusion in football and athletics and also in a third sport, which is very popular in certain Member States. Of all the selected sports, only football clubs and federations reported the existence of discriminative, racist, and xenophobic examples in their sport (FRA, 2010). Thus, only football establishes detailed legislation, and also detailed penalties, for discrimination. Other branches, including athletics, basketball, and volleyball, state that there are no reported cases of discrimination or even assert the non-existence of such problems.

In fact, only European football, Union of European Football Associations (UEFA), has clear disciplinary procedures against racism and discrimination in sports (FRA, 2010, p. 7). For example, a UK football club, Liverpool, banned 40 discriminative words for fans in the stadium, including 'Jewish', 'gypsy', 'Muslim', 'Paki', 'homo', 'that's gay', 'she-man', and 'ladyboy' (Fanatik, 2013).

The sports club also announced that fans will face punishments, including even lifelong disqualification from the stadium, if they use any of these 40 words.

Although the Euroleague Basketball launched campaign 'Not in my house' against any kind of discrimination and violence in sport, and especially in basketball, in 2018, efforts in basketball remain limited with regards to the fight against discrimination, as its policies and sanctions continue to suffer from various shortcomings (Eurohoops, 2018).

In further research, discrimination will be investigated in every branch of sport in Europe because unreported cases involving men, women, and LGBTIQ+ persons in both professional and amateur sports may be uncovered through more detailed research.

1.3. Who is Accused of Discrimination in Sports?

In general, fans, officials of clubs and federations, referees, players, and sports media are accused of various kinds of discrimination in sports. According to the reported cases, most discriminative events originate from, or are instigated by, fans/spectators. Nevertheless, certain officials of clubs and federations are also accused of discrimination. For instance, the former president of Austrian football club SK Sturm Graz insulted his Bosnian coach and some players with ex-Yugoslavian backgrounds. The coach initiated legal proceedings against the former president, and the court decided in his favour (FRA, 2010, p. 38). Moreover, the owner of a Romanian club, Steaua Bucharest, was penalised by the Romanian Football Federation due to racist, anti-gypsy, and Islamophobic comments he made regarding the Hungarian community in Romania (FRA, 2010, p. 38).

On the one hand, referees and players/athletes may themselves be affected by racism. On the other hand, they may exhibit racist or discriminative attitudes towards other players or athletes. They may even engage in racist or discriminative behaviour, which can exert devastating effects on other players or athletes.

Sports media also represent an important realm that can engender direct or indirect discrimination. For example, the media tends to attribute the success of black players/athletes to the athletic black body alone.

1.4. Recommendations for the Development of an Improved EU Sports Policy

In terms of recommendations for the development of an improved EU sports policy that is capable of increasing diversity and equal participation in European sports, people and institutions accused of discrimination in sports could be given non-discrimination training. The aim of such trainings is to educate people on the behaviours, slogans, cheers, announcements, and broadcasting that are legally defined as discriminatory on 'sex, race, colour, language, religion, political or other opinion, national or social origin, association with a national minority, property, birth, or other status'. Such training may be called 'Training on Anti-Discrimination in Sports'. Moreover, a 'Discriminating Signs and Symbols Guide in Sports' that includes all kinds of discrimination, alongside examples, could be prepared and delivered to players, administrators, security personnel, associations, and sports club fans (FARE, 2016). Thus, preventive measures against discrimination could be planned and implemented both inside and outside sports facilities. Other prohibitive measures (such as making announcements against discrimination both inside and outside the facility, controlling fans' banners and flags before the competition, making it a condition for season-ticket (if it exists) holders that they do not participate in racist abuse, and taking disciplinary action against players who engage in racial abuse) should continue to be harshly implemented.

Through this 'Training on Anti-Discrimination in Sports', an EU Policy on Anti-Discrimination in Sports could be prepared, and discrimination in every branch of sports could be abolished. Sports governing bodies should also prepare anti-discrimination and equality regulations and should implement them effectively.

2. CONCLUSION

Given the fact that legislations for discrimination in sports for the member states of the United Nations, Council of Europe and the EU are not binding, there is still a tendency to ignore discrimination in sports; this is seen in the lack of implementation of the existing binding and non-binding legislation, the lack of treatment of fans, referees, players/athletes, sports clubs, and federations regarding which behaviour constitutes discrimination, and unawareness of players and athletes about filing an action after a discriminative event. Although the EU has created legislation to enforce anti-discrimination measures in sport, neither the legal arrangements nor their applications in Member States serve to end any kind of discrimination in the realm of sports. Thus, the aim of this chapter was to raise awareness of this crucial and unrelenting problem.

Although some EU Member States have raised awareness of racism and discrimination in sport by establishing or using already-established institutions, such as, the Centre for Equal Opportunities and Opposition to Racism (CEOOR) in Belgium, Anti-Discrimination Agencies (ADAs) in the Netherlands and the Spanish State Commission against Violence in Sport, the number of reported and registered cases remains limited. Thus, players/athletes must be treated fairly and equally in sport and if there is any kind of discrimination, they must be encouraged to report the case to a governmental or non-governmental body, or even file an action about it. By doing so, discriminative cases in sport will surface easily and spread rapidly, so an anti-discrimination policy in sports can be established in more detail by the EU or by the Member and Candidate States.

REFERENCES

Bradbury, S. (2011). *Representation and structural discrimination in football in Europe: The case of minorities and women [full report]*. Loughborough: Loughborough University.

CAS. (2018, January 19). *Athletics – Dutee Chand case*. Lausanne: Court of Arbitration for Sport. Retrieved from https://www.tas-cas.org/fileadmin/user_upload/Media_Release_3759_Jan_2018.pdf. Accessed on August 11, 2019.

Council of Europe. (1950, November 4). ECHR. Retrieved from https://www.echr.coe.int/Documents/Convention_ENG.pdf. Accessed on August 3, 2019.

Council of Europe. (2001, May 16). *Recommendation No. R (92) 13 on the revised European sports charter*. Strasbourg: Council of Europe. Retrieved from https://rm.coe.int/16804c9dbb. Accessed on August 11, 2019.

Council of Europe. (2008, December 19). *ECRI general policy recommendation no.12 on combating racism and racial discrimination in the field of sport*. Strasbourg: Council of Europe. Retrieved from https://rm.coe.int/ecri-general-policy-recommendation-no-12-on-combating-racism-and-racia/16808b5ae7. Accessed on August 9, 2019.

Diken. (2019, March 26). UEFA, Karadağ'ı ırkçı tezahürat nedeniyle disipline sevk etti. *Diken*. Retrieved from http://www.diken.com.tr/uefa-karadagi-irkci-tezahurat-nedeniyle-disipline-sevk-etti/. Accessed on August 21, 2019.

DG for Culture and Education. (2010). Council of the EU, Press Release: Education, Youth and Culture, p. 10. Retrieved from https://www.consilium.europa.eu/uedocs/cms_data/docs/pressdata/en/educ/114361.pdf.

Durban Declaration and Programme of Action Report. (2014). Retrieved from https://www.un.org/en/development/desa/population/migration/generalassembly/docs/globalcompact/A_RES_68_151.pdf

DW. (2019, March 22). Gündoğan'a ırkçı tezahürat: Üç zanlı teslim oldu. *DW*. Retrieved from https://www.dw.com/tr/gündoğana-ırkçı-tezahürat-üç-zanlı-teslim-oldu/a-48028493. Accessed on August 11, 2019.

Eurohoops. (2018, November 8). Euroleague basketball launches campaign against discrimination. *Eurohoops*. Retrieved from https://www.eurohoops.net/en/euroleague/771194/euroleague-basketball-launches-campaign-against-discrimination/. Accessed on August 11, 2019.

European Commission's White Paper on Sport. (2007). Retrieved from https://eur-lex.europa.eu/legal-content/EN/TXT/?uri=CELEX%3A52007DC0391.

European Court. (1974, December 12). Judgment of the court of 12 December 1974. *EUR-Lex*. Retrieved from https://eur-lex.europa.eu/legal-content/EN/TXT/?uri=CELEX%3A61974CJ0036. Accessed on August 12, 2019.

European Court. (1976, July 14). Judgment of the court of 14 July 1976. *EUR-Lex*. Retrieved from https://eur-lex.europa.eu/legal-content/EN/TXT/?uri=CELEX%3A61976CJ0013. Accessed on August 11, 2019.

European Court. (1995, December 15). Judgment of the court of 15 December 1995. *EUR-Lex*. Retrieved from https://eur-lex.europa.eu/legal-content/EN/TXT/?uri=CELEX%3A61993CJ0415. Accessed on August 13, 2019.

European Court. (2000a, April 13). Judgment of the court (sixth chamber) 13 April 2000. *CURIA*. Retrieved from http://curia.europa.eu/juris/showPdf.jsf;jsessionid=DB9FCBDD87E878D9F0 87C039DCE79CEE?text=&docid=45242&pageIndex=0&doclang=en&mode=lst&dir=&occ= first&part=1&cid=7822740. Accessed on August 11, 2019.

European Court. (2000b, April 13). Judgment of the court (sixth chamber) of 13 April 2000. *EUR-Lex*. Retrieved from https://eur-lex.europa.eu/legal-content/EN/TXT/?uri=CELEX%3A61996CJ0176. Accessed on August 3, 2019.

European Court. (2010, March 16). Judgment of the court (grand chamber) of 16 March 2010. *EUR-Lex*. Retrieved from https://eur-lex.europa.eu/legal-content/EN/TXT/?uri=CELEX%3A62008CJ0325. Accessed on August 9, 2019.

European Sports Charter. (1992). Retrieved from https://rm.coe.int/16804c9dbb.

European Sports Law and Policy Bulletin. (1/2010). *The Bernard case, sports and training compensation*. Italy: Sports Law and Policy Centre. Retrieved from http://www.sportslawandpolicycentre.com/Bulletin%20I_2010.pdf

European Union (EU). (2000a, June 29). Council directive 2000/43/EC of 29 June 2000 implementing the principle of equal treatment between persons irrespective of racial or ethnic origin. *EUR-Lex*. Retrieved from https://eur-lex.europa.eu/legal-content/en/TXT/?uri=CELEX%3A32000L0043. Accessed on August 11, 2019.

European Union (EU). (2000b, December 18). Charter of fundamental rights of the European Union. *Official Journal of the European Communities*. Retrieved from https://www.europarl.europa.eu/charter/pdf/text_en.pdf. Accessed on August 8, 2019.

European Union (EU). (2008, November 28). Council framework decision 2008/913/JHA on combating certain forms and expressions of racism and xenophobia by means of criminal law. *Official*

Journal of the European Union. Retrieved from https://eur-lex.europa.eu/legal-content/en/ALL/?uri=CELEX%3A32008F0913. Accessed on August 11, 2019.

European Union (EU). (2012, October 26). Consolidated version of the treaty on the functioning of the EU. *Official Journal of the European Union.* Retrieved from https://eur-lex.europa.eu/legal-content/EN/TXT/PDF/?uri=CELEX:12012E/TXT. Accessed on August 1, 2019.

European Union Agency for Fundamental Rights (FRA). (2010). Racism, ethnic discrimination and exclusion of migrants and minorities in sport: A comparative overview of the situation in the European Union. Retrieved from https://fra.europa.eu/sites/default/files/fra_uploads/1207-Report-racism-sport_EN.pdf

Fanatik. (2013, August 6). 40 Yasaklı Kelime. *Fanatik.* Retrieved from https://www.fanatik.com.tr/40-yasakli-kelime-haber-fotograf-328383-2. Accessed on August 8, 2019.

FARE. (2016, June). Monitoring discriminatory signs and symbols in European football. *FARE Network.* Retrieved from https://www.farenet.org/wp-content/uploads/2016/10/Signs-and-Symbols-guide-for-European-football_2016-2.pdf. Accessed on July 17, 2019.

Hannelin, H. (2016). Professional team sports: Nationality discrimination and EU law. *Helsinki Law Review, 10*(1), 78–98.

International Charter on Physical Education and Sport. (1978). Retrieved from https://unesdoc.unesco.org/ark:/48223/pf0000216489.

Istanbul Declaration. (2004). Retrieved from https://www.nato.int/docu/pr/2004/p04-096e.htm.

Racial Equality Directive. (2000). Retrieved from https://eur-lex.europa.eu/legal-content/en/TXT/?uri=CELEX%3A32000L0043.

Schwab, B. (2018). Embedding the human rights of players in world sport. *The International Sports Law Journal, 17,* 214–232.

Treaty of Lisbon. (2009). Retrieved from https://eur-lex.europa.eu/legal-content/EN/TXT/?uri=celex%3A12007L%2FTXT.

UEFA. (2002, October 10). UEFA publishes 10 point plan on racism. *UEFA.* Retrieved from https://www.uefa.com/newsfiles/37757.pdf. Accessed on August 22, 2019.

World Conference against Racism, Racial Discrimination, Xenophobia and Related Intolerance Declaration. (2001). Retrieved from https://www.ohchr.org/Documents/Publications/Durban_text_en.pdf.

World Players Association (WPA). (2017, December 14). Universal declaration of player rights. *UniGlobalUnion.* Retrieved from https://www.uniglobalunion.org/sites/default/files/files/news/official_udpr.pdf. Accessed on August 16, 2019.

CHAPTER 14

AN ASSESSMENT OF INNOVATION EFFICIENCY IN EECA COUNTRIES USING THE DEA METHOD

Rustem Barıs Yesilay and Umut Halac

ABSTRACT

Introduction – *In recent years, there has been a growing interest in innovation, not only in developed countries but also in developing countries. However, there has been limited literature for the developing countries.*

Purpose – *The literature on national innovation systems (NIS) mainly consists of case studies or qualitative researches aiming to explain the patterns of innovation, while the quantitative analysis are limited in explaining the innovation capability and efficiency of innovation. This study is unique in a sense that it compares the innovation efficiencies of the EECA countries. This chapter aims to measure the efficiency of NIS via data envelopment analysis (DEA) method.*

Methodology – *DEA is used to consider a sample of 18 Eastern European and Central Asian (EECA) countries and Turkey. One of the main issues is to determine the input and output variables because the available data for some of these countries were limited. Therefore, research and development expenditure (% of GDP), government expenditure on education, total (% of GDP), imports of goods and services (% of GDP) and foreign direct investment, net inflows (% of GDP) were determined as input variables. Output variables were as follows; patent applications both residents and non-residents, high-technology exports (% of manufactured exports) and scientific and technical journal articles.*

Contemporary Issues in Business, Economics and Finance
Contemporary Studies in Economic and Financial Analysis, Volume 104, 203–215
ISSN: 1569-3759/doi:10.1108/S1569-375920200000104014

Findings – *Based on the key findings it can be noted that Kazakhstan, Turkey, Latvia and Uzbekistan are more efficient in innovation performance compared to other EECA countries. Throughout the results of the DEA, these countries may develop new policies about their innovation systems to reach out the higher performance.*

Keywords: Innovation efficiency; national innovation system; data envelopment analysis; Eastern European and Central Asian (EECA) countries; innovation; input and output

1. INTRODUCTION

Innovation, as a vital factor for growth and sustainable economic development, as well as, for increasing the welfare of society, is broadly appreciated. Numerous theoretical concepts and policy approaches have been developed and implemented to build and maintain the country's capacity for innovation (Acemoglu, Aghion, & Zilibotti, 2006; Meissner, 2015). Most of the countries have therefore devoted more efforts to research and development (R&D) and have tried to create a complimentary innovation environment by enforcing intellectual property rights to promote innovations. Nevertheless, using R&D resources inefficiently may result in lagging technological progress and diminish the complementary effect brought on by other innovative activities. Hence, understanding the nature of R&D efficiency and its determinants is needed for designing R&D policies that effectively cultivate innovation and foster technological development (Chen, Hu, & Yang, 2011).

According to Guellec and Van Pottelsberghe (2004), the importance of the R&D expenditures for economic growth has been affirmed by the literature. Therefore, the efficient usage of R&D expenditures becomes vital. Countries are exposed to high levels of competition in domestic and foreign markets for innovative products. Especially in a globalised world, nations have to continuously update their innovative capabilities and capacities. Countries utilising their R&D resources inefficiently will be penalised with a growth discount (Cullmann, Schmidt-Ehmcke, & Zloczysti, 2009).

With this chapter, we aim to determine the efficiency levels of countries using the variables covered in the national innovation systems (NIS). A sample of 18 Eastern European and Central Asian (EECA) countries and Turkey is used and analysed throughout data envelopment analysis (DEA) method. In the first section of the chapter, the importance and elements of the NIS will be discussed. Throughout the following section, we will mention the concepts of 'efficiency' in NIS. As a bridge section, concepts of 'inputs' and 'outputs' will be summarised so we can pass through the methodological section. The last two sections relate to the DEA on the base of the methodology and empirical results. The chapter will be concluded with the final remarks and conclusion section.

2. WHAT IS 'THE NIS'?

According to Afzal (2014):

> the National Innovation System (NIS) of a country is composed of different subsystems, rang-
> ing from the economic regime, financial structure and physical infrastructure, to the education
> system, cultural traditions and so on.

The NIS concept dates back to the late 1980s (Dosi, Freeman, Nelson, Silverberg, & Soete, 1988; Freeman, 1987) and was developed further in later years (Edquist, 1997; Lundvall, 1992; Nelson, 1993). Lundvall (1992, p. 36) defines the NIS as the elements and relationships that interact in the production, diffusion and use of new and economically useful knowledge and are either located within or rooted inside the borders of a nation state. Nowadays, the concept of NIS, as a useful approach, has become widely recognised by researchers to compare the countries' innovation activities within a structured model (Meissner, 2015).

Sharif (2006) points out that the NIS is about both academic and policy-making contexts. It is thought-out as a useful and auspicious analytical tool for academic policy and for the evolution of innovation policy-making, cultivating an understanding of key determinants of innovation and its processes (Edquist, 1997; Furman, Porter, & Stern, 2002; Guan & Chen, 2012; Lundvall, 2007). Most public policies influencing innovation activities are still designed and implemented at the national level, innovation processes are also increasingly being considered from regional perspectives consequent upon the ascendancy of the globalisation phenomenon (Abbasi, Hajihoseini, & Haukka, 2011; Humbert, 1994; Lundvall, 1992).

According to Nasierowski and Arcelus (2003), an NIS can be defined as the:

> network of agents, policies and institutions that affect the introduction of technology that is
> new to the economy. NISs are formed in order to foster development, application, and diffusion
> of technology, thereby improving productivity. Within this scope, efficiency relates to an NIS's
> ability to transform R&D inputs into R&D outputs.

Furthermore, NIS results from the interaction between the embedded innovation environment represented by framework conditions and the knowledge innovation process besides infrastructure affiliated to government intervention (Faber & Hesen, 2004; Furman et al., 2002; Guan & Chen, 2012; OECD, 2005). Cooke, Uranga, and Etxebarria (1998) define 'embeddedness' to represent the interdependent relationship between the institutional environment and the innovation process system.

As Edquist (1997) has indicated, an underlying production system and an institutional set-up geared towards innovation are the main characteristics of an NIS. In terms of its physical structure, an NIS is a bunch of interacting actors/institutions (e.g. industries, universities and governments) that produce and carry out knowledge innovation (Guan & Chen, 2012). These actors provide the national innovation production skeleton within which governments implement and form policies to affect the innovation process. Through intermediate organisations (Howells, 2006) or interface structures (Molas-Gallart,

Castro-Martínez, & Fernández-de-Lucio, 2008), actors in separate organisational and cultural contexts are connected through an NIS, and these connections stretch the institutionally embedded relationship between the innovation environment and innovation production (Guan & Chen, 2012). From this perspective, the NIS should be accepted as a special sector with specific inputs 'human and financial resources' and particular outputs 'patents, scientific publications' (Cai, 2011; Carayannis, Grigoroudis, & Goletsis, 2016; Hu, Yang, & Chen, 2014; Matei & Aldea, 2012; Pan, Hung, & Lu, 2010; Sharma & Thomas, 2008).

3. EFFICIENCY OF NIS

The studies on innovation systems have been getting significant attention, due to the important role of innovation policies in the economic growth and welfare. According to Carayannis et al. (2016):

> Innovation should be considered as a complex and dynamic, socio-technical, socio-economic, socio political phenomenon. In this context, measuring the performance and the efficiency of innovation systems remains a high priority in order to develop integrated benchmarking systems in the knowledge- based economies.

Innovation environment is an important element that affects the efficiency and productivity of the innovation process in all countries. A better innovation environment enables countries to conduct R&D more efficiently and consequently stimulates more innovations, whereas an inferior one may induce the inefficient use of R&D resources and result in slower technological progress. As highlighted by Hollanders and Esser (2007) and Abbasi et al. (2011), efficiency is an important concept, also in innovation because of the outputs of the innovation process that matter for society. The NIS proposed by Lundvall (1992), Nelson (1993), and Edquist (1997) focuses on the interplay among the government, higher education institutions and industries that encourage innovative behaviour in a specific nation, which may significantly affect R&D efficiency of various innovative outputs (Chen et al., 2011).

Governments, which are national innovation policy-makers, interest themselves with innovation efficiency as closely as they would to the innovation input/output ratio and highlight the outcome of public policy intervention on the innovation efficiency. Efficient innovation (Hollanders & Esser, 2007) is affiliated with the notion of productivity, which is improved when less innovation input is needed to produce the same innovation output or when the same amount of innovation input generates more innovation output. This notion involves comparing the observed input to the minimum potential input required to produce the output or, alternately, comparing the observed output to the maximum potential output obtainable from the input. In this context, in the two comparisons, the optimum is defined in terms of production possibilities, and efficiency is technical (Fried, Lovell, & Schmidt, 2008). In this context, efficient NISs are running at their production possibility frontier or 'transformation curve', which implies the maximum amount of innovation output that can be produced with a given input. The innovation efficiency of an NIS is measured by the ability to transform innovation input into output and create profits (Guan & Chen, 2012).

Assessing innovation efficiency helps us both to give directions to improve efficiency by highlighting fields of weakness and to identify the best innovative countries for benchmarking. In empirical management, in countries seeking to enhance policy learning and in order to develop more suitable policy recommendations, cases of 'best practices' are currently employed. Moreover, the effect of innovation environment on the innovation process is related to the effectiveness of the innovation policy instruments shaped by governments. If the aim is to foster effective innovation policy-making, it may be advised to further investigate the effect of factors embedded in the innovation environment on the efficiency of the NIS based on system logic. Principal studies (Dosi et al., 1988; Edquist, 1997; Fernández-de-Lucio, Gutiérrez-Gracia, Jiménez-Sáez, & Azagra-Caro, 2001; Fernández-de-Lucio, Rojo, & Castro 2003; Freeman, 1987; Fritsch & Slavtchev, 2007, 2010; Furman et al., 2002; Lundvall, 1992; Nelson, 1993) have empirically demonstrated or indicated that the differences in the innovation performance of geographic units are closely affiliated to variation in the innovation climate embedding the innovation process (Chen & Guan, 2012).

4. NIS INPUTS AND OUTPUTS

The literature on NIS mainly consists of case studies or qualitative research aiming to explain the patterns of innovation, while the quantitative analysis is limited to explaining the innovation capability and efficiency of innovation. DEA is an approach based on linear programming (LP) technique. Throughout this technique, the basis of efficiency measure, that is, production frontier can be determined. So multiple inputs and multiple outputs can be evaluated simultaneously (Lu, Kweh, & Huang, 2014). With these attributes, the DEA as an econometric approach needed to be used to reduce the subjective factors as far as possible and get a more objective and reliable judgement on the NIS of the countries.

In the context of NIS, inputs (resources) are transformed into outputs (results) (Kotsemir, 2013). The efficiency of the R&D process depends on the major inputs such as R&D expenditure and R&D personnel (Kou, Chen, Wang, & Shao, 2016; Sharma & Thomas, 2008). Due to the lack of data, in this chapter, R&D personnel indicator is not included in the model. One of the most important points is that the NIS inputs reflect each country's ability to improve technology.

The inputs used in this chapter are listed as follows: R&D expenditure (% of GDP), researchers in R&D (per million people), imports of goods and services (% of GDP) and foreign direct investment, net inflows (% of GDP). The outputs are the number of patent applications,[1] both residents and non-residents, articles in scientific and technical journals and high-technology exports (% of manufactured exports). All indicators are defined in the World Bank's Data Catalog (2019).

5. METHODOLOGY

There are different econometric approaches to efficiency estimation and one of them is related with employing procedures of the mathematical LP. One of the widespread deterministic techniques involves DEA, registering a large variety of applications (Cooper, Seiford, & Zhu, 2004). DEA was formally developed by Charnes, Cooper, and Rhodes (1978), but it is based on the work of Farrell (1957) seeking for better models on productivity evaluation. So, DEA can be defined as: 'a non-parametric method for measuring efficiency of decision-making units (DMUs) using linear programming techniques to envelop observed input-output vectors as close as possible' (Boussofiane, Dyson, & Thanassoulis, 1991).

DEA is built on a piecewise linear convex frontier that envelopes input and output data, relative to which input is minimised or output is maximised. Then, efficiency scores are calculated from the frontiers generated by a sequence of linear programs. We do not want to get lost into the complex theoretical part of the DEA but primarily focus on the empirical side of the method.

Decision-making units (DMUs) have the capacity to control and process the inputs and outputs. Each DMU is using different amounts of inputs and producing different amounts of output. Assume that, n indicates the number of DMU, m indicates the inputs and 's' indicates the outputs. The relative efficiency[2] score p of a DMU will be obtained by solving a fractional program defined by extremal optimisation of the ratio of weighted sum of outputs to weighted multiple input, subject to the constraints of non-decreasing weights and efficiency measuring less than or equal to 1. This involves finding the optimal weights so that efficiency measure is maximised.

Formally, this fractional form is defined as:

$$\max \frac{\sum_{k=1}^{s} v_k y_{kp}}{\sum_{j=1}^{m} u_j x_{jp}} \tag{1}$$

$$\text{s.t.} \frac{\sum_{k=1}^{s} v_k y_{ki}}{\sum_{j=1}^{m} u_j x_{ji}} \le 1 \quad \forall_i, \, v_k, \, u_j \ge 0 \quad \forall_k, \, j.$$

where $k=1,\ldots,s,\, j=1,\ldots,m,\, i=1,\ldots,n$ and y_{ki} denotes output k produced by DMU i, x_{ji} stands for input j used by bank i, v_k and u_j are weights given to output k and input j.

Fractional form (1) is converted through Charnes–Cooper transformation into the multiplier form as in LP.

$$\max \sum_{k=1}^{s} v_k y_{kp}$$

$$\text{s.t.} \sum_{j=1}^{m} u_j x_{jp} = 1, \quad \sum_{k=1}^{s} v_k y_{ki} - \sum_{j=1}^{m} u_j x_{ji} \tag{2}$$

$$\le 0 \quad \forall_i, \, v_k, \, u_j \ge 0 \quad \forall_k, \, j.$$

Solving the multiplier form for each DMU (*n*-times) gives us the relative efficiency scores *p* of all DMUs. Because it is subject to fewer restrictions, the multiplier form has to be turned into the so-called envelopment form.

$$\min \theta_p$$

$$\text{s.t.} \sum_{i=1}^{n} \lambda_i x_{ji} - \theta_p x_{jp} \leq 0 \; \forall_j, \; \sum_{i=1}^{n} \lambda_i y_{ki} - y_{kp} \qquad (3)$$

$$\geq 0 \; \forall_k, \lambda_i \geq 0 \; \forall_i,$$

where θ is the efficiency score, and λ_i are dual variables. The original model of Charnes et al. (1978) was the envelopment form (3), which assumes constant returns to scale (CRS), but Banker, Charnes, and Cooper (1984) developed a model imposing a restriction on λp to be equal to 1 for $p = 1,...,n$, This model allows for variable returns to scale.

All efficient DMUs, including those boundary points sited on the section of the piecewise linear frontier that is parallel to axes, are on the efficiency frontier. The boundary points, where one can decrease the use of an input and still produce the same output (input-slack), or vice versa (output-slack), are weakly efficient (Rousseau & Rousseau, 1997). The weak efficiency indicates the existence of non-zero slacks.

Another thing needs to be clarified, which is the difference between input-orientation and output-orientation. The input-orientation improves efficiency through proportional reduction of input quantities, without changing output quantities. The output-orientation improves in efficiency through proportional expansion of output quantities without altering the inputs used.[3]

6. APPLICATION OF DEA

As mention before, our study is focussed on the EECA Economies, which includes Albania, Bosnia and Herzegovina, Croatia, Czech Republic, Estonia, Georgia, Hungary, Kazakhstan, Latvia, Lithuania, Moldova, West Macedonia, Poland, Romania, Serbia, Slovak Republic, Slovenia, Uzbekistan and in addition to these, Turkey. Our DEA model is built upon these 19 countries, and as a base year we selected the year 2017, for which we have the best available data for these countries. According to our empirical approach, we have two sets of variables; input variables and output variables.

As inputs variables, the [rd] indicates the total R&D expenditure of GDP and measures the R&D intensity. The [rrd] is the number of R&D researchers per million people, which measures the number of experts in the R&D sector. The [im] indicates the total of imports as a ratio of GDP. The [fdi] denotes the total value of foreign direct investment of GDP.

As output variables, the [pat] and the [nonpat] denote the number of residents patent applications and nonresidents patent applications, respectively, and this is used as a measure of innovative activity. The [htx] indicates the magnitude of the high-technology exports with high R&D intensity, such as in aerospace, computers, pharmaceuticals, scientific instruments and electrical machinery. In addition, the [scie] is the number of scientific and technical journal articles.

6.1. CRS Output-oriented Single-stage DEA Model

In this subsection, we perform empirical tests to determine the efficiency levels of the DMUs (countries). Our DEA specifies a CRS, output-oriented one-stage model. We have the following results, as seen in Table 1.

On the base of the results provided in Table 1, Kazakhstan, Turkey, Latvia, and Uzbekistan are the efficient DMUs, and are referent for all other countries. However, within these referent countries, Kazakhstan is just one-step ahead from other countries. All thetas of these four countries equal to 1 but Kazakhstan is referent to more countries than the other efficient countries.

According to the results in Table 1, West Macedonia, have respectively, the worst efficiency level on the base of the thetas. Thus, the performance or the efficient score of the West Macedonia Albania, Serbia, and Hungary are 0.1176, 0.1289, 0.1948, and 0.2124, respectively. And we can calculate the efficiency gap between all these countries and Kazakhstan as the reference country. For example, if Poland wants to reach the efficiency level of Kazakhstan, she needs to increase the efficiency level by 5.1% (1 to 0.948199). Using the similar calculation, West Macedonia needs to increase the efficiency level by 88.2%. The question arises here is how these countries can increase their efficiency levels to reach the reference country. To analyse this situation, we can make use of different tools such as input-slack and output-slack.

Table 2 shows the results of the DEA model on the base of the input-slack. Input-slack indicates the magnitude of the idle or underused the inputs in the

Table 1. Results of the CRS Input-oriented Two-stage DEA Model.

	Rank	theta	ref: KAZ	ref:LVA	ref:TUR	ref: UZB
Albania	18	0.128942	0.021002		0.004677	
Bosnia and Herzegovina	13	0.395816	0.050584		0.010748	0.225938
Croatia	7	0.754195	0.176208	0.461499	0.094402	
Czech Republic	8	0.662277	0.205955	0.522018	0.442005	
Estonia	11	0.457415	0.109797	0.519987	0.019364	
Georgia	10	0.4624	0.407163			0.383312
Hungary	16	0.212382	0.451102		0.162295	
Kazakhstan	1	1	0	1	1	1
Latvia	3	1	1	0	1	1
Lithuania	9	0.644907	0.607269	0.731755	0.034031	0.044609
Moldova	15	0.339469	0.034501		0.003387	0.439977
West Macedonia	19	0.117672	0.046913		0.011151	0.110118
Poland	5	0.948199	0.171253	0.989395	0.961169	
Romania	6	0.812386	0.178022	0.007961	0.287788	0.515844
Serbia	17	0.19484	0.073345	0.084677	0.142506	
Slovak Republic	12	0.415678	0.130524	0.42828	0.136187	
Slovenia	14	0.357181	0.05808	0.350065	0.084830	
Turkey	2	1	1	1	0	1
Uzbekistan	4	1	1	1	1	0

Table 2.   Results of the Input-Slacks on DEA Model.

	islack:rd	islack:rrd	islack:im	islack:fdi
Albania	0.0127719		5.18444	0.867188
Bosnia and Herzegovina	0.0208209		12.2505	
Croatia	0.333151	378.242		
Czech Republic	0.461467	816.425		
Estonia	0.323142	581.091		
Georgia		147.665	4.44572	
Hungary	0.04912	54.3842		5.85932
Kazakhstan	0		0	
Latvia	0	1.93E-12		
Lithuania	0.174639	614.867		
Moldova	0.0110218		9.93653	
West Macedonia	0.010333		2.82382	
Poland		602.063	11.0509	
Romania			6.18582	
Serbia		56.4116	0.560884	
Slovak Republic		139.92	5.44686	
Slovenia	0.477027	689.694		
Turkey	0	0		0
Uzbekistan	0	1.03E-11	0	

model. In addition, it provides the information about the amount of the slack on any variables. The first column of Table 2 represents the amount of the slack in R&D expenditure of any countries in this model. As noted, reference countries have no slack on this matter but some of the other countries have the slack on R&D expenditure. Slovenia has the highest slack position for this variable, at 0.477. We can argue this number as, Slovenia can decrease the R&D expenditure by 0.477 without any changes on output amounts. Also, Czech Republic scores 0.461 slack in R&D expenditure, likewise, Czech Republic can reduce the R&D expenditure by 0.46 without reducing the output.

On the base of the number of researchers in R&D, Czech Republic has the highest slack (816.4 people out of a million) and Slovenia has the second highest slack (689.69 people out of a million). Therefore, these countries can reduce the amount of researchers in R&D and getting the same output. The third column indicates the amount of the slack for import variable. According to these results, Bosnia and Herzegovina and Poland have the highest slacks on import, where the amounts of the slacks are 12.25 and 11.05, respectively. On the base of the foreign direct investment amounts, Hungary has the highest slack and she can reduce this variable by 5.86% without any changes on the output. In addition, we can analyse the efficiency of the countries on the base of output-slack, as well. Table 3 provides the amount of the slacks for the output variables in this DEA model.

According to Table 3, Poland has the highest slack (500.3) for patent applications of non-residents. Poland has to increase the patent applications of non-residents by 500 without any changes on input variables. Following Poland, Czech Republic has 283.1 output-slack for the variable of non-residential patent applications. On the other hand, Poland and Romania have the biggest numbers

Table 3.   Results of the Output-slacks on DEA Model.

	oslack: nonpat	oslack:pat	oslack:htx	oslack:scie
Albania	3.74184	28.9923		
Bosnia and Herzegovina	61.8074	122.258		
Croatia	94.3515	631.941		
Czech Republic	283.131	2215.8		
Estonia	45.6898	250.065		
Georgia		418.707	10.2586	167.639
Hungary	155.503	843.044		
Kazakhstan	0			0
Latvia	0	0		
Lithuania		259.679		
Moldova	42.4177	91.0729		
West Macedonia	37.8441	105.77		
Poland	500.343	1906.54		
Romania	274.089	1114.01		
Serbia	85.5359	776.691		
Slovak Republic	107.023	798.739		
Slovenia	61.1424	149.418		
Turkey		0		0
Uzbekistan			0	0

for residential patent applications. On the lines of high-tech product export and scientific papers, only Georgia has output-slacks.

7. CONCLUSION

It is generally accepted that innovation is the key motive for sustainable economic development and growth. And there are numerous researches about the determinants and effects of innovation. As a contemporary approach, NIS is one of the mostly recognised and accepted method to analyse the countries' innovative levels. In this chapter, we want to shed a light onto the efficiency of innovative capacity for selected countries using the variables covered by NIS. We have executed the DEA for 18 EECA countries and Turkey.

It is interesting to note that, Kazakhstan is one-step ahead as the leader country on the base of the efficiency and Turkey, Latvia, Uzbekistan follow, respectively. The results indicate that performance of Kazakhstan needs to be investigated in detail; probably she has risen above the ashes of the former Union of Soviet Socialist Republics. On the other hand, West Macedonia and Albania have the worst performance recorded. From the point of view of the input-slack, countries like Slovenia, Czech Republic, Poland, Bosnia and Herzegovina, and Hungary have the biggest slacks for different variables. It shows that these countries have to recheck their policies about the innovation process because they are using a lot of inputs and they are not producing enough outputs. With the proper policies, they can decrease the amount of the inputs used in the innovation process while they can keep up the same level of output. On the other hand, Poland, Czech Republic, Romania, and Georgia have the biggest output-slacks for different variables. This is an evidence of the inefficiency for these countries. So, these countries can increase the output performance with new innovation policies. But the most shocking result is that Poland and Czech Republic have common elements for input-slack and output-slack. These two countries are highly ineffective on both sides. They need urgent and rational policies to change their directions.

NOTES

1. Patents are widely recognised as a proxy for innovative output (Griliches, 1990; Hsu, 2011). Nasierowski and Arcelus (1999) define patent applications by nonresidents as a 'measure of a country's involvement in international business cooperation and export activities' and patent applications by residents, as a 'measure of the effort of the locals in the investment in solutions for one country's internal demand'.

2. A DMU is relatively fully efficient or Farrell-efficient 'on the basis of available evidence if and only if the performance of other DMUs does not show that some of its inputs or outputs can be improved without worsening some of its other inputs or outputs' (Cooper et al., 2004).

3. According to the findings of Coelli and Perelman (1999) there are a strong correlation between input and output orientation, because of that there won't be any significant differences sourced from the choice of orientation.

REFERENCES

Abbasi, F., Hajihoseini, H., & Haukka, S. (2011). Use of virtual index for measuring efficiency of innovation systems: A cross-country study. *International Journal of Technology Management and Sustainable Development, 9*(3), 195–212.

Acemoglu, D., Aghion, P., & Zilibotti, F. (2006). Distance to frontier, selection, and economic growth. *Journal of European Economic Association, 4*(1), 37–74.

Afzal, M. N. I. (2014). An empirical investigation of the national innovation system (NIS) using data envelopment analysis (DEA) and the TOBIT model. *International Review of Applied Economics, 28*(4), 507–523.

Banker, R., Charnes, A., & Cooper, W. (1984). Some models for estimating technical and scale inefficiencies in data envelopment analysis. *Management Science, 30*, 1078–1092.

Boussofiane, A., Dyson, R. G., & Thanassoulis, E. (1991). Applied Sata envelopment analysis. *European Journal of Operational Research, 52*, 1–15.

Cai, Y. (2011). *Factors affecting the efficiency of the BRICS' national innovation systems: A comparative study based on DEA and panel data analysis.* Economics (open e-Journal), Economics Discussion Papers, No. 2011-52.

Carayannis, E. G., Grigoroudis, E., & Goletsis, Y. (2016). A multilevel and multistage efficiency evaluation of innovation systems: A multiobjective DEA approach. *Expert Systems with Applications, 62*, 63–80.

Charnes, A., Cooper, W. W., & Rhodes, E. (1978). Measuring efficiency of decision-making units. *European Journal of Operations Research, 2*, 429–440.

Chen, C. P., Hu, J. L., & Yang, C. H. (2011). An international comparison of R&D efficiency of multiple innovative outputs: The role of the national innovation system. *Innovation: Management, Policy and Practice, 13*(3), 341–360.

Chen, K., & Guan, J. (2012). Measuring the efficiency of China's regional innovation systems: Application of network data envelopment analysis. *Regional Studies, 46*(3), 355–377.

Coelli, T., & Perelman, S. (1999). A comparison of parametric and nonparametric distance functions: With application to European railways. *European Journal of Operational Research, 117*(2), 326–339.

Cooke, P., Uranga, M. G., & Etxebarria, G. (1998). Regional systems of innovation: An evolutionary perspective. *Environment and Planning, 30*, 1563–1584.

Cooper, W., Seiford, L., & Zhu, J. (2004). Data envelopment analysis: History, models and interpretations. In W. Cooper, L. Seiford, & J. Zhu (Eds.), Handbook on data envelopment analysis. Boston, MA: Kluwer Academic Publishers.

Cullmann, A., Schmidt-Ehmcke, J., & Zloczysti, P. (2009). *Innovation, R&D efficiency and the impact of the regulatory environment: A two-stage semi-parametric DEA approach.* Discussion Paper, No. 883. German Institute for Economic Research, Germany.

Dosi, G., Freeman, C., Nelson, R. R., Silverberg, G., & Soete, L. (1988). *Technical change and economic theory.* London: Pinter.

Edquist, C. (1997). Systems of innovation: Technologies, institutions, and organizations. London: Pinter.

Faber, J., & Hesen, A. B. (2004). Innovation capabilities of European nations cross-national analyses of patents and sales of product innovations. *Research Policy, 33*(3), 193–207.

Farrell, J. M. (1957). The measurement of productive efficiency. *Journal of the Royal Statistical Society, 120*(1), 253–290.

Fernández-de-Lucio, I., Gutiérrez-Gracia, A., Jiménez-Sáez, F., & Azagra-Caro, J. M. (2001). Las debilidades y fortalezas del sistema valenciano de innovación. In M. Olazarán, & M. G. Uranga (Eds.), *Sistemas Regionales de Innovación* (pp. 251–278). Bilbao: Servicio Editorial de la Universidad del País Vasco.

Fernández-de-Lucio, I., Rojo, J., & Castro, E. (2003). *Enfoque de Políticas Regionales de Innovación en la Unión Europea.* Madrid: Academia Europea de Ciencias y Artes.

Freeman, C. (1987). *Technology policy and economic performance: Lessons from Japan.* London: Pinter.

Fried, H., Lovell, C. A. K., & Schmidt, S. (2008). Efficiency and productivity. In H. Fried, C. A. K. Lovell, & S. Schmidt (Eds.), *The measurement of productive efficiency and productivity change* (pp. 3–91). New York, NY: Oxford University Press.

Fritsch, M., & Slavtchev, V. (2007). *What determines the efficiency of regional innovation systems?* Jena Economic Research Papers No. 2007-06. Friedrich-Schiller-University Jena, Jena.

Fritsch, M., & Slavtchev, V. (2010). How does industry specialization affect the efficiency of regional innovation systems? *The Annals of Regional Science, 45*(1), 87–108.

Furman, J. L., Porter, M. E., & Stern, S. (2002). The determinants of national innovative capacity. *Research Policy, 31*(6), 899–933.

Griliches, Z. (1990). Patent statistics as economic indicators: A survey. *Journal of Economic Literature, 28*(4), 1661–1707.

Guan, J., & Chen, K. (2012). Modeling the relative efficiency of national innovation systems. *Research Policy, 41*(1), 102–115.

Guellec, D., & van Pottelsberghe, B. (2004). From R&D to productivity growth: Do the institutional settings and the source of funds of R&D matter? *Oxford Bulletin of Economics and Statistics, 66*(3), 353–378.

Hollanders, H., & Esser, F. C. (2007). *Measuring innovation efficiency. EuropeanCommission. European Innovation Scoreboard* INNO-Metrics Thematic Paper 2007.

Howells, J. (2006). Intermediation and the role of intermediaries in innovation. *Research Policy, 35*(5), 715–728.

Hsu, Y. (2011). Cross national comparison of innovation efficiency and policy application. *African Journal of Business Management, 5*(4), 1378–1387.

Hu, J. L., Yang, C. H., & Chen, C. P. (2014). R&D efficiency and the national innovation system: An international comparison using the distance function approach. *Bulletin of Economic Research, 66*(1), 55–71.

Humbert, M. (1994). Strategic industrial policy in global industrial system. *Review of International Political Economy, 1*(3), 445–463.

Kotsemir, M. (2013). *Measuring national innovation systems efficiency: A review of DEA approach.* National Research University Higher School of Economics Research Paper Series, No. WP BRP, 16, Moscow, Russia.

Kou, M., Chen, K., Wang, S., & Shao, Y. (2016). Measuring efficiencies of multi-period and multi-division systems associated with DEA: An application to OECD countries' national innovation systems. *Expert Systems with Applications, 46*, 494–510.

Lu, W. M., Kweh, Q. L., & Huang, C. L. (2014). Intellectual capital and national innovation systems performance. *Knowledge-Based Systems, 71*, 201–210.

Lundvall, B. (1992). *National systems of innovation.* London; New York, NY: Pinter.

Lundvall, B. (2007). National innovation systems: Analytical concept and development tool. *Industry and Innovation, 14*(1), 95–119.

Matei, M. M., & Aldea, A. (2012). Ranking national innovation systems according to their technical efficiency. *Procedia-Social and Behavioral Sciences, 62*, 968–974.

Meissner, D. (2015). *Measuring innovation: A discussion of innovation indicators at the national level.* Swiss Science and Innovation Council Secretariat, *SSRN Electronic Journal*, Working Paper, 3.

Molas-Gallart, J., Castro-Martínez, E., & Fernández-de-Lucio, I. (2008). *Interface structures: Knowledge transfer practice in changing environments.* INGENIO (CSIC-UPV) Working Papers Series, No. 2008-4. Valencia, Spain.

Nasierowski, W., & Arcelus, F. J. (1999). Interrelationships among the elements of national innovation systems: A statistical evaluation. *European Journal of Operational Research, 119*, 235–253.

Nasierowski, W., & Arcelus, F. J. (2003). On the efficiency of national innovation systems. *Socio-Economic Planning Sciences, 37*, 215–234.

Nelson, R. R. (1993). *National innovation systems: A comparative analysis.* Oxford: Oxford University Press.

OECD. (2005). *Published by Oslo manual: Guidelines for collecting and interpreting innovation data* (3rd ed.). Paris: OECD Publishing.

Pan, T. W., Hung, S.V., & Lu, W. M. (2010). DEA performance measurement of the national innovation system in Asia and Europe. *Asia-Pacific Journal of Operational Research, 27*(3), 369–392.

Rousseau, S., & Rousseau, R. (1997). Data envelopment analysis as a tool for constructing scientometric indicators. *Scientometrics, 40*(1), 45–56.

Sharif, N. (2006). Emergence and development of the national innovation systems concept. *Research Policy, 35*(5), 745–766.

Sharma, S., & Thomas, V. J. (2008). Inter-country R&D efficiency analysis: An application of data envelopment analysis. *Scientometrics, 76*(3), 483–501.

World Bank's Data Catalog. (2019). Retrieved from https://datacatalog.worldbank.org/. Accessed on April 26 2019.

CHAPTER 15

TESTING THE OVERREACTION HYPOTHESIS ON THE BIST30 INDEX AND DOW JONES: THE CASE OF THE 2008 FINANCIAL CRISIS PROCESS*

Ercan Özen and Metin Tetik

ABSTRACT

Introduction – *Emerging markets are under the influence of many external factors in global market conditions. International interest rates and price fluctuations in major stock market indices are also among these factors. The FED policies shape the international capital movements in particular, which significantly affects the emerging markets. For this reason, emerging stock markets may show different reactions especially in times of crisis.*

Purpose – *The purpose of this study is to investigate whether the BIST30 index acted in accordance with the overreaction hypothesis (ORH) against the return changes in the Dow Jones Industrial Average (DJIA) index in the process of the 2008 global financial crisis.*

Methodology – *The data set of the study was analysed by dividing it into two periods. The first period is the monetary expansion period between 17 August 2007, when the Federal Reserve (FED) reduced the interest rate for the first time, until 22 May 2013 when the FED announced that it would reduce the bond purchases.*

* This chapter is a revised version of the paper that was presented in 21th Finance Symposium held on 19–21th October 2017 in Balıkesir, Turkey.

Contemporary Issues in Business, Economics and Finance
Contemporary Studies in Economic and Financial Analysis, Volume 104, 217–234
Copyright © 2020 by Emerald Publishing Limited
All rights of reproduction in any form reserved
ISSN: 1569-3759/doi:10.1108/S1569-375920200000104015

The second period is the monetary contraction period including the dates between 23 May 2013 and 1 June 2017. An error correction model (ECM) was established in both periods for the indices, determined as cointegrated. The validity of the ORH was tested by Cumulative Abnormal Return (CAR) Analysis.

Findings – *According to the ECM, the authors identified that the effect of short-term changes in the DJIA return in the monetary expansion period on BIST30 index return was higher than that in the monetary contraction period. However, according to the findings obtained from the CAR analysis results, the BIST30 index did not generally act in accordance with the ORH against the DJIA. Findings can be appreciated as a decision-making tool especially for investment specialists and investors interested in securities investments.*

Keywords: Overreaction Hypothesis; Stock Market; BIST; Dow Jones; Financial Crisis; FED; Monetary Policy

JEL classification: F21; F32; F65; O16

1. INTRODUCTION

The world has recently gained momentum in terms of globalisation, social, cultural, economic and financial factors with the effect of increasing commercial, tourism and industrial activities. As a result, the interaction among the markets and the sensitivity for events has increased. In this process, the United States has become the world's largest economy and the New York Stock Exchange index and the Dow Jones Industrial Average (DJIA) have become important indicators for the world stock markets and financial system. All stock exchanges in the world have different reactions to an important development in DJIA.

Macroeconomic developments stand out as the leading events which generally affect the developments in the index of world stock exchanges. The United States is the country which has the greatest gross domestic product (GDP)[1] and dominates the world's economy. The Federal Reserve (FED), the Central Bank of the United States, also has an important effect on the general situation of the US economy.

The greatest event affecting the world economy in the last decade is the 2008–2009 global financial crisis, which spread to all the world from the US markets. The 6% interest rate in 2000 decreased to 1% in 2003 as a result of welfare increasing policies and consumption promotion. These promotions were mostly in the housing market and mortgage loans with high return risk, which reached to amounts. In this process, securities based on high-risk mortgages were produced and they were sold in the world markets with prices well above their actual values. Therefore, financial risk spread and the fragility in markets increased. That being said, increasing prices created the inflationist pressure and the FED began to increase interest rates in 2004. Therefore, in this process, due to the mortgage loans sensitivity to the increasing interest rate, dead loan problems began to occur.

Investors began to lose their trust due to the pay-back problem and the demand for mortgage products decreased, while the demand for bonds increased. Since stockbrokers collateralised these derivative products for short-term cash needs, a liquidity shortage began. The FED interest rate increased to 5,25% in 2007.[2] This time the FED's increase in interest rate (in order to control the inflation) led to mortgage dead loans and a liquidity crisis which led to high interest rates.

In order to solve the liquidity shortage, the FED decided to decrease the interest rate for the first time on 17 August 2007 and established the Term Auction Facility which met a fixed amount of term funding for various collateralisations in the same year. In spite of the FED activating different austerity packages later, the bankruptcy of Lehman Brothers on 15 September[3] 2008 led the crisis to peak. In December 2008, the interest rate was decreased to the range of 0–0.25% and in the process mortgage bond programme reached 100 billion $ per month and the bond repurchase programme reached 85 billion $ per month.

Through this process the FED provided liquidity, and positive effects of the abundance of money in global markets, especially in developing markets, were observed. Therefore, developing countries obtained more funds and macroeconomical effects were also observed. The DJIA saw positive returns and this was also reflected in other stock exchanges like the Istanbul Stock Exchange (BIST) and the correlation among the stock exchanges was enhanced. The increase in the DJIA led to the increase in other developing stock exchange indices like BIST. Excessive amounts of liquidity and low interest rates began to have positive impacts on the US economy. Therefore, the improving growth rate, along with the decrease in unemployment rates (3.9%) in the USA, reached 2% in June 2018. Due to the increase in inflation caused by this growth, on 22 May 2013 the FED announced that it would decrease 85 billion $ of monthly bond purchases. The FED decreased the bond purchase gradually and increased the interest rate on 22 May 2015. The FED interest rates were between the ranges of 2.25–2.50% by December 2018.[4]

While the DJIA peaked with the recovery in the US economy, these developments did not lead to the same impact for developing countries like Turkey. The scarcity of money in the global markets led to a reduction in supply compared to the demand needed by local economies. Since this change influenced the economies of countries negatively, the relation between stock exchanges such as Borsa Istanbul and Dow Jones Stock Exchange weakened. The high degree of relationship which occurred in monetary expansion period weakened in the second period, the monetary contraction period. In the first period, similar events for Dow Jones and other stock exchanges started to have different a meaning in the second period.

When an event with the same meaning for two markets happens, a stock exchange can react in the same direction as another stock exchange. This reaction can sometimes be over-optimism and it can sometimes be over-pessimism. After these extreme price changes, it can be seen that after a certain period, the prices are back to their previous level. While investors who anticipate such actions may profit through an appropriate investment strategy, the investors who buy at high prices or sell at low prices may have considerable losses. The incidence of excessive increase or decrease in prices reveals the 'Overreaction Hypothesis' (ORH) and this contradicts the 'Efficient Markets Hypothesis' (EMH).

Investors can suffer significant losses due to the rapid decline in prices after a certain period where prices in the stock market rise, and therefore the ORH is valid. In such cases, investors need to know whether the market response is normal or excessive. Thus, investors who understand the characteristics of market behaviour are less likely to suffer. The validity of the ORH in the market is needed to reduce the likelihood that small investors will suffer losses in stock markets.

The purpose of this study is to investigate whether the reactions of the Istanbul Stock Exchange 30 index (BIST30) against the DJIA Index are compatible with 'ORH' or not. After the introduction section of the study, ORH is explained in the second section. In the third section, one finds the literature review, in the fourth section one can find the methods and findings, and the study ends with the conclusion and evaluation section.

2. OVERREACTION HYPOTHESIS

According to the EMH, developed by Fama (1970), prices do not change until new information arrives in the market. However, some events that are not compatible with the EMH happen in the ORH. After the information arrives in the market, prices move upwards or downwards fast, depending on the type of information received. However, in the following days, although no new information arrives in the market, the prices move in the opposite direction of the first information and are observed to be back to the previous level.

The EMH is based on information-based efficiency, which means validation of all information in the market is done by prices and it has three different versions. According to the weak form of efficiency, investors cannot obtain excessive returns using past market prices. Semi-strong form of efficiency claims that investors cannot obtain more returns than the market returns using both past prices and publicly disclosed information. A strong form of market efficiency suggests that the people who also learn non-disclosed intrinsic information along with the disclosed information cannot obtain higher returns than the market.

In case of overreaction, investors are highly sensitive to the new information (De Medeiros, 2005, p. 2). Prices of the securities respond to the disclosed information either by increasing or by decreasing excessively (Barak, 2008a, p. 159). According to the ORH, due to some information arriving in the market, returns of the securities increase upwards or downwards well over the average market returns. However, returns reach more reasonable levels at a later stage (Fig. 1). According to DeBondt and Thaler (1985, p. 795), opposite movements follow the excessive movements in securities. In addition, DeBondt and Thaler (1985) suggest that corrections of high return movements will also be high. An investor who predicts this situation may get higher returns than the market, contrary to the weak form of market efficiency. According to Tufan (2008, p. 80) one of the reasons for this situation is that investors act in accordance with the herding behaviour.

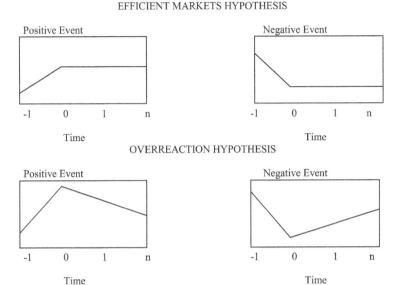

Fig. 1. Market Reactions According to EMH and ORH. *Source*: Brown, Harlow, and Tinic (1988) and Shachmurove (2002).

3. LITERATURE REVIEW

There are various studies investigating whether the ORH is valid in BIST. While many studies indicated the existence of overreaction in Borsa Istanbul (BIST), in a few studies, opposite results were obtained. Barak (2008b), Durukan (2004), Yücel & Taşkın (2007), Doğukanlı and Bahadır (2011), Doğukanlı, Vural, and Ergün (2012) and Tunçel (2013) in their studies revealed that ORH existed in BIST. While the majority of the studies were index-based, a small number of studies were analysed on the stocks. Contrary to these studies, Akkoç and Özkan (2013) also used stock exchange indices in their studies between the 2004 and 2011 period and could not get the findings conforming the ORH.

When we analyse the stock exchanges out of BIST, there are a lot of academic studies indicating evidence about overreaction. Some of this evidence is observed in the studies of Piccoli, Chaudhury, and Souza (2017), DeBondt and Thaler (1985), Brown and Harlow (1988), Dissanaike (1997), Shachmurove (2002), Bauman, Conover, and Miller (1999), Brown et al. (1988) and De Medeiros (2005).

DeBondt and Thaler (1985), Bremer and Sweeney (1991), Brown et al. (1988) and Brown and Harlow (1988) indicate that people are very sensitive to unexpected news and therefore they overreact. In all four studies it is revealed that previously losing portfolios had better performance than previously winning ones. Similarly, Dissanaike (1997) studied the monthly data of FT500 index belonging to 1975–1991 period and identified that the obtained results were compatible with the ORH. Similar results were obtained also for Indonisian Stock Exchange for 2005–2015 period (Sembiring, Rahman, Effendi, & Sudarsono, 2016).

Shachmurove (2002) reported that irrational behaviours were observed more frequently in small markets. The author investigated the validity of the ORH using the data of 1996 and earlier in small- or medium-scale stock exchanges of 13 countries and found out that ORH was valid in Turkey, Luxembourg, Norway and the Netherlands.

Bauman et al. (1999) in their study analysing the market to book value ratio and earnings per share, indicated that there was overreaction in stock exchanges. According to the study, share returns increase more than profit growth per share and small company effect is observed. The companies whose market value is smaller than their book value obtained more returns than big companies.

Piccoli et al. (2017) calculated the cumulative abnormal returns (CAR) and tested whether there were excessive returns in BOVESPA for the 2000–2013 period. The authors determined that the market overreacted against internal and external shocks after positive and negative events and the overreaction was stronger when the market volatility was low. Alwathnani, Dubofsky, and Haitham (2017) tested the ORH in the market after the dividend notice and revealed that the market overreacted against surprise windfall profits.

There are many studies analysing whether markets overreacted or not during the 2008 global crisis period. Da Costa (2017) used the data of the 2007–2014 period in his study on US share and fixed income exchange traded fund market. Da Costa (2017) called the period between 9 October 2007 and 9 March 2009 as the crisis period and the period between 9 March 2009 and 31 December 2014 as the recovery period. Accordingly, the size of overreaction in the markets in the crisis period was higher than in the recovery period. In addition, while investors were over-pessimistic with the positive news in bull market periods in which the market expectations improved, they reacted in a stronger manner to the negative events than the positive ones because they were over-pessimistic in bear market periods.

While the studies here measure the overreactions of stock exchanges against general economic events, there are a few studies measuring the reactions of stock exchanges against the improvements in other stock exchange indices. These are the studies of De Medeiros (2005) and Tetik and Ozen (2016). De Medeiros (2005) and Tetik and Ozen (2016) investigated whether the price movements in DJIA led to an overreaction in the stock exchanges of other countries or not. De Medeiros (2005) identified that Bovespa overreacted for the positive actions derived from DJIA for 1994 and 2005 period; however, it reacted weakly for the negative shocks and revealed that Bovespa did not meet the efficient market conditions. Tetik and Ozen (2016) also revealed whether the movements in DJIA for 2010 and 2016 period led to an overreaction on BIST100 index or not. The authors found out that the reaction by BIST100 index was compatible with ORH.

The literature research shows that there are many studies on the validity of ORH. However, a limited number of studies investigate the response of an index to DJIA, one of the most important indices in the world. The present study expands the literature on this aspect. In addition, the response of one index to the other index is investigated by different FED policy periods. Thus, the impact of FED policy changes on inter-stock exchange relations and the impacts of investor decisions on the results will be revealed. This shows the originality of the Study. The purpose of this study is to identify whether the shocks in DJIA led to an effect on BIST in accordance with ORH similar to the studies of De Medeiros (2005) and Tetik and Ozen (2016).

4. METHOD AND FINDINGS

The purpose of the study is to determine how the short-term changes in DJIA Index returns affected the BIST index returns in the periods when the FED implemented expanding and contracting policies and also to reveal whether the BIST30 overreacted for the positive and negative shocks occurring in DJIA or not. For that reason, the study was divided into two periods: the monetary expansion period and monetary contraction period. In the analysis, the daily closing prices of the two indices between 17 August 2007 and 22 May 2013 and between 23 May 2013 and 1 June 2017 were used as the data in both periods separately. Data were collected from both the DJIA and the BIST30 by investing.com.[5] In the study, Borsa İstanbul 30 (BIST30) index was chosen instead of 100 (BIST100) index, which is the main indicator index of Borsa İstanbul. This is due to the fact that stocks out of the top 30 in the BIST100 index are relatively shallow, which will adversely affect the analysis.

While the error correction model (ECM) was used in the study in order to identify the effects of short-term changes, a structure similar to the studies of Brown et al. (1988), Shachmurove (2002), De Medeiros (2005) and Tetik and Ozen (2016) was used for the analysis of overreaction. BIST30 index was handled for overreaction analysis and DJIA was utilised in order to calculate the positive and negative excessive returns of BIST30 index. Later, CAR and volatility of BIST30 after an event were measured. In the study, BIST30 ($I_t^{BIST-30}$) index and DJIA (I_t^{DJIA}) daily closing price data were used by considering the periods between 17 August 2007 and 22 May 2013, and 23 May 2013 and 1 June 2017 separately. In order to calculate the CAR of BIST30 after an event, a methodology was utilised similar to the study of Brown et al. (1988) Daily return rates of BIST30 index and DJIA determined as cointegrated were calculated.[6] Then a simple regression equation between the obtained BIST30 return and DJIA was formed and some definitions on the obtained residuals ($\hat{u}_t = R_t - \hat{R}_t$) were made as follows:

If $\hat{u}_t \geq 0.025$, it represents the days with positive events.

If $\hat{u}_t \leq -0.025$, it represents the days with negative events

If $-0.025 \leq \hat{u}_t \leq 0.025$, it represents the days without events.

After the abnormal return (AR*td*) of BIST30 index in *t* day following an unexpected *d* event was calculated like this, CAR of the index was calculated as follows:

$$CAR_t = CAR_{t-1} + \overline{AR}_t$$

Here $\overline{AR}_t$ is the average of the abnormal returns of BIST index. The statistical significance of the obtained CAR was determined by *t* test. The diagrams of BIST30 and DJIA data used in the analysis in monetary expansion and monetary contraction periods are as in Fig. 2.

Before the regression equation between BIST30 return and DJIA index was established, in order to identify the positive and negative factors on BIST30 index, The authors checked whether the series were stationary or not. According to ADF test results, it was confirmed that BIST30 and DJIA variables and their logarithms were not stationary at 1% level of significance; however, the first differences of the variables were stationary.[7] This demonstrated to us that the series are cointegrated (Table A1).

The Johansen cointegration test technique was used in order to determine whether there was a long-term cointegration relationship between the levels of the series (see Table 1 and Table 2). The Lag length of the variables necessary for Johansen cointegration test was tested. In order to determine the Lag length, Akaike Information Criterion (AIC), Schwarz Information Criterion (SC), Hannan–Quinn information criterion (HQ) and Final Prediction Error criterion

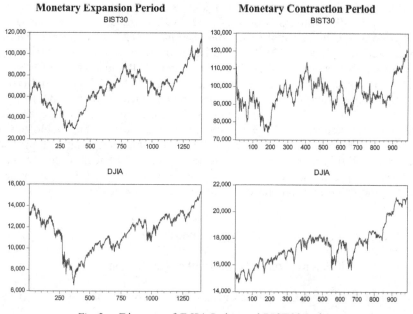

Fig. 2.   Diagram of DJIA Index and BIST30 Index.

Table 1. Johansen Cointegration Test Values for Expansion Period.

Hypothesised No. of CE(s)	Eigenvalue	Trace Statistic	0.05 Critical Value	Prob.**
None *	0.312137	521.2388	15.49471	0.0001
At most 1	1.88E−05	0.026206	3.841466	0.8713
Hypothesised No. of CE(s)	Eigenvalue	Max-Eigen Statistic	0.05 Critical Value	Prob.**
None *	0.312137	521.2126	14.26460	0.0001
At most 1	1.88E−05	0.026206	3.841466	0.8713

Note: The * and ** the significance at 1% and 5% levels, respectively, for Expansion Period.

(FPE) stand out in the literature as methods that can be used. When we look at the information criteria for both two periods, it was determined that the optimum Lag length for both periods was two (Table A2 and Table A3).[8]

According to Johansen cointegration Trace and Max-Eigenvalue test results, it is understood that there is a cointegration between series since the test statistics are bigger than 5% of critical value in both two periods. Therefore, there is a long-term relationship between these variables in both periods. However, a potential imbalance between these variables in the short term was determined and how much this imbalance was corrected was analysed through ECM. In Tables 3 and 4 estimation results of the ECM for both two periods are presented.

According to the ECM, short-term changes in Dow Jones index return (R_t^{DJIA}, i.e., DLOGDJIA) in the monetary expansion period have a 0.58 unit of positive significant effect on BIST return ($R_t^{BIST-30}$, i.e., DLOGBIST30). According to Table 4, the effect of the short-term changes in DJIA return in the monetary contraction period on BIST30 return decreased and regressed to 0.52. While approximately 18% of the changes in BIST30 in the monetary expansion period was explained by DJIA return according to the ECM, this explanation rate decreased approximately to 8.4% in the monetary contraction period.

If the error correction term in the ECM is negative, we can say that there is a long-term relationship between the variables. With reference to Table 4, we can say that there is a long-term relationship between the BIST and Dow Jones index returns in both two periods. In addition, statistically significant error correction

Table 2. Cointegration Test Values for Contraction Period.

Hypothesised No. of CE(s)	Eigenvalue	Trace Statistic	0.05 Critical Value	Prob.**
None*	0.019029	19.25676	15.49471	0.0129
At most 1	0.000398	0.390662	3.841466	0.5320
Hypothesised No. of CE(s)	Eigenvalue	Max-Eigen Statistic	0.05 Critical Value	Prob.**
None*	0.019029	18.86610	14.26460	0.0087
At most 1	0.000398	0.390662	3.841466	0.5320

Note: The * and ** the significance at 1% and 5% levels, respectively, for expansion period.

Table 3. ECM for Monetary Expansion Model.

Dependent Variable: DLOGBIST30
Method: Least Squares
Sample (adjusted): 21,397
Included observations: 1,396 after adjustments

Variable	Coefficient	SE	t-Statistic	Prob.
C	0.000422	0.000482	0.875707	0.3813
DLOGDJIA	0.582033	0.033274	17.49234	0.0000
U(−1)	−0.002297	0.002466	−0.931609	0.3517
R-squared	0.180145	Mean dependent var		0.000488
Adjusted R-squared	0.178968	SD dependent var		0.019889
SE of regression	0.018022	Akaike info criterion		−5.192303
Sum squared resid	0.452435	Schwarz criterion		−5.181040
Log likelihood	3,627.228	Hannan–Quinn c riter.		−5.188092
F-statistic	153.0403	Durbin–Watson stat		2.112153
Prob (F-statistic)	0.000000			

term indicates how much a potential derivation in long-term balance is corrected in every period (since daily data is worked on, this can be established every day). While we cannot talk about this situation in the monetary expansion period, the statistically significant −0.0031 coefficient estimated in the monetary contraction period means that approximately 3.1% of a potential deviation in long-term balance is corrected every day.

4.1. CAR Analysis

The residuals obtained from the ECM were determined to represent the days with positive events (if it is $\hat{u}_t \geq 0.025$), the days with negative events (if it is, $\hat{u}_t \leq -0.025$), and the days without events (if it is $-0.025 \leq \hat{u}_t \leq 0.025$), respectively. Therefore, we observed that there was 87 positive and 91 negative events in the

Table 4. ECM for Monetary Contraction Period.

Dependent Variable: DLOGBIST30
Method: Least Squares
Sample (adjusted): 2 985
Included observations: 984 after adjustments

Variable	Coefficient	SE	t-Statistic	Prob.
C	−0.000114	0.000479	−0.238890	0.8112
DLOGDJIA	0.519604	0.061796	8.408339	0.0000
U(−1)	−0.031722	0.007105	−4.464616	0.0000
R-squared	0.084129	Mean dependent var		5.93E−05
Adjusted R-squared	0.082262	SD dependent var		0.015680
SE of regression	0.015021	Akaike info criterion		−5.555697
Sum squared resid	0.221342	Schwarz criterion		−5.540784
Log likelihood	2,736.403	Hannan–Quinn criter.		−5.550025
F-statistic	45.05605	Durbin–Watson stat		2.140123
Prob (F-statistic)	0.000000			

monetary expansion period. The authors identified that there was 38 positive and 39 negative events in the monetary contraction period.[9] The reaction of BIST30 index average CAR obtained from the study for the positive and negative events in the monetary expansion and contraction periods are indicated in Fig. 3 separately.

When we look at the behaviours of BIST30 index average CAR in the monetary expansion period, it approximately goes up +0.0385 unit, that is, 3.8% (significant at the level of 1%) in case of a positive event in DJIA. When we analyse the BIST30 index CAR up to 60 days, the stock prices fluctuate ambivalently. Therefore, when the reaction of the stock prices up to 30 days is analysed, given that the BIST30 index return is observed to become stable around a new threshold value in case of a positive event, we can say that this behaviour is a practice of efficient market hypothesis (EMH). Similarly, BIST30 index average CAR in the monetary expansion period approximately goes up +0.0366 unit, that is, –3.6% (significant at the level of 1%) in case of a negative event. When the process of BIST30 index CAR up to 60 days is observed, since the prices are observed to become stable around a threshold value between −2% and −4% in the reaction level of the first day in case of a positive event, we can say that this behaviour is also a practice of EMH. Both positive and negative events in DJIA in monetary expansion period indicate that BIST30 does not overreact in this situation; therefore, the EMH is valid.

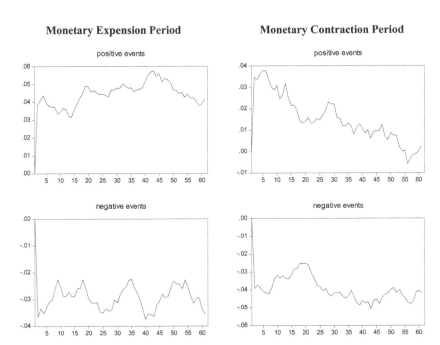

Fig. 3. CAR after Positive and Negative Events in Monetary Expansion and Contraction Periods.
Note: 5% of Significance Levels of CAR* can be seen in Tables A4 and A5.

When we look at the behaviours of the BIST30 index average CAR in the monetary contraction period, it approximately goes up $+0.0349$ unit, that is, 3.5% (significant at a level of 1%) in case of a positive event in DJIA. When the process of BIST30 index CAR up to 60 days is observed, it can be said that there is an overreaction in 0th day since the prices go down. In this case it can be said that the behaviour of BIST30 index return confirms the ORH in case of a negative event. In this case, when there are positive events in the DJIA in the monetary contraction period, BIST30 overreacts in this situation. This indicates that EMH is not valid. However, the relationship becomes statistically insignificant after the 16th day. For that reason, we cannot speak about the overreaction. The BIST30 index average CAR in the monetary contraction period goes up approximately $+0.0390$ unit, that is, -3.9% (significant at the level of 1%) in case of a negative event. When the process of the BIST30 index CAR up to 60 days is observed, since the prices are observed to become stable around a threshold value between -2% and -5% in the reaction level of the first day in case of a positive event, we can say that this behaviour is a practice of EMH.

5. CONCLUSION AND EVALUATION

Relations between international financial markets are closely followed by also investors, as well as, governments and companies. Internationally increasing integration also affects stock exchanges. Stock exchanges can be affected in a similar or different way during various events, depending on the geographical and developmental characteristics of the countries. These forms of effects provide data for investors to make decisions about risk management and to create international portfolios. The degree to which a stock exchange is affected by another one and the discovery of whether there is an overreaction can be appreciated as a tool to contribute to decision-making.

Whether the BIST30 index acts in accordance with the ORH for the changes in DJIA Index during the 2008 global financial crisis was investigated in this study. Since the FED implemented expansion and contraction policies in the process of the crisis, the data set was analysed as two sets. An ECM was established for the indices determined as cointegrated in both periods. The validity of the ORH was tested through CAR analysis. According to the ECM, it was identified that the effect of short-term changes in DJIA index return on BIST30 index return in the monetary expansion period was higher when compared to the monetary contraction period. However, according to the findings obtained as a result of CAR analysis results, it was identified that BIST30 index did not generally act in accordance with the ORH against the DJIA. During the monetary expansion period, the response of BIST30 to the positive and negative news from DJIA maintained its persistency and acted in accordance with the EMH instead of the ORH. In the second period, BIST30 overreacted to the positive return changes from DJIA according to CAR results. However, the results lose their significance after the 16th day. In the second period, no overreaction is observed in the BIST30 against the DJIA originated negative events. In addition, the degree of the reaction by BIST30 to DJIA in the expansion period differentiates. While BIST30 attributed 3.85% of positive reactions to the positive events derived from DJIA on the first day in expansion period, it attributed 3.66% of negative reactions to the negative events. In this period, the BIST30 reacted to the positive events more than the negative ones. However, in the contraction period, while BIST30 ascribed 3.49% of reaction to the positive events, the reaction to the negative events was 3.90 %. In this case, the power of the reaction by BIST30 varied according to the period.

According to the study, the relationship between the BIST30 and the DJIA weakened in the second period when the FED implemented contraction policies as compared to the first period of expansion policies. This is because the effect of liquidity contraction policies implemented by the FED in the second period on Turkey's developing economy is different.

The findings of the study reveal the following policy recommendations for investors: In the FED's expansion policy period, BIST30 responds to DJIA in compliance with EMH as opposed to ORH. In this case, the risks of investors are reduced. The results of FED's policy in the second policy period reveal different effects on the economy of Turkey and BIST30. In the second policy period, while the DJIA is on the increase, the BIST30 overreacts against the DJIA. So BIST30 acts in accordance with ORH. However, the response of BIST30 to the decreases in DJIA during this second period is in line with EMH.

These results indicate that the BIST30 index's response to DJIA's price movements during FED's expansion periods is correct and investors are likely to make appropriate investments. In the contractionary policy period, BIST30 investors should be careful, since during this period, the rise in DJIA leads to over reactions in BIST30.

Other important policy findings of the study are: (i) During the FED expansion period, BIST30's response to positive events in DJIA is greater than its response to negative events; (ii) On the other hand, in the FED's contractionary policy period, in contrast to the expansion period, BIST30's response to negative events in DJIA is greater than its response to positive events.

These findings show that while BIST30, one of the emerging markets exchanges, has a high positive level of exposure to DJIA during the FED expansion period; it has a high level of negative impact in the contractionary policy period.

The study of De Medeiros (2005) and Tetik and Ozen (2016) suggested that stock exchanges overreacted against Dow Jones stock exchange. This study revealed different results from the study of Tetik and Ozen (2016) on BIST30 index. There are two main reasons for that. The first one is that the index used in the first study is different. The stocks of big companies in BIST30 index are integrated with international markets contrary to BIST100 index. The other reason is that the study is divided into two periods in which the FED implemented expansion and contraction policies.

Further studies may cover not only Turkey, but also other developed and developing countries. So, we can see the properties of other countries' response to the FED's policies. The findings of this study will be a guide for academics, companies and investors. When the literature is analysed, there is a limited amount of studies handling whether there is an overreaction among stock exchanges. Studies in the future can be expanded by including the stock exchanges of different countries.

NOTES

1. According to IMF data; GDP of United States is 21.34 trillion USD and GDP of China is 14.22 trillion USD as of April 2019. imf.org/external/datamapper/NGDPD@ WEO/OEMDC/ADVEC/WEOWORLD/USA. Accessed on October 15, 2019.

2. http://www.bloomberght.com/haberler/haber/1481863-analiz-fedin-buyuk-resesyon-yolculugu. Accessed on June 12, 2018.

3. See Washingtonpost.com.

4. http://www.bloomberght.com/haberler/haber/1481863-analiz-fedin-buyuk-resesyon-yolculugu. Accessed on June 12, 2018.

5. https://www.investing.com/indices/major-indices. Accessed on July 15, 2017.

6. $R_t^{\text{BIST}-30} = \log \dfrac{I_t^{\text{BIST}-30}}{I_{t-1}^{\text{BIST}-30}}$ ve $R_t^{\text{DJIA}} = \log \dfrac{I_t^{\text{DJIA}}}{I_{t-1}^{\text{DJIA}}}$ was calculated.

7. ADF test results are are presented in Table A1.

8. Lag length test results are presented in Table A2.

9. In the Appendices, the average CAR table obtained as a result of the positive and negative events detected between these periods and the t-statistics indicating their significance are presented.

REFERENCES

Akkoç, S., & Özkan, N. (2013). An empirical investigation of the uncertain information hypothesis: Evidence from Borsa Istanbul (In Turkish). *BRSA (BDDK) Banking and Financial Markets, 7*(2), 101–119.

Alwathnani, A. M., Dubofsky, D. A., & Haitham, A. A. Z. (2017). Under-or-overreaction: Market responses to announcements of earnings surprises. *International Review of Financial Analysis, 52*, 160–171.

Barak, O. (2008a). *Behavioral finance theory practice*. Ankara: Gazi Press.

Barak, O. (2008b). Overreaction anomaly in ISE and its evaluation in the scope of behavioral finance modeling (In Turkish). *Gazi University Journal of Economics and Administrative Sciences, 10*(1), 207–229.

Bauman, W. S., Conover, C. M., & Miller, R. E. (1999). Investor overreaction in international stock markets. *Journal of Portfolio Management, 25*, 102–111.

Bloomberg.com. (2014, January 9) Retrieved from http://www.bloomberght.com/haberler/haber/1481863-analiz-fedin-buyuk-resesyon-yolculugu. Accessed on December 6, 2018.

Bremer, M., & Sweeney, R. J. (1991). The reversals of large stock price decreases. *Journal of Finance, 46*(2), 747–754.

Brown, K. C., & Harlow, W. V. (1988). Market overreaction: Magnitude and intensity, *Journal of Portfolio Management, 14*(2), 6–13.

Brown, K. C., Harlow, W. V., & Tinic, S. M. (1988). Risk aversion, uncertain information, and market efficiency. *Journal of Financial Economics, 22*(2), 355–385.

Da Costa, A. I. V. (2017). *Overreaction of equity and fixed income ETF during the 2007/2008 financial crisis*. Dissertation for Master of Finance. Retrieved from https://repositorio-aberto.up.pt/handle/10216/104401?locale=en. Accessed on June 18, 2017.

DeBondt, W. F., & Thaler, R. H. (1985). Does the stock market overreact. *Journal of Finance, 40*, 793–805.

De Medeiros, O. R. (2005). Reaction of the Brazilian stock market to positive and negative shocks. Retrieved from http://ssrn.com/abstract=868464; http://dx.doi.org/10.2139/ssrn.868464. Accessed on June 4, 2016.

Dissanaike, G. (1997). Do stock market investors overreact? *Journal of Business Finance & Accounting*, *24*(1), 27–49.

Doğukanlı, H., & Bahadır, E., (2011). Behavioral finance against effective markets: Investigation of the overreaction hypothesis on the ISE (In Turkish). *Ç.U. Journal of Social Sciences Institute*, *20*(1), 321–336.

Doğukanlı, H., Vural, G., & Ergün, B. (2012), Using various portfolio formation and test periods: An examination of overreaction in ISE. *The ISE Review*, *13*(49), 1–17.

Durukan, M. B. (2004). Overreaching hypothesis: Evidence from the Istanbul stock exchange (In Turkish). In *VIII. National Finance Symposium*, İstanbul, Turkey.

Fama, E. F. (1970). Efficient capital markets: A review of theory and empirical work. *The Journal of Finance*, *25*(2), 383–417.

International Monetary Fund. imf.org/external/datamapper/NGDPD@WEO/OEMDC/ADVEC/WEOWORLD/USA. (2019, May 15). Accessed on September 15, 2019.

Piccoli, P., Chaudhury, M., & Souza, A. (2017). How do stocks react to extreme market events? Evidence from Brazil. *Research in International Business and Finance*, *42*, 275–284.

Sembiring, F. M., Rahman, S., Effendi, N., & Sudarsono, R. (2016). Capital asset pricing model in market overreaction conditions: Evidence from Indonesia Stock Exchange. *Polish Journal of Management Studies*, *14*(2), 182–191.

Shachmurove, Y. (2002). The behavior of secondary European stock markets to positive and negative shocks. *International Journal of Business*, *7*(2), 1–16.

Tetik, M., & Ozen, E. (2016). Overreaction hypothesis and reaction of Borsa Istanbul to Dow-Jones. *Business and Economic Research*, *6*(2), 412–423.

Tufan, E. (2008). *Behavioral finance (In Turkish)*. Ankara: Imaj Press.

Tunçel, A. K. (2013). Test of excessive response hypothesis: The case of Borsa İstanbul. Uludag University (In Turkish). *Journal of the Faculty of Economics and Administrative Sciences*, *1*(32), 113–122.

Washingtonpost.com. A guide to the financial crisis — 10 years later. (2018, September 10). Retrieved from https://www.washingtonpost.com/business/economy/a-guide-to-the-financial-crisis--10-years-later/2018/09/10/114b76ba-af10-11e8-a20b-5f4f84429666_story.html. Accessed on June 12, 2018.

Yücel, T., & ve Taşkın, F. D. (2007). Overreaction hypothesis and evidence from the Istanbul stock exchange (In Turkish). *Economics Business and Finance*, *22*(260), 26–37

APPENDICES

Table A1.   Stationarity Tests of Indexes by Periods.

Indexes	Expansionary Period ADF Value	Contractionary Period ADF Value	J 1%	5%	10%
LDJIA	−1.05	−0.93	−3.43	−2.86	−2.57
LBİST30	−0.49	−2.50	−3.43	−2.86	−2.57
LDDJIA	−41.24	−31.05	−3.43	−2.86	−2.57
LDBİST30	−35.90	−18.49	−3.43	−2.86	−2.57

Note: *The *D* symbol indicates that the first difference is obtained.

Table A2.   Lag Length Test for Expansion Period.

Lag	LogL	LR	FPE	AIC	SC	HQ
0	−33843.61	NA	5.01e+18	48.73378	48.74132	48.73660
1	−26986.62	13684.36	2.60e+14	38.86627	38.88889	38.87473
2	**−26931.92**	**109.0128**	**2.41e+14***	**38.7932***	**38.83096***	**38.80736***
3	−26929.54	4.724851	2.42e+14	38.79560	38.84838	38.81534
4	−26929.33	0.418695	2.43e+14	38.80106	38.86891	38.82643
5	−26928.53	1.597037	2.44e+14	38.80566	38.88859	38.83667
6	−26920.17	16.56216*	2.43e+14	38.79938	38.89740	38.83604
7	−26917.43	5.425845	2.43e+14	38.80119	38.91429	38.84349
8	−26916.72	1.406032	2.44e+14	38.80593	38.93410	38.85386

Note: * Indicates the length of the lag selected by the criterion; the lag length was determined as 2.

Table A3.   Lag Length Test for Contraction Period.

Lag	LogL	LR	FPE	AIC	SC	HQ
0	−22920.44	NA	8.20e+17	46.92414	46.93414	46.92794
1	−19094.50	7628.394	3.28e+14	39.10030	39.13030*	39.11172
2	**−19085.56**	**17.77641***	**3.25e+14***	**39.0902***	**39.14020**	**39.10922***
3	−19085.10	0.912216	3.27e+14	39.09745	39.16744	39.12408
4	−19081.90	6.341680	3.28e+14	39.09909	39.18908	39.13333
5	−19079.26	5.230116	3.29e+14	39.10186	39.21185	39.14371
6	−19078.98	0.545796	3.31e+14	39.10948	39.23947	39.15894
7	−19077.23	3.444139	3.33e+14	39.11409	39.26408	39.17116
8	−19075.51	3.387605	3.34e+14	39.11875	39.28873	39.18343

Notes: * Indicates the length of the lag selected by the criterion; The lag length was determined as 2.

Table A4.   Market Response to Positive and Negative Shocks in Expansion Period.

Day	Market Response to Positive Events CAR	Market Response to Negative Events CAR	Day	Market Response to Positive Events CAR	Market Response to Negative Events CAR
1	0.038534964*	−0.036623589*	31	0.050216782*	−0.026259647*
2	0.041060976*	−0.033452657*	32	0.049380902*	−0.025526925*
3	0.04361961*	−0.035222691*	33	0.048007723*	−0.022962983*
4	0.039863997*	−0.03293048*	34	0.048206329*	−0.022443144*
5	0.037722681*	−0.030897687*	35	0.045914409*	−0.025637645*
6	0.037205406*	−0.030069968*	36	0.046878884*	−0.027354873*
7	0.037333129*	−0.025960315*	37	0.047225053*	−0.029903166*
8	0.033409775*	−0.022617513*	38	0.048188959*	−0.033512419*
9	0.034647437*	−0.025275803*	39	0.05154007*	−0.037437017*
10	0.036602541*	−0.028795451*	40	0.055219763*	−0.035394502*
11	0.036090512*	−0.028745295*	41	0.056823957*	−0.035830577*
12	0.032334143*	−0.027262276*	42	0.05773488*	−0.036374318*
13	0.031520514*	−0.028862816*	43	0.054587078	−0.0321474*
14	0.035737748*	−0.028968784*	44	0.056136974*	−0.030523492*
15	0.039043258*	−0.025887569*	45	0.051633985*	−0.028093612*
16	0.042203176*	−0.025912727*	46	0.053298292*	−0.029339445*
17	0.0449003*	−0.022678836*	47	0.052718753*	−0.029039554*
18	0.0491842*	−0.025687074*	48	0.051114667*	−0.025547308*
19	0.049026299*	−0.029584528*	49	0.04693228*	−0.0232321*
20	0.045872217*	−0.031209599*	50	0.046631045*	−0.024170882*
21	0.046539447*	−0.031320168*	51	0.04488592*	−0.024405232*
22	0.045428627*	−0.03113738*	52	0.045414715*	−0.026000312*
23	0.04452212*	−0.034659703*	53	0.042702785*	−0.02279612*
24	0.044791336*	−0.035054924*	54	0.044578319*	−0.025482788*
25	0.044084018*	−0.033479895*	55	0.042237608*	−0.028754781*
26	0.043014488*	−0.034359839*	56	0.04251333*	−0.031454131*
27	0.046738189*	−0.03401409*	57	0.040696574*	−0.029523822*
28	0.046718988*	−0.03019844*	58	0.03800061*	−0.029527673*
29	0.048122176*	−0.031093874*	59	0.038926803*	−0.033748634*
30	0.047900983*	−0.028247597*	60	0.041546496*	−0.035477149*

Note: * represents the %5 level of significance.

Table A5. Market Response to Positive and Negative Shocks in Contraction Period.

Day	Market Response to Positive Events CAR	Market Response to Negative Events CAR	Day	Market Response to Positive Events CAR	Market Response to Negative Events CAR
1	0.034929339*	−0.03905843*	31	0.015600139	−0.041432711*
2	0.033807732*	−0.03732428*	32	0.012024868	−0.043491595*
3	0.036282466*	−0.038680505*	33	0.011825852	−0.044717857*
4	0.037845723*	−0.040714417*	34	0.013325052	−0.043209234*
5	0.037970553*	−0.041670743*	35	0.011900451	−0.040414029*
6	0.034300682*	−0.042090708*	36	0.00804371	−0.044096824*
7	0.030376461*	−0.039129479*	37	0.011477576	−0.047268755*
8	0.028925875*	−0.033462297*	38	0.012903241	−0.048549485*
9	0.0310221*	−0.031932818*	39	0.011063268	−0.045980656*
10	0.024743058*	−0.033235532*	40	0.008598676	−0.047383399*
11	0.026458719*	−0.032006187*	41	0.010117111	−0.04664959*
12	0.031803521*	−0.033487424*	42	0.00620338	−0.050706644*
13	0.025397287*	−0.033789805*	43	0.00942911	−0.045900548*
14	0.02154917*	−0.031739277*	44	0.009530064	−0.045237748*
15	0.021736308*	−0.028244352*	45	0.009757376	−0.047657346*
16	0.019737538	−0.028238375*	46	0.0127001626	−0.044003267*
17	0.014551568	−0.025183583*	47	0.007312426	−0.042422406*
18	0.013314452	−0.025381697*	48	0.005462815	−0.041751897*
19	0.013967291	−0.025172638*	49	0.008801744	−0.039871178*
20	0.015987065	−0.026107438*	50	0.007555547	−0.038872878*
21	0.013051254	−0.030584162*	51	0.007463182	−0.041583036*
22	0.013667271	−0.033608806*	52	0.002278912	−0.039932657*
23	0.015559733	−0.03749977*	53	8.76116E−05	−0.043041791*
24	0.014743458	−0.038213144*	54	0.000470151	−0.044291756*
25	0.016973783	−0.040370979*	55	−0.005720912	−0.047022613*
26	0.019140583*	−0.039323699*	56	−0.003046382	−0.047742175*
27	0.02313219 *	−0.042545107*	57	−0.001563018	−0.046702983*
28	0.02217623*	−0.043389496*	58	−0.001060537	−0.041400673*
29	0.022222558*	−0.041680901*	59	0.000299685	−0.040483026*
30	0.01592751	−0.041637268*	60	0.00266822	−0.041851963*

Note: * represents the %5 level of significance.

CHAPTER 16

THE DETERMINANTS OF BANK'S STABILITY: EVIDENCE FROM LATVIA, A SMALL POST-TRANSITION ECONOMY[*]

Ramona Rupeika-Apoga, Inna Romānova and Simon Grima

ABSTRACT

Introduction – *Stability of commercial banks is on the back stone of a country's economy and its development, making bank stability one of the main concerns of financial regulators. The bank stability models for large and small economies differ significantly.*

Purpose – *In this chapter we examine the determinants of bank stability in a small post-transition economy, based on the case of Latvia. Latvia has a well-organized banking system, providing a wide range of services to local and international customers. Besides, the Latvian banking sector is quite unique in Europe as it comprises two sets of banks with radically different target groups of customers and sources of revenue.*

Methodology – *To carry out this study we analysed panel data of the quarterly financial statements of Latvian banks operating during the period 2012-2017.*

Findings – *We found evidence of a negative significant relationship between size and bank stability, negative significant impact of liquidity risk on bank*

---

[*] This chapter was edited by Ercan Özen and Hakan Boz.

Contemporary Issues in Business, Economics and Finance
Contemporary Studies in Economic and Financial Analysis, Volume 104, 235–253
Copyright © 2020 by Emerald Publishing Limited
All rights of reproduction in any form reserved
ISSN: 1569-3759/doi:10.1108/S1569-375920200000104016

stability, a positive significant relationship between capital adequacy and bank stability, as well as a positive significant relationship between credit risk and stability. These results increase the importance of a sufficient level of capital adequacy ratio and liquidity to maintain bank stability. In general, the results of the study confirm the results of other studies on bank stability of small economies, with some exceptions due to the unique situation in term bank business models applied by Latvian banks. The current study provides valuable policy implications to small post-transition economies and stakeholders in general.

Keywords: Bank stability; credit risk; liquidity risk; bank size efficiency; profitability; Latvia; commercial banks; small economies

1. INTRODUCTION AND MOTIVATION

Following the restoration of the country's independence on the 4 May, 1990, The Republic of Latvia began to transform its economy from a centrally planned system to a market system. The Latvian banking sector has undergone various phases of development, including rapid development, privatisation process, responses to the domestic banking crises (1994–1995), the 1998 financial crisis in Russia and the last global crisis in 2008. During the first four years, the Bank of Latvia (Central Bank of Latvia) granted licences to 67 banks (14 banks in 1991, 36 in 1992, 16 in 1993, 1 in 1994).

An analysis of the banking operations during the period 1991–1995, as well as the research carried out by Latvian and foreign scholars (Hansson & Tombak, 1999; Körnert, & Romānova, 2014; Saksonova, 2003; Shteinbuka, Sniegs, & Kazaks, 1995; Vaidere, 2006) allowed the identification of the main imbalances that have occurred and led to the banking crisis: weak management of bank liquidity and bank asset-liability term mismatch, bad loan quality and insufficient loan collateral, insufficient control of bank opening foreign exchange position, unprofessional and/or unethical behaviour of bank shareholders as well as lack of experience and insufficient regulation of the banking sector.

Out of 55 banks licensed by the end of 1994, only 47 were able to submit their annual financial statements for 1994. However, only 16 of these banks showed a profit at the end of the year. The Bank of Latvia revoked the licences of 15 banks. The number of banks decreased drastically, and by the end of 1995, only 40 banks were operating.

The first local banking crisis had shown that Latvian financial system is unstable because insufficient local capital and foreign investment is crucial for the further development (Rupeika-Apoga, Zaidi, Thalassinos, & Thalassinos, 2018).

The next challenge for bank development after the 1994–1995 banking crisis was the financial crisis in Russia, in 1998. Nevertheless, the banking sector remained stable. The external and global shocks have stimulated the shift of bank focus towards consolidation, increased attention to liquidity and asset allocation, investing more in longer-term assets.

According to the data of the Financial and Capital Market Commission (FCMC) at the end of 2017, the Latvian banking system consisted of

16 commercial banks and 5 foreign bank branches. Nordic capital was strongly represented on the Latvian market with 54% of the total paid authorised capital of the banks. Nordic-owned banks mostly concentrate on the provision of banking services to Latvian residents. However, 19% of the capital was owned by Latvian residents and 27% held by EU member states, US and CIS countries. These banks orient on provision of services to non-residents, mostly from CIS countries (FCMC, 2018). Therefore, up until 2017, in terms of banking business models, Latvian banks could be clearly divided into two groups: (1) banks with resident clients-oriented bank business models and (2) non-resident-clients-oriented bank business models. This makes the Latvian banking sector unique in Europe since it comprises two sets of banks with radically different target groups of customers and sources of revenue (Bojāre & Romānova, 2017). This peculiarity motivated us to carry out a study on bank stability in Latvia.

The situation of Latvian banking sector is unique due to the large number of clients from the countries of the former Soviet Union. At the end of 2015, 56% of total bank deposits belonged to the non-residents from CIS countries. The high proportion of non-resident money represents a reputational risk since banks and supervisors have to be able to manage and control these cash flows. The first problems in the field of money laundering appeared in 2000, with 'VEF bank' and 'Multibanka'. Starting from 2010, the banking segment of non-residents-oriented banks has been a subject to higher individual capital adequacy and liquidity requirements. Therefore, banks that were classified as a high-risk business catering for non-residents were forced to capitalise and raise liquidity ratios (LRs). The introduction of more stringent anti-money laundering (AML)/ counter terrorism funding (CTF) requirements has contributed to the reviewing of the foreign customer base, which resulted in the banks discontinuing cooperation with customers who do not meet the new requirements. Table 1 presents FCMC sanctions imposed on Latvian banks until the end of 2017, due to the non-fulfilment of AML/CTF requirements. From all cases of financial sanctions that were applied to banks, only one Nordic-owned bank, Swedbank, was sanctioned. The main reasons for sanctions were for violations of (1) the regulation on the Prevention of Money Laundering, (2) the Proceeds from Criminal Activity (Money Laundering) and Terrorist Financing and (3) the FCMC's regulatory requirements: (a) deficiencies in the bank's internal control system and (b) insufficient customer due diligence and monitoring of transactions (FCMC, 2018). Additionally, another Nordic-owned bank – Skandinaviska Enskilda Banken (SEB) – was warned for violations of FCMC regulations.

For supervision purposes the FCMC carries out regular assessment of bank performance and risks using the rating system: 1.0 to 4.0, where 1.0 is the highest, and 4.0 is the lowest rating. FCMC ratings and rating methodology are not publicly available. However, the general results are adapted in Table 2. The ratings are assigned for 2016 and 2017, the supervisory review and evaluation process (SREP) carried out by the FCMC was considerably enhanced, taking into account the European Banking Authority (EBA) guidelines for the SREP, as well as the ECB framework with respect to the SREP of less significant banks. In 2016, the key risks identified for banking activities comprised of credit risk, liquidity risk, reputation

Table 1. Sanctions Imposed by FCMC due to AML/CTF.

Date	Bank	Fine amount, EUR
02.07.2014.	JSC "Reģionālā investīciju banka"	70000
15.05.2015.	JSC "Rietumu Banka"	35000
23.10.2015.	JSC Expobank	105 000
27.11.2015.	Bank M2M Europe JSC	55 000
25.11.2015	JSC "PrivatBank"	2 016 830
03.03.2016.	JSC "TRASTA KOMERCBANKA"	Withdrawal of authorisation (ECB decision)
09.03.2016	JSC "Baltic International Banka"	1 100 000
26.05.2016	ABLV Bank	3 166 682
25.07.2016	"Latvijas pasta banka"	305 000
22.11.2016.	**"Swedbank" AS**	**1 361 954**
26.06.2017.	JSC "Baltikums Bank"	35 575
26.06.2017	JSC "Privatbank"	35 575
26.06.2017	JSC "Reģionālā investīciju banka"	570 364
17.07.2017.	JSC "Rietumu banka"	1 566 604
19.07.2017.	AS "NORVIK BANKA"	1 324 667
08.11.2017.	AS "Meridian Trade Bank"	889651

Source: Authors' own table. Adapted from FCMC (2018).

Table 2. FMCS's Ratings Assigned in 2017.

Rating Scale	1.0–1.7	1.8–2.5	2.6–3.3	3.4–4.0
A number of banks, including the banks under the direct supervision of the ECB.	0	6	8	1

Source: Authors' own table. Adapted from the Financial and Capital Market Commission (2018).

risk, strategy risk and business risk (FCMC, 2018). Special attention was paid to the operational strategies, business models and the earning capacity of banks.

In this study, we investigate empirically the determinants of Latvian bank stability, including bank-specific and macroeconomic factors. The bank-specific variables are bank size, capital adequacy risk, liquidity risk, credit risk, compliance risk, profitability, concentration and efficiency of bank operations. Macroeconomic variables are represented by inflation rate and GDP growth rate.

The findings of this study will provide useful insights for regulators, practitioners, policy makers and researchers. Taking into account unique institutional and market infrastructure in Latvia, this research contributes to the academic literature of bank stability. Comparing to the existing research on the bank stability in Latvia, this study investigates large number of aspects, including competition, compliance, etc. For policy makers and bank management, it will be useful to control those aspects that can destabilise the banking system. We focus on identification of factors determining bank stability taking a sample of 16 banks in the period from 2012 to 2017. The valuable contribution is that in this research we present evidence from a small post-transition economy, such as Latvia, which formed part of the Soviet Union till 1991 and joined the EU in 2004. Despite the ongoing debate on the importance of the relationship between stability and risk, there are no empirical studies on the impact of credit, liquidity and compliance risks and efficiency, capital adequacy, concentration and profitability on bank stability in the post-transition economy.

2. METHODOLOGY

2.1. Variables

A summary of the variables used for analysing bank stability is presented in Table 3.

2.2. Dependent Variable

Similarly, to previous studies by Adusei (2015), Ghenimi, Chaibi, & Omri (2017), Köhler (2015) and Rupeika-Apoga et al. (2018), the *z*-score of the accounting measures of profitability, leverage and volatility is used as a measure for bank stability. The *z*-score is considered as a standard measure of bank stability. Its widespread use is due to its relative computational simplicity and the fact that it can be computed using publicly available accounting data only. It can, therefore, be used to complement share-market-based approaches and can be the main risk measure for markets where share prices are not available, as in the Latvian case.

Table 3.   Explanatory Variables Definition and Predicted Signs.

Variable	Measure	Notation	Expected sign
	Dependant variable		
Bank stability	Natural logarithm of the Z-score	***Z_Score***	
	Independent variables		
Bank size	Natural logarithm of total assets	***Size***	Negative/Positive
	Natural logarithm of equity	***SizeQ***	
	Natural logarithm of total deposits	***SizeD***	
	The ratio of assets of bank in total assets	***WTA***	
Capital adequacy risk	Percentage of a bank's risk-weighted credit exposures	***CAR***	Positive
Credit risk	Total loans divided by total assets	***CR***	Negative
	Natural logarithm of total loans	***Loans***	
Operational efficiency	Cost to income ratio	***CIR***	Negative/Positive
Liquidity risk	Ratio of all assets with maturity up until 1 month to current liabilities with maturity up until 1 month	***LR***	Positive/Negative
	Total loans divided by total deposits	***L_D***	
	Total deposits divided by total assets	***D_A***	
Profitability	Return on equity ratio	***ROE***	Positive
	Return on assets ratio	***ROA***	
Concentration	Assets of three largest banks as a share of total commercial banks assets	***CR3***	Positive/Negative
Compliance Risk	Dummy that takes the value of 1 if the i-bank got fine from FCMC and 0 otherwise.	***ComR***	Negative
Economic growth	Quarterly GDP at current prices	***GDP***	Positive/ Negative
Inflation	Quarterly inflation rate	***INF***	Positive/Negative

Source: Authors' own table.

The bank stability is competed using the following equation:

$$Z\_Score_{i,t} = \left| \frac{ROA_{i,t} + \frac{E_{i,t}}{A_{i,t}}}{\sigma ROA_{ip}} \right|, \tag{1}$$

where $Z\_Score_{i,t}$ is the stability z-score of bank i in quarter t, $ROA_{i,t}$ is the return on assets ratio, E/A is the equity-to-asset ratio of bank i in quarter t and σROA_{ip} is the standard deviation of the ROA of bank i over the whole sample period p (Köhler, 2015).

As the z-score is highly skewed (Liu, Molyneux, & Wilson, 2013), in this study we use the natural logarithm of the z-score.

2.3. Independent Variables

In this study, we include a number of bank-specific independent variables. Bank size is one of the independent variables that provide a measure for a bank market power, returns to scale and diversification benefits. The bank size is vitally important to distinguish between the risk effects of diversification and risks of expected bailouts. *Size* is measured as the natural logarithm of total assets (Amidu & Wolfe, 2013; Laeven, Ratnovski, & Tong, 2016; Rupeika-Apoga et al., 2018). Total asset is a variable frequently used by regulators and researchers. It represents the nominal volume of bank activities; nevertheless, it contains valuation problems, since it does not take into account individual bank business models or differences between financial systems. This is the reason why we include also other measures of bank size. The second proxy of bank size is deposits of bank clients *SizeD* (Adusei, 2015). The third measure is the natural logarithm of equity capital *SizeQ*. Equity is relatively stable and mostly immune to measurement problems as it represents the book value of a bank. Nevertheless, the measure of total equity is less current and does not reflect the volume of bank business (Schildbach, 2017). Additionally, we decided to add the share of assets of bank i in the total assets WTA. This helps to estimate the differences in individual bank business models. The academic literature provides controversial assessment of the effect of bank size on its stability. From one point of view, bank growth may ensure efficiency gains and larger diversification resulting in higher bank stability. Whereas larger banks may take unnecessary risks due to the guarantee associated with the 'too-big-to-fail' argument. There is a strand of literature showing a negative impact (Köhler, 2015; Laeven et al., 2016), whereas others do not confirm the statistical significance of the impact on bank stability (Altaee, Talo, & Adam, 2013). Therefore, the expected impact on bank stability is questionable.

The second independent measure is a capital adequacy risk, which is measured using capital adequacy ratio (CAR). CAR is often used as a valuable tool for assessing the safety and soundness of banks (Abou-El-Sood, 2016; Mayes & Stremmel, 2012). Capital ratio is an internationally recognised measure for bank risk of insolvency from excessive losses. In Latvia CAR is significantly higher than the minimal required rate of 8%, fluctuating around 20% within for the last 5 years. It is, therefore, expected that the CAR will impact bank stability positively.

The third independent variable is a credit risk. In this chapter we use two measures of credit risk, the traditional measure CR, the ratio of total loans to total assets (Adusei, 2015; Curak, Poposki, & Pepur, 2012) and the natural logarithm of total loans.

Loans. The Basel Committee on Banking Supervision defines credit risk as the potential that a bank borrower (or counter party) will fail to meet its obligations according to the agreement with the bank. Empirical research shows that credit risk contributes to bank instability (Adusei, 2015; Ghenimi et al., 2017), therefore we expect a negative impact on bank stability.

The next variable is bank efficiency or managerial ability. It is measured as the ratio of operating costs to operating income (CIR) (Madi, 2016; Petria et al., 2015; Xu, Hu, & Das, 2019). Lower ratios are generally seen as indicators of higher efficiency. However, there are a number of factors affecting it as bank size and business model. Universal banks generating its income mostly as interest income in general tend to have lower CIR ratios comparing to investment banks. Banks with lower values of CIR are less likely to experience distress (Lindblom et al., 2014). Therefore, we expect a positive impact of CIR on the probability of bank distress.

Academics offer different proxies for liquidity risk assessment; in this article we use three proxies for the bank liquidity risk: the LR, the ratio of total loans to deposits (L_D) and the ratio of total deposits to assets (D_A). LR is measured as the ratio of total assets with maturity up to 1 month to current liabilities with maturity up to 1 month and D_A is the ratio of total deposits to assets. LR and D_A represent inverse measure of the liquidity risk and expected to have a positive impact on stability (Lindblom et al., 2014; Rupeika-Apoga et al., 2018). Liquidity risk L_D measured as the ratio of total loans to deposits (Curak et al., 2012) is expected to have a negative impact on bank stability (Ghenimi et al., 2017; Rupeika-Apoga et al., 2018). Whereas some researchers consider the main liquidity indicators (e.g. liquid assets to deposits and short-term loans to deposits) as less predictive for bank stability (Betz, Opricǎ, Peltonen, & Sarlin, 2014). Nevertheless, considering the Latvian situation, where the total deposits dominate non-resident deposits and the requirement for banks to insure liquidity is twice as high as in the EU 28, we are expecting any outcome of liquidity risk, as positive or negative, on bank stability.

Profitability is measured using the common measures of bank profitability, that is, ROA and ROE (Adusei, 2015; Betz et al., 2014; Ghenimi et al., 2017). We expect a positive impact on bank stability for both profitability proxies.

The next variable included in the study is bank-industry-specific–the concentration ratio. The concentration ratio measures the competition in terms of the number and size distribution of banks. Three-bank concentration ratio is calculated as the total assets of the three largest banks divided by the total assets of the banking sector. The concentration ratio is a measure of industry structure and bank competition. Nevertheless, high industry concentration does not apply automatically low competition between banks (Tan & Tan, 2016). Again, we expect the impact of concentration to have any outcome, positive or negative, on bank stability.

The introduction of more stringent AML/CTF requirements has contributed to the reviewing of the bank business models and has a huge impact on bank stability. According to the Bank for International Settlements (BIS) compliance risk is defined as the risk of legal or regulatory sanctions, material financial loss, or loss of reputation a bank (BIS, 2018). The bank supervisory authority in Latvia FCMC imposes sanctions on Latvian banks due to not meeting AML/CTF requirements. As compliance risk is very hard to measure without access to internal information, we use as a proxy for compliance risk a dummy variable ComR, with a value of 1 if the bank has been fined by the FCMC and 0 if it has not been fined. The expectation is that compliance risk has a negative impact on bank stability.

Two external variables are used to check the robustness of the findings. These are inflation and gross domestic product (GDP). GDP is used to measure the overall state of the economy and is usually seen as positively related to bank stability. Some researchers argue that GDP growth stimulates competition within banks, which in turn reduce profitability and can imply a reduction in bank stability (Tan & Floros, 2012). On the other hand, the impact of inflation on bank performance depends on the expectancy of inflation. In fact, there are two opposite views regarding the effect of inflation on bank stability. Some researchers find a positive relationship while the others – the negative (Betz et al., 2014; Diaconu & Oanea, 2014; Lindblom et al., 2014).

2.4. Data Sources

The sample of the study covers banks operating in Latvia between 2012Q2 and 2017Q4. Due to the reorganisation and liquidation process, the number of commercial banks varies between 20 and 16 banks during the period of the research (Table 4). Data of 16 banks that were active during all period were used for modelling. The bank-specific variables have been extracted from the quarterly reports of commercial banks covering 2012Q2–2017Q4. Macroeconomic variables are obtained from the Statistic Office Database of Latvia.

2.5. Data Analysis Technique

To investigate the determinants of bank stability in Latvia, we use a Panel Data Analysis technique, which is widely used to analyse the time series in each cross-section of the data set (Adusei, 2015; Bakkeri, 2018; Eissa et al., 2019; Rupeika-Apoga & Syeda, 2018). Panel data are a data set in which the behaviour of entities (states, companies, individuals or countries) is observed across time. In this research, we chose banks. We then use the following model to analyse the relationship of the independent variables to bank stability using the below formulae:

$$Z\text{-Score} = C + \beta_1 S + \beta_2 CAR + \beta_3 CR + \beta_4 CIR + \beta_5 LR \\ + \beta_6 P + \beta_7 CR3 + \beta_8 ComR + \beta_9 GDP + \beta_{10} Inf + \mu, \qquad (2)$$

where z-Score = bank stability; S = bank size; CAR = capital adequacy risk; CR = credit risk; CIR = operational efficiency; LR = liquidity risk; P = profitability;

Table 4. Banks in the Study and the Results of Exits and Mergers from 2012 to 2017.

	2012	2013	2014	2015	2016	2017
Banks in the sample	19	20	17	16	16	16
ABLV	□	□	□	□	□	□
Baltik International Bank	□	□	□	□	□	□
Baltikums/ Blue Orange	□	□	□	□	□	□
LBB/Bank M2M Europe	□	□	□	□	□	□
Citadele	□	□	□	□	□	□
DnB	□	□	□	□	□	□
Latvijas Pasta Banka	□	□	□	□	□	□
Ekspobank	□	□	□	□	□	□
Meridian Trade Bank/SMP/	□	□	□	□	□	□
Norvik Banka	□	□	□	□	□	□
Privatbank	□	□	□	□	□	□
Regional Investment Bank	□	□	□	□	□	□
Rietumu banka	□	□	□	□	□	□
Rigensis bank	□	□	□	□	□	□
SEB	□	□	□	□	□	□
Swedbank	□	□	□	□	□	□
GE Money Bank	□	□	Reorganisation/Citadele			
Unicredit Bank	□	□				
Latvijas Hipoteku un Zemes banka	□	□	Reorganisation/ Swedbank			
Trasta bank	□	□	□	Liquidation/ AML		

Source: Authors' own table *created based on bank financial reports (2012–2017)*.

CR3 = concentration; ComR = compliance risk; GDP = gross domestic product; Inf = inflation rate; μ = random error term.

A two-stage approach is used to choose the variables for the model. The first stage implicates the correlation test between all proxies since we included several proxies for bank size, profitability, credit risk and liquidity. The second stage involves the correlation test between variables chosen in the first stage. The robustness of the results is checked by adding macroeconomic variables.

3. RESULTS AND DISCUSSION

We apply the correlation test to check the degree of association between independent variables. The correlation coefficients between three proxies of bank size are very high; the same is true for credit risk, liquidity risk and profitability. We chose the one that has the smallest correlations with other independent variables. The best performance for bank size is the WTA proxy, for credit risk is the CR proxy, for liquidity risk is the D_A proxy and for profitability is the ROE proxy (See Table 5).

The results of the correlation analysis show that the model has passed the multicollinearity test (see Table 6) and Tolerance Variance Inflation Factor (VIF) tests are also positive.

Table 5. Pearson Correlation Analysis.

	Size	SizeQ	SizeD	WTA	CAR	CR	Loans	CIR	LR	L_D	D_A	ROE	ROA	CR3	ComR	GDP	INF
Size	1.00																
SizeQ	0.95	1.00															
SizeD	0.95	0.85	1.00														
WTA	0.87	0.90	0.77	1.00													
CAR	−0.43	−0.18	−0.53	−0.14	1.00												
CR	0.54	0.58	0.44	0.54	−0.26	1.00											
Loans	0.96	0.91	0.91	0.82	−0.50	0.72	1.00										
CIR	0.19	0.10	0.27	0.04	−0.54	0.13	0.25	1.00									
LR	−0.57	−0.42	−0.71	−0.29	0.70	−0.41	−0.63	−0.47	1.00								
L_D	0.23	0.34	−0.01	0.33	0.11	0.73	0.35	−0.13	0.14	1.00							
D_A	−0.03	−0.17	0.23	−0.08	−0.24	−0.26	−0.07	0.14	−0.20	−0.57	1.00						
ROE	0.37	0.25	0.44	0.24	−0.40	−0.01	0.34	0.17	−0.41	−0.21	0.16	1.00					
ROA	0.49	0.33	0.62	0.19	−0.62	0.21	0.53	0.43	−0.78	−0.21	0.23	0.69	1.00				
CR3	−0.02	−0.01	0.02	0.01	0.03	0.01	0.00	−0.09	0.01	−0.06	0.24	−0.02	0.06	1.00			
ComR	−0.02	0.01	−0.04	−0.06	0.06	−0.15	−0.03	0.03	0.00	−0.11	−0.15	0.04	0.09	0.19	1.00		
GDP	−0.02	−0.01	−0.01	0.00	0.02	0.01	−0.02	0.01	0.01	−0.02	0.00	−0.03	−0.03	−0.14	0.02	1.00	
INF	0.00	0.05	−0.06	0.00	0.03	0.03	0.01	0.08	−0.02	0.09	−0.29	−0.14	−0.04	−0.07	0.31	0.13	1.00

Source: Authors' own table.

Table 6.   Pearson Correlation Analysis.

	WTA	CAR	CR	CIR	D_A	ROE	CR3	ComR	GDP	INF
WTA	1.00									
CAR	−0.14	1.00								
CR	0.54	−0.26	1.00							
CIR	0.04	−0.54	0.13	1.00						
D_A	−0.08	−0.24	−0.26	0.14	1.00					
ROE	0.24	−0.40	−0.01	0.17	0.16	1.00				
CR3	0.01	0.03	0.01	−0.09	0.24	−0.02	1.00			
ComR	−0.06	0.06	−0.15	0.03	−0.15	0.04	0.19	1.00		
GDP	0.00	0.02	0.01	0.01	0.00	−0.03	−0.14	0.02	1.00	
INF	0.00	0.03	0.03	0.08	−0.29	−0.14	−0.07	0.31	0.13	1.00

Source: Authors' own table.

The descriptive statistics is available in Table 7. The total number of observations is 367. Higher value of *z-Score* indicates higher bank stability. The mean *z-Score* is 2.57, measured as the natural logarithm of the z-score. This is similar to the findings by Köhler (2015) of a z-score for banks in the EU (2.58).

The largest bank share in total assets is 22%, and the mean value is 6%, indicating that the market is diversified, with both large and small banks. The CAR on average is 23%, which is significantly higher than the minimal regulatory requirement of 8%. The mean of the credit risk is showing 39% that is low for EU 28 standards. On average, the efficiency ratio is 57%, which means that the banks in Latvia are managing their operations efficiently (a low-efficiency ratio is always desirable). The Deposits to Assets ratio is very high, on average 76%, compared to 59% in EU 28 for the same period (European Banking Federation, 2018). Profitability of banks considerably differs with an average of 10% return on equity. The mean of bank concentration is 51%, indicating the presence of bank competition. On average the inflation rate remains 1% during the period of the study, whereas the GDP growth rate fluctuated significantly from −15% to 13%.

3.1. Panel Data Analysis

The suitability of the panel model was checked by performing the Hausman test and the likelihood ratio test.

Table 7.   Descriptive Statistics.

	Z_SCORE	WTA	CAR	CR	CIR	D_A	ROE	CR3	ComR	GDP	INF
Mean	2.57	0.06	0.23	0.39	0.57	0.76	0.10	0.51	0.23	0.02	0.01
Maximum	4.36	0.22	1.33	0.92	2.48	1.86	0.70	0.53	1.00	0.13	0.03
Minimum	−2.61	0.00	0.08	0.01	−0.72	0.01	−0.46	0.48	0.00	−0.15	−0.01
Std. Dev.	0.90	0.06	0.14	0.20	0.29	0.28	0.14	0.01	0.42	0.09	0.01
Skewness	−1.39	0.94	4.08	0.76	2.00	1.37	−0.87	−0.76	1.31	−0.79	0.66

Source: Authors' own table.

Correlated Random Effect-Hausman Test: The results of the *F*-value and Chi-square are significant suggesting that the fixed effect model is appropriate for this panel data analysis (see Table 8).

Redundant Fixed Effects-Likelihood Ratio: A redundant fixed effects test is applied to choose which model between the common effect model and the fixed effect model is the most suitable for our panel data analysis. The results of *F*-value and Chi-square are significant indicating that the fixed effect model is the most appropriate for this panel data analysis (see Table 9).

The null hypothesis can be rejected as the difference between the coefficient of the fixed and RE models is not significant. Therefore, we apply the fixed effect panel regression model for this analysis.

The empirical results are reported in Table 10.

Table 8. Correlated Random Effect-Hausman Test.

Test Summary	Chi-Sq. Statistic	Chi-Sq. d.f.	Prob.
Cross-section random	107.140644	8	0.0000

Source: Authors' own table.

Table 9. Redundant Fixed Effects-Likelihood Ratio.

Effects Test	Statistic	d.f.	Prob.
Cross-section F	190.450999	(15,344)	0.0000
Cross-section Chi-square	814.548507	15	0.0000

Source: Authors' own table.

Table 10. Regression Results.

Variable	Coefficient	Std. Error	*t*-Statistic	Prob.
WTA	−5.690365	1.342382	−4.239007	0.0000
CAR	2.024421	0.152706	13.25695	0.0000
CR	0.468022	0.143594	3.259344	0.0012
CIR	0.138023	0.050269	2.745704	0.0064
D_A	−0.323853	0.054266	−5.967919	0.0000
ROE	1.000889	0.126518	7.911034	0.0000
CR3	3.841155	1.010294	3.802017	0.0002
ComR	0.055586	0.034517	1.610404	0.1082
C	0.374266	0.484398	0.772643	0.4403
Effects Specification				
Cross-section fixed (dummy variables)				
R-squared	0.944428	Mean dependent var		2.572571
Adjusted *R*-squared	0.940702	S.D. dependent var		0.896500
S.E. of regression	0.218309	Akaike info criterion		−0.142654
Sum squared resid	16.34693	Schwarz criterion		0.112737
Log-likelihood	50.17707	Hannan-Quinn criteria.		−0.041179
F-statistic	253.4435	Durbin-Watson stat		1.976233
Prob(*F*-statistic)	0.000000			

Source: Authors' own table.

The value of R^2 is 94%, the value of F-statistic is 253.443. And therefore, the model is a good fit.

To check collinearity, the VIF test was used. The diagnosis shows no multicollinearity problem (below 2.0). Also, results of Durbin Watson test (1.97) confirm no autocorrelation problems of data. Additionally, the test of residuals shows that both Skewness (0.053) and Kurtosis (0.256) are close to zero and the Shapiro-Wilk test confirms the normality of the residuals distribution. Thus, the model and results are reliable.

3.2. Robustness Check

The model of bank stability is checked by adding macroindicators (GDP and inflation). The Hausman test and likelihood ratio test are used to check the suitability of the panel model. In this case, the random effect test is the most suitable for the analysis of the current data. The results are available in Table 11. As shown in the table, the diagnostics confirms the reliability of the results.

The proxy of bank size (WTA) is positive under all models, but is statistically insignificant. The robustness check indicates no statistically significant effect of the bank size on its stability. As a result, we are unable to confirm that size of a bank has a significant impact on bank stability. All other control variables have maintained their effects on bank stability, confirming the robustness of results in Table 10. We haven't found a statistically significant impact of GDP or/and inflation on bank stability.

4. DISCUSSION OF KEY FINDINGS

The results of the study indicate a negative and significant relationship between size and bank stability. This implies that large banks are not more stable than smaller banks. Since the effect of size on bank stability has so far not been completely and satisfactorily resolved in literature, our expectations were not skewed in any direction. That is positive, negative or non-significant impact. Our findings confirm the findings of the previous research by Laeven et al. (2016) that large banks, on average, create more individual and systemic risk than smaller banks. However, we were unable to corroborate the findings by Köhler (2015) that bank size has a significant negative impact on bank stability, meaning larger banks are less stable than smaller banks since the robustness test on bank size in our study resulted insignificant.

Moreover, the proxy used in this model for compliance risk ComR is not statistically significant, but another proxies of compliance risk should be found for further research.

Capital adequacy shows positive significant impact on bank stability. The CAR is an indicator to depositors of a bank safety net, higher CAR is seen as a guarantee of bank ability to meet its financial obligations. This confirms our a priori assumption of a positive impact of bank capital on bank stability.

The model shows a positive and significant relationship between credit risk and stability. This finding contradicts the traditional theory since credit risk

Table 11. Results of Robustness Analysis with Inflation and GDP as Additional Control Variables.

Variable	GDP			Inflation			GDP and Inflation		
	Coefficient	t-Statistic	Prob.	Coefficient	t-Statistic	Prob.	Coefficient	t-Statistic	Prob.
WTA	1.138855	1.173822	0.2412	1.094858	1.128808	0.2597	1.105201	1.138825	0.2555
CAR	2.083010	13.85118	0.0000	2.084823	13.89441	0.0000	2.080922	13.83947	0.0000
CR	0.682728	5.043361	0.0000	0.678160	5.013048	0.0000	0.676492	4.994544	0.0000
CIR	0.144754	2.884760	0.0042	0.133426	2.626561	0.0090	0.134673	2.645794	0.0085
D_A	−0.296884	−5.479698	0.0000	−0.280571	−5.099934	0.0000	−0.283585	−5.123833	0.0000
ROE	0.978554	7.791247	0.0000	1.007298	7.884145	0.0000	1.006975	7.873587	0.0000
CR3	3.331035	3.270543	0.0012	3.360092	3.323211	0.0010	3.439953	3.364291	0.0009
ComR	0.042526	1.236050	0.2173	0.031806	0.890655	0.3737	0.031021	0.867143	0.3864
C	0.100006	0.201335	0.8406	0.072141	0.145887	0.8841	0.033341	0.066699	0.9469
GDP	0.087343	0.710771	0.4777				0.068670	0.554294	0.5797
INF				1.396793	1.253481	0.2109	1.316859	1.170717	0.2425
R-squared	0.430933			0.432371			0.432663		
F-statistic	30.03806***			30.21462***			27.14931***		
Durbin-Watson stat	1.548279			1.553454			1.549407		

Source: Authors' own table.

should have a negative effect on the bank's stability. However, we can explain our results with the specific situation in the Latvian credit market. Providing loans for clients is a main function of every bank, and it is normal that a significant part of the bank's assets is in loans, whereas the mean of credit risk proxy (loan-to-asset ratio) in Latvia is only 39%, that is very low comparing to the 60% in eurozone in 2017 (European Banking Federation, 2018). In Latvia, banks use two business models. The main loan market players in Latvia are with Nordic capital, with the share of 70% in 2017, however, the second business model with local capital specialise mostly in providing services to high-income clients and non-residents, mostly from Russia, Ukraine and other CIS states, with market share in loan market about 30% at the end of 2017 (Rupeika-Apoga et al., 2018). As the loan-to-asset ratio is so low, there is no negative effect from it to bank stability, since the amount of assets is significantly larger than loans.

Traditionally, the proxy of liquidity risk (D_A) and bank stability should have a positive relationship, but our model shows a negative and significant impact. This proxy also characterises bank funding, considering deposits as a source of funding. The model results can be again explaining by the specific situation in the Latvian market. The total LR of the Latvian banking sector in 2017 reached 60%, while the minimum regulatory requirement is 30%. Moreover, to ensure better stability of the banking sector the financial regulator, FCMC, in 2013 has introduced the individual LR depending on the share of non-resident bank assets funded by non-resident deposits (see Table 12).

On average capital and LRs of Latvian banks are higher in comparison to the European average. In Latvia, banks are pushed to create additional liquidity, since non-residents' deposits are considered risky. As a result, the share of deposit liabilities over total assets for a period between 2012 and 2017 in Latvia was 69% compared to 51% in the EU 28 (European Banking Federation, 2018). Some banks need to ensure current liquidity at the extremely high level of 70%, which pushes them to additional risks and negatively affects the stability of banks.

The relationship between operational efficiency and stability is positive and significant. This positive relationship can be explained by the high effectiveness of Latvian banks. Also, the rise in costs has a positive impact on bank stability. While, the mean of *CIR* in Latvia is 57% that is lower in comparison to European banks, the possibilities to improve cost efficiency are limited (European Banking Federation, 2018).

The study confirms positive and statistically significant impact of ROE on bank stability. Also, Xu et al. (2019) analysing 431 publicly traded banks (US, advanced Europe, and GSIBs) from 2004 to 2017 found that profitability is negatively associated with a contribution to both, idiosyncratic and systemic risks, and consequently the expected default frequency of banks.

Table 12.   Individual Liquidity Ratio from 2013 in Latvia, % (OECD, 2016).

Non-resident deposits to total assets ratio	From 20% up to 40%	Greater than 40% up to 70%	Greater than 70%
Individual liquidity ratio	40%	50%	60%

Source: Authors' own table.

In general, the bank profitability is considered to be good in Latvia. In 2016 weighted average ROE of Latvian banks was 14.3% comparing to 3.3% average ROE in the EU (EBA, 2017). However, the situation in 2017 changed; the ROE in Latvia dropped to 7.6%, while profitability in the 50 largest European banks improved to 7.1%. According to Banking Hub, ability of European banks to keep this level of profitability in nearest future is highly unlikely (Holländer, 2018).

The concentration ratio has a positive and significant impact on bank stability, implying that low competition has a positive effect on bank stability in Latvia. Academic literature provides two opposite views of the impact of competition on bank stability. On the one hand, increasing competition can ruin bank net present value of profits. The leading market players tend to be more prudent in risk-taking to avoid adverse selection when taking up risky investments (Fiordelisi & Mare, 2014; Shijaku, 2017). On the other hand, low competition is considered to lead to high systemic risk, but low idiosyncratic risk (Xu et al., 2019). As the mean value of concentration ratio in Latvia is 51 %, that is close to the share of total assets held by the five largest EU banks, it shows that concentration in Latvia is average and not as high as in Estonia and Lithuania (about 90%), but not as low as in Germany and Luxembourg (about 30%) (European Central Bank, 2017).

5. CONCLUSIONS, PROPOSALS, RECOMMENDATIONS

Stability of commercial banks is the back stone of a country's economy and its development, making bank stability one of the crucial prerequisites for the economic development of any country, especially for small post-transition economies. The study is based on quarterly financial statements data of Latvian banks operating in the period between 2012 and 2017. It investigates the main determinants of banks' stability applying panel data analysis of 16 banks operating in Latvia.

The study results identify important issues for policy makers and regulators. Firstly, the results imply the need for control of bank consolidation processes. The study shows a positive and significant impact of capital adequacy on bank stability, proving that banks with a higher CAR are considered to suffer less and most likely to meet their financial obligations.

Moreover, the model shows a positive and significant impact of credit risk on bank stability. Due to the specific situation in the Latvian credit market, credit risk contrary to the traditional theory view wherein a negative effect on bank stability was found. These results increase the importance of a sufficient level of CAR and liquidity to maintain bank stability. The model suggests a negative and significant impact of liquidity risk on bank stability. Both capital and LRs are high in Latvian banks. The LR of Latvian banks is on average twice as high as the minimum requirements and above the European average.

The study shows a positive and significant relationship between bank operational efficiency (CIR) and stability. Consequently, profitability (ROE) shows a positive significant impact on bank stability. Finally, the analysis shows a positive and statistically significant relationship between the concentration ratio and the bank stability, implying the positive effect of lower competition on bank stability in Latvia.

In general, the results of the study confirm the results of other studies on bank stability of small economies (countries with less than 3 million population) (Xuereb, Grima, Bezzina, Farrugia, & Marano, 2019) specifically Latvia in this case, with some exceptions due to the unique situation in the term bank business models applied by Latvian banks (liquidity and credit risks).

The results of the study have important implications for the regulators and policy makers since larger countries are mainly represented in the decision process, and most of the time take over and sometimes dictate the final decisions. Also, the concept of proportionality is not clear and is not effectively managed, at the disadvantage of the smaller countries. A proportionate approach would mean tailoring regulatory and policy requirements to (1) firm's size, (2) systemic importance, (3) complexity and risk profile, to avoid excessive compliance costs and regulatory burden for smaller and non-complex organisations that could unduly reduce their competitiveness without justification. Most policies and regulations are drawn-up by representatives of larger countries and a one-size-fits-all approach is taken (Xuereb et al., 2019).

Therefore, this article is important since it highlights the effects/impact of certain factors on smaller countries and allows for an understanding of the impact and implications of new policies and regulations to smaller jurisdictions, in this case within Latvia (Xuereb et al., 2019).

Beyond the scope of this study, future research can be conducted using more determinants for bank stability or based on the comparative analysis of bank groups classified in terms of the business model.

REFERENCES

Abou-El-Sood, H. (2016). Are regulatory capital adequacy ratios good indicators of bank failure? Evidence from US banks. *International Review of Financial Analysis*, *48*, 292–302. https://doi.org/10.1016/J.IRFA.2015.11.011

Adusei, M. (2015). The impact of bank size and funding risk on bank stability. *Cogent Economics & Finance*, *3*(1), 1–19. https://doi.org/10.1080/23322039.2015.1111489

Altaee, H. H., Talo, I. M. A., & Adam, M. H. (2013). Testing the financial stability of banks in GCC countries: Pre and post financial crisis. *International Journal of Business and Social Research*, *3*(4), 93–105.

Amidu, M., & Wolfe, S. (2013). Does bank competition and diversification lead to greater stability? Evidence from emerging markets. *Review of Development Finance*, *3*(3), 152–166. https://doi.org/10.1016/J.RDF.2013.08.002

Bakkeri, A. (2018). Contribution of governance to ensure the stability of Islamic banks: A panel data analysis. *International Journal of Accounting and Financial Reporting*, *8*, 140. doi:10.5296/ijafr.v8i3.13333

Bank for International Settlements. (BIS). (2018). Retrieved from www.bis.org

Betz, F., Oprică, S., Peltonen, T. A., & Sarlin, P. (2014). Predicting distress in European banks. *Journal of Banking & Finance*, *45*, 225–241. https://doi.org/10.1016/J.JBANKFIN.2013.11.041

Bojāre, K., & Romānova, I. (2017). The factors affecting the profitability of banks: The case of Latvia. *European Research Studies Journal*, *20*(3A), 922–936.

Curak, M., Poposki, K., & Pepur, S. (2012). Profitability determinants of the Macedonian banking sector in changing environment. *Procedia Social and Behavioral Sciences*, *44*, 406–416. https://doi.org/10.1016/J.SBSPRO.2012.05.045

Diaconu, R.-I., & Oanea, D.-C. (2014). The main determinants of bank's stability. Evidence from Romanian banking sector. *Procedia Economics and Finance, 16*, 329–335. https://doi.org/ 10.1016/S2212-5671(14)00810-7

Eissa A. Al., Homaidi, M. I., Tabash, N. H. F. & Faozi A. A. (2019). The determinants of liquidity of Indian listed commercial banks: A panel data approach, *Cogent Economics & Finance, 7*, 1.

European Banking Authority. (2017). *Risk assessment of the European banking system.* https://doi.org/ 10.2853/816166

European Banking Federation. (2018). Banking in Europe: EBF facts & figures 2018. *EBF Economic Outlook, 43.*

European Central Bank. (2017, October). *Report on financial structures* (p. 87). https://doi.org/10.2866/901897

Financial and Capital Market Commission. (2018). Retrieved from www.fktk.lv

Financial Reports of Latvian commercial banks from 2012 to 2017.

Fiordelisi, F., & Mare, D. S. (2014). Competition and financial stability in European cooperative banks. *Journal of International Money and Finance, 45*, 1–16. https://doi.org/10.1016/ J.JIMONFIN.2014.02.008

Ghenimi, A., Chaibi, H., & Omri, M. A. B. (2017). The effects of liquidity risk and credit risk on bank stability: Evidence from the MENA region. *Borsa Istanbul Review, 17*(4), 238–248. https://doi. org/10.1016/J.BIR.2017.05.002

Hansson, A. H., & Tombak, T. (1999). Banking crisis in the Baltic states: Causes, solutionas and lessons. In M. I. Blejer & M. Skreb (Eds.), *Financial sector transformation: Lessons from economies in transition* (pp. 195–236). Cambridge: Cambridge University Press.

Holländer, D. (2018). European banking study. *ZEB*. Retrieved from https://www.bankinghub.eu/ banking/research-markets/european-banking-study

Köhler, M. (2015). Which banks are more risky? The impact of business models on bank stability. *Journal of Financial Stability, 16*, 195–212. https://doi.org/10.1016/J.JFS.2014.02.005

Körnert, J., & Romānova, I. (2014). Entwicklungen im Bankensystem Lettlands seit 1991 [Developments in the Latvian Banking System since 1991]. *Bank-Archiv: Zeitschrift für das gesamte Bank- und Börsenwesen, 4*, 237–245.

Laeven, L., Ratnovski, L., & Tong, H. (2016). Bank size, capital, and systemic risk: Some international evidence. *Journal of Banking & Finance, 69*, S25–S34. https://doi.org/10.1016/ J.JBANKFIN.2015.06.022

Li, X., Tripe, D., & Malone, C. (2017, January). Measuring bank risk: An exploration of z-score. Retrieved from https://pdfs.semanticscholar.org/9b73/f7655c5088ba83c7c98589d6dce247032ddf. pdf?_ga=2.217254230.1567185320.1588745579-1039786335.1585583623

Lindblom, T., Sjögren, S., & Willesson, M. (Eds.). (2014). *Governance, regulation and bank stability.* London: Palgrave Macmillan. https://doi.org/10.1057/9781137413543

Liu, H., Molyneux, P., & Wilson, J. O. S. (2013). Competition and stability in European banking: A regional analysis. *Manchester School, 8*(2), 176–201.

Madi, M. E. S. (2016). Determinants of financial stability in UK banks and building societies-Are they different? *Journal of Business Studies Quarterly, 8*(2), 78–89.

Mayes, D. G., & Stremmel, H. (2012, November). The effectiveness of capital adequacy measures in predicting bank distress. *Ssrn* 1–45. Vienna: SUERF (SUERF Studies: 2014/1). Retrieved from https://www.suerf.org/studies/3991/the-effectiveness-of-capital-adequacy-measures-in-predicting-bank-distress.

OECD Report. (2016). *Latvia: A review of the financial system.* Rerieved from https://www.oecd.org/ finance/Latvia-financial-markets-2016.pdf

Petria, N., Capraru, B., & Ihnatov, I. (2015). Determinants of banks' profitability: Evidence from EU 27 banking systems. *Journal of Economics and Finance, 20*, 518–524.

Rupeika-Apoga, R., & Syeda H. Z. (2018). The determinants of bank's stability: Evidence from Latvia's banking industry. In *New challenges of economic and business development-2018*: Productivity and Economic Growth, Riga, Latvia, May 10-12 (pp. 579–586).

Rupeika-Apoga, R., Zaidi, S. H., Thalassinos, Y. E., & Thalassinos, E. I. (2018). Bank stability: The case of Nordic and non-Nordic banks in Latvia. *International Journal of Economics and Business Administration, 6*(2), 39–55.

Saksonova S. (2003). *The stages of the development of Latvian commercial banks' asset structure and their analysis* (pp. 286–296). Riga: University of Latvia.

Schildbach, J. (2017). Large or small? How to measure bank size. *EU Monitor Global Financial Markets*, 1–24. Retrieved from http://www.dbresearch.com/PROD/RPS_EN-PROD/PROD0000000000443314/Large_or_small%3F_How_to_measure_bank_size.PDF

Shijaku, G. (2017). Does bank competition affect bank stability after the global financial crisis? *Bank of Albania*, *34*, 175–208.

Shteinbuka, I., Sniegs, E., & Kazaks, M. (1995). Factors and consequnces of banking crisis in Latvia. *Bulletin of the Ministry of Finance of the Republic of Latvia*, *2*, 6–17.

Tan, Y., (Ed.). (2016). The Measurement of Bank Efficiency and Bank Competition in China. In *Efficiency and Competition in Chinese Banking* (Ch. 5, pp. 93–116). Oxford: Chandos Publishing. https://doi.org/10.1016/B978-0-08-100074-8.00005-4.

Tan, Y., & Floros, C. (2012). Bank profitability and GDP growth in China: A note. *Journal of Chinese Economic and Business Studies*, *10*(3), 267–273. https://doi.org/10.1080/14765284.2012.703541

Vaidere, I. (2006), *Banku sistēmas attīstība Latvijā* [*Development of banking system in Latvia*] (p. 99). Riga: University of Latvia.

Xu, T., Hu, K., & Das, U. (2019). Bank profitability and financial stability. *IMF Working Papers*, *19*(5), 54. https://doi.org/10.5089/9781484390078.001

Xuereb, K., Grima, S., Bezzina, F., Farrugia, A., & Marano, P. (2019). The impact of GDPR on the financial services industry of small European states. *International Journal of Economics and Business Administration*, *VII*(4), 243–266.

INDEX